An International His

The aim of this book is to provide readers with the tools to understand the historical evolution of terrorism and counterterrorism over the past 150 years.

To appreciate the contemporary challenges posed by terrorism, it is necessary to look at its evolution, at the different phases it has gone through and the transformations it has experienced. The same applies to the solutions that states have come up with to combat terrorism: the nature of terrorism changes but still it is possible to learn from past experiences, even though they are not directly applicable to the present.

This book provides a fresh look at the history of terrorism by providing an in-depth analysis of several important terrorist crises and the reactions to them in the West and beyond. The general framework is laid out in four parts: terrorism prior to the Cold War, the Western experience with terrorism, non-Western experiences with terrorism and contemporary terrorism and anti-terrorism. The issues covered offer a broad range of historical and current themes, many of which have been neglected in existing scholarship; it also features a chapter on the waves phenomenon of terrorism against its international background.

This book will be of much interest to students of terrorism studies, political violence, international history, security studies and international relations.

Jussi M. Hanhimäki is Professor of International History at The Graduate Institute of International and Development Studies, Geneva, Switzerland, and author of several books.

Bernhard Blumenau is a Researcher at The Graduate Institute of International and Development Studies, Geneva, Switzerland.

Political Violence
Series Editor: David Rapoport

This book series contains sober, thoughtful and authoritative academic accounts of terrorism and political violence. Its aim is to produce a useful taxonomy of terror and violence through comparative and historical analysis in both national and international spheres. Each book discusses origins, organisational dynamics and outcomes of particular forms and expressions of political violence.

Aviation Terrorism and Security
Edited by Paul Wilkinson and Brian M. Jenkins

Counter-Terrorist Law and Emergency Powers in the United Kingdom, 1922–2000
Laura K. Donohue

The Democratic Experience and Political Violence
Edited by David C. Rapoport and Leonard Weinberg

Inside Terrorist Organizations
Edited by David C. Rapoport

The Future of Terrorism
Edited Max Taylor and John Horgan

The IRA, 1968–2000
Analysis of a secret army
J. Bowyer Bell

Millennial Violence
Past, present and future
Edited by Jeffrey Kaplan

Right-Wing Extremism in the Twenty-First Century
Edited by Peter H. Merkl and Leonard Weinberg

Terrorism Today
Christopher C. Harmon

The Psychology of Terrorism
John Horgan

Research on Terrorism
Trends, achievements and failures
Edited by Andrew Silke

A War of Words
Political violence and public debate in Israel
Gerald Cromer

Root Causes of Suicide Terrorism
The globalization of martyrdom
Edited by Ami Pedahzur

Terrorism versus Democracy
The liberal state response, second edition
Paul Wilkinson

Countering Terrorism and WMD
Creating a global counter-terrorism
network
Edited by Peter Katona, Michael D.
Intriligator and John P. Sullivan

Mapping Terrorism Research
State of the art, gaps and future
direction
Edited by Magnus Ranstorp

The Ideological War on Terror
Worldwide strategies for counter-
terrorism
Edited by Anne Aldis and Graeme P. Herd

The IRA and Armed Struggle
Rogelio Alonso

Homeland Security in the UK
Future preparedness for terrorist
attack since 9/11
Edited by Paul Wilkinson

Terrorism Today, Second Edition
Christopher C. Harmon

**Understanding Terrorism and Political
Violence**
The life cycle of birth, growth,
transformation, and demise
Dipak K. Gupta

Global Jihadism
Theory and practice
Jarret M. Brachman

**Combating Terrorism in Northern
Ireland**
Edited by James Dingley

Leaving Terrorism Behind
Individual and collective
disengagement
Edited by Tore Bjørgo and John Horgan

**Unconventional Weapons and
International Terrorism**
Challenges and new approaches
*Edited by Magnus Ranstorp and Magnus
Normark*

International Aviation and Terrorism
Evolving threats, evolving security
John Harrison

Walking Away from Terrorism
Accounts of disengagement from
radical and extremist movements
John Horgan

Understanding Violent Radicalisation
Terrorist and *jihad*ist movements in
Europe
Edited by Magnus Ranstorp

**Terrorist Groups and the New
Tribalism**
Terrorism's fifth wave
Jeffrey Kaplan

Negotiating with Terrorists
Strategy, tactics, and politics
*Edited by Guy Olivier Faure and I. William
Zartman*

Explaining Terrorism
Causes, processes and consequences
Martha Crenshaw

The Psychology of Counter-Terrorism
Edited by Andrew Silke

Terrorism and the Olympics
Major event security and lessons for
the future
*Edited by Anthony Richards, Peter Fussey
and Andrew Silke*

**Irish Republican Terrorism and
Politics**
A comparative study of the official and
the provisional IRA
Kacper Rekawek

Fault Lines in Global *Jihad*
Organizational, strategic and
ideological fissures
*Edited by Assaf Moghadam and Brian
Fishman*

**Militancy and Political Violence in
Shiism**
Trends and patterns
Edited by Assaf Moghadam

Islamist Radicalisation in Europe
An occupational change process
Daniela Pisoiu

An International History of Terrorism
Western and non-Western experiences
*Edited by Jussi M. Hanhimäki and
Bernhard Blumenau*

Democracy and Terrorism
Friend or foe?
Leonard Weinberg

An International History of Terrorism

Western and non-Western experiences

Edited by
Jussi M. Hanhimäki and
Bernhard Blumenau

Routledge
Taylor & Francis Group

LONDON AND NEW YORK

First published 2013
by Routledge
2 Park Square, Milton Park, Abingdon, Oxon, OX14 4RN

Simultaneously published in the USA and Canada
by Routledge
711 Third Avenue, New York, NY 10017

Routledge is an imprint of the Taylor & Francis Group, an informa
business

British Library Cataloguing in Publication Data
A catalogue record for this book is available from the British Library

Library of Congress Cataloging in Publication Data
An international history of terrorism : Western and non-Western
experiences / edited by Jussi M. Hanhimäki and Bernhard Blumenau.
p. cm. — (Political violence)
Includes bibliographical references and index.
1. Terrorism—History. 2. Terrorism—Prevention—History.
I. Hanhimäki, Jussi M., 1965– II. Blumenau, Bernhard, 1984–
HV6431.I5466 2013
363.32509—dc23
2012028084

ISBN: 978-0-415-63540-0 (hbk)
ISBN: 978-0-415-63541-7 (pbk)
ISBN: 978-0-203-09346-7 (ebk)

Typeset in Baskerville
by FiSH Books Ltd, Enfield

Printed and bound in Great Britain by
TJ International Ltd, Padstow, Cornwall

Contents

Contributors   ix
Preface   xii

Introduction   1

PART I
Terrorism prior to the Cold War   15

1   **The first global wave of terrorism and international
    counter-terrorism, 1905–1914**   16
    RICHARD BACH JENSEN

2   **'Methods which all civilized opinion must condemn':
    the League of Nations and international action against terrorism**   34
    CHARLES TOWNSHEND

3   **A blueprint for successfully fighting anarchist terror?:
    Counter-terrorist communities of violence in Barcelona
    during the *pistolerismo***   51
    FLORIAN GRAFL

PART II
Western experiences with terrorism   65

4   **The United Nations and West Germany's efforts against
    international terrorism in the 1970s**   66
    BERNHARD BLUMENAU

5   **The absent terrorism: Leftist political violence and the
    French state, 1968–1974**   86
    MARKUS LAMMERT

6   **The success of Italian anti-terrorism policy**   100
    TOBIAS HOF

7   Quid pro quo: state sponsorship of terrorism in the Cold War   115
    THOMAS RIEGLER

8   The hijacking of TWA-847: A strategic analysis   133
    RICHARD C. THORNTON

PART III
Non-Western experiences with terrorism   149

9   Bengal terrorism and the ambiguity of the Bengali Muslims   150
    RASHED UZ ZAMAN

10 SWAPO, the United Nations, and the struggle for national
    liberation   169
    SHALOMA GAUTHIER

11 The 'Claustre Affair': a hostage crisis, France and civil war in
    Chad, 1974–1977   189
    NATHANIEL K. POWELL

12 Reagan and Libya: a history of pre-emptive strikes and (failed)
    regime change   210
    MATTIA TOALDO

PART IV
Contemporary terrorism and anti-terrorism   229

13 *Al Qaeda* and the reinvention of terrorism: social sciences and the
    challenge of post-globalization transnational political violence   230
    MOHAMMAD-MAHMOUD OULD MOHAMEDOU

14 The US response to contemporary terrorism   245
    ABRAHAM R. WAGNER

15 Terrorism in the twenty-first century: a new era of warfare   263
    SEAN N. KALIC

PART V
Concluding essay   281

16 The four waves of modern terror: international dimensions and
    consequences   282
    DAVID C. RAPOPORT

    Index   311

Contributors

Bernhard Blumenau is currently completing his PhD on West Germany's multilateral initiatives against terrorism in the 1970s at the Graduate Institute of International and Development Studies in Geneva. His research and publication interests include the history of terrorism, transatlantic relations, German history and politics, and the Cold War. He is also a Research Associate at the Pierre du Bois Foundation for Current History. He is currently working as researcher and project coordinator for a project entitled 'International Terrorism, the West, and the Cold War, 1970–1992' funded by the Swiss National Science Foundation.

Shaloma Gauthier is a PhD candidate at the Graduate Institute of International and Development Studies in Geneva. She is completing her PhD on 'International Organizations and their Endeavour to Supervise and Administer State-Building'. Her research interests include the mandate system under the League of Nations, the United Nations trusteeship system, state-building initiatives by the United Nations, humanitarian intervention and peacekeeping. From 2008–2012, she was a research assistant for a project entitled 'From Relief to Rehabilitation, The History of Humanitarian Organizations' Programmes on Behalf of Civilian Populations in the Aftermath of the First World War (1918–1930)', funded by the *Fonds national Suisse de la recherche scientifique*. She is currently a Research Associate at the *Fondation Pierre du Bois pour l'histoire du temps présent*.

Florian Grafl is currently completing his PhD on 'Urban Violence in Barcelona during the Interwar Years' and is a member of the research group 'Gewaltgemeinschaften', which is based at the University of Gießen. His research and publication interests focus on various aspects of modern Spanish history, especially concerning urban and political violence in Catalonia.

Jussi M. Hanhimäki is a Professor of International History at the Graduate Institute of International and Development Studies in Geneva. His books include *The Flawed Architect: Henry Kissinger and American Foreign*

Policy (2004); *The United Nations: A Very Short Introduction* (2008); and *Transatlantic Relations Since 1945: An Introduction* (2012).

Tobias Hof, PhD, is a Research Fellow at the Institut für Zeitgeschichte (IfZ) in Munich and an assistant lecturer at the Ludwig-Maximilians Universität in Munich. He is currently a scholar of the Gerda Henkel Foundation and is working on a biography on Galeazzo Ciano. He just published a book on *Staat und Terrorismus in Italien 1969–1982* (2011).

Richard Bach Jensen is a professor of history at the Louisiana Scholars' College at Northwestern State University. His forthcoming book *The Battle against Anarchist Terrorism: An International History, 1878–1934* will be published by Cambridge University press.

Sean N. Kalic, PhD, is an associate professor in the Department of Military History at the US Army's Command and General Staff College in Fort Leavenworth, Kansas. He is a Cold War scholar, who has written on terrorism, military thought, and US space policy.

Markus Lammert, MA, is a PhD candidate (Paris/Munich) and a Research Fellow at the Institut für Zeitgeschichte (IfZ) in Munich. He studied history, politics, and French literature at Freie Universität Berlin, Université de Provence, Universität Leipzig, and Sciences Po Paris. He worked as an assistant in the French Parliament and as a curator at Schlesisches Museum Görlitz.

Mohammad-Mahmoud Ould Mohamedou is a Visiting Professor at the Graduate Institute of International and Development Studies and Head of the Programme on the Middle East and North Africa at the Geneva Centre for Security Policy. Previously, he was the Associate Director of the Program on Humanitarian Policy and Conflict Research at Harvard University.

Nathaniel K. Powell is a PhD candidate at the Graduate Institute of International and Development Studies in Geneva. He is also a Research Associate at the Pierre du Bois Foundation. Currently, he is completing his PhD on French diplomacy and security policy in Central Africa during the 1970s.

David C. Rapoport is Professor Emeritus in Political Science at UCLA and the founding Editor of *Terrorism and Political Violence*, and the founder of 'The Study of Religion', UCLA. He taught the first American terrorism course in 1970. Rapoport has published 65 academic articles and seven books including *Assassination and Terrorism* (1971), *Morality of Terrorism* (1989), *Inside Terrorist Organizations* (2001), *The Democratic Experience and Political Violence* (2001), *Terrorism: Critical Concepts in Political Science* (2006), and the forthcoming book *The Four Waves of Modern Terror*. A festschrift in his honour has recently been edited by Jean E. Rosenfeld: *Terrorism Identity and Legitimacy* (2011).

Thomas Riegler studied history and politics at Vienna and Edinburgh Universities. He has published on a wide range of topics, including terrorism and film studies. He is the author of *Terrorismus. Akteure, Strukturen, Entwicklungslinien* (2009) and *Im Fadenkreuz: Österreich und der Nahostterrorismus* 1973 bis 1985 (2010).

Richard C. Thornton is Professor of History and International Affairs at George Washington University in Washington, D.C., where he teaches the strategic history of the Cold War. He earned his BA from Colgate University in 1961, where he was Phi Beta Kappa, and his PhD from the University of Washington in 1966 where he specialized in American, Russian, Chinese, and Japanese history.

Mattia Toaldo is a post-doctoral fellow for the British School in Rome and the Society for Libyan Studies. He earned his PhD in Diplomatic History at Roma 3 University. His most recent book is *The Origins of the US War on Terror.*

Charles Townshend is a Professor of International History at Keele University and a Fellow of the British Academy. He has specialised in the study of political violence and civil emergency and the history of modern Ireland and Palestine. Amongst his previous publications are *Terrorism: A Very Short Introduction* (revised edition 2011), and *Easter 1916: the Irish Rebellion* (2005). His most recent book was *When God Made Hell: the British Invasion of Mesopotamia and the Creation of Iraq 1914–1921* (2010, published in the USA as *Desert Hell*, 2011).

Rashed Uz Zaman teaches at the Department of International Relations, University of Dhaka. He has been educated at Dhaka, Hull, and Reading. He was an Alexander von Humboldt post-doctoral fellow at the University of Erfurt, Germany, from 2009–11. His areas of interest include strategic studies and South Asian politics.

Abraham R. Wagner is currently a Professor of International and Public Affairs at Columbia University, School of International and Public Affairs. He is also a Senior Research Fellow at Columbia's Saltzman Institute of War and Peace Studies, and the author of several books and numerous articles on terrorism, national security, and intelligence.

Preface

On behalf of the Pierre du Bois Foundation for Current History, it is a great privilege and pleasure for me to introduce this Routledge volume on *An International History of Terrorism: Western and non-Western Experiences*. This is the second book that Routledge has published as the outcome of a scientific international conference organized by the Graduate Institute of International and Development Studies, Geneva, Switzerland, in partnership with the Foundation.

The Foundation carries the name of Pierre du Bois, my husband, who was a Professor of International History and Politics at the Graduate Institute of International Studies for 15 years. He was an expert in European integration, security issues, and contemporary international relations. Pierre du Bois left us prematurely, suddenly, and extremely sadly in June 2007, at the age of 64.

In keeping with his wishes, the Foundation was established, which aims at promoting and supporting research in the area of current history. The Foundation supports the organization of public conferences and lectures, encourages interaction between young researchers and recognized scholars, and contributes to the creation of academic networks. It offers scholarships, research and publication grants, as well as the Pierre du Bois Prize. The research and interest focus of the Foundation are, to start with, Europe and the challenges of European construction, security issues in all forms, and Latin America, always from a multidisciplinary angle.

This book fits perfectly within the framework of security-related issues. It is edited by Professor Jussi M. Hanhimäki, from the Graduate Institute of International and Development Studies, and Bernhard Blumenau, who is completing his PhD under the supervision of Professor Hanhimäki. Jussi M. Hanhimäki is one of the foremost specialists in transatlantic relationships after 1945, the history of the Cold War, and American foreign policy. He is the editor of *The Routledge Handbook of Transatlantic Security* and his most recent book deals with *Transatlantic Relations since 1945: An Introduction*. Bernhard Blumenau is working on West Germany's strategies against international terrorism in the 1970s. In preparing this book, the editors did not intend to offer a comprehensive history of terrorism.

Rather, they intended to demonstrate that the twenty-first century did not invent the phenomenon of terrorism but certainly renewed it, with new challenges, actors, battlefields, and methods.

The international conference where most of the chapters of this volume were originally presented brought together many brilliant scholars from all over the world, both well-known historians and young and promising researchers. Their gathering on the theme of terrorism at the Graduate Institute of International and Development Studies confirms the strengthening of Geneva as a hub for expertise on security and foreign policy issues. The Conference dinner took place at the Hôtel Beau-Rivage on the shores of Lake Geneva. This location has particular historical relevance as the Empress Elisabeth of Austria was assassinated in 1898 by the Italian anarchist Luigi Lucheni a few metres in front of the hotel. She had been staying incognito at the Hôtel Beau-Rivage. Today, one can still visit her former apartment.

I would like to express my deep gratitude to Professor Jussi M. Hanhimäki and Bernhard Blumenau; they have brilliantly designed, planned, organized, and animated the conference and edited this book.

I am grateful for this second volume resulting from the association between Routledge and the Foundation and for the partnership between the Graduate Institute of International and Development Studies and the Pierre du Bois Foundation for Current History and hope that it will be followed by many more publications in the future.

Irina du Bois
President of the Pierre du Bois Foundation for Current History

Fondation Pierre du Bois
pour l'histoire du temps présent

Introduction

Jussi M. Hanhimäki and Bernhard Blumenau

'Two hours that shook the world', was how the late Fred Halliday summed up the meaning of the 11 September 2001 (9/11) terrorist attacks on New York and Washington.[1] In many ways, he was entirely correct. The collapse of the twin towers of the World Trade Center in New York after two hijacked commercial airplanes had hit them on that Tuesday morning – with another plane striking into the Pentagon and one crashing in rural Pennsylvania after the passengers tried to gain back control – prompted a sustained global response that, in the years that followed, transformed international relations. No stone was to be left unturned in rooting out those responsible for these acts, the American president, George W. Bush, declared on 20 September 2001. The United States (US) was going to 'direct every resource at our command, every means of diplomacy, every tool of intelligence, every instrument of law enforcement, every financial influence, and every necessary weapon of war, to the disruption and to the defeat of the global terror network'. With these unyielding words, Bush declared what would be dubbed the 'Global War on Terror'. It was to be 'a lengthy campaign, unlike any other we have ever seen'. The Global War on Terror was to be a total war, a conflict in which every nation would need to choose whether 'you are with us or with the terrorists'.[2] There were to be no shades of grey.

Little over a decade later, the war that Bush had declared looks immensely more complicated than the black-and-white rhetoric had suggested in 2001. The terrorist network that had organized the 9/11 attacks – *al Qaeda* – has lost most of its masterminds, including its founder, Osama Bin Laden, who was killed by American troops on 1 May 2011. But *al Qaeda* still exists and its 'affiliates' have proliferated; terrorist attacks take place, regularly, in many parts of the world. Many countries that initially signalled their sympathy and support for the Bush administration in the wake of 9/11 became gradually more critical about the way in which the Global War on Terror was waged. Indeed, by 2003 many Europeans seemed to be implying that US policies, like the terrorist networks, presented a serious threat to international security. Or worse, certain American policies – such as the invasion and occupation of Iraq – seemed to increase, rather than extinguish, the appeal of the causes for which such transnational networks as *al Qaeda* claimed they were fighting. The selective use of torture to gain information from suspected terrorists and the denial of legal rights to others further inflamed public opinion about a war that, unlike what Bush had implied, had no clear end.

The problems with declaring and fighting a war on terrorism were manifold. For one, combating an 'ism' is by nature far more complicated than confronting a physical entity (such as a country). For another, this was a particular kind of 'ism': terrorism was not an ideology but rather a method of using violence to advance political goals. Or to put it differently: terrorists were united only by their use of indiscriminate violence to promote certain political goals. Although *al Qaeda* was the most talked about transnational terrorist organization of the early twenty-first century, it had no monopoly or copyright on 'terrorism'. These – and many other – problems of definition, strategy, and goals have been discussed vehemently since September 2001. They are likely to be debated for some time to come.

Yet much of the discussion regarding terrorism and counter-terrorism during the early twenty-first century has proceeded from the presumption, explicit or implicit, that something unique in human history had occurred in those two hours on the morning of 11 September 2001. Was this truly the case? This is the basic question at the heart of this book. The answer that emerges from a study of the international history of terrorism is, by and large, negative.

Terrorism has existed in different forms for far longer than the grand declarations of the early twenty-first century would lead one to believe. In the first century AD, the Zealots in Judea, modern day Israel, targeted the Roman occupiers as well as their Jewish collaborators. In the thirteenth century, the Assassins, a Shia Islam group based in Northern Iran, employed killers who, in the manner of twenty-first century suicide bombers, would target an enemy even at the price of their own lives. The term 'terrorism' itself was finally coined during the French Revolution and the so-called Reign of Terror in 1793–94. Given that the term referred to a purge of the (presumed) internal enemies of the revolutionary government, another complicated question is raised related to the modern definition of terrorism: sometimes acts of terror are sanctioned by the nation state either within or outside its borders. It has touched, at one time or another, almost every nation on earth. In the late nineteenth and early twentieth centuries, for example, the Russian Czar Alexander II in 1881, French President Marie-Francois Sadi Carnot in 1894 and American President William McKinley in 1901 were assassinated as part of a global wave of anarchist attacks.

If the anarchists were generally content with targeting high-profile individuals (including the empress and crown prince of Austria in 1898 and 1914, respectively), the century that preceded ours saw the gradual increase of terrorist activities with an increased human toll. Throughout the twentieth century, various national liberation movements used terrorist tactics – targeted and random assassinations and bombings in particular – to advance their goals. The Irish Republican Army in Ireland, the Zimbabwe African National Union in Rhodesia, various Zionist groups in Israel before 1947 and Palestinian factions in the last six decades, a number of Hindu and Muslim groups in South Asia, the Fuerzas Armadas Revolucionarias de Colombia in Colombia are but a miniscule sampling of the hundreds of organizations that have, at one point or another, orchestrated or condoned terrorist acts in various parts of the globe. In the Cold War era, yet another headline-grabbing terrorist method emerged: the hijacking of commercial airplanes.

In short, terrorism is not a phenomenon that emerged unexpectedly in the early twenty-first century. Nor is it likely that any declaration of a war (global or otherwise) on terror is going to be followed, at some specific juncture, by a credible statement expounding that terrorism no longer exists. To be sure, the Obama administration may have stopped using the term 'war on terror' but the phenomenon lives on as television newscasters and newspaper headlines inform us virtually on a daily basis.

Given that terrorism has a long history, this fact prompts a number of questions. What do we mean by (international) terrorism? How has terrorism – as well as the reactions to it and the impact it has had on the evolution of international relations – changed over time? What did the notion of 'terrorism' mean to people during different historical epochs? What acts were committed, why were they committed, and by whom at different times and in different places? What were the responses of states, international organizations and the international community at large? What were the successes and shortcomings in responding to terrorism? How far were states themselves involved in committing or sponsoring terrorist acts? What are the current and future challenges posed by terrorism?

These are some of the key questions that will be addressed in the chapters of this book. Before summarizing the contents, however, a few words about the definition of terrorism itself are necessary.

In some dictionaries, such as *Webster's*, terrorism is simply defined as 'the use of violence and threats to intimidate or coerce, especially for political purposes'. Such a formulation does, quite naturally, lead to further demand for specificity, particularly in regard to agency and goals. Who can be described as a terrorist? Deranged individuals and fanatical groups motivated by ideology or religion? The broad definition does not, for example, exclude governments as possible perpetrators of terrorism. Nor does the definition say anything about the possibility of 'just cause'; a formulation that has clouded discussion about terrorism for as long as terrorist acts have been committed. Were the above-mentioned Zealots or rather the Roman legionaries that hunted Jewish resisters down and crucified them the real 'terrorists' of the first century AD? Do the assassination attempts against Hitler (or Mussolini or Franco) qualify as (failed) terrorist acts? Indeed, one needs only to recall the term 'balance of terror' – popular during the Cold War as a description of the Soviet–American nuclear arms race – or the Reign of Terror during the French Revolution to highlight the virtual impossibility of laying down a straightforward definition of terrorism.[3]

There are, naturally enough, plenty of competing and overlapping definitions of terrorism. In a 1999 book, Walter Laqueur, for example, counted over 100 different definitions and went on to dryly observe that these postulations had but one common denominator: they all cited the use or the threat of the use of violence (bringing us, more or less, back to *Webster's*). Laqueur's own preferred definition – 'the illegitimate use of force to achieve a political objective when innocent people are targeted'[4] – comes as close to how most people understand terrorism in the early twenty-first century as possible. Yet, even this is not without its pitfalls: words such as 'illegitimate' and 'innocent' are subject to certain normative relativism in specific contexts. Accordingly, in 2004, Bruce Hoffman, one of the foremost experts on terrorism, came up with a far lengthier description. Similarly to Laqueur, he defined terrorism, as the 'deliberate creation and exploitation of fear through violence or the threat of violence in the pursuit of political change'.[5] But, perhaps given that he was writing in the highly charged and increasingly complex post-9/11 world, Hoffman further pontificated:

> Terrorism is specifically designed to have far-reaching psychological effects beyond the immediate victim(s) or object(s) of the terrorist attack. It is meant to instill fear within, and thereby intimidate, a wider 'target audience' that might include a rival ethnic or religious group, an entire country, a national government or political party, or public opinion in general. Terrorism is designed to create power where there is none or to consolidate power where there is very little. Through the publicity generated by their violence, terrorists seek to obtain the leverage, influence and power they otherwise lack to effect political change on either a local or an international scale.[6]

Many other scholars have given similarly lengthy definitions. Yet, for the purposes of this book, it may suffice to note that in most of the various formulations a few things stand out: a) the use or threat of violence; b) the victims of terrorist acts are often chosen at random to cause an impact; c) the intention to create psychological effects beyond the immediate targets; and d) a political change (normally by groups that lack influence or power) is expected to follow the act. Even such a list is hardly satisfactory, open to (mis)interpretation and lacking in specificity. But it surely applies to the cases of terrorism from the late nineteenth to the early twenty-first century that are studied in this book.

When contemplating the battle of definitions, it is important to acknowledge the other side of the coin: the debates about the correct measures to be taken to deflect, prevent, punish or destroy those responsible for these acts of violence. In fact, definitions of terrorism are, in many cases, produced by those who try to conceive the appropriate counter-terrorist strategy to prevent, say, hijackings of commercial airplanes or the assassination of political leaders. While individual states have traditionally been the main counter-terrorism actors, moreover, the increasingly transnational nature of various anarchist and terrorist networks throughout the twentieth and early twenty-first centuries has prompted a number of international efforts in this arena. It is interesting to note, however, that efforts to negotiate comprehensive counter-terrorism treaties have not been great successes. As early as 1937, the League of Nations concluded the Convention for the Prevention and Punishment of Terrorism. But only one country (India) ultimately ratified the Convention before the onset of the Second World War condemned the entire issue, as well as the League itself, into temporary obscurity. Even before German tanks entered Poland in September 1939, however, the full ratification had been rendered virtually impossible by a simple obstacle: the states involved in the negotiations could not agree on what could be considered as a terrorist act.[7]

In the past five decades, the United Nations (UN) and its agencies have developed a wide range of international legal agreements aimed to help suppress terrorism and bring those responsible to justice. As of May 2012, there were no less than twenty-seven global or regional instruments pertaining to the subject of international terrorism. The first of these, dealing with the hijacking of airplanes, dates to 1963; others address such 'sectoral' questions as the financing of terrorism or terrorist organizations and weapons of mass destruction. In 1996, the General Assembly passed a resolution establishing an Ad Hoc Committee to draft the *Comprehensive Convention on International Terrorism* after similar efforts had failed to lead to any serious outcome in the 1970s. As of this writing and despite 9/11 and the Global War on Terror – or perhaps because of them – the negotiations have failed to produce such a document. Instead, a deadlock on a key issue of definition reigns: many countries wish to make a clear distinction between 'terrorism' on the one hand and armed struggle to resist foreign occupation on the other. In simpler terms: one man's (or country's) terrorist is still another's freedom fighter.

This suggests a key practical problem that arises from the seemingly mundane question of defining terrorism: if one cannot find a common definition of the problem, it is extremely difficult to agree on how to counter it. In other words, given the complexity of international terrorism and the lack of a universally acceptable definition for the phenomenon, it is virtually impossible to find a common response or strategy on how to combat, let alone defeat, it. On a broad level, most everyone would agree that it would be good if there were no politically motivated acts of violence.

But there will always be debates about the motivations behind such acts. This, in turn, assures that there will certainly be disagreements about the proper set of responses to terrorist acts. Anyone who has followed the ups and downs of the Global War on Terror in the first decade of the twenty-first century would find it hard to disagree with this.

The history of terrorism is indeed filled with normative challenges and contextual complications. The tricky distinction between freedom fighters and terrorists, for example, is hardly new. The Zealots of Judea and the Patriots of the American Revolution were not regarded kindly by the Roman or British imperial authorities. In retrospect, they are heralded as heroes. Similar examples abound all over the world. An illustrative case is that of a young Finnish anarchist named Eugene Schauman, who assassinated the Russian Governor General Nikolai Bobrikov in Helsinki in 1904 and then proceeded to kill himself. The Russian government, which ruled over Finland at the time, had a clear view: Schauman was an anarchist, a criminal who had escaped his due only by shooting himself in the chest. Many Finns saw it differently. After Finland gained its independence in 1917, Schauman quickly claimed his place in the pantheon of Finland's national heroes, becoming a secular martyr of sorts. Today, a memorial plaque commemorates the event, adorned with the Latin words '*Se Pro Patria Dedit*' (given himself for his country). The assassin became a symbol of Finland's eventually successful struggle for independence – that is, until the early twenty-first century when the question of the centenary of the assassination arrived. The Finnish Prime Minister at the time, Matti Vanhanen, bluntly announced that Schauman's deed had been 'purely an act of political terrorism, and altogether deplorable'. But the plaque remains in place.[8]

It should be clear by this point that the purpose of this book is not to come up with a 'one-size-fits-all' definition of terrorism or make moral judgments. Rather, it is to emphasize two aspects about the phenomenon. First, terrorism has, over time, taken many shapes and forms, been used for many different causes, been driven by religious fanatics and atheist ideologues alike. Depending on the period in question, 'terrorism' has been used by governments to justify policies of repression and aggression – as well as what can be viewed as perfectly legitimate steps taken to ensure the safety of the masses from acts of violence. Second, terrorism, like so many other terms, has specific resonance and meaning depending on the time and place. It follows that only by looking at the evolution of terrorism, the different phases it has gone through and the transformations in its causes and consequences can we fully begin to appreciate the challenges that terrorism presents to our contemporary world.

As the book will show, the nature of terrorism has changed over time. The full complexity of the phenomenon can, however, only be fully understood by exploring not only different time periods but also several geographical areas, for the historical experience with terrorism, in Europe alone, has been quite varied. In the early decades of the twentieth century anarchist violence touched some countries – such as Spain, Russia, and Italy – quite frequently but was notably absent in others. In the early 1970s, Italy and West Germany were hard hit by terrorism while the situation was remarkably different in France. Only in the 1980s did France experience similar problems. The same holds true when assessing the characteristics of the terrorist threat. Using the examples of France and West Germany in the 1970s again highlights an important lesson: domestic terrorism committed by German terrorist groups was a major feature of the early 1970s; at the same time, France was preoccupied with terrorist acts committed against its civilian citizens in other parts of the world, such as Africa.[9]

To help readers to better appreciate the historical evolution of and notably different experiences with terrorism, the essays selected for this book thus cover a wide spectrum of case studies across time and space. The chronological span extends from the last quarter of the nineteenth century to the present. In addition to Europe, the regional areas examined include the Indian subcontinent, the US, sub-Saharan Africa and the Middle East. Moreover, the book will delve into the role of international organizations in various efforts to combat terrorism and assess a number of other pertinent questions, such as human rights, the right to self-determination and state terrorism.

These are all issues with much contemporary and historical interest that have already been treated by scholars in some detail. Indeed, while most works on terrorism – whether general overviews or more specific analyses of some aspect thereof – look at the phenomenon through a contemporary lens, the history of terrorism is a growing, but somewhat underdeveloped, subfield of international history. Among the notable overviews are books by: Gérard Chaliand and Arnaud Blin, Michael Burleigh and Randall Law, Walter Laqueur, James and Brenda Lutz, Bruce Hoffman, Albert Parry, Ben Saul, and Paul Wilkinson.[10] This present book complements the aforementioned studies by looking both at Western and non-Western experiences over a time span of roughly 150 years. There are also many articles and books that deal with terrorism in a more limited, national or temporal, context. For these and other useful sources for understanding the historical evolution of terrorism, readers are advised to consult the individual chapters that form the content of the present volume.

An International History of Terrorism is divided into four major parts that illustrate the evolution of terrorism and counter-terrorism from the late nineteenth century to the present.

The first part consists of three essays on different aspects of terrorism in the pre-Cold War era. In Chapter 1, Richard Jensen discusses the first global wave of terrorism and counter-terrorism in the decade preceding the outbreak of the First World War. Equated by contemporaries with anarchism (albeit sometimes falsely), at an international level this phenomenon

originated mainly from Russia and Spain and led to a massive wave of 'assassinationism' that affected five continents. Jensen further evaluates the
limited success in the efforts to combat – at both the national and international level – this anarchist and nihilist violence before the outbreak of the
Great War. Indeed, as Charles Townshend points out in Chapter 2, the first
attempt to establish an international convention against terrorism was
made at Geneva in 1937. Like subsequent efforts, however, this convention
failed to establish a useful definition of terrorism. As Townshend illustrates,
one of the main reasons for this failure was the unexpected resistance of
Great Britain. Although widely seen as a supporter of international action
through the League of Nations, the British feared that the convention
would be used to suppress legitimate protest in illiberal states (such as the
Soviet Union and Nazi Germany). Indeed, the Brits, perhaps surprisingly,
given the country's twenty-first century approach to counter-terrorism,
argued that, in some states, necessary political reforms could be advanced
via violent means. To complete Part I, Florian Grafl provides a case study of
anarchism in turn-of-the-century Barcelona, Spain, which was struck by a
series of anarchist bomb attacks. The authorities reacted by prompting a
long-term campaign of anti-anarchist violence that effectively legitimized
local paramilitary groups and, ultimately, spiralled out of control, culminating in the so-called era of *pistolerismo* (1917–23). Not for the last time,
counter-terrorism produced unintended violent consequences.

Part II of the book explores different aspects of the 'Western' experience
with and responses to terrorism in the Cold War era. Bernhard Blumenau
focuses on West Germany's efforts to foster international cooperation
against terrorism at the UN in the 1970s, a decade that saw the proliferation of terrorist acts – assassinations, hijackings, bombings – directed at the
citizens of the Federal Republic. As Blumenau illustrates, the energetic
West German campaign to prompt an international consensus on anti-
terrorist measures, while successful on occasion, ran into serious obstacles
at the UN in large part due to questions about the legitimate use of force
by national liberation movements (an interesting parallel to the 1930s and
the discussions at the League of Nations explored in Townshend's chapter). Markus Lammert, in Chapter 5, explores the French response to leftist
political violence and its effects on French society in the years after 1968.
Lammert pays particular attention to the student riots of May 1968 that, he
argues, shaped French perceptions of threats to public order. Ultimately,
however, France witnessed a broad demand for liberalization and a new
emphasis on civil rights in the public sphere. Meanwhile in Italy, as Tobias
Hof illustrates in Chapter 6, the anti-terrorism strategies of the 1970s were
inspired by a flexible double strategy. On the one hand, the government,
particularly after the kidnapping and killing of former Prime Minister Aldo
Moro in 1978, introduced repressive legislation. On the other hand, Italian
authorities were willing to give reduced sentences to captured terrorists in
exchange for cooperation.

In Chapter 7, Thomas Riegler analyzes another controversial issue of the 1970s and 1980s: state sponsorship of terrorist groups. While many enlisted groups were used to conduct surrogate operations against rival states, internal enemies or dissidents, Riegler does not sign up for the view that the relationship between terrorist groups and their state benefactors was a purely hierarchical one (that is, that the terrorists were ultimately hired guns at the service of select governments). Instead, he suggests that the terrorist groups and networks often successfully co-opted and manipulated their state sponsors. The question of state sponsorship is, in fact, at the core of the next chapter, in which Richard Thornton discusses the difficulties faced by the Reagan administration in trying to ascertain the true motives behind the hijacking of flight TWA-847 on 14 June 1985. The chapter illustrates how both the assessment of the presumed identity of the state sponsors of the hijacking and their alleged motives shifted during the seventeen-day crisis. Having originally suspected Syria and Iran, the administration soon honed in on Libya and the Soviet Union as the puppet masters behind the hijacking. Americans also came to believe that the objective of the hijackers was not so much the public demand to swap passengers for prisoners held by Israel but was an attempt to prevent any possible improvement in relations between the US and Iran or the US and Algeria.

In Part III, the geographic focus shifts from Europe to the developing world. Rashed Uz Zaman explores terrorist activities in Bengal (modern-day Bangladesh). Taking a broad chronological approach, the author traces the historical evolution of the pre-1947 terrorist activities that were aimed at forcing the British rulers of India to concede political power to Indians. Indeed, the early decades of the twentieth century were strongly influenced by Hindu religious symbolism to which Bengali Muslims had little connection. After the partition of the subcontinent, however, Bengali Muslims gradually moved to oppose the ideology of the new Pakistan state (that was politically dominated by West Pakistan with Bengalis inhabiting the East, or what today is known as Bangladesh) with extremist factions embracing terrorist methods in their campaign for independence.

Two subsequent chapters focus on terrorism and counter-terrorism in Africa. In Chapter 10, Shaloma Gauthier examines the relationship between the South West Africa People's Organization (SWAPO) and the UN. Armed struggle was invoked by this movement of national liberation as a means to further the cause of self-determination. Contemporary Western jurists pointed to the dangers of a sweeping application of the principle of self-determination that, not unlike in Bengal, cost the lives of individuals not associated with either side of the struggle. Disturbingly, SWAPO also directed some of this violence and repression towards individuals within its organization. In Chapter 11, Nathaniel Powell focuses on the little-known case of Northern Chad, where local rebels took a number of French hostages between 1974 and 1977, prompting the French government to make numerous and sometimes covert attempts to free them. Powell argues that these attempts seriously jeopardized France's strategic position in the region by empowering anti-government Chadian rebels and providing a major opening for Libyan expansionist policies. The long-term consequences for the region were dire: fuelling an intermittent conflict that persists to the twenty-first century.

In his chapter, Mattia Toaldo examines the prolonged confrontation between Libya and the US from 1981 to 1986 as a case study of counter-terrorism. The chapter describes the rationale behind the first confrontations in 1981, as well as the efforts at regime change between the summer of 1985 and the summer of 1986 (including the April 1986 US bombing of Libya). Making use of recently declassified records, Toaldo argues that Libya was a testing ground for American anti-terrorism policy that, while tempered by Cold War constraints, included such goals as 'regime change' that would later be associated with the Global War on Terror in the early twenty-first century. Toaldo's chapter thus provides an interesting transformation towards the discussion on contemporary terrorism and counter-terrorism that are at the heart of the three essays that follow.

The focus of Part IV of the book is, not surprisingly, on 9/11 and its consequences. In his chapter, Mohammad-Mahmoud Ould Mohamedou focuses on the best-known post-Cold War transnational terrorist group, *al Qaeda*. In the past decades, this non-state armed group, led by the Saudi-born Osama Bin Laden, revolutionized contemporary terrorism. The chapter provides a contextualized, comparative, and critical analysis of *al Qaeda*'s methods and goals and argues that the significance of *al Qaeda* in the history of terrorism is consequential particularly as the group has managed to turn itself (*al Qaeda*) into an ideology (*al Qaedism*). The other chapters consider the response to the most spectacular act of terrorism in the modern era. According to both Abraham Wagner and Sean Kalic, the 11 September 2001 *al Qaeda* attacks did indeed dramatically change the international security environment. Wagner evaluates the US response, focusing on a number of organizational changes, such as the creation of the Department of Homeland Security, the methods used to gather intelligence on terrorist operations and the treatment of captured terrorists. In contrast, Kalic takes a broader, systemic perspective and argues that the US and the West have struggled with transnational terrorism, specifically *al Qaeda*, because it symbolizes a new era of warfare. While the Westphalian system, established in 1648, has long dominated the structure and laws of the international community, global terrorism has emerged as the central issue in international security in the twenty-first century. In this context, the major question is how a coalition of nations can conduct a 'Global War on Terrorism' against a transnational non-state actor, within the context of an international system established for and by nation states.

In the concluding chapter of the book, David Rapoport employs his well-known theory of 'terrorist waves' to provide a long-term perspective on the historical evolution of terrorism. He argues that modern non-state terror emerged in the 1880s, as a consequence of technological developments. Since the late nineteenth century, Rapoport argues, there have been four 'waves' of international terrorism: the anarchist, anti-colonial, new left, and religious. The impact on the international system varied dramatically in each wave. For example, a terrorist act (the assassination of Austrian Archduke Franz Ferdinand) precipitated the First World War and the second wave helped to extinguish overseas empires. Rapoport further maintains that each of these waves lasted roughly four decades and predicts that the current, religious, wave that began in 1979 will probably disappear around 2025.

As the above description implies, the essays in this volume do not provide a complete or definitive international history of terrorism. However, we hope that readers seeking to understand the phenomenon that has dominated headlines and prompted unprecedented military activities around the globe in the first decade of the twenty-first century will, at the minimum, come to appreciate two salient facts. First, that terrorism as a phenomenon has been around for a long time and has affected, at one point or another, most parts of the globe. While the causes and goals of terrorist acts have changed – as generalized by Rapoport's 'waves' or as can be concluded by reading the other individual essays herein – the general phenomenon itself has endured. A quick glance at the daily news in 2012 gives little hope that it is about to become extinct. Second, countering terrorism has been another timeless and constantly mutating endeavour with mixed success. The key problem is that historically the application of terror has been a means to a surprising number of different ends (bringing about social and economic change; bringing about the end of colonial rule; creating some form of new political-religious entity, and so on). Most such causes have found large numbers of supporters – as 'freedom fighters' or 'the vanguard of revolution' – even if the extreme methods have been condemned. As much as one might wish for a world free of terrorism, it is difficult to envision such Utopia in the near future. Like outlawing war or extinguishing poverty, eradicating terrorism remains a goal that everyone may agree is desirable but no one knows how to achieve.

The essays in this book were originally presented at a two-day conference on 'Terrorism and International Politics: Past, Present and Future' held in late September 2011 at the Graduate Institute of International and Development Studies in Geneva and sponsored by the Pierre du Bois Foundation for Current History. Organized close to the tenth anniversary of the *al Qaeda* attack of 11 September 2001, the conference offered a forum for a frank exchange of views on the past, present and (possible) future of terrorism and counter-terrorism. Rather than searching for clues for the developments in the first decade of the twenty-first century, however, the participants – a selection of seasoned experts and younger scholars – were encouraged to take a historical approach on the issue of terrorism. Our overall goal was to assess the long-term evolution of a phenomenon rather than ask 'why did 9/11 happen?'. The end result, this book, is a compilation that, the editors hope, provides a wide range of readers with the tools to understand the historical evolution of terrorism and counter-terrorism over the past one hundred and fifty years.

The editors would like to express their heartfelt thanks to the Graduate Institute in Geneva, the Pierre du Bois Foundation and the Swiss National Science Foundation for their generous support for this undertaking. We are particularly grateful to the efforts of Irina du Bois, whose commitment made the conference not only possibly but into a truly memorable occasion.

We would also like to express our gratitude to those who were instrumental in bringing this book into fruition. At the Graduate Institute we owe a special thanks to Lisa Komar for her copyediting efforts. Last, but in no way least, we wish to acknowledge the encouragement and support of the teams at Routledge and FiSH Books, in particular Andrew Humphrys, Annabelle Harris and Mark Livermore, as well as Jane Moody for an expert job at copy editing.

Notes

1   F. Halliday, *Two Hours That Shook the World. September 11, 2001: Causes and Consequences,* London: Saqi Books, 2001. Halliday borrowed his formulation from the American journalist John Reed's *Ten Days That Shook the World,* New York: Boni and Liveright, 1919, a first-hand account of the Russian Revolution.
2   G.W. Bush, 'Address Before a Joint Session of the Congress on the United States Response to the Terrorist Attacks of September 11', 20 September 2001. Available online: www.presidency.ucsb.edu/ws/index.php?pid=64731&st= &st1=#ixzz1vPRLneeZ (accessed 19 May 2012).
3   For a discussion of the problem of defining 'terrorism' see, for instance, A.P. Schmid, 'The Definition of Terrorism', Alex P. Schmid (ed.) *The Routledge Handbook of Terrorism Research,* London/New York: Routledge, 2011.
4   W. Laqueur, *The New Terrorism: Fanaticism and the Arms of Mass Destruction,* New York: Oxford University Press, 1999, p. 6.
5   B. Hoffman, *Inside Terrorism,* New York: Columbia University Press, 2006, p. 40.
6   Ibid., pp.40–1.
7   On the League of Nations and terrorism see B. Saul, 'The Legal Response of the League of Nations to Terrorism', *Journal of International Criminal Justice,* 2006, vol. 4, 78–102. See also C. Townshend, '*Methods which all civilized opinion must condemn': The League of Nations and International Action against Terrorism',* Chapter 2 in this volume.
8   Aittokoski, H. 'Finland shaken 100 years ago by murder of Governor-General Bobrikov', *Helsingin Sanomat International Edition,* 15 June 2004. Available online: www.hs.fi/english/article/1076153076611 (accessed 20 May 2012). Linguistically talented readers interested in this case may consult S. Zetterberg, *Viisi laukausta senaatissa. Eugen Schaumanin elämä ja teko,* Helsinki: Otava, 1986.

9   For more information on these differences see, for instance, B. Blumenau, 'The United Nations and West Germany's Efforts against International Terrorism in the 1970s' (Chapter 4), M. Lammert, 'The Absent Terrorism: Leftist Political Violence and the French State 1968–74' (Chapter 5), and N. Powell, 'The 'Claustre Affair': A Hostage Crisis, France, and Civil War in Chad, 1974–7'(Chapter 11), in this volume.

10 G. Chaliand and A. Blin (eds), *Histoire du Terrorisme. De L'Antiquité à Al Qaida,* Paris: Bayard, 2004, translated into English as: *The History of Terrorism. From Antiquity to Al Qaeda,* Berkeley: University of California Press, 2007; M. Burleigh, *Blood and Rage. A Cultural History of Terrorism,* London: Harper Press, 2008; R. Law, *Terrorism: A History,* London: Polity, 2009; W. Laqueur, *A History of Terrorism,* New York: Transaction Books, 2001, and W. Laqueur, *The Age of Terrorism,* Boston and Toronto: Little, Brown and Company, 1987; J.M. Lutz and B.J. Lutz, *Terrorism. Origins and Evolution,* New York: Palgrave Macmillan, 2005, and J.M. Lutz and B.J. Lutz, *Global Terrorism,* 2nd ed., London and New York: Routledge, 2008; Hoffman, op cit.; *A. Parry, Terrorism: From Robespierre to Arafat,* New York: Vanguard Press, 1976; B. Saul, *Defining Terrorism in International Law,* Oxford: Oxford University Press, 2006; P. Wilkinson, *Terrorism Versus Democracy: The Liberal State Response,* 3rd ed., London: Routledge, 2011. For a synopsis of the current state of the literature on terrorism, see for example, G. Duncan and A.P. Schmid, 'Bibliography of Terrorism', in Alex P. Schmid (ed.) *The Routledge Handbook of Terrorism Research,* London and New York: Routledge, 2011, pp. 475 –597.

Part I
Terrorism prior to the Cold War

1   The first global wave of terrorism and international counter-terrorism, 1905–14

Richard Bach Jensen

Arguably, history's first global wave of terrorism took place between about 1905 and 1914. This chapter will focus on the causes, contours of, and government responses to this largely anarchist- and nihilist-identified era of terrorism. Because of the wave's worldwide reach and astounding number of victims, particularly in Russia, I will suggest that this wave be considered as important as the more famous era of anarchist terrorism during the 1890s. Stepped up policing efforts, both nationally and internationally, paralleled and followed in the wake of anarchist and nihilist acts of violence, but the results of these efforts were decidedly mixed.

David Rapoport, whose four-wave conception of the history of modern terrorism is at present the most convincing overarching analysis of the historical evolution of modern terrorism, speaks of an 'anarchist wave' of terrorism between the 1880s and the 1920s. This was 'the first global or truly international terrorist experience in history'.[1] I would propose that several distinct currents or phases developed within this larger wave. Between 1878 and 1901, anarchist terrorism primarily affected Europe, although three notable violent episodes stunned the United States (US) and a few incidents took place in the Ottoman Empire and India. After the assassination of American President McKinley in September 1901 – and in some countries a few years before the assassination, in other words, around the turn of the century – a pause occurred in anarchist bombings and assassinations on both sides of the Atlantic. The pause was often attributed to a combination of the effects of a popular backlash against the terrorists, police repression, a reviving economy after the great depression of the nineteenth century, and increasing anarchist involvement in the labour movement through anarcho-syndicalism.[2] In several countries, for example in Italy, France, and the US, the emergence of strong, progressive governments that were politically more inclusive of dissenters and friendlier to the actions of labour was also a factor in the decline of anarchist violence. After about 1905, however, a new wave of mostly anarchist- and nihilist-identified violence began, but this time with global, not just north Atlantic, dimensions. The new wave severely affected countries and colonies on five continents: Europe, North and South America, and Asia; even Africa was involved.

The causes of this new outbreak of terrorism were multiple. It took place against the background of the first great period of economic globalization between 1890 and 1914 when the 'greatest international migration of people in history' took place, not equalled even in our present time.[3] This development was especially pronounced after 1900.[4] Most of the relevant migration was from Europe to the rest of the world, but occasionally it went the other way. Chinese, particularly Chinese students, who had journeyed to Paris (and also to Tokyo) began the transfer of anarchist ideas back to China, where anarchists began plotting assassinations around 1905. Young Indians travelled to Paris where they learned bomb making from émigré Russian revolutionists and brought the information back to India for deadly use.[5] While Paris was a significant transmission point, at the heart of the post–1905 wave of terrorism were Russia and Spain, two of the most politically backward and dysfunctional states in Europe. The actions of radicalized Russian and Spanish migrants and the activities and fate of Francesco Ferrer y Guardia, the Spanish educator and revolutionist, were two of the most important factors, either directly or indirectly, in spurring on global terrorism.

The mass media contributed to the sense of an international terrorist wave by identifying many assassinations and other violent deeds as 'anarchist' even if committed by non-anarchists. The police and government authorities were just as liable to such mislabelling. Even some of the anarchists and revolutionaries were confused and prone to misidentification. For example, in China and Japan aspiring anarchists tended to treat Russian 'nihilism', that is, the actions, and especially the terrorist acts, of the Socialist Revolutionary Party, as synonymous with the deeds of Western European anarchists.[6]

The media, the police, and the authorities usually dressed the terrorist wolf in anarchist clothing, not only because of the powerful impression left on the mentality of the age by the experience of anarchist terrorism during the 1890s, but also because violent anarchist acts were considered as non-political, as crimes against humanity and the law of nations. While Russian revolutionaries or rebelling nationalists might earn international sympathy and protection as political dissidents, violent anarchists could rarely hope for either sympathy or asylum.

A series of assassinations just before and after the onset of the Russian Revolution of 1905 and the revolution itself were especially important in prompting a new global wave of terrorism. Before the revolution, anarchists were considered unimportant inside Russia, where the populists or 'nihilists', and later, the Socialist Revolutionaries engineered most of the terrorist incidents. Unlike the anarchists, the Socialist Revolutionaries exercised tight, central control over terrorist acts, and beginning in 1901, targeted hated Tsarist officials, such as Interior Minister Plehve, assassinated in July 1904, and Grand Duke Sergei, murdered in February 1905. These killings helped unleash a decade of 'assassinationism' throughout the world. While the careful organization and conspiratorial method of these terrorist acts (that is, the so-called 'Russian method') greatly impressed revolutionaries and potential terrorists, it also needs to be pointed out that the latter continued to be inspired by the 'anarchist mystique': the myth of the powerful individual assassin striking down tyrants, and also by local traditions of political violence.[7]

The 1905 Revolution transformed Russian terrorism in a diffuse and unpredictable manner. Anarchist groups, in the words of a contemporary, 'sprang up like mushrooms after a rain'.[8] Many became deeply involved in a vicious, criminal, and 'motiveless' mass terrorism that lacked any ideological and ethical constraints. During 1906–07, the anarchists and the Socialist Revolutionaries killed 4,000 people.[9] According to Anna Geifman, anarchists were responsible for the majority of the 17,000 Russian casualties from terrorism between 1901 and 1916.[10] While these statistics are open to dispute, it is probably true to say that during this period in Russia more people were killed by anarchists or those identified as anarchists than throughout the rest of the world during the entire forty-year period from 1880 to 1920.

Russians fleeing Tsarist repression after the collapse of the 1905 Revolution brought terrorism, in a few scattered cases, to France and Switzerland, to the US, to Britain, and, perhaps most spectacularly, to Argentina. Many Russian revolutionaries went to Paris, where, around 1907, the French police reported, although presumably they exaggerated, that nearly 1,500 Russian 'terrorists' were living in the city. There they collaborated with Spanish anarchists and gave bomb-making lessons and manuals to Indians fighting British domination of the subcontinent.[11] Paris became a 'grand headquarters' – or at least a refuge and networking centre – for violent revolutionaries and terrorists from many lands.[12] There they were closely (although not closely enough!) monitored by both the French security forces and the Russian overseas police. More generally, the 1905 Russian Revolution excited and energized anarchists and socialists throughout the world since they believed it might be a model or inspiration for revolutions in their own countries.[13]

This was certainly true of the US, where, in 1908, a dozen violent incidents led to a major anarchist scare and, in the words of the *New York Times*, a declaration by the US government of 'open war on Anarchists'.[14] In April 1908, President Theodore Roosevelt declared that 'compared with the suppression of anarchy, every other question sinks into insignificance'. The outbreak of violence was due not only to the direct or indirect impact of the 1905 Revolution and Tsarist repression, but also to a severe economic crisis and unemployment during the winter of 1907–08. Newspapers and police officials linked together the unrelated violent deeds of an Italian anarchist in Denver (who had recently arrived from Argentina) and Russian immigrants in Chicago and New York City and made them into a vast anarchist plot.[15]

In Britain, the connection between Tsarist repression, the Revolution of 1905, and an outbreak of violence was even more direct. Latvian revolutionists who had escaped from the Russian Empire carried out a series of crimes, beginning with two robberies attended by several deaths (at Tottenham on 23 January 1909 and at Houndsditch on 16 December 1910) and climaxing in London's spectacular and bloody Sidney Street siege in January 1911. Although at the time these Baltic extremists were often identified as 'anarchists', they were mostly members of the Latvian Social Democratic Party. Their actions reflected the extremist, quasi-criminal or criminal attitudes of many opponents of the Tsarist regime as unleashed by the 1905 Revolution.[16]

Several incidents took place in France and Switzerland. In 1906, a young Russian woman killed a man in Interlaken, mistaking him for a former Russian interior minister.[17] On May Day 1907, a Russian anarchist with American citizenship fired at some French cuirassiers in Paris, wounding a police agent.[18] More serious was an incident on 18 September 1907, when Russians attempted to rob a branch of the Montreux bank in Veytaux, Switzerland, killing a bank clerk and a bystander and wounding several others. Intriguingly, the Russian initially identified themselves as Spanish.[19] Russian 'anarchists' also tried to extort money from wealthy compatriots residing in Switzerland.[20]

The second great source of global terrorism in the early twentieth century was Spain – especially the city of Barcelona – and the controversial Francisco Ferrer. In 1903, after a five-year pause, anarchist assassinations and bombs resumed in Spain. Between 1903 and 1909, over eighty bombs exploded in Barcelona, killing at least eleven people and injuring over seventy. In terms of casualties, these numbers far exceeded the more famous French terror of the mid-1890s. Panic gripped the population of the great port, which came to be referred to as the 'city of bombs'.[21] While Ferrer's connections to this bombing campaign are obscure or non-existent, he and his close associates have been linked to two of the era's most famous assassination attempts.

In some ways, Ferrer could be compared to Osama Bin Laden since for several years he bankrolled anarchist revolution and assisted would-be terrorists determined to overthrow the Spanish monarchy. His wealth made him very unusual among the anarchists, who generally had little or no money. Juan Avilés Farré's recent definitive biography of Ferrer demonstrates that he was fundamentally a revolutionary. This is in sharp contrast with earlier historiography that has portrayed Ferrer as essentially an idealistic educational reformer who founded fifty 'Modern Schools' in Spain and was the innocent victim of a reactionary, priest-ridden Spanish government eager to find a scapegoat for the country's social problems and rampant terrorism.

The first of the assassination attempts in which Ferrer was alleged to be involved occurred in Paris in May 1905, when an attempt was made on King

Alfonso XIII's life while he was riding in a carriage together with the French President. A much more significant attack occurred on 31 May 1906. Shortly after Alfonso's wedding, the king and his new bride proceeded down the Calle Mayor in Madrid when a powerful bomb was thrown at the royal procession, injuring about one hundred and thirty people: twenty-three to thirty-three killed and over one hundred wounded.[22] Once again, the young Spanish king (as well as his consort) escaped unharmed. In terms of the total number of casualties, this was the bloodiest act of anarchist terrorism up until this point. It was also one of the most famous, since it took place in full view of thousands of people and in the glare of the international media. Mateo Morral, who Ferrer had hired as a librarian and publishing assistant at the Modern School in Barcelona, was the assassin. Spanish historians think that Morral was also involved in the Paris bombing of 1905. In addition, there may be a Russian connection. According to a Spanish informer and the Barcelona police, Russian terrorists were involved in both the 1905 and 1906 attempts on the king. Indeed, Morral's girlfriend at the time was the Russian Nora Falk, described by a friend of Morral's as a 'nihilist' who had fled Tsarist persecution and who Avilés Farré suspects was a terrorist.[23]

As for Ferrer, he probably knew about the 1905 bombing, since he was friends with all of the suspects (although they were acquitted after a politically charged trial). Although conclusive proof is still lacking, Avilés Farré provides much evidence that Ferrer was deeply involved in the 1906 assassination attempt.[24] In 1909, Ferrer was finally condemned to death by a military tribunal for a crime he certainly did not commit: plotting and instigating 'Tragic Week', a bloody 1909 revolt in Barcelona. Ferrer's execution led to massive, sometimes violent, demonstrations throughout Europe and the Americas. Ferrer became a heroic martyr, not only to the anarchists, but also to progressives of all kinds.

The desire to avenge Ferrer's execution motivated two assassination attempts in Spain. The first was the murder of Prime Minister Canalejas in November 1912 by Manuel Pardiñas, who had travelled to Spain after living in Cuba and Tampa, Florida. The second was an unsuccessful attack on King Alfonso XIII in April 1913.[25]

During 1909–10, the two major sources of global terrorism – the reaction to Tsarist repression in Russia and to conditions in Spain, especially the execution of Ferrer – came together in a single stream in Argentina. Historians have largely overlooked the important phenomenon of terrorism prior to the First World War in Argentina. By the early twentieth century, Buenos Aires had become the largest single anarchist centre in the world with perhaps ten thousand or more anarchists, a daily anarchist newspaper, and a multitude of anarchist organizations. Between 1905 and 1910, Russian, Spanish, and Argentinean anarchists made two attempts on the life of the President of Argentina, carried out eight or more bombings, including bombing the Cathedral of Buenos Aires and the great Colon opera house, and assassinated Ramon Falcon, the powerful, iron fisted police chief of the capital. In 1908, an Argentina periodical accused Abraham Hartenstein, a nineteen-year-old boiler – and sometime bomb – maker from Odessa, Russia, of founding the 'Black Gang' and introducing terrorism into Argentina. The latter claim seems exaggerated, given the two previous assassination attempts on Argentine presidents. Nonetheless, terrorism now entered a new and more menacing phase with the arrival of the Russians. In 1909, the Italian minister to Argentina wrote that 'the anarchist element [has been] immeasurably increased in recent times by adherents exiled from Russia'.[26] The Buenos Aires police declared that they had discovered a chemical laboratory, bombs, and evidence that Hartenstein's Black Gang was planning to blow up the public water works and the main electrical power plant of Buenos Aires.[27] Hartenstein soon returned to Europe where, in February 1909, he killed two police officers in Ghent.[28]

In October and November 1909, a bombing and an attempted bombing were carried out against Spanish targets in Argentina in protest against Ferrer's execution. Catalonians were responsible for the 14 October bombing of the Spanish consulate in Rosario and Russians for the failed attempt on the Carmen chapel in Buenos Aires. In the most sensational act of violence, on 14 November 1909, Simon Radowisky assassinated the police chief of Buenos Aires. Radowisky had fled Russia after being injured and arrested as an anarchist during the 1905 Revolution. His victim, Falcon, was arguably a pillar of the Argentine state and his assassination caused enormous alarm. In a sign of both protest and solidarity, leading cabinet ministers together with two hundred thousand other people paraded past Falcon's open coffin. Moreover, the government declared sixty days of martial law and arrested thousands of real or suspected anarchists, some of whom were tortured and many more deported. Newspapers and union officers were closed down and censorship imposed.[29]

Other violent acts by real or alleged anarchists that gave the 1905–14 wave of terrorism a global dimension can be quickly summarized. In 1907–09 anarchist terrorist incidents, leading to three deaths, took place for the first time in Sweden. A Swedish anarchist, perhaps thwarted in his attempt to assassinate the Tsar who was visiting Stockholm, ended up killing a Swedish major. This anarchist had been in active contact with anarchists from Russia who had taken refuge in Stockholm. This was the first political assassination in Swedish history since the eighteenth century.[30] Beginning in 1905, Indian 'anarchists' (actually nationalists but so-called by the newspapers and British government authorities) assassinated and bombed in India and London.[31] Real or alleged anarchist incidents also occurred in Italy, Belgium, Germany, Denmark, France, and the Ottoman Empire. In March 1913, an 'educated anarchist' shot to death King George I of Greece.[32] Several Japanese dissidents, radicalized by their opposition to the Russo-Japanese war, became anarchists and advocated assassination.

Before being arrested in 1910, they had talked about murdering government figures, blowing up buildings, and consummating a 'revolution of terror'. They also apparently conspired to kill the emperor. This was the first such plot against the emperor in perhaps thirteen hundred years of Japanese history.[33]

In China, 'assassinationism', a product of anarchist and Russian nihilist influence as well as nationalist sentiment, came into vogue between 1905 and 1912. Besides individual attacks, at least four 'assassination squads' or 'corps' were organized to carry out the murder of Manchu officials. One such bombing attack in October 1911 led to the death of 20 people and the partial or complete destruction of seven to eight buildings.[34] The assassination of a leading Manchu noble in January 1912 'as much as anything' convinced the imperial court to abdicate.[35] Tellingly, the one and only assassination attempt against the British governor of Hong Kong occurred during this period (4 July 1912).[36]

In May 1910, Butrus Ghali, the prime minister of Egypt and a Christian, was assassinated by Ibrahim Nasif al-Wardani, a Moslem and Egyptian nationalist who for two years had studied in Switzerland where, according to evidence produced at his trial, he had associated with Russian 'revolutionaries and anarchists' and read anarchist literature. This was the 'first public assassination of a prominent political figure in Egypt in more than a century'.[37]

The climactic and concluding event of the first global wave of terrorism, as well as of four years of assassination attempts in the Balkans, was the June 1914 murder of Archduke Franz Ferdinand.[38] Although the Young Bosnians were mostly south Slav nationalists, rather than anarchists, they were routinely identified as the latter by the Austrian authorities.[39] At least temporarily, and in most countries, the First World War put an end to the era of terrorism that had begun around 1905.

Government responses to the 1905–14 terrorist wave

Nations responded to the new wave of anarchist, anarchist-identified, and nihilist *attentats* in several different ways. Calls went out for a new international accord to prevent and repress anarchist crimes, but these proved fruitless. Repeated efforts were undertaken to render the 1904 anti-anarchist St Petersburg Protocol, signed by a dozen European states, a functioning and more effective agreement, although attempts to increase its membership failed. Italy, in particular, but also Austria, Spain, Russia, and Argentina, expanded their networks of policemen and informers operating throughout Europe and abroad.[40] Between 1908 and 1912, Spain carried out some of the most important police reforms in its history. These led to the foundation of a modern police force.[41] Continued international pressure on Switzerland led it to pass new anti-anarchist legislation, agree to extradition accords aimed at the anarchists, and expel terrorists and violent revolutionaries. Britain and other countries made efforts to reduce bureaucratic delays and improve communications regarding the exchange of information about the anarchists. Various North and South American countries signed multilateral treaties to expedite the extradition of anarchists and to improve police cooperation. By 1913–14, however, the St Petersburg Protocol gave signs of coming unravelled. The remainder of this chapter will focus primarily on the evolution of that agreement.[42]

The anti-anarchist league led by Germany and Russia was the most important multilateral anti-terrorist association created prior to the signing of several conventions among the European states in the late 1970s.[43] The system laid down by the Protocol, however, proved to be a continual work in progress.[44] By June of 1904, Russia, Rumania, Serbia, Bulgaria, the Ottoman Empire, Austria–Hungary, Germany, Denmark, Sweden–Norway, Spain, and Portugal had adhered to the agreement. Switzerland became a de facto member of the group and, in May 1904, Luxembourg concluded a trilateral anti-anarchist accord (based on the St Petersburg Protocol) with Germany and Russia alone. The 1904 Protocol specified procedures for expulsion, called for the creation of central anti-anarchist offices in each country, and in general, regularized inter-police communication regarding anarchists.

The bloody Madrid bombing of May 1906 spurred new efforts toward international cooperation. Spain called for an 'international accord for the repression and prevention of anarchist crimes'.[45] The Spanish interior minister emphasized that 'in order to be effective, the surveillance of the anarchists must be worldwide, because it is a universal social evil'.[46] But the death of the Duke of Almodóvar del Rio, the able Spanish Foreign Minister, and the reluctance of other European powers, such as Italy, to sign a new accord led to the initiative's failure.[47]

Nevertheless, Berlin thought that now might be the time to achieve closer anti-anarchist cooperation with London, if possible getting it to adhere to the St Petersburg Protocol or at least a modified version of it. On 7 June 1906, the Germans asked the British Foreign Secretary 'whether the British government would change its attitude with regard to measures for dealing with anarchists'.[48] The British refused since they objected to having their 'hands tied by the stipulation of a convention'. Nonetheless, an internal Foreign Office memo made the significant admission that 'practically we carry out most of the provisions of the general protocol signed . . . on March 1, 1904' and that Britain had 'adopted her [Switzerland's] attitude as our model'.[49] If the Continental Powers had more fully realized and appreciated that this was British policy, they might have been less prone to their constant criticizing of England for harbouring anarchists.

The British also rebuked Russian feelers for closer cooperation, refusing its request of 21 November 1906 for direct inter-police communications regarding the anarchists. The head of the Metropolitan Police objected to the extra work that such communication would demand of his department and the difficulties presented by Russian and Polish names.[50] In 1909, following the Tottenham outrage, the Russians once again thought of approaching the British regarding adherence to the St Petersburg Protocol. They ultimately decided against taking this step, however, since they realized that the increasingly strained relations between London and Berlin made the former loath to become involved in an international agreement signed by the Germans.[51]

The failure to secure new international measures involving Britain, Italy, and other states in the aftermath of the Madrid bloodbath was perhaps the last chance for such an accord or for an enlargement of the anti-anarchist league. Nonetheless, the system set up by the St Petersburg Protocol continued to be fine-tuned and in some cases strengthened.

In February 1907, Switzerland agreed to improve the procedures calling for prior notification before anarchists were expelled across the Austro-Hungarian and German borders. These procedures were spelled out in writing but, counter to what has been alleged, this did not mean that Switzerland formally signed the St Petersburg Protocol.[52] The negotiations leading up to this highly secret agreement were set in motion by an incident in August 1905 when Switzerland expelled the anarchists Siegfried Nacht and Josef Urban. Despite Swiss efforts to forewarn Vienna, the anarchists managed to evade the Austrian authorities and enter Tyrol, where the Emperor Franz Joseph was observing army manoeuvres. Taken aback by the Austrian emperor's possible exposure to an attack from supposedly dangerous anarchists, the Swiss agreed on a proposal whereby a Swiss Justice Department employee would by word of mouth inform an official of the Austrian embassy about an impending expulsion. Switzerland would also provide the Austrians with photographs and detailed descriptions of the deportees. To mask what was essentially an act of administrative extradition, the anarchists would be escorted to the border by detectives in civilian clothes, rather than by police and officials in uniform, as was done with other expelled or extradited persons.[53] On 15 June 1907, Switzerland followed up its Austrian accord with a German agreement designating border places for the exchange of expelled anarchists.[54] Neither the cantonal governments nor the Swiss parliament were informed of these agreements since it was feared they would become the subject of vociferous objections from radicals and socialists.

In other ways as well, after 1905, Switzerland toughened its approach to anarchists and violent revolutionaries and adopted harsher public policies of expulsion, extradition, and repression. In 1906, two Italian anarchists were expelled for spreading anti-militarist propaganda.[55] In November, a Swiss court applied the recently passed law penalizing support for anarchist crimes and sent the Swiss publicist Luigi Bertoni to jail for a month for commemorating the actions of the assassin Bresci.[56] Also in 1906, to avoid punishment for a similar deed in Italy, Armando Borghi, editor of the weekly anarchist publication *Aurora*, fled to Switzerland. He was stopped at the border 'as a dangerous anarchist, due to an international convention against the anarchists of which I don't know the year'. The Swiss also informed the Italian police, who arrested Borghi.[57]

In June 1906, May 1907, June 1908, and September 1909, the Swiss judiciary ordered the extradition back to their homeland of four Russian revolutionaries.[58] In each case, the Swiss federal tribunal refused to accept the argument that their violent deeds were political crimes. On 22 February and 18 March 1908, Bern also signed agreements with, respectively, Russia and Italy that provided for the extradition of persons guilty of the abusive use of explosives.[59] Switzerland was no longer an automatic place of asylum for anarchists or terrorists, as it seemingly once had been. This change in Swiss practice, which was also probably due to the reaction against such bloody incidents as the Interlaken murder and the Veytaux bank robbery, deeply impressed international opinion.[60]

Besides integrating the Swiss more closely into their anti-anarchist pact, Germany and Russia worked to make the provisions of the St Petersburg Protocol operational. This took a surprisingly long time. Almost ten years after the signing of the agreement, some of the signatories had not yet designated either the border points or the authorities who were to receive expelled anarchists or both.[61] In January 1914, Berlin noted that the German federal states often observed neither the St Petersburg Protocol nor the regulations governing the internal German anti-anarchist system as promulgated in the circulars of 28 November 1898 and 23 May 1908.[62]

Why these delays and omissions? While it is not entirely clear why simple administrative decisions should have taken such a long time to implement and communicate, one can offer several plausible explanations. Perhaps the predominant reason was that the countries and the German states that had failed to comply with the requirements of the St Petersburg Protocol were not important centres of anarchist activity (aside from Russia, which frequently confused the issue by making no distinction between anarchists and revolutionary socialists). Nor – with the possible exception of Berlin – were the cities of these countries centres of large-scale Russian immigration with active revolutionary subcultures. Moreover the outbreak of the Russo-Japanese War in February 1904 and the subsequent 1905 revolution diverted the attention of the Russian government from the anarchist threat abroad. Finally, the friendly relations between Germany and Russia that had been crucial in the creation of the St Petersburg Protocol became increasingly strained after the conclusion of an Anglo-Russian Entente in August 1907.

Several further attempts were made to expand the number of nations participating in the St Petersburg Protocol. Germany renewed its invitation to Italy but, in August 1908, Prime Minister Giolitti turned down Berlin's suggestion that Rome adhere to the Protocol on the same abridged terms as Switzerland or Luxembourg.[63] Another failed initiative involved Japan. In February 1909, Tokyo approached Berlin about possibly adhering to the Protocol. Japan expressed concern about anarchists arriving in the country from the American Northwest (referring, perhaps, to the establishment in 1906 by Kotoku Shusui, the leading Japanese anarchist, of a Social Revolutionary Party among Japanese Americans in San Francisco and Oakland).[64] In 1909, Germany responded to the Japanese request by first sounding out Russia, which raised no objections to Tokyo's adherence, and then consulting the other members of the anti-anarchist pact.[65] Some eight months later, after examining the Protocol, Japan informed Germany that regretfully, as things stood in Japan, it was 'not in a position' [*nicht in der Lage*] to join the Protocol. Why Japan declined is unclear. It may have been because the US was not a member or because Japan did not yet possess a political police force capable of carrying out the systematic communications with the European states that were required by the Protocol.

In late November 1913, Spain wished to return to the question of enlarging the anti-anarchist league and making it more effective. A year earlier, the assassination of Prime Minister Canalejas had led to a reorganization and centralization of the Spanish police under a *Direccion General de Seguridad* (DGS). At the request of the DGS, the Spanish government suggested to Germany that Italy and the US, as well as the Latin American countries of Argentina, Brazil, Cuba, and Panama, be invited to adhere because they were 'very important centres [*focos importantisimos*] of the universal anarchist movement'.[66] Spain also asked for more effective and continuous exchange of information about the anarchists (including their actions in organizing revolutionary strikes), the use of a single language when communicating, and the establishment of the requirement that, at the request of consular officials, captains keep track of the anarchists on board their ships. Little seems to have come of the Spanish proposals; nor did those countries of interest to Spain subsequently adhere to the Protocol. Berlin informed Madrid that, given their earlier flat refusals, it was pointless to ask the US and Italy to join the Protocol again.[67]

Decline of the St. Petersburg 'system'

Before the First World War, signs appeared that anti-anarchist cooperation between the European states was diminishing. At the end of September 1913, Switzerland refused to transport Italian anarchists expelled from Germany directly into the hands of the Italian police, as it had done in the past. The Swiss also insisted that henceforth a return be made to the former practice used prior to the St Petersburg Protocol; that is, that communications regarding anarchists be made via the diplomatic route rather than directly through police channels.[68] At the beginning of the next year, Sweden, Norway, and Portugal (which in 1910 had become a republic after overthrowing its monarchy) informed Berlin that, like Switzerland, they wished to rely exclusively on diplomatic channels when communicating about anarchist expulsions.[69] In July 1914, apparently subscribing to the view that the assassins of the Archduke Franz Ferdinand were anarchists, the influential head of the Austro-Hungarian army urged his government to threaten to cancel the 1904 St Petersburg Protocol with Russia, in order to pressure the Tsar into withholding his support from Serbia during Vienna's confrontation with Belgrade.[70]

Conclusion

During the period 1905–14, the occurrence of assassinations or attempts in Sweden, Croatia, Japan, Hong Kong, and Egypt, for the first time in over a century or more, is striking. Striking as well is the number of these and other assassinations and bombings that were connected globally to the Russian revolutionary diaspora, especially after the 1905 Revolution, and to Ferrer and his fellow Spanish anarchists – or inspired by Russian terrorism and Ferrer's martyrdom.

It must also be emphasized that Russian and Spanish anarchists and revolutionaries, or the influence of their violent deeds, spread terrorism only to countries and territories where local conditions favoured its outbreak. There may have been thousands of so-called Russian 'terrorists' in Paris, but they rarely bombed purely French targets, except on two occasions when bombs went off by accident.[71] Large numbers of Russian émigrés moved to Italy and Switzerland but after 1901 they carried out no bombings (although in Switzerland, admittedly, one bloody robbery and one assassination against a non-Swiss target). This was because political and socio-economic conditions were unfavourable to such actions. In order to preserve their asylum in Switzerland, exiled Russian socialists went so far as to try to prevent 'expropriations' and even to send dangerous anarchists back to Russia.[72] But where economic malaise and social repression exacerbated discontent and where government authoritarianism and brutality made peaceful protest ineffectual or impossible, Russian and Spanish revolutionaries and anarchists found an eager audience and fertile ground for extreme actions. In terms of world terrorism, it usually took two to tango: an 'exporting' country characterized by political, social, and economic malfunction and an 'importing' country with its own particular configuration of discontents.

Government responses to anarchist and nihilist violence between 1905 and 1914 were of some importance at the national and bilateral level, but in the international and multilateral arena usually ineffectual. The modernization of the Spanish police between 1908 and 1912 was groundbreaking. The change in Swiss policies after 1905 was also notable, as was the British admission that for the most part they followed the Swiss anti-anarchist model and had adhered *de facto* to the St Petersburg Protocol. The multilateral response, however, proved weak, since national interests and political rivalries usually trumped the desire for a coordinated international effort against the terrorists. What genuine progress was made, as for example between the Swiss and the Austrians and Germans regarding the St Petersburg Protocol, often had to be carried out in utter secrecy.

Notes

1   D. Rapoport, 'The Four Waves of Modern Terrorism', in A. K. Cronin and J. M. Ludes (eds) *Attacking Terrorism: Elements of a Grand Strategy*, Washington, DC: Georgetown University Press, 2004, pp. 46–73.

2   J. Romero Maura, 'Terrorism in Barcelona and its Impact on Spanish Politics, 1904–1909', *Past and Present*, 1968, vol. 41: 130–83; R. Núñez Florencio, *El terrorismo anarquista (1888–1909)*, Madrid: Siglo veintiuno, 1983, p. 59.

3   E. J. Hobsbawm, *The Age of Empire, 1875–1914*, New York: Vintage, 1989, p.153.

4   For example, the average number of emigrants from Italy to the rest of the world was twice as large annually in the 1901–05 period as during the 1890s. C. Seton-Watson, *Italy from Liberalism to Fascism*, London: Methuen, 1967, p. 314.

5   R. J. Popplewell, *Intelligence and Imperial Defence. British Intelligence and the Defence of the Indian Empire, 1904–1924*, London: Frank Cass, 1995, p. 104; P. Heehs, *The Bomb in Bengal: The Rise of Revolutionary Terrorism in India, 1900–1910*, Delhi/Oxford: Oxford University Press, 1993, pp. 90–1.

6   'The most influential of the books published [in Chinese on anarchism] in 1903, *Modern Anarchism* [. . .] described the Russian populist movement instead of theoretical anarchism'. For several years 'Chinese publicists' used 'anarchism and nihilism interchangeably'. E. Krebs, *Shifu, Soul of Chinese Anarchism*, New York: Rowman and Littlefield, 1998, pp. 36–7; also pp. 4, 33–5.

7   In my view, S. G. Marks, *How Russia Shaped the Modern World: from Art to Antisemitism, Ballet to Bolshevism*, Princeton: Princeton University Press, 2003, exaggerates the influence of 'the Russian method' on the development of international terrorism (see Chapter 1: 'Organizing Revolution: The Russian Terrorists'). During the 1890s, when no significant assassinations or terrorist acts had taken place inside Russia nor – with one possible exception – had Russian terrorists operated outside the country, a powerful image had emerged of the Western European anarchist assassin. Even the exception, the Polish Stanislaw Padlewski's assassination of the ex-head of the St. Petersburg police, General Seliverstov, may have been a case of police provocation by the Okhrana. A. Butterworth, *The World That Never Was*, New York: Pantheon, 2010, pp. 276, 376. For the anarchist mystique, see R. B. Jensen, 'Daggers, Rifles and Dynamite: Anarchist Terrorism in Nineteenth Century Europe', *Terrorism and Political Violence*, 2004, vol. 16, pp. 116–53.

8   P. Avrich, *The Russian Anarchists*, Princeton: Princeton University Press, 1967, p. 42.

9   P. Avrich, *The Russian Anarchists*, Princeton: Princeton University Press, 1967, p. 64.

10   A. Geifman, *Thou Shalt Kill: Revolutionary Terrorism in Russia, 1894–1917*, Princeton: Princeton University Press, 1995, pp. 124–5.

11   P. Heehs, *The Bomb in Bengal: The Rise of Revolutionary Terrorism in India, 1900–1910*, Delhi/Oxford: Oxford University Press, 1993, pp. 90–1. According to French police estimates for Paris in 1907, 550 Russian émigré 'anarchists' and some 900 'revolutionaries', of whom 200 were maximalists, were unqualified advocates of violence. Nicolas Safranski, identified by the Paris police as an 'anarchist', but actually a maximalist member of the Socialist Revolutionary Party, instructed the Indians on explosives.

12   Paris police report on 'Russian revolutionary schemings' in France, December 1907. R. H. Johnston, *New Mecca, New Babylon: Paris and the Russian Exiles*,

1920–1945, Kingston/Montreal: McGill-Queen's University Press, 1988, p. 17.

13 'If it is true that because of its geographical distance, its evolution and its outcome the Russian Revolution of 1905 did not succeed in putting profound roots into the mental habits of the Italian anarchists of the epoch, it is just as certain that it revitalized the revolutionary instincts and the dreams of change that continued to nurture themselves from a past always more out of focus [. . .].' M. Antonioli, 'Gli anarchici italiani e la rivoluzione russa del 1905', in *Sentinelle perdute: Gli anarchici, la morte, la Guerra*, Pisa: BFS edizioni, 2009, p. 41. Italian anarchist publications wrote of the excitement produced by the assassination of Grand Duke Sergei (p. 48) and the feeling that the revolution in Russia would be 'the signal of a explosion of a series of revolts in other nations' (p. 50).

14 *New York Times*, 4 March 1908.

15 R. J. Goldstein, 'The Anarchist Scare of 1908: A Sign of Tensions in the Progressive Era', *American Studies*, 1974, vol. 15, pp. 50–75.

16 For more information on the Tottenham, Houndsditch, and Sidney Street episodes, see F. B. Clarke, *Will-o'-the Wisp: Peter the Painter and the Anti-Tsarist Terrorists in Britain and Australia*, Melbourne: Oxford University Press, 1983, pp. 33–7. The Social Democratic Party repudiated the actions of the Tottenham robbers while the English press frequently identified them as 'foreign Anarchists'. D. Rumbelow, *The Houndsditch Murders and the Siege of Sidney Street*, London: W. H. Allen, 1988, pp. 32, 43, 45.

17 M. Vuilleumier, *Immigrés et réfugiés en Suisse: Aperçu historique*, 2nd ed., Zurich: Pro Helvetia, 1989, p. 57.

18 *The Times* (London), 2, 3 May 1907, p. 5.

19 This incident is apparently referred to in P. Avrich, *The Russian Anarchists*, Princeton: Princeton University Press, 1967, pp. 51, 53, 70, although he mistakenly locates the robbery in Montreux rather than nearby Veytaux. A Parisian newspaper identified the robbers as Paul Nilista and Maxime Danieloff, although these may well have been aliases. *Le Gaulois*, 19 September 1907. See also *The Times* (London), 19 September 1907, p. 3.

20 A. Geifman, *Thou Shalt Kill: Revolutionary Terrorism in Russia, 1894–1917*, Princeton: Princeton University Press, 1995, pp. 37–8.

21 R. Núñez Florencio, *El terrorismo anarquista (1888–1909)*, Madrid: Siglo veintiuno, 1983, p. 75.

22 For a detailed narrative of the assault, see A. J. Calvert, *The Spanish Royal Wedding: An Account of the Marriage of H.M. Alfonso XIII of Spain and H.R.H. Pincess Victoria Eugénie of Battenberg*, Taunton: Phoenix, 1906.

23 J. Avilés Farré, *Francisco Ferrer y Guardia: pedagogo, anarquista y mártir*, Madrid: Marcial Pons Ediciones de Historia, 2006, pp. 152, 168–9, 189–90.

24 See J. Avilés Farré, *Francisco Ferrer y Guardia: pedagogo, anarquista y mártir*, Madrid: Marcial Pons Ediciones de Historia, 2006, ch.7.

25 With Canalejas, it is a question of probability, rather than certainty, since the assassin committed suicide immediately after the murder. S. Sueiro Seoane, 'El asesinato de Canalejas y los anarquistas españoles en Estados Unidos', in J. Avilés and Á. Herrerín (eds), *El nacimiento del terrorismo en occidente*, Madrid: Siglo XXI, 2008, pp. 159–88; E. Comin Colomer, *Un siglo de atentados políticos en España*, Madrid: [Editorial N.O.S.], 1951, pp. 209–10.

26 Macchi di Cellere, Buenos Aires, to Tittoni, Rome, 4 December 1909. IFM, Z–contenzioso, f. 49, folder 908.

30   *Richard Bach Jensen*

27   J. Moya, 'The Positive Side of Stereotypes: Jewish Anarchists in Early-Twentieth-Century Buenos Aires', *Jewish History*, 2004, vol. 18, p. 30.
28   Hartenstein used a number of aliases; for example, Vladimir Seliger (or Zelinger), Alexander Sokolof. J. Moulaert, *Le mouvement anarchiste en Belgique*, trans. S. Haupert, Ottignies, Belgium: Quorum, 1996, p. 299.
29   *Buenos Aires Herald*, 16 November 1909; J. Suriano, *Trabajadores, anarquismo y Estado represor: de la Ley de residencia a la Ley de defensa social (1902–1910)*, Buenos Aires: CEAL, 1988, p. 16; A. J. Capelletti, 'Anarquismo Latinoamericano', in C. M. Rama and A. J. Cappelletti (eds), *El Anarquismo en América Latina*, Caracas, Venezuela : Biblioteca Ayacucho, 1990, p. xxxii, gives a figure of more than 2,000 detained and deported.
30   K. Lithner, 'Assassination in Sweden', in J. F. Kirkham *et al.* (eds), *Assassination and Political Violence: Report to the National Commission on the Causes and Prevention of Violence*, New York: Praeger, 1970, pp. 731–2.
31   P. Heehs, *The Bomb in Bengal: The Rise of Revolutionary Terrorism in India, 1900–1910*, Delhi/Oxford: Oxford University Press, 1993, pp. 90–1; *The Times* (London), 4 May 1908); 'Indian Anarchism', *The Times* (London), 12 February 1909.
32   Although often dismissed as simply a 'madman', several witnesses attest to Aleko Schinas's intelligence and commitment to anarchist ideas. See 'King's Murderer is Educated Anarchist', and 'The Assassin Lived Here', *New York Times*, 20 March 1913, p. 3.
33   I. L. Plotkin, *Anarchism in Japan: A Study of the Great Treason Affair 1910–1911*, Lewiston, Queenstown and Lampeter: Edwin Mellen, 1990, pp. 13–14, 24–7, 108; C. Tsuzuki, 'Kotoku, Osugi, and Japanese Anarchism', *Hitotsubashi Journal of Social Studies*, 1966, vol. 3: 30–42. After Kotoku met Miyashita Takichi, the most active conspirator in the assassination plot against the emperor, he said that with a terrorist like him: 'Japan would become somewhat like Russia'. Tsuzuki, op cit., p. 36).
34   Two of the assassination corps cooperated in killing Fengshan, who had been sent to restore order in Guangzhou. Krebs, op cit., p. 69.
35   Liangbi, a leading proponent of resistance to a republican takeover, was from the collateral line of the imperial family. E. J. M. Rhoads, *Manchus and Han: Ethnic Relations and Political Power in Late Qing and Early Republican China, 1861–1928*, Seattle: University of Washington Press, 2000, pp. 21, 23, 154–5, 222. For a list of bombings and assassination attempts during the final years (1905–12) of the Ch'ing, see D. Tretiak, 'Political Assassinations in China, 1600–1968', in J. F. Kirkham *et al.* (eds), *Assassination and Political Violence: Report to the National Commission on the Causes and Prevention of Violence*, New York: Praeger, p. 644.
36   N. J. Miner, 'The Attempt to Assassinate the Governor in 1912', *Journal of the Royal Asiatic Society Hong Kong Branch*, 1982, vol. 22, pp. 279–84.
37   M. Badrawi, *Political Violence in Egypt 1910–1924: Secret Societies, Plots and Assassinations*, Richmond, Surrey: Curzon Press, 2000, pp. 28, 32, 37–8, 46. The Western press, however, labelled the crime as 'nationalist'. *The Times* (London), 21–4 February 1910; *New York Times*, 21–2 February 1910.
38   For information on these Balkan assassination attempts and Young Bosnia's connection to Socialist Revolutionary and anarchist groups and influence, see V. Dedijer, *The Road to Sarajevo*, New York: Simon and Schuster, 1966, pp. 181, 200, 226, 236, 357, 435.

39 V. Dedijer, *The Road to Sarajevo*, New York: Simon and Schuster, 1966, pp. 226, 275.

40 R. B. Jensen, 'The International Campaign Against Anarchist Terrorism, 1880–1930s', *Terrorism and Political Violence*, 2009, vol. 21: 89–109 (especially pp. 96–7).

41 A. Viqueira Hinojosa, *Historia y Anecdotario de la policía española 1833–1931*, Madrid: San Martin, 1989, p. 110; M. Turrado Vidal, *Estudios sobre historia de la policía*, Madrid: Ministerio del Interior, 1986, vol. 1, pp. 37–8.

42 This section of the essay is a revised and condensed version of a chapter that will appear in my forthcoming book, *The Battle against Anarchist Terrorism: An International History, 1878–1934*, Cambridge University Press.

43 See Chapter 4 of P. Romaniuk, *Multilateral Counter-Terrorism: The Global Politics of Cooperation and Contestation*, London: Routledge, 2010.

44 For the basic history of the St. Petersburg Protocol, which was a sequel to the 1898 international anti-anarchist conference of Rome, see R. B. Jensen, 'The International Campaign Against Anarchist Terrorism, 1880–1930s', *Terrorism and Political Violence*, 2009, vol. 21, pp. 97–9.

45 This phrase, referring to the foreign minister's instructions in his telegram of 14 June, can be found in: Duke of Arcos, Rome, to Foreign Minister, Madrid, 19 June 1906, SFM. OP. L. 2751/336.

46 Count de Romanones, interview in *Le Journal*, 6 June 1906, cited by E. González Calleja, *La razón de la fuerza. Orden público, subversión y violencia política en la España de la Restauración (1875–1917)*, Madrid: Consejo superior de investigaciones científicas, 1998, p. 376.

47 Duke of Arcos, Rome, to foreign minister, Madrid, 19 June 1906, SFM. OP. L. 2751

48 Copy, extract from dispatch, FO to Sir F Lascelles, Berlin, n. 149, 7 June 1906, in HO144/757/118516/15, PRO; Stumm, German Embassy, London, to Von Bülow, Reich Chancellor, Berlin. 8 June 1908, GFO, Eur.gen.91, Bd. 4.

49 W.E. Davidson, 8 June 1908, FO371/78; A.H. D[ixon], 'Memorandum as to the Protocol of 1904 respecting Anarchist Crimes', 13 July 1906, HO144/757/118516, PRO.

50 The Russian note was dated 21 November 1906. Copy of this and Secretary Gladstone's reply in PRO. HO144/757/118516/47 and /51. B. Porter, *The Origins of the Vigilant State: The London Metropolitan Police Special Branch Before the First World War*, London: Weidenfeld and Nicolson, 1987, p. 159.

51 See the Russian diplomatic notes of 30 January and 17 April 1909, cited in R. Johnson, *The Okhrana Abroad, 1885–1917*, Columbia University, PhD, 1970, pp. 65–6; and F. Zuckerman, *The Tsarist Secret Police Abroad: Policing Europe in a Modernising World*, Houndmills, Basingstoke, Hampshire: Palgrave Macmillan, 2003, p. 65.

52 H. Liang, *The Rise of Modern Police and the European State System from Metternich to the Second World War*, Cambridge: Cambridge University Press, 1992, p. 174; and, citing Liang, P. Romaniuk, *Multilateral Counter-Terrorism: The Global Politics of Cooperation and Contestation*, London: Routledge, 2010, p. 26. The St Petersburg Protocol called for the prior notification of anarchist expulsions.

53 Heidler, Bern, to Aehrenthal, Vienna, secret, 7 February 1907, HHStA. Adm. Reg. F52/9.

54 Schmidt-Dargitz, Foreign Ministry, to Interior Ministry, Berlin, 8 January 1914, GCSAP, Interior Ministry, 13689. F. 449.

55 F. J. Saint-Aubin, *L'extradition et le droit extraditionnel: Théorique et Appliqué*, Paris: A. Pedone, 1913, vol.1, p. 440.

56 According to G. Casagrande, 'Mises en fiche du début du siecle: le cas Luigi Bertoni', in *Cent ans de police politique en Suisse (1889–1989)*, Lausanne: Editions d'enbas, 1992, p. 76.

57 A. Borghi, *Mezzo Secolo di Anarchia*, Naples: Edizioni scientifiche italiane, 1954, pp. 97, 129–30.

58 R. Corbaz, *Le Crime Politique et la Jurisprudence du Tribunal Fédéral Suisse en matière d'extradition*, Lausanne: G. Vaney-Burnier, 1927, pp. 102–25.

59 *Repertoire de droit international privè et de droit penal international*, 1929, s.v. 'Anarchiste', 1:429; [Polizeidirektion, Vienna], *Die sozialdemokratische und anarchistische Bewegung im Jahre 1908*, Vienna: Druck der kaiserlich-königlichen Hof- und Staatsdruckerei, 1909, p. 69, Amtsbibliothek der Polizeidirektion, Wien; C. Lardy, 'Notes historiques sur L'extradition en Suisse', *Zeitschrift Für Schweizerisches Recht*, 1918, vol. 38, p. 322.

60 M. Vuilleumier, *Immigrés et réfugiés en Suisse: Aperçu historique*, 2nd ed., Zurich: Pro Helvetia, 1989, p. 57. Writing ca. 1910 in the authoritative *Enciclopedia giuridica italiana*, P. Lanza observed that: 'recently Switzerland has conceded to Russia extradition for common crimes connected to political ones which, until some years ago, it would not have dreamed of conceding', S.v. 'Estradizione', p. 548n. See also the *Journal de doit international privé* [*Clunet*], 1906, vol. 33: 767–8; and F. J. Saint-Aubin, *L'extradition et le droit extraditionnel: Théorique et Appliqué*, Paris: A. Pedone, 1913, vol. 1, pp. 440, 442.

61 Mss. German foreign office, Berlin, to von Lucius, St. Petersburg, 11 October 1913. GCSAP. 35972; mss. German foreign office to von Tschirschky, Vienna, Secret! 8 January 1914. Russia provided its *points-frontière* on 13 December 1913, copy, Sazonov, St. Petersburg to German Foreign Ministry, nr. 130, GCSAP, Bd. 35,no. 72, 35972. German ministry, Denmark, to Bethmann Hollweg, Secret! 8 January 1914; Tschirschky, Vienna, to Bethmann Hollweg, Berlin, 8 June 1914, GCSAP, bd. 35, no. 72, 35972.

62 Copy, Schmnidt-Dargitz, German Foreign Ministery, to Interior Ministry, Berlin, secret, 8 January 1914, CGSAP, Interior Ministry 13689. For the 23 May 1908 circular, see Interior Ministry to German Federal States, secret!, GCSAP, 13689.

63 Wedel, German embassy, Rome, to secretary general, Italian foreign ministry, 20 June 1908; Giolitti, interior ministry, DGPS, to foreign minister, Rome, 30 August 1908, IFO, ser. P. b. 47.

64 I. L. Plotkin, *Anarchism in Japan: A Study of the Great Treason Affair 1910–1911*, Lewiston, Queenstown and Lampeter: Edwin Mellen, 1990, pp. 26–7.

65 Von Schoen, Berlin, 7 February 1909 to German legation Bern, GFO, Pol.An, Anarchistisches, Gesandtschaft Bern, bd 7.

66 Director general, DGS, to undersecretary, Spanish foreign ministry, 12 August 1913; Marques de Lema (Madrid) to Spanish ambassador (Berlin), 22 November 1913, SFM, *Orden Publico*, L. 2753.

67 See confidential German memorandum forwarded by Spanish embassy, Berlin, to Spanish foreign minister, n. 329, 24 December 1913, SFM, *Orden Publico*, L. 2753.

68 *Note*, Department IIIb. Foreign Ministry, Berlin, 13 November 1913, *Auswärtiges Amt*, GCSAP, Band 3, n. 19, 35515.

69 Mss. Foreign Office, Berlin, to Staatsministerium, Munich, 8 January 1914, GFO, bd. 35, 72/35972.

70 H. Liang, *The Rise of Modern Police and the European State System from Metternich to the Second World War*, Cambridge: Cambridge University Press, 1992, p. 188.

71 In May 1896 and May 1907. P. Heehs, 'Foreign Influences on Bengali Revolutionary Terrorism 1902–1908', *Modern Asian Studies*, 1994, vol. 28: 550.

72 A. Geifman, *Thou Shalt Kill: Revolutionary Terrorism in Russia, 1894–1917*, Princeton: Princeton University Press, 1995, p. 272 n. 159.

2 'Methods which all civilized opinion must condemn'

The League of Nations and international action against terrorism

Charles Townshend

On 9 October 1934, King Alexander of Yugoslavia was assassinated, while riding with the French foreign minister, Jean Louis Barthou, along the seafront in Marseille at the start of a state visit. They were shot dead by a Macedonian terrorist (aided by Croatian separatists) and Yugoslavia accused Hungary of sheltering the Croat rebels. Although the circumstances differed from those of the assassination of the Habsburg Archduke Franz Ferdinand in Sarajevo in 1914, this sort of incident could certainly precipitate a major international crisis. It took its place in a grim chain of deadly attacks on heads of state and prominent international figures over the previous half century (since the assassination of Czar Alexander by Russian terrorists in 1881). Around the turn of the century, Presidents McKinley of the United States (US) and Sadi Carnot of France were assassinated by anarchists, as was King Umberto of Italy. Heads of state were especially iconic targets but, of course, anarchists (particularly in France) also targeted less exalted or even completely ordinary people: Auguste Vaillant threw a bomb into the French Chamber of Deputies in 1893 and, around the same time, another anarchist, Emile Henry, bombed a Paris café – with the chilling declaration, '*il n'y a pas d'innocents*'.

The terrorist wave of the 1890s seemed to many like an assault on civilization itself.[1] Its internationalism was striking: Carnot was killed by an Italian, McKinley by a Pole. Although the wave subsided in the early twentieth century, the sense of destabilization and insecurity did not disappear. But there were significant changes, not least in the international system, in the two decades between the Sarajevo assassination and the killings in Marseille in 1934. Most obviously, the creation of the League of Nations provided an alternative paradigm of conflict resolution and a potentially global framework for implementing it. One thing that remained constant, though, was the sense that the killing of a head of state was a uniquely violent assault on the civilized order, coupled with the fear that such incidents could provoke dangerous international conflicts. It was this which led to the attempt to achieve through the League a coherent and comprehensive international response. The fate of this response offers some interesting insights into the problems which still confront this kind of international action.

I

The League Council addressed the issue on 10 December, two months after the attack. There was a clear general sense that some action needed to be taken, some punitive or if possible preventive strategy and machinery developed, but also a realization that this would not be straightforward. 'The rules of international law concerning the repression of terrorist activity are not at present sufficiently precise to guarantee efficiently international cooperation in this matter', as the Council noted. It therefore took the decision to set up 'a Committee of Experts to study this question', and draw up 'a preliminary draft of an international convention to assure the repression of conspiracies or crimes committed with a political or terrorist purpose'.[2] Drawn from eleven countries,[3] this committee met in April–May 1935 and again in January 1936. The basis for its discussion was a set of proposals drawn up by the French government, with observations from another eleven countries, including China, India, Turkey, and the US (although the last of these was not a member of the League).[4] It also received a draft convention from the Executive Bureau of the International Criminal Police Commission. On this basis, the Experts drew up a draft 'containing the essential provisions'[5] of an international convention, together with a preliminary draft of articles instituting an International Criminal Court.

During the eight months that elapsed between the Committee's two meetings, a further three countries (Argentina, Egypt, and the Netherlands) contributed their views, and the eventual draft convention was then circulated to all the members of the League to consider before the question was placed on the agenda of the 1936 General Assembly. (As a result, nineteen governments presented written criticisms or proposals for amendments.) The Assembly's First Committee had four meetings to give 'exhaustive consideration' to the draft conventions and the observations, before the Assembly as a whole resolved to ask the Experts to revise their conclusions in the light of the governments' critiques. Only after this 'lengthy preparation' did the Council finally instruct the Secretary General on 27 May 1937 to invite the members of the League 'and certain non-member states' to a diplomatic conference to consider the two draft conventions.[6] That conference met in Geneva on 1–16 November.

The whole process was well described by the conference president, Count Carton de Wiart of Belgium, as 'a history of patient and painstaking endeavour'.[7] It was certainly not a quick fix. Yet any hope that the painstaking preparations and extensive consultations had cleared the path for international agreement at the conference was to prove vain. Just as a start, for example, the conference had trouble with the terms of the convention's title. While the Venezuelan delegate favoured calling it the 'Convention for the International Prevention and Repression of Terrorism', others wanted to incorporate the idea of 'international terrorism', which the Soviet

Union for instance thought was 'very important'. The conference Rapporteur pointed out that the phrase 'international prevention and repression' implied 'repression carried out, as it were, internationally', whereas the convention was really concerned to secure action by national authorities. 'There might be some misunderstanding on the point'. Discussion was deferred to the second reading. When the USSR reiterated the need for the term 'international terrorism', the Rapporteur suggested that this expression was 'inadequate and heavy', though he admitted that alternatives such as 'terrorism having an international character' were too long. Though the conference was billed as for 'the international repression of terrorism', this title, he said, had 'simply been chosen for the benefit of the public'; it could not be used in legal texts.[8]

The final draft of the Convention for the Prevention and Punishment of Terrorism consisted of twenty-nine Articles; the Convention for the Creation of an International Criminal Court contained fifty-six. These were complex measures, but the essence of the main convention was relatively straightforward. The first article defined 'acts of terrorism' as 'criminal acts which are directed against a State and which are intended or calculated to create a state of terror among individuals, groups of persons or the general public', and committed states ('High Contracting Parties' in diplomatic language) to cooperate 'for the prevention and punishment of such acts when they are of an international character'. It reminded states that it was in any case their duty 'to refrain from any act designed to encourage terrorist activities directed against the safety and public order of another State'. Article 2 clarified the nature of terrorist acts to be punished, focusing on their targets – principally heads of state, or persons holding public positions 'when the act is directed against them in their public capacity'. Damage to public property was also included, as was the supplying of arms, explosives, or harmful substances with a view to the commission of a terrorist act. Article 3 brought conspiracy or incitement to commit terrorist acts within the scope of the convention. Other articles bound states to treat terrorist acts against others as seriously as those against themselves. Three articles (7–9) dealt with the issue of making terrorist acts 'extradition crimes'.

The conference made the right gestures at the grand level. The president noted at the start that, whilst they were 'entitled to claim that, thanks to the efforts and sacrifices of succeeding generations, our civilization has succeeded' – at least 'in many spheres' – 'in toning down the savagery and brutality of primitive times', it was cause for 'shame and disquiet' that 'advancing knowledge and improved communications' had actually helped to promote 'acts designated by that new term, "terrorism"'. The gravity and contagious nature of these acts made them not only prejudicial to the interests of particular individuals or states, but a danger to 'mankind as a whole'. If the conference could 'forge a legal and diplomatic instrument whereby the community of States can achieve its purpose', it would have 'rendered to civilization a service for which all honest men must forever be indebted to you'.[9] The French delegate stressed that France's interest in framing a convention was not purely selfish, but 'had in view the general interests of society'. Poland deplored the repercussions of terrorist conspiracies 'which were calculated to disturb good relations between the peoples', and invoked 'the general reprobation of terrorist crimes in all civilized countries'. Belgium (surely thinking of 1914) pointed out that 'the crime was calculated to cause international difficulties which might result in the direst catastrophe'. Other delegates spoke of protecting 'the common heritage of the whole civilized world – security of life and limb, health, liberty and public security', (Czechoslovakia) and invoked 'the interdependence of States not only in intellectual matters but also in the sphere of internal peace and security' (Haiti).[10]

The devil here, though, was to materialize not just in the detail, but also in the headline principles of the proposal. What, at the most fundamental level, was terrorism? 'In current usage', the Yugoslav delegate thought, 'the term "terrorism" both in the Latin and other languages, had always been taken to refer to acts of violence committed, with intent to intimidate, against persons and property', but because these offences had never been defined, 'psychological interpretations of the term had held the field'. This had led '(as was to be expected) to misunderstanding'. The ground for a legal definition had been cleared by the work of the International Office for the Unification of Criminal Law, which had held a series of conferences (the last in Copenhagen in 1935). No wholly satisfactory result had yet been attained, but he thought that 'sufficient information was at last available to enable a definitive legal text to be drafted'. If this was optimistic, his next observations indicated some reasons for caution. To 'arrive at a clear and accurate picture of terrorism' it was not enough, however, 'merely to define its different forms.' 'It was necessary in the first place to define terrorism in general, by establishing the elements common to every particular form of terrorism.' This was 'such a highly delicate matter' that the definition must appear in the legislative text. To this steep undertaking was added another – the Polish demand that the convention should 'make it impossible for terrorist crimes to go unpunished'. Komarnicki, the head of the Polish delegation, deplored the fact that the draft convention 'now contained very little trace of the principle *aut dedere aut judicare*, which should have been the keystone of the whole Convention'.[11]

Despite the urgency of the Yugoslav challenge, the question of definition would, in the event, take up less of the conference's attention than the issue of extradition. But there was a crucial connection between the two, well identified by the Belgian delegate, who noted that terrorist outrages 'often went unpunished because the countries concerned did not agree as to their real nature'. The reason was that many countries refused to grant extradition for political crimes, and 'certain aspects of terrorism were closely related to political crime'. 'That was the difficulty.' Noting that the

Spanish constitution precluded extradition for 'political – and even social
– offences', the Spanish delegate called for precise definitions of both
'terrorism' and 'extradition'. He suggested that 'it was impossible to find a
definition of terrorism that was in no way subjective', but essential 'at any
rate to eliminate from any definition the considerations of motive'. Later,
though, during the discussion of Article 1, he admitted that 'no definition
could ever hope to be perfect'. Nor, he now suggested, was a definition
absolutely necessary 'seeing that the purpose of the Convention was to
confer an international character on acts which were known to all crimi-
nologists'. In any definition of terrorism, he finally decided, 'it would be
difficult to avoid tautology'.[12]

Apparently supporting the Spanish view, the Rapporteur (Pella of
Romania) added that 'while one might have quite a clear idea as to what
constituted an act of terrorism, it was not easy to find a legal definition'.
'Terrorism was not so much an offence *sui generis* – that was to say an
offence having characteristics invariably the same – as a manifestation *sui
generis* of criminality.' In other words it took the form of various criminal
acts, all of them currently punishable under the criminal law of most countries. But which acts exactly? Pella did not list them, merely suggesting that
it was possible to distinguish between terrorism and political crimes, which
were not 'anti-social and did not shake the foundations of social life'. They
were merely 'anti-governmental', so they 'conflicted only with the principles of quite special morality' – that is, forms of government.[13]

The Yugoslav delegate reiterated his point about the definition of terrorism when the conference at last moved on to discuss Article 1. Indeed he
added a demand that the word 'terrorist' should also be defined. He was
concerned to stress both the objective and subjective dimensions of the
issue, and proposed two definitions accordingly. The first, objective definition described acts of terrorism as 'having, by their nature or object, the
capability of terrorizing (individuals, groups of persons or the general
public) which is utilized by the authors of the acts as a means of injuring
the interests of the State'. The subjective definition substituted 'capability
of intimidating' for 'terrorizing'.[14] This approach found no backers, and
others moved to challenge the wording of the article in relation to intention, suggesting instead of 'intended to create a state of terror' the phrase
'the intention, nature or result of which is to create a state of terror'.[15]

The definition eventually put together at Geneva – 'criminal acts
directed against a state and intended or calculated to create a state of
terror in the minds of particular persons, or a group of persons or the
general public' – was, as Ben Saul has recently argued, robust enough to
influence subsequent attempts to define terrorism.[16] But Saul also notes its
circularity (defining terrorism by reference to terror) and its narrow focus
on anti-state violence. The adjective 'criminal', which trumpeted this state
perspective, seemed to support those who argued that no new legislation
was actually needed, since terrorist acts were ipso facto illegal under

existing criminal law. On the crucial question of extradition, several countries were evidently queasy about Article 8. Many were proud to have exceptions for political crimes. It was pointed out to them that Belgium, in 1856, had adopted 'a restrictive definition of political offences from which terrorist outrages were excluded' and several countries had followed suit more recently – for instance, Finnish law in 1922 refused to regard murder or attempted murder as a political crime, unless it was committed in the course of open hostilities.[17] These precedents, however, did little to persuade sceptical delegates that the process of extradition could be regularized across legal boundaries.

II

It was the issue of extradition, above all, that would drive the biggest wedge into the faltering international consensus on the convention by revealing Britain as the strongest dissentient. The evolution of the British viewpoint is particularly illuminating. The United Kingdom (UK) government's initial attitude seems to have been quite positive. Sir John Simon, the Foreign Secretary, suggested that the first meeting of the Committee of Experts 'may furnish an occasion for considering whether an international police bureau could not usefully be established (under League auspices) to act as a clearing house for information such as that contained in these reports'.[18] This was, admittedly, a cautious proposal. He made clear that 'such an organization must necessarily avoid interference in national police administrations, and would depend for its efficacy on the loyal cooperation of the governments involved'.[19] (It would, in other words, not have any powers.)

> Initially, therefore, its efforts might not be attended with any great success. But eventually it might be expected to act as a certain check both on undesirable subterranean activities encouraged by certain governments... and on the circulation of wild and unsubstantiated reports of such activities.[20]

It could 'provide a channel through which such suspicions could be ventilated without involving the prestige of governments'. The British police authorities also sounded optimistic about the capacity of the proposed convention to 'promote wider police cooperation'. They noted, apparently with approval, the French government's suggestion that the Convention should also consider measures for coordinated activity against forgery and abuse of passports and identification documents.[21]

From this point, however, British discussion of the proposals sounded a heightening tone of scepticism. Noting with some distaste that the so-called 'Report of the *Commission Internationale de Police Criminelle*' had actually been submitted by the Vienna Police Directorate, one official described the draft convention unflatteringly as 'a pot-pourri of the Convention on Counterfeiting Currency, the French proposals *en bloc*, and a few ideas of the authors about extradition'.[22] This was, to say the least, unpromising.

But Britain did have its own agenda to bring to the convention. At least, its epigone the government of India did. It believed that 'the potential danger of Indian terrorist would be reduced very considerably if steps were taken to prevent him arming himself with revolvers and pistols'. In the 1930s, the upsurge of terrorism in Bengal had posed really serious problems, and Sir Findlater Stewart at the India Office felt 'that at the moment – with the French in their present mood – there is a golden opportunity to get something effective done'.[23] There is an unmistakable hint here of the British sense of having a special grasp of what constitutes 'effective' action, as against windy rhetoric and empty gesture. There was a definite cultural, indeed ethnic, dimension to this. When the draft convention took shape, the Foreign Office thought that it was time to 'warn people like the French and Romanians that we have serious difficulties with the present draft'. It would be a good idea to 'endeavour to ascertain what attitude people like the Dutch and Scandinavians are likely to adopt'. The key tactical question would be whether the British line would also be adopted by 'a fair number of respectable countries'.

Britain's 'difficulties' lay in two vital spheres. One was that of legal tradition or culture. 'The administration of criminal law in this country differs *toto caelo* from its administration abroad', one Home Office official wrote, 'and it is impossible by international treaties to produce corresponding results'. In other words, British law was already more effective than anything that foreigners were likely to come up with. The corollary was crystal clear: 'So I should like the scope of what is contemplated reduced to a minimum.' The second difficulty lay in the concept of political crime. Here, British officials were from the start remarkably positive about the need to keep open the possibility of violent revolution against tyrannical regimes. L.S. Brass, the Home Office deputy legal adviser (who would be part of the UK delegation at Geneva) pondered the problem in mid-1936 thus: 'The general principles should be, in effect, that all States should repress terrorist activities and should bring, and cooperate in bringing, to justice persons concerned in such activities.' So far, so good. But it was necessary to preserve 'a State's right to afford asylum to a person who has taken part in a *bona fide* revolution (e.g. Venizelos) and had taken refuge in its territory'. It was also necessary to preserve 'the liberty of proper freedom of speech', and to ensure that the activities to fall under the ban of the terrorism convention 'should not include ordinary strikes'.[24]

There was a real political gulf here, as Brass made clear to a senior police officer at the same time.

> If all states were at all times decently governed, presumably anyone
> who attempted by force to overthrow an existing government should

be a *hostis humanae generis*; but when the government is itself a terrorist government, I think the person who endeavours to overthrow it by the only means available is not necessarily to be so regarded.[25]

He urged the Foreign Office that, however difficult it might be to draw the line, 'the Convention should be directed against acts of terrorism and not against open insurrectionary movements'. 'Preparations for a rebellion or insurrection or coup d'état' should be excluded, since the object was – or should be – 'not to make it more difficult to change Governments by revolutionary methods', but only to discountenance the use of 'methods which all civilized opinion must condemn'. The Foreign Office reluctantly agreed: 'It is unfortunately necessary to recognize', Sir Alexander Maxwell noted, 'that in some states remedial changes can only be secured by methods involving some violence'.

Where such a line might be drawn became a kind of speculative parlour game for these officials: one ruminated that 'though the Convention is not designed to apply when there is a state of civil war, it would apply to activities in the earlier stages of a political movement which may develop into civil war'. 'The crux of the problem is that the Convention would place us under an obligation to punish sympathisers here who encourage or help oppressed minorities abroad to secure political liberty, if other than purely peaceful means are employed.' In such cases, he thought it was likely that peaceful means 'would probably be useless'.[26] Thinking about possible implications of Article 2(1)c, another official wondered 'might not an attack on [Mosley] by the Communists be regarded as an act of terrorism directed against Italy?' And the term "damage" employed in Article 2(2) was very wide: might it include painting the Swastika on the Soviet Embassy? As he frankly admitted, 'I find some difficulty in getting into the atmosphere of the Convention'.[27]

The sense that some states (whether or not 'terrorist governments', as Brass had put it) were looking for international assistance in choking off internal opposition ran through all these British speculations. The draft of Article 2, for instance, seemed 'oddly arranged'. Between the 'two appalling catastrophes' – 'the overthrow of a Government... or a disturbance in international relations' – was sandwiched 'an interruption of the working of public services, which many people would consider to be of a much lower order of magnitude, and in many cases to be quite well justified'. The British thus persuaded themselves that the Convention might present them with the prospect of being required to extradite strikers. This focused the weight of their doubts about it on the twin concepts of territoriality and extradition, and it was on these issues that they finally decided to declare that they would not sign it.

Abstention was not an easy position to take. The Foreign Office was initially dismayed by the 'very cold douche' thrown on the convention by the Home Office; Roger Makins fretted that it would be 'a very serious step for us to indicate that we could in no circumstances become parties' to it.[28] For one thing, the Rapporteur of the League Assembly who had originally proposed setting up the Expert Committee, Anthony Eden, was British. Britain was widely assumed to be a leading supporter both of strong action against terrorism and of international cooperation via the League. The British representative on the Expert Committee, the lawyer Sir John Fischer Williams, had taken part in drawing up the draft Convention. But he was deeply sceptical about its efficacy and acutely conscious that it might set precedents with undesirable potential consequences. Acceptance of the Convention 'must mean at least such an amendment to our criminal law as to make it a criminal offence to conspire here to commit a terrorist act abroad'. And what use, really, would the Convention be? 'Such value as it has is largely as a gesture of willingness to cooperate in international action.' Criminalization of conspiracy to commit terrorist offences in other countries, and tighter passport restrictions might, he believed, 'occasionally prevent the execution of a terrorist plot'. No bad things in themselves, but 'no fervent terrorist will be deterred from action by the reflection that in the event of his success punishment is certain or severe'.[29]

By July 1937, five months before the conference was due to meet, the British were already planning their exit strategy. Territoriality and extradition were seen as insuperable obstacles, and the government was becoming more worried about its ability to get new legislation through Parliament. The Home Office Permanent Secretary pointed out that while 'we might possibly carry a bill making it an offence to conspire in this country with intent to cause explosions in foreign countries, I do not think we could go further than that'. He suggested to the Home Secretary that,

> if you agree that HMG cannot ratify the proposed Convention unless it is drastically limited – limited, in fact, in such a way that some supporters of the Convention will regard the proposed amendments as wrecking amendments – we will discuss with the FO what is the best tactical line to take.[30]

The Attorney General reinforced this by saying that 'it would be necessary that any legislation' on the proposed offence of conspiracy to cause grievous bodily harm 'should contain an exception for civil war, and he thought that such an exception would be open to criticism in view of the difficulty of knowing when a civil war begins'. The conclusion was 'that we should contrive to disentangle ourselves from the Geneva proposals'.

The next question was whether Fischer Williams would be ready to undertake the 'delicate business', as Maxwell put it, of 'extricating His Majesty's Government from signing a Convention, while at the same time placing no obstacle in the way of other States (who may be willing to do so) concluding a Convention on the lines of the Draft'.[31] After suitable fee arrangements had been agreed (a 50-guinea *per diem* honorarium), Fischer

Williams at last headed off to Geneva, although he seems to have been less than wholly convinced about the official line that the Convention would involve an unacceptable list of additions to domestic law. He anxiously queried Brass, 'are you quite sure that the inclusion of terrorist crimes in our obligation for extradition means legislation?' It had not done so, he pointed out, in the case of the Forged Currency Convention a few years earlier. (He noted that [Sir James] 'Stephen in his History of the Criminal Law says "almost any offence may be made an extradition crime", and when he says "make" I think he means "make by treaty". You might look the point up before you start for Geneva.'[32]).

III

Britain elected, rather unhelpfully, to launch its formidable manifesto of reservations even before the conference began to debate the provisions of the draft convention. On the basis of a thirteen-page set of government instructions, Fischer Williams delivered a comprehensive critique of the draft convention on the afternoon of the first day, immediately after the ratification of the delegates' credentials. While protesting that it was 'most anxious to abstain from any step which would hinder the achievement' of international cooperation, Britain regretted that 'the difficulties of dealing with the matter on the lines suggested in certain articles of the Convention would be grave' – 'perhaps greater in the UK than in many other countries'. This was because 'while the existing law of the UK was thought to be sufficient to enable effective steps to be taken ... the result was attained by methods different from those proposed'. If Britain were to accede to the convention it would have to make 'changes of a very substantial character' in the form of its criminal law; the necessary legislation 'would involve departures from British traditions'.[33]

A major difficulty was that such legislation 'would raise the question of restricting the free expression of public opinion which, especially in the political sphere, had for centuries been zealously safeguarded in Great Britain'. Moreover, Fischer Williams explained, because English criminal jurisprudence followed the territorial principle, any proposal that might seem to extend the rare exceptions to that principle 'would not secure general approval in the absence of any circumstances clearly calling for such a change'. Equally difficult was the question of extradition, since 'English courts placed a very narrow construction upon offences of a political character'. The government was only authorized to grant extradition 'in respect of limited classes of crimes, and it felt unable to ask Parliament to extend those classes'.[34] (The government noted that even if British law should be found insufficient 'the natural course in the UK would be to take any necessary legislative steps to stop any gaps by amendments of the existing system rather than by legislation on the lines suggested in the Draft Convention'.[35])

The British government's trump card was public opinion. The Home Office had long argued that opinion 'might be opposed to treating such [that is, revolutionary] activities as crimes...if there are no constitutional means of changing a bad government'.[36] Fischer Williams could not put things quite so bluntly, but he suggested that 'the people of the United Kingdom would be reluctant to accept' departures from established legal traditions. This argument was less plausible, however, in relation to the proposed International Criminal Court, to which the government was even less well disposed than it was to the Convention. Here, Britain developed a different argument: 'the time had not yet arrived for the creation of such a Court', since 'the work which [it] would perform could generally be done more efficiently by national courts'. Being limited to a single class of crime, the court would seldom be used, and it was doubtful whether creating it 'would at the present time be conducive to improved international cooperation'. Indeed, it would have the reverse effect. In the British government's opinion 'harm was done to international institutions generally by the establishment of an institution not supported by the general assent of public opinion'.[37]

But the bedrock of the British position was the pragmatic and, to other countries, alarmingly conservative belief that 'existing arrangements have been found in practice to be sufficient to deal with any attempt in the UK to promote terrorist activities – as that expression is normally understood – in another country'.[38] (Although Fischer Williams stopped short of sharing with the conference his extreme pessimism over the possibility of deterrence.) A series of delegates expressed polite bafflement about the British arguments. Several stressed that the Convention would and could not infringe the legal sovereignty of any state. Likewise with the proposed International Court, as the French delegate pointed out, every state remained 'free to decide upon its own course of action: it might try the individual itself, or extradite him, or hand him over to the International Criminal Court'. 'Countries which were not attracted by the idea – it was really a question of feeling rather than of principle – were free not to take part in it.'[39] Others urged a more imaginative approach: the Spanish delegate admitted that 'it was true that the law ought to be in accordance with the stage of development of a people, and in the present case the stage of development of the international community', but it should also be understood that 'laws and conventions were in themselves educational'. The present was 'a happy moment' for giving this idea a trial – and even if it failed, could it really do any harm?[40]

Britain remained impervious to such persuasion. The Home Office representative reported from Geneva on 8 November that the League conference was going nowhere. The convention 'seems to find a good deal of favour in the Eastern European states, who are supported by France (no doubt for political reasons)'. But 'apart from these, the general atmosphere of the Conference seems to be one of apathy'. It was impossible at that point to predict the final form of the convention – 'There are two tendencies at work in opposite directions and it is by no means clear what will be the final outcome'. He noted that what he called 'Geneva language' was part of the problem. His view was that 'we had better keep out of the whole thing and not sign'.[41] A week later, he noted disapprovingly that 'our friends across the Channel have seemed ready to accept practically any amendment', but he did not interpret this as a desire to be accommodating. Rather 'this makes me wonder whether they will ever ratify'. Holland, he noted sniffily, was going to accept the convention because it would enhance the international role of the Hague. Poland wanted every separate provision to be subject to strict reciprocity – a proposal he regarded as 'monstrous'. Again, he interpreted it not (as the Polish delegation had argued) as a sign of commitment, but as a device to turn the convention into 'a Convention for providing States with defences for inaction'.[42]

By the end of November, the Home Office felt that the UK had created the impression that it wished the convention well, but thought it better to abstain than to press for amendments. Fisher Williams and Brass reported that there had been 'no sign whatever of any criticism or resentment' of the British course of action.[43] Williams was believed to have 'extricated' the UK from the convention 'without creating any unfavourable impression'.[44] The Home Secretary thanked him for successfully steering a course between 'the risk of committing our Government to legislation that would have run contrary to our traditions and the risk of appearing unsympathetic towards measures for the repression of terrorism'. It 'cannot have been easy', he added feelingly – and not unjustly.[45] Though it had proved impossible to get the International Criminal Court convention 'cut out', the British had 'succeeded in severing the Court from the League of Nations'. (Judges were to be nominated by governments and appointed by the Permanent Court of International Justice at the Hague.)

British objections were not, of course, the only obstacles to agreement. The discussion of the issue of 'conspiracy' to commit terrorist acts, for example, revealed uneasy divergences of approach. The conference limped to an unsatisfactory conclusion, typified by the perfunctory debate on Poland's proposed article (18bis) requiring full reciprocity. In contrast with Britain's hyperbolic denunciation of the Polish proposals as 'monstrous' (though in public they spoke less bluntly of the 'rather dangerous character' of the amendment, which 'would raise difficulties at every turn'), the conference president was more emollient. 'He paid a tribute to the Polish delegation for its whole-hearted efforts to perfect the text of the Convention', but concluded that 'the fact that the Polish proposal had not been supported by any other delegation, the Conference did not accept that proposal'.[46] The Poles, however, were unimpressed. At the close of the conference on 16 November 1937, they announced gloomily, but not inaccurately, that 'the text, as finally framed, unfortunately does not represent any real advance on the present situation as determined by bilateral conventions and the practise of States'.[47]

IV

When initially dangling before the delegates the prospect of 'rendering a service to civilization for which all honest men must be forever indebted to you', Count Carton de Wiart had noted more sombrely that 'against the common peril' of terrorism, 'international solidarity is but a vain and hollow formula. Some means must be found whereby that solidarity may assert itself'.[48] Here, indeed, was the rub.

The League of Nations reported that thirty-five states had sent plenipotentiaries to its conference on the repression of terrorism; by July 1938, twenty-three had signed the terrorism convention and twelve the convention establishing the International Criminal Court.[49] (Bizarrely, the government of India ratified the Convention although the UK did not.[50]) By that time, however, one of the states that had attended the conference, Venezuela, had quit the League in protest against its ineffectiveness. The Soviet Union had, uniquely, ratified the Convention while entering an official Reservation (duly approved by all the signatories) that 'with regard to the settlement of disputes relating to the application of the present Convention, the Government of the USSR assumes only such obligations as are incumbent upon it as a member of the League of Nations'.[51]

The year 1938 was not a propitious one to be building international solidarity, and nothing perhaps better demonstrated this than the lack of harmony over the terrorism question between Britain on the one hand, and France and Poland on the other. The Convention and the League were heading in the same direction, towards irrelevance. On the surface, the terrorism issue might have seemed to be independent of the conflicts propelling the international system into a return to the old world order. All states saw something that they recognized as 'terrorism' as being a serious threat. What that thing was, however, remained a question of a political rather than a legal nature. The underlying reasons for the ineffectiveness of the League and its Convention were essentially the same. The League's crippling weakness was that, being based on the international status quo, it could not accommodate forces of change. Legal reforms foundered on the entrenched commitment of states to their own traditions. Paradoxically, though, the state which dug in its heels most cantankerously over the terrorism convention, the UK, did so on the grounds not only of preserving its own system, but of permitting violent political change in the wider world.

The Terrorism Convention does not even rate a passing mention in the few histories of the League that have been written since its demise.[52] Its place in studies of international action against terrorism is not much larger, though its labours on the problem of definition are beginning to receive recognition as precursors of subsequent (hardly more successful) efforts.[53] Another thirty-five years of inaction would follow before the United Nations (UN) returned to the issue in 1972. Resolution 3034 then led to the creation of three committees, to (1) define terrorism, (2) examine the causes of terrorism, and (3) propose measures to prevent terrorism. The failure of the first necessarily entailed the failure of the others.[54] Again, the Fifth UN Congress on Prevention of Crime and Treatment of Offenders in 1975 would record that 'the attention of the participants was focused on the phenomenon of "terrorism" which has no accepted definition in any legal code, resulting in real difficulties in considering it in the context of criminal justice processes'.[55] Although international terrorism once again became 'a major concern of the world community', concrete action remained elusive.[56] Not until 1984, for instance, did the General Assembly of the International Criminal Police Organization (Interpol) agree to remove the restrictions on sharing information on terrorism between its one hundred and thirty-six members. The process of ratifying the European Convention on the Suppression of Terrorism, agreed in January 1977, was inexplicably long drawn-out.[57] Even a decade after 9/11, while the UN found it possible to respond to the Secretary General's urging that it 'should project a clear, principled and immutable message that terrorism is unacceptable' – in September 2010 the General Assembly once again 'reiterate[d] its strong and unequivocal condemnations of terrorism in all its forms and manifestations' – the term still remained undefined.[58]

One leading writer on terrorism, judging that 'the United Nations has proved a broken reed on the whole subject', adds that 'it has proved as useless as the League of Nations before it'. The problem remains the same: member states 'are unable to agree even on a basic working definition of terrorism'. The reason, he suggests, is ideological: 'they are deeply divided in their attitude to violence in general'.[59] The ideological divide has been fairly straightforward – whereas for liberal states 'terrorism is anathema', for third-world states in the first flush of 'national liberation', terrorism is 'the essential handmaiden of revolt against oppression', and revolutionary violence is morally legitimate. This was, broadly speaking, true of the post-war years. It has been noticeable that since Britain became the target of 'terrorist' movements in Palestine, in many colonial territories, and eventually in Ireland, it has conformed to this liberal formula. Its uncompromising hostility to terrorism has been especially prominent since the 'War on Terror' was launched in September 2001. In the process it has seemed resigned to, if not positively enthusiastic about, the erosion of its old legal safeguards in favour of 'security'. The British state now sees the 'balancing' of freedom and security as problematic; it does not see the first as undergirding or reinforcing the second.[60] Unlike Tony Blair's administration, however, the government of Stanley Baldwin was not prepared to accept that 'the rules of the game had changed'.

Notes

1   See, for instance, F. Ford, *Political Murder: From Tyrannicide to Terrorism*, Cambridge, MA: Harvard University Press, 1985, ch.11.
2   League of Nations Council resolution 10 December 1934. *Proceedings of the International Conference on the Repression of Terrorism* (C.94.M.47.1938.V), League of Nations, Geneva, 1 June 1938, Annex 1, p. 183.
3   Belgium, Britain, Chile, France, Hungary, Italy, Poland, Romania, Spain, Switzerland, and the USSR.
4   The others were Austria, Cuba, Denmark, Estonia, Guatemala, Latvia, and Yugoslavia.
5   League of Nations Council resolution 10 December 1934. *Proceedings of the International Conference on the Repression of Terrorism* (C.94.M.47.1938.V), League of Nations, Geneva, 1 June 1938, Annex 1, p. 183.
6   Ibid.
7   Ibid.
8   Ibid., pp. 70, 146–7.
9   League of Nations Conference, draft minutes. National Archives, London, FO 371/22564.
10 League of Nations Council resolution 10 December 1934. *Proceedings of the International Conference on the Repression of Terrorism* (C.94.M.47.1938.V), League of Nations, Geneva, 1 June 1938, Annex 1, pp. 50, 56, 57, 60, 62.
11 Ibid., p. 57.
12 Ibid., pp. 63,80.
13 Ibid., pp. 65, 66.
14 Ibid., pp. 71–2.
15 Comment by delegate for Haiti, League of Nations Council resolution 10 December 1934. *Proceedings of the International Conference on the Repression of Terrorism* (C.94.M.47.1938.V), League of Nations, Geneva, 1 June 1938, Annex 1, p. 75.
16 B. Saul, 'The Legal Response of the League of Nations to Terrorism', *Sydney Law School Legal Studies Research Paper* No.11/50, University of Sydney, August 2011.
17 League of Nations Council resolution 10 December 1934. *Proceedings of the International Conference on the Repression of Terrorism* (C.94.M.47.1938.V), League of Nations, Geneva, 1 June 1938, Annex 1,0 pp. 60, 67.
18 Secretary of State, Foreign Affairs, to Under Secretary, Home Office, 13 February 1935. National Archives, London, HO 45/18080. The reports concerned alleged plots to assassinate King Peter II of Yugoslavia, the Prince Regent, and the Yugoslav Ministers of War and Marine.
19 Ibid.
20 Ibid.
21 Kendal (Scotland Yard) to L.S. Brass (Home Office), 6 March 1935. National Archives, London, HO 45/18080.
22 Makins to L.S. Brass, 18 March 1935. National Archives, London, HO 45/18080.
23 Stewart (India Office) to Sir R. Scott, 16 April 1935. National Archives, London, HO 45/18080.
24 Memo by L.S. Brass, Home Office, 17 June 1936. National Archives, London, HO 45/18080.

25 L.S. Brass to Kendal (Scotland Yard), 20 March 1935. National Archives, London, HO 45/18080.

26 Minute by L.S. Brass, 20 March 1937. National Archives, London, HO 45/18080.

27 CR to L.S. Brass, 25 June 1937. National Archives, London, HO 45/18081.

28 Minute of 17 July 1936. National Archives, London, FO 371/20486.

29 Fischer Williams to Maxwell (Home Office), 24 September 1937. National Archives, London, HO 45/18081.

30 Under-secretary to Secretary of State, Home Office, 20 July 1937. National Archives, London, HO 45 18080. (Two days later he indeed proposed going forward by 'wrecking amendments' as a strategy for the conference.)

31 Maxwell to Malkin, 29 July 1937, National Archives, London, HO 45/18081; 'Instructions for United Kingdom Delegation at Diplomatic Conference,' 28 October 1937. National Archives, London, DO 35/569(7).

32 Fischer Williams to L.S. Brass, 27 October 1937. National Archives, London, HO 45/18081.

33 The Attorney General drew up a six page memorandum listing 'Changes required to bring the Draft into conformity with existing law', 25 October 1937. National Archives, London, DO 35/569(7).

34 League of Nations Council resolution 10 December 1934. *Proceedings of the International Conference on the Repression of Terrorism* (C.94.M.47.1938.V), League of Nations, Geneva, 1 June 1938, Annex 1, p. 53.

35 Instructions for UK Delegation, p. 4.

36 Minute by L.S. Brass, 3 April 1935. National Archives, London, HO 45/18080.

37 League of Nations Council resolution 10 December 1934. *Proceedings of the International Conference on the Repression of Terrorism* (C.94.M.47.1938.V), League of Nations, Geneva, 1 June 1938, Annex 1, p. 54.

38 Instruction for UK Delegation, p. 2.

39 League of Nations Council resolution 10 December 1934. *Proceedings of the International Conference on the Repression of Terrorism* (C.94.M.47.1938.V), League of Nations, Geneva, 1 June 1938, Annex 1, p. 68.

40 Ibid., p. 63.

41 L.S. Brass to O.F. Dawson (Home Office), 8 November 1937. National Archives, London, HO 45/18081.

42 Ibid.

43 Report, 10 December 1937. National Archives, London, FO 371/21251.

44 Maxwell (Home Office) to Craig (Treasury), 12 December 1937. National Archives, London, HO 45 18080.

45 Secretary of State, Home Affairs, to Fischer Williams, 4 December 1937. National Archives, London, HO 45 18081.

46 League of Nations Council resolution 10 December 1934. *Proceedings of the International Conference on the Repression of Terrorism* (C.94.M.47.1938.V), League of Nations, Geneva, 1 June 1938, Annex 1, pp. 158–9.

47 Ibid., p. 161.

48 Conference draft minutes. National Archives, London, FO 371/22564.

49 League of Nations, *Report on the Work of the League 1937/8*, Part I (Geneva, 18 July 1938), pp. 175–8.

50 Secretary General, League of Nations, to Secretary of State for Foreign Affairs, 22 September 1938. National Archives, London, FO 371/22565.

51   National Archives, London, FO 371/22565.
52   See, for example, F.S. Northedge, *The League of Nations: its Life and Times 1920–1945*, Leicester: Leicester University Press, 1986.
53   B. Saul, 'The Legal Response of the League of Nations to Terrorism', *Sydney Law School Legal Studies Research Paper* No.11/50, University of Sydney, August 2011, pp. 16–17.
54   D.M. Schlagheck, *International Terrorism*, Lexington, MA: Lexington Books, 1988, p. 122.
55   U.N. Information Centre Report BR/73/37 (Sep. 1975), pp. 3–4.
56   M. Crenshaw, *Terrorism and International Cooperation*, Institute for East-West Security Studies, Occasional no. 11, 1989, p. 13.
57   J. Lodge, 'Terrorism and the European Community: Towards 1992', *Terrorism and Political Violence*, vol. 1, 1989, pp. 28–47.
58   'Uniting Against Terrorism', Statement of the Secretary General; General Assembly Resolution 64/297, 8 September 2010.
59   P. Wilkinson, *Terrorism and the Liberal State*, 2nd ed., London: Macmillan, 1986, p. 284.
60   See, for example, *Counter-Terrorism Powers. Reconciling Security and Liberty in an Open Society*, Cm6147. Home Office, February 2004.

3 A blueprint for successfully fighting anarchist terror?

Counter-terrorist communities of violence in Barcelona during the *pistolerismo*

Florian Grafl

Introduction

In 1888, Barcelona staged its first Great Exhibition in order to overshadow the then dominant capital Madrid.[1] However, it was not this event but rather the anarchist terror starting five years later for which the Catalan city for the first time gained attention outside the borders of the Iberian Peninsula.[2] At that time, Barcelona, the industrial centre of Spain, was struck by the first wave of terrorism in the 1890s.[3] According to the dogma of 'propaganda by deed' the anarchists started a series of determined bomb attacks.[4]

The first major upset was caused on 24 September 1893, when a bomb exploded during a military parade on the occasion of the *Fiesta de Merced*. Paulino Pallás was found responsible and executed. His prediction that his death would be avenged by further acts of terror soon came true. On 7 November, just over one month later, Santiago Salvador dropped a bomb in the *Liceo* opera house, a popular meeting point of Barcelona's upper class, killing twenty people. Another spectacular bomb attack occurred in the *Calle de Cambios Nuevos* during a religious procession on 7 June 1896.[5] Already the first terror attacks in 1893 evoked a strong reaction from the state starting with '*La Campaña de Montjuich*', when many innocent anarchists were tortured and executed. This policy of countering violence with violence remained the preferred method to deal with terrorism for the next 30 years.[6]

The second phase of terrorism in Barcelona lasted until 1907 and was rather different. In the 1890s, the terror attacks were directed against clearly defined targets, such as the military, the upper class, and the church. In the first decade of the new century, the anarchists opted for a new strategy: bombs exploded randomly at various places in the city in order to create fear among the citizens. The case of Juan Rull, a well-paid police confidant who nevertheless planted many of the bombs in order to 'stay in business', demonstrated two tendencies that gained even more relevance later: the helplessness of the police as well as the economic aspect of terrorism.[7]

In 1909, the authorities completely lost control in Barcelona for the first time. The call for Catalan reinforcements for the unpopular war being fought in Morocco caused a general strike that resulted in collective violence. From 25 July to 2 August, which became known as 'Tragic Week', many religious buildings were set on fire. When order was finally restored in the city with the help of the army, the punishment by the Spanish state was once again severe.[8] The executions that followed, especially that of Francisco Ferrer, the founding father of the '*Escuela Moderna*', were seen by most contemporaries as even more violent than the events of Tragic Week and provoked a massive protest not only in Spain but also abroad.[9]

After this culmination of violence, the second decade of the twentieth century in Barcelona began rather peacefully.[10] Spain experienced an economic boom during the First World War, owing to its neutrality and the possibility of delivering goods to both sides of the conflict.[11] Nevertheless, a new source of conflict was already established. In 1910, the CNT (*Confederación Nacional del Trabajo*) was founded, which rapidly became the most important trade union with more than 700,000 members by 1919. This new organization was created by a variety of different political factions, which also included some of the leading anarchists.[12]

The new wave of violence starting at the end of the 1910s was therefore not only politically motivated but also had social reasons, such as the poor conditions of the working class. The two general strikes in 1917 and 1919, as well as a lockout by the factory owners, created an atmosphere of mutual distrust and hate among the upper class and the workers, and the stage was set for the most violent episode in the history of Barcelona. Representatives of both sides of the social conflict fell victim to assassinations. When the period of the '*pistolerismo*' came to an end in 1923 with the beginning of the dictatorship of Primo de Rivera, more than 800 people had been attacked in the streets.[13]

It is true that research has already extensively dealt with the *pistolerismo*, not only because there were so many victims but also because it was a unique phenomenon in the history of Spain.[14] Most of the works so far have focused on the reasons for this massive bloodshed. In this chapter however, a different, rather micro-historical approach is attempted with the intention of shifting the attention to the perpetrators. Of course, it is impossible to focus on each single bomber or *pistolero*. Therefore, *Gewaltgemeinschaften* (communities of violence) acting on both sides of the conflict will be identified and analyzed, with a special focus on the counter-terrorist groups using violence with the intention of finding out how effective they were in re-establishing law and order in the city.[15] Although there is plenty of evidence that terror attacks in other Spanish cities were planned in Barcelona as well, in this chapter these groups are taken as an urban phenomena and the focus will be on their actions in Barcelona only.[16]

The terrorist network in Barcelona

So far, the victims of the *pistolerismo* have always been put in the context of the developments of the social struggle.[17] Here, the violence should not be structured by its causes, but by the different forms in which it was executed.[18] This has only been done very superficially, because this period has been linked almost exclusively with assassinations, although bomb attacks were still a common terrorist tool.[19] Although it seems obvious to associate violence in Barcelona during this period exclusively with political motives, the current research on political violence in the twentieth century accepts the fact 'that much which might appear political in fact had other causes'.[20] This more ambiguous view on the motivation to use violence should also be applied in the case of Barcelona, because one cannot deny that, from the middle of 1921 onwards, the assassinations were more and more replaced by raids.[21]

In dividing the violence in Barcelona by its forms, it is logical to focus at first on bomb attacks, since they were the form of aggression that the city had already experienced the most frequently. So it was not surprising that when, in November 1919, in only twelve hours three explosive devices detonated in the *Capitania General* in the *Calle de Simón Oller* and one bomb was found at the monument of Doctor Robert near the *Plaza de la Universidad*, the Republican newspaper *El Diluvio* saw the first signs of the re-establishment of terrorism.[22]

At first, the perpetrators, as in the 1890s, seemed to operate on their own, but in contrast to Paulino Pallás or Santiago Salvador, they did so in a rather amateurish way. The explosion of a bomb in the *Calle del Consulado* on 15 December 1919 was caused accidentally by the twenty-seven-year-old syndicalist Salvador Francisco Clascar Vidal, who lost his right arm in the explosion.[23] As will become clear later in the text, this was by no means a single case.[24] For the most spectacular bomb attack in 1919 in the *Paseo de Gracia*, which already happened on 6 August, Joaquín Caballé was convicted, a boy of only 14 years. He seemed to be addicted to alcohol rather than anarchism or working-class ideas and earned money through robberies. So it is rather likely that he dropped the bomb because he was paid to do so and not for political reasons.[25]

While examples of perpetrators who acted on their own are rather easy to find, it is much more difficult to identify anarchist activist groups. Mainly owing to their clandestine character, little is known about the members of these communities of violence, although as already indicated the political violence during the period of investigation has been researched intensively especially for the case of Barcelona.[26] Nevertheless, it seems that at least three terror groups can be identified in the first phase of the *pistolerismo*.

The first group was located in the old district of *Santa Caterina* and was led by Lluís Dufur. The second group frequented the bar of Francisco Martínez Valles in the *Calle de Valencia 108* for their conspirations. The third group had approximately twenty to forty members and therefore was supposedly the biggest group. They met in the *Calle de Toledo 10* and appeared to be led by Vicente Sales and Roserio Benavente.[27] Since this information does not provide insight into the structure of these communities of violence, it is necessary to try to examine them a little bit deeper.

It seems difficult to gather information about the first group, disregarding the fact that its leader, Lluís Dufur, was shot by the police on Christmas Eve in 1920.[28] So it is necessary to focus on the remaining groups. According to the court reports of contemporary newspapers, the supposed leader of the second group, Francisco Martínez Valles, along with ten other men, was accused of fabricating bombs. Indeed, it seemed that the thirty-two-year-old stonecutter was the leading figure of the group, because its members not only met in his bar as already indicated, but also stored the bombs in the quarry he owned in the Montjuich, the small mountain next to the city. According to the press, the other defendants were also about thirty years old, whereas only three of them were younger than twenty-five.[29] Later, Andrés Masdeu Batista and José Saletas Pla were captured for having brought the bombs to the Montjuich from outside the city, while Alfredo Gómez Franquet, an anarchist who had already taken part in the social struggles in Paris before the First World War, was accused of having used the bombs for terror attacks on the Café Continental and the *Circulo de Cazadores* at the *Plaza Catalunya* on 30 June 1921.[30] So it seems that this group operated on a large scale, with various categories of persons who fulfilled different tasks in order to carry out the bomb attacks in the city.

Another part of the terror network in Barcelona was revealed on 2 May 1921 after a huge explosion in the house of 73 year old Vincente Sales Ortiz in the *Calle de Toledo 10*. Sales lived there with his twenty-four-year-old son Vicente Sales Mollner and the son's lover Rosario Benavente, the leaders of the third and biggest terror group acting in Barcelona at that time. It seems that the explosion was accidental, because among the victims, in addition to Benavente, were nineteen-year-old Miguel Tonijuan as well as eighteen-year-old Juan Avante, both of them suspected terrorists according to the local press. Seemingly, the house of Vincente Sales Ortiz served as a shelter for young anarchists and it was reported that it had been frequented by many young people. In the following trial, Vicente Sales Mollner and a friend of his, twenty-year-old Antonio Rubin, were convicted, whereas the third defendant, Rosario Segarra, a woman aged twenty-three, who fled to France after the explosion, was set free.[31]

Rosario Segarra was also on trial for a bomb attack that occurred only one week before the accident on 24 April in the *Paseo de Gracia* during a celebration of the *Somaten*.[32] The defendants were accused of having met in the house of Juan Bautista Acher Peiró in the *Calle de Galileo* in Sans, preparing the terror attack, which was executed by putting a bomb in a car that was then parked in the *Paseo the Gracia* and later exploded. While Rosario Segarra was once again set free, her twenty-three-year-old lover

Juan Elias Saturnino was convicted to six years in prison, whereas Archer Peiró was sentenced to death.[33] He was also supposed to meet with Laureano Laviña, a friend of Martínez Valles, and others in the bar '*Petit Canaletas*' in the *Calle de Poniente*.[34]

Although this gives the impression that the anarchist network specialized in explosions that were rather well organized, the main weapon to fight the other side of the social conflict was not bombs but assassinations. These, however, could also be interrelated, as the case of the Rodenas brothers shows. While Volney Rodenas was convicted because the police found explosives in his house, Progreso Rodenas was supposed to have taken part in various assassinations as well as shoot-outs with the police.[35] The twenty-six-year-old electrician was accused of a shoot-out with the police on 9 December 1919, together with Francisco Enrich, Antonio Vicente Gómez, and Pecho Ubach, as well as an assassination attempt on police inspector Leon with Samuel Perez on 23 April 1920.[36]

Unfortunately, in contrast to the anarchist terror groups previously mentioned, the communities of violence performing the assassinations of factory owners are very difficult to identify. It seems that even the leaders of the *Sindicatos Unicos*, local branches of the CNT, did not know exactly who was part of these groups of *pistoleros*.[37] Although some sources on these communities of violence exist, it is questionable how reliable they are.[38] On the other hand, biographical and fictional literature suggests that the members of the groups did not know each other well, so it is rather doubtful that one can speak of communities here.[39]

While it seems that Rodenas mainly followed his anarchist convictions, there can be no doubt that some of the *pistoleros* murdered for financial reasons, although their number is difficult to verify.[40] It seems that the CNT spent a part of the workers' contributions as payment.[41] When the CNT was prohibited and became illegal in 1921, there was not a sudden drop in the number of assassinations, while, on the other hand, raids became a daily practice.

One example of this is a group captured in August 1921. The gang consisted of nine men who were described as only being between fifteen and twenty years of age. While some of its members were also blamed for the possession of bombs, they mainly focused on raids, which they committed in different areas of the city. It seems that these crimes were not carried out by the gang as a whole. Instead, each crime was perpetrated by a few of the group's members.[42] That the gang was a rather closed community is made obvious by the fact that one of its members was murdered by the others because he was allegedly a spy for the police.[43]

Although a new series of assassinations started when Salvador Segui, one of the most important labour leaders, was killed in March 1923, it cannot be denied that raids had become the predominant form of violence. The most spectacular one happened in September 1922, when a train was robbed in Pueblo Nuevo.[44] It is true that raids have also been linked to the political context, suggesting that the poor living conditions in some cases left little choice but to resort to criminality.[45] But the brutal and egoistic attitude of the perpetrators, who did not pay special attention to the safety of innocent bystanders and seemed to use the money for themselves instead of the anarchistic cause, seems to show that these new form of violence were often motivated by financial interests.[46]

That the raids became a daily practice was realized by the fact that the police suffered greatly during these shoot-outs with the *pistoleros* and were even less potent than at the beginning of this period.[47] It also seems that, in contrast to the police, the communities of violence acting in Barcelona became stronger and more influential. Although it cannot be denied that, as already stated, economic motives played a major role, important anarchist groups still existed who mainly fought for the political cause. The most famous example is '*Los Solidarios*', headed by Buenaventura Durruti. They not only focused on terror attacks but also accumulated a lot of money through bank robberies. According to one of its members, Ricardo Sanz, at the end of 1923 the group bought weapons for 200,000 pesetas. Together with the fact that they committed assassinations not only in Barcelona but in many different parts of Spain, it becomes obvious that the anarchist groups became very powerful until they had to leave the country during the first years of the Primo de Rivera dictatorship.[48]

Counter-terrorist communities of violence in Barcelona

Facing this direct attack on law and order in the city, four measures were tried to stop terrorism. Soon after the first attacks, it became apparent that the justice system was not able to handle the terrorists on its own. Of the seventy trials concerning the assassinations that took place between 1920 and 1923, eighty per cent of the accused perpetrators were absolved.[49] In 1923, the governor attested to the poor state of the courts by having to admit that the judges set the anarchists free because they feared them and released the *pistoleros* out of sympathy.[50]

It was not only the judges but also the police who were to blame for the fact that law and order was no longer in the hands of the state. The most important reason for this was the very low number of policemen.[51] Because of their often unjustified aggressions on citizens, the police were highly unpopular. Hatred of the police began to increase even more at the end of 1920. When it became obvious that suspected terrorists could not be arrested owing to the inefficiency of justice, civil governor Martínez Anido and the chief of police Arlegui tried to eliminate them without legal justification. In November 1920, they enacted the '*ley de fugas*' (law of fugitives). This law, which was applied for the first time on 5 December 1920, enabled the police to shoot suspects when they tried to escape their imprisonment. Between 19 and 21 January 1921, twenty men fell victim to this practice.[52]

Since the forces of the state were rather helpless to secure law and order, it is not surprising that the upper class, who had the most interest in maintaining the status quo in the city, called for help from non-state forces. The most numerous of them were the '*Somaten*'. This rural militia with traditions dating back to medieval times was turned into an urban paramilitary formation.[53] In supporting the police, however, the members of the *Somaten* often adopted violent measures themselves.[54]

While the *Somaten* were an official paramilitary unit, the most violent groups operated underground. The most influential of these paramilitary groups was the '*Banda Negra*' (the Black Gang), which was founded in 1919 and was led by Manuel Bravo Portillo.[55] He had been the chief of police in Barcelona until mid-1918, when it was revealed that he co-operated with the German secret service in the city and helped to locate Spanish ships with goods for the Allies, which were later torpedoed by German submarines.[56]

The task of the gang was to gather information on syndicalists, with the aim of arresting or even killing them. Bravo Portillo recruited the members of the gang from the lower classes, so the forty to fifty men who formed the gang consisted of former prisoners and pimps, as well as police officers who had been disgraced. They were organized into three subgroups. The men with the best appearance and the most intelligence were sent into the bars, where their task was to gather information from the conversations of workers. A similar function was fulfilled by the second subgroup, who took part in the meetings of the trade unions. The result of the work of these two groups were gathered together in the '*Fichero Lasarte*', a paper listing the names and place of residence of all syndicalists who were presumed to be dangerous.

The third subgroup was led by former prisoner Antonio Soler, and included the most unscrupulous of Bravo Portillo's men. Only they were allowed to carry weapons. Their tasks were to provoke unrest among the workers in order to justify reprisals by the factory owners and assassinations of dangerous syndicalists. Every member of the gang received a daily wage of 50 pesetas, which was much more than a normal worker could expect. Although the gang collaborated closely with the police, the main sponsor was the *Federación Patronal*, the employers' association.[57]

The first victim of Bravo Portillo's gang was the secretary of the CNT union of construction, Pedro Massoni, who was attacked on 23 April 1919. While Massoni escaped with injuries, the first murder of the *Banda Negra* was Pablo Sabater, secretary of the union of dyers, committed on 19 July. The modus operandi of the assassination was the same as with Massoni: three men, disguised as police, came to Sabater's house late at night, pretending to arrest him. Instead of taking him to a police station, they brought him to a quiet place in order to shoot him without eyewitnesses.[58] While forty-five-year-old Luis Fernández García was convicted of the crime, it must have been clear to most of the syndicalists that Bravo Portillo pulled the strings and in fact he was killed in an act of revenge not even two months later.[59]

The new chief of the gang was a German named Fritz Stallmann. He was born in Potsdam and like many criminals came to Barcelona during the First World War. There he changed his name to Baron von König, pretending to be aristocratic. He soon became a close friend of Bravo Portillo, from whom he took over the leadership of the gang.[60] Under von König, the violence used by the group also took on a greater intensity. There was no pretence that the victims were to be arrested. They were simply shot in the street. Whereas his predecessor had made the gang relatively loyal to the police and their employers, von König mainly followed his own ambition to earn as much money as possible. Thus, he not only continued with the contract killing of syndicalists but also started to blackmail factory owners.[61]

However, in doing so, step by step he lost the protection of the authorities and he was expelled from Spain without a trial in June 1920.[62] In the absence of its leader, it did not take long before the *Banda Negra* completely collapsed. Antonio Soler tried to escape to Cuba but was shot on the way to Puerta Rico by a syndicalist.[63] At the beginning of 1922, *La Vanguardia* reported that Mariano Sans Pau remained the only member of von König's gang in Barcelona, whereas all of the others had either been shot or left the city.[64]

After von König's expulsion, the policy of fighting violence with counter-violence continued in the form of the *Sindicato Libres*. This new trade union, which was under the influence of the factory owners, was founded in 1919 to split the workers. From the beginning, this organization was threatened by the *Sindicatos Unicos* with assassinations. Of its thirty-three founding fathers, thirty were attacked.[65] On 11 August, the *Libres* struck back for the first time and, from November 1920 onwards, the numbers of victims of the *Sindicatos Unicos* were greater than those of the *Libres*.[66] The perpetrators are even more difficult to identify than the *pistoleros* of the other side, because the police, as already indicated, had little interest in capturing them. It is, however, likely that they were also mainly interested in money. The contemporary journalist Jaime Passarell stated in an article that for the assassinations of the lawyer Francisco Layret, who defended many syndicalists, and Salvador Segui, only 65,000 pesetas were paid.[67]

Conclusion

The *pistolerismo*, the most violent period in the history of Barcelona, has already been thoroughly examined, but this chapter has introduced a new approach in two ways. First, in order not just to condemn but rather to evaluate the counteractive measures of the state properly, it was necessary to identify the violence used by the anarchists. This was thoroughly investigated when it first occurred in the 1890s and the beginning of the twentieth century, but neglected so far in the period after the First World War. Second, the intention of this chapter was to provide more details on the perpetrators and how they were organized in communities of violence.

Although the sources, which mainly consisted of contemporary newspaper articles and court reports, do not seem to be completely reliable, it has become clear that the anarchist terror groups in Barcelona that already existed in the beginning of the 1920s should not be underestimated. At least two terrorist groups played a significant role in the events of the *pistolerismo*. The first group was led by Francisco Martínez Valles. It consisted of more than ten adult men who mostly shared the same profession. The group had three different components. One part of the group delivered the bombs to Barcelona, others were responsible for their storage at the Montjuich, while the most radical of its members executed the bomb attacks in the city centre. The second group, which was uncovered by the explosion in the *Calle de Toledo* had quite a different character. It seems that its members were significantly younger and were tied together by personal relations rather than by being fellow workers, so that young women were also involved. Already at this time, the terror network in Barcelona seemed to be well organized, which was made clear by the fact that the groups cooperated. Until 1923, these communities of violence had a lot of influence as the example of *Los Solidarios* has shown and it seems that economic aspects largely contributed to the growing number of these gangs.

After having described the dimensions of terrorism in Barcelona in the beginning of the 1920s and the rather poorly developed police force and the court system, it became obvious that it was nearly impossible to combat terrorism in a legal way. The *ley de fugas* clearly showed that the authorities had lost confidence in the judges. Considering the helplessness of the state, it is understandable that any hope to restore peace in the city lay in paramilitary organizations. While the vigilante force, the *Somaten*, using violence as well, was of great support to the police, the counter-communities of violence who did not respect the law at all were the most influential. Since the *pistoleros* of the *Sindicatos Libres* are very hard to identify, because they were hardly ever taken to court and judged, only the *Banda Negra*, as an example of a counter-terrorist community of violence, could be examined in greater detail.

Nevertheless, examination of this group is quite instructive. With forty to fifty members, it was even larger than the biggest anarchist terror group and it was well organized. In comparison to the *Somaten*, the members of the *Banda Negra* were only attracted by the money they got as a wage. So it is not surprising that after the death of Bravo Portillo, who was relatively loyal to the state, the gang followed its own interests more and more and had to be demobilized in the summer of 1920. Just like the *pistoleros* of the *Sindicato Libres* later, the *Banda Negra* was able to eliminate numerous persons who were considered to be terrorists. However, in doing so, they provoked the *pistolerismo*, when assassinations were used in the place of law and order. It is not completely unjustified that not only contemporary socialists but also many historians referring to these events speak of state terrorism rather than just an overreaction by the state.

Notes

1   For a recent article on the Great Exhibitions and their impact on Barcelona
     see: M. Baumeister, 'Alteuropäische Städte auf dem Weg in die Moderne.
     Großausstellungen und metropolitane Identitäten in Barcelona und Turin
     1884 bis 1929', *Historische Anthropologie*, 2002, vol. 10, pp. 449–63.
2   A. Smith, 'Barcelona through the European mirror: From Red and Black to
     Claret and Blue', in A. Smith (ed.) *Red Barcelona: Social Protest and Labour
     Mobilization in the Twentieth Century*, London: Routledge, 2002, p. 7.
3   For a more comprehensive picture of this period of terrorism see the chapters
     in this book by Richard Bach Jensen (Chapter 1) and David Rapoport (Chapter
     16), as well as the recent article by H.G. Haupt and K. Weinhauer, 'Terrorism
     and the State', in D. Bloxham and R. Gerwarth (eds) *Political Violence in
     Twentieth-century Europe*, Cambridge: Cambridge University Press, 2011, pp.
     176–209.
4   For 'propaganda by deed' as well as the specifics of violence in Spanish anar-
     chism see the articles of W. Bernecker, 'Strategien der „direkten Aktion" und
     Gewaltanwendung im spanischen Anarchismus', in W. Mommsen and J.
     Hirschfeld (eds) *Sozialprotest, Gewalt, Terror. Gewaltanwendung durch politische
     und gesellschaftliche Randgruppen*, Stuttgart: Klett, 1982, pp. 108–34, as well as U.
     Linse, '„Propaganda der Tat" und „Direkte Aktion". Zwei Formen anarchistis-
     cher Gewaltanwendung', in W. Mommsen and J. Hirschfeld (eds) *Sozialprotest,
     Gewalt, Terror. Gewaltanwendung durch politische und gesellschaftliche Randgruppen*,
     Stuttgart: Klett, 1982, pp. 237–69.
5   For the most recent overview on the bomb attacks at the end of the nineteenth
     century in Barcelona see: R. Núñez Florencio, 'El terrorismo', in J. Casanova
     (ed.) *Tierra y libertad, Cien años de anarquismo en España*, Barcelona: Crítica,
     2010, pp. 61–88, as well as T. Abelló, 'Anarchism in the Catalan-speaking
     Countries: Between Syndicalism and Propaganda (1868–1931)', *Catalan
     Historical Review*, 2010, vol. 3, pp. 87–102.
6   For the Montjuich trials, see the extensive work by A. Dalmau, *El Procés de
     Montjuïc. Barcelona al final del segle XIX*, Barcelona: Ajuntament de Barcelona,
     2010.
7   The case of Juan Rull was recently fully examined by A. Dalmau, *El Cas Rull.
     Viure del terror a la ciutat de les bombes (1901–1908)*, Barcelona: Columna edicions,
     2008. See also his recent article, A. Dalmau, 'La oleada de violencia en la
     Barcelona de 1904–1908', *Ayer* 2012, vol. 85, pp. 157–73.
8   With the 100th anniversary of the Tragic Week, many new works have been
     published; for example: A. Domínguez Álvarez, *La Setmana Tràgica de Barcelona
     1909*, Valls: Cossetània, 2009, as well as: D. Marin, *La Semana Trágica. Barcelona
     en llamas, la revuelta popular y la Escuela Moderna*, Madrid: La Esfera de los
     Libros, 2009, and D. Martínez Fiol, *La Setmana Tràgica*, Barcelona: Pòrtic, 2009.
9   Although it cannot be denied that Ferrer was an innocent victim of the events
     following the Tragic Week, the recent work on his life by J. Avilés Farré,
     Francisco Ferrer y Guardia. Pedagogo, anarquista y mártir, Madrid: Marcial Pons
     Ediciones de Historia, 2006, makes clear that Ferrer at least had been in
     contact with some terrorists before.
10   J. Casanova remarked in his article that in 1910 only one bomb exploded while
     the following five years were completely free of any acts of terror. J. Casanova,

'Terror and Violence: The Dark Face of Spanish Anarchism', *International Labor and Working-Class History*, 2005, vol. 67, pp. 87.

11 For the influence of the First World War on Spain see the works of F. Romero Salvadó, *Spain 1914–1918: Between War and Revolution*, London: Routledge, 1999, as well as: F. Romero Salvadó, *The Foundations of Civil War: Revolution, Social Conflict and Reaction in Liberal Spain 1916–1923*, London: Routledge, 2008.

12 For a recent article on the CNT, see: K. Biberauer, 'Anarchismus mit oder versus Syndikalismus. Die ideologische Entwicklung der CNT (1910–1936)', in F. Edelmayer (ed.) *Anarchismus in Spanien. Anarquismo en España*, Wien: Verlag für Politik und Geschichte, 2008, pp. 109–61.

13 For detailed statistics of the victims, see: A. Balcells, *El pistolerisme. Barcelona (1917–1923)*, Barcelona: Pórtic, 2009, p. 56.

14 E. González Calleja, *El máuser y el sufragio. Orden público, subversión y violencia política en la crisis de la Restauración 1917–1931*, Madrid: Consejo superior de investigaciones científicas, 1999, p. 54, makes clear that Barcelona in this respect was by far the most violent city during that time.

15 The concept of *Gewaltgemeinschaften* is based on the work of a research group of historians at the University of Giessen, who focus on communities from ancient times up to the Second World War that constitute themselves mainly by using violence. For a more detailed explanation of this concept, see: H.J. Bömelburg and H. Carl (eds), *Lohn der Gewalt. Beutepraktiken von der Antike bis zur Neuzeit*, Paderborn: Ferdinand Schöningh, 2011, as well as the article by W. Speitkamp, 'Gewaltgemeinschaften', in M. Christ, C. Gudehus and H. Welzer (eds) *Gewalt. Ein interdisziplinäres Handbuch*, Stuttgart: Verlag J.B. Metzler, 2012.

16 The most important case of a terror attack planned in Barcelona but executed elsewhere was the assassination of Prime Minister Eduardo Dato, see for example: F. Sánchez Ferrera, *Cinco Asesinatos que macaron la historia de España*, Madrid: Aldeberan, 1998, pp. 113–40; F. Lenger, 'Die europäische Stadt in der Moderne. Eine Herausforderung für Sozialgeschichte, Stadtgeschichte und Stadtsoziologie', in C. Benninghaus *et al.* (eds) *Unterwegs in Europa. Zur vergleichenden Sozial- und Kulturgeschichte Europas*, Frankfurt: Campus, 2008, pp. 357–76, shows that violence is an important topic among urban historians at the moment, although, as the article makes clear, Southern European cities have been rather neglected so far.

17 P. Gabriel, 'Red Barcelona in the Europe of War and Revolution 1914–1930', in A. Smith (ed.) *Red Barcelona: Social Protest and Labour Mobilization in the Twentieth Century*, London: Routledge, 2002, pp. 44–65, and recently: F. Romero Salvadó, '"Si vis pacem para bellum". The Catalan Employers' Dirty War 1919–23', in F. Romero Salvadó and A. Smith (eds) *The Agony of Spanish Liberalism: From Revolution to Dictatorship 1913–1923*, London: Palgrave Macmillan, 2010, pp. 175–201.

18 Another very interesting way to present the events of the *pistolerismo* in a different way than in the context of the class conflict was recently shown in M. Domínguez López, 'El pistolerisme a L'Hospitalet', *Quaderns d'estudi*, 2012, vol. 25: 87–126, which can be seen as the first step towards a topography of the *pistolerismo*.

19 P. Gabriel, 'Red Barcelona in the Europe of War and Revolution 1914–1930', in A. Smith (ed.) *Red Barcelona: Social Protest and Labour Mobilization in the Twentieth Century*, London: Routledge, 2002, p. 59, mentions the explosion in the music

hall Pompeya, which killed six people and injured twelve. This incident might be the most spectacular bomb attack, although it is not completely clear who exactly was to blame for it.

20   M. Conway and R. Gerwarth, 'Revolution and Counter-revolution', in D. Bloxham and R. Gerwarth (eds) *Political Violence in Twentieth-century Europe*, Cambridge: Cambridge University Press, 2011, p. 140.
21   A. Balcells, *El pistolerisme. Barcelona (1917–1923)*, Barcelona: Pórtic, 2009, p. 15.
22   *El Diluvio*, 27 November 1919, p. 10.
23   For the details of this bomb attack, see for example: *El Noticiero Universal* 15 December 1919, p. 4, and for the proceedings against Francisco Clascar Vidal: *El Diluvio* 9 April 1920, p. 16, *El Diluvio* 14 April 1920, p. 10.
24   Apart from the examples given in the text, another spectacular bomb explosion in the *Calle de Metges* in August 1921 was caused by accident; see for example, *El Diluvio* 6 August 1921, p. 15.
25   For the proceedings against Joaquín Caballé: *El Diluvio* 7 March 1920, p. 13; *El Diluvio* 10 March 1920, pp.12, 24; *El Diluvio* 11 March 1920, p. 12.
26   This problem of sources was already formulated by J. Romero Maura, 'Terrorism in Barcelona and its Impact on Spanish Politics 1904–1909', *Past and Present*, 1968, vol. 41, p. 130.
27   M.A. Pradas Baena, *L'Anarquisme i les lluites socials a Barcelona 1918–1923. La repressió obrera i la violència*, Barcelona: Publicacions de l'Abadia de Montserrat, 2003, pp. 86–8.
28   The trial of the shoot-out is documented in: *El Noticiero Universal*, 19 November 1923, p. 12.
29   *El Diluvio*, 19 May 1922, p. 26.
30   *El Noticiero Universal* 27 February 1922, p. 10; *El Diluvio* 4 August 1921, p. 10.
31   For detailed information about what happened in the *Calle de Toledo 10*, see: *El Noticiero Univeral* 3 May 1921, p. 5; *El Noticiero Univeral* 4 May 1921, p. 5; *El Noticiero Univeral* 5 May 1921, p. 7; *El Noticiero Univeral* 9 May 1921, p. 7; *El Noticiero Univeral* 20 July 1921, p. 5; *El Noticiero Univeral* 30 July 1921, p. 8; *El Noticiero Univeral* 24 March 1922, p. 8; *El Noticiero Univeral* 25 March 1922, p. 10; *El Diluvio* 20 July 1921, p. 10; *El Diluvio* 5 August 1921, p. 7.
32   This urban paramilitary unit will be closer examined later in the text.
33   *El Diluvio* 12 October 1922, p. 16; *El Diluvio* 17 October 1922, p. 13; *El Noticiero Universal* 14 October 1922, p. 9
34   *El Noticiero Universal* 27 February 1922, p. 10.
35   *El Diluvio* 3 July 1921, p. 17.
36   *El Diluvio* 10 January 1922, p.10; *El Noticiero Universal* 9 January 1922, p. 7.
37   K.J. Nagel, *Arbeiterschaft und nationale Frage in Katalonien zwischen 1898 und 1923*, Saarbrücken: Verlag für Entwicklungspolitik, 1991, p. 462, with reference to the writings of the contemporary journalist Francisco Madrid.
38   See the memoirs of A. Pestaña, *Lo que aprendí en la vida*, Algorta: Zero, 1971, and A. Pestaña, *Terrorismo en Barcelona. Memorias inéditas*, Barcelona: Edición Planeta, 1979, as well as: J. León Ignacio, *Los años del pistolerismo. Ensayo para una Guerra civil*, Barcelona: Edición Planeta, 1981.
39   See, for example: M. Mir, *Diario de un pistolero*, Barcelona: Ediciones Destino, 2006, pp. 23–31.
40   One example is documented in *El Noticiero Universal* 5 May 1922, p. 9; *El Noticiero Universal* 12 June 1922, p. 11.

41 K.J. Nagel, *Arbeiterschaft und nationale Frage in Katalonien zwischen 1898 und 1923*, Saarbrücken: Verlag für Entwicklungspolitik, 1991, p. 462.
42 *El Diluvio*, 6 August 1921, p. 14.
43 *El Diluvio*, 9 August 1921, p. 9.
44 For a detailed description of this event, see for example the reports on the trial in *El Diluvio* 1 September 1926, p. 7–8.
45 C. Ealham, *Anarchism and the City: Revolution and Counter-revolution in Barcelona, 1898–1937*, Oakland: AK Press, 2010, pp. 155–9.
46 One example would be the raid on the *Casa Salisachs*, which is documented among others in: *El Diario de Barcelona* 30 August 1923 p. 5436; *El Diario de Barcelona* 31 August 1923, p. 5477.
47 AHN 54A(8) shows that from the force of 1,409 men only 816 were serviceable.
48 *Los Solidarios* are still best documented in M. Enzensberger, *Der kurze Sommer der Anarchie*, Frankfurt: Suhrkamp, 1972, pp. 38–49.
49 A. Balcells, *El pistolerisme. Barcelona (1917–1923)*, Barcelona: Pórtic, 2009, pp. 110–1.
50 AHN 58A(13).
51 According to A. Balcells, *El pistolerisme. Barcelona (1917–1923)*, Barcelona: Pórtic, 2009, p. 21, on average, there was only one policeman for every 5,000 citizens.
52 K.J. Nagel, *Arbeiterschaft und nationale Frage in Katalonien zwischen 1898 und 1923*, Saarbrücken: Verlag für Entwicklungspolitik, 1991, S. 461.
53 F. Romero Salvadó, '"Si vis pacem para bellum". The Catalan Employers' Dirty War 1919–23', in F. Romero Salvadó and A. Smith (eds) *The Agony of Spanish Liberalism: From Revolution to Dictatorship 1913–1923*, London: Palgrave Macmillan, 2010, p. 180.
54 K.J. Nagel, *Arbeiterschaft und nationale Frage in Katalonien zwischen 1898 und 1923*, Saarbrücken: Verlag für Entwicklungspolitik, 1991, p. 455 states that members of the *Somaten* were responsible for assassinations of labour leaders in Hospitalet. That the *Somaten* used violence in Barcelona as well, can be seen for example in: *El Diluvio* 30.11.1919, p. 8–9.
55 K.J. Nagel, *Arbeiterschaft und nationale Frage in Katalonien zwischen 1898 und 1923*, Saarbrücken: Verlag für Entwicklungspolitik, 1991, p. 454.
56 G. Brenan, *The Spanish Labyrinth: The Social and Political Background of the Spanish Civil War*, Cambridge: Cambridge University Press, 1943 (8th edn 2009), p. 69.
57 The gang is documented in the most detail in the memoires of former police officer M. Casal Gómez, *La Banda Negra. Origen y actuación del pistolerismo en Barcelona 1918–1921*, Barcelona: Icaria, 1977.
58 For a more detailed description of these assassinations, see M.A. Pradas Baena, *L'Anarquisme i les lluites socials a Barcelona 1918–1923. La repressió obrera i la violència*, Barcelona: Publicacions de l'Abadia de Montserrat, 2003, p. 95.
59 G. Brenan, *The Spanish Labyrinth: The Social and Political Background of the Spanish Civil War*, Cambridge: Cambridge University Press, 1943 (8th edn 2009), p. 69.
60 For more information on this person, see again M. Casal Gómez, *La Banda Negra. Origen y actuación del pistolerismo en Barcelona 1918–1921*, Barcelona: Icaria, 1977, as well as the article by J. Ventura Subirats, 'La verdadera Personalidad del "Baron de König"', *Cuadernos de Historia Económica de Cataluña*, 1971, vol. 5, pp. 103–18.

61   F. Romero Salvadó, '"Si vis pacem para bellum". The Catalan Employers' Dirty War 1919–23', in F. Romero Salvadó and A. Smith (eds) *The Agony of Spanish Liberalism: From Revolution to Dictatorship 1913–1923*, London: Palgrave Macmillan, 2010, p. 181.

62   Von König's expulsion of Spain is documented in: AHN 34A (3).

63   *La Vanguardia*, 21 July 1920, p. 4.

64   *La Vanguardia*, 6 January 1922, p. 6, although A. Balcells, *El pistolerisme. Barcelona (1917–1923)*, Barcelona: Pórtic, 2009, p. 63, states that only when Benet Armengol was shot in May 1923 was the last member of the *Banda Negra* eliminated.

65   E. González Calleja, *El máuser y el sufragio. Orden público, subversión y violencia política en la crisis de la Restauración 1917–1931*, Madrid: Consejo superior de investigaciones científicas, 1999, p. 176.

66   A. Balcells, *El pistolerisme. Barcelona (1917–1923)*, Barcelona: Pórtic, 2009, p. 67

67   See his articles in *El Mirador* of 19 and 26 November 1931. Both can be found in the recent edition of his major works by V. Soler (ed.), *Jaume Pasarell. Bohemis, Pistolers, Anarquistes i altres ninots*, Barcelona: Acontravent, 2010.

Part II

Western experiences with terrorism

4   The United Nations and West Germany's efforts against international terrorism in the 1970s

Bernhard Blumenau

[In the fight against international terrorism, we have to] convince governments that they should stand together or they will hang separately.[1]

Robert S. Ingersoll, 1975

Introduction

The 1970s marked a height of international terrorist activity. As the above quotation shows, it was a serious – albeit controversial – issue for the international community and perceived as a grave threat, at least by Western countries. For the Federal Republic of Germany (FRG), it was most certainly an important concern.

Yet, to date, studies of West German foreign policy in the 1970s are predominantly focused on matters such as *Ostpolitik* and détente, economic summits, as well as on the neutron bomb and the NATO double-track decision. The problems deriving from international terrorism do not appear in most academic assessments. However, as this chapter will demonstrate, efforts against international terrorism were an important aspect of Bonn's foreign policy, especially in the second half of the 1970s. This text will shed light on this often neglected concern for the federal government and Auswärtiges Amt (AA) and will assess why and how the threat of terrorism was mirrored in West German foreign policy strategies.

Literature on German foreign policy in the 1970s is bourgeoning. However, the aspect of how West German diplomacy attended to terrorism has not yet been examined aside from a few topical assessments, and no study has been published thus far in English.[2] Likewise, the importance that terrorism did have for the United Nations (UN) in the 1970s is not yet reflected enough in academic literature. This study will thus contribute to closing these gaps.

As far as sources are concerned, this chapter draws heavily upon documents from the West German AA, documents from United States (US) archives, and secondary sources, such as memoirs and interviews.

West Germany's encounter with terrorism

To understand the important role that anti-terrorism efforts played in Bonn's foreign policy, it is essential to look at West Germany's domestic experience with terrorism. Like most Western countries, the FRG was hit by an unprecedented wave of, partly very violent, student protests in the mid and late 1960s.[3] However, with a new social-democratic government formed by Willy Brandt and his promise to 'risk more democracy', the majority of the protesters tired of revolution. Yet, some of the more radical members of these groups went underground and continued their fight by more violent means. This was the case in West Germany, but also in the US with the Weathermen Underground and in Italy with the Red Brigades. In the FRG, the *Rote Armee Fraktion* (Red Army Faction, RAF) is the most infamous example but there were others too: the Berlin-based *Bewegung 2. Juni* (Movement Second of June) and the *Revolutionäre Zellen* (Revolutionary Cells).[4]

The RAF was founded in 1970 and was led by Andreas Baader and Gudrun Ensslin. Ulrike Meinhof provided the broader public with 'ideological' justifications for RAF attacks but was not involved in the key decision making which lay with Baader, the undisputed commander-in-chief. They began their activism with arson in a Frankfurt shopping mall in 1968. Following the recommendations in Carlos Marighella's *Mini-manual of the Urban Guerrilla*, they then escalated their actions to include bank robberies, theft, and – eventually – attacks against American and West German offices and officials. However, owing to the introduction of new methods of man hunting, such as the use of computers and grid searches, the *Bundeskriminalamt* (Federal Criminal Office) under its president, Horst Herold, managed to arrest all key leaders of the first generation of the RAF in the summer of 1972. Still, soon after that, a new generation emerged whose preoccupation was to free their mystified leaders from prison. As far as the ideological basis of the RAF was concerned, it was practically nonexistent. As Audrey Kurth Cronin quite pointedly put it: 'To say that they had an ideology would be an overstatement'.[5] The few hints of ideology had then completely disappeared when the second generation took over. The first big action of this new generation of the RAF was a raid on the West German embassy in Stockholm in April 1975. It was in this year, 1975, that the official government position on terrorism emerged.

Some months before the Stockholm attack, members of the *Bewegung 2. Juni* had kidnapped Peter Lorenz, a Christian-conservative politician running for the office of mayor of West Berlin. Upon pressure from the Christian-conservative opposition party leader, Helmut Kohl – and with Chancellor Helmut Schmidt being bedridden with influenza – the federal government decided to give in to the kidnappers' demands and released several terrorists from prison. They were flown to Southern Yemen and each of them was furnished with a considerable amount of money.[6]

According to his own testimony, Schmidt always had doubts about giving in to terrorist demands and regretted this decision afterwards: 'It was my biggest mistake that I backed down during the Lorenz kidnapping'.[7] He therefore decided that henceforth, the German government would no longer concede to terrorist demands. The litmus test for this new policy came with the above mentioned raid on Bonn's embassy in Sweden in April 1975. Several RAF terrorists occupied the building and held all diplomats hostage, while executing two of them to show the seriousness of their intentions. They demanded the release of the RAF leadership from prison in exchange for the diplomats. This time, however, Bonn stood firm and Schmidt explained to a startled Olof Palme, Prime Minister of Sweden, that 'we do not negotiate. We are lifting extraterritoriality'.[8] The responsibility for the solution of the crisis therefore shifted from the West Germans to the Swedes. While the Swedish police were thus preparing to storm the embassy, the explosives that had been planted by the terrorists suddenly detonated. The hostages were saved and the terrorists arrested and extradited to Germany.[9] As Schmidt explained in hindsight:

> Once again, as in the case of the kidnapping of the member of the Berlin parliament Peter Lorenz, we had to balance two considerations: On the one hand, to save directly threatened lives while on the other hand, to counter threats to the most vital function of every state: to provide security for the lives of all its citizens.[10]

Schmidt continued by stressing that had he given in at Stockholm 'we could have soon been at the end of all security'.[11] Consequently, by late April 1975, a new West German policy line on terrorism had been established – that the government would not meet terrorists' demands. This has remained the official policy on terrorism until today.

In light of the failed blackmailing attempt in Stockholm, increasing pressure from their imprisoned leadership forced the RAF to commit a new series of attack in what was to enter the history books as the 'German Autumn' of 1977. It started with the assassinations of federal prosecutor-general Siegfried Buback in early April 1977 and Dresdner bank manager Jürgen Ponto in late August. The 'German Autumn' found its climax in the double crisis of September and October 1977. First, on 5 September, Hanns Martin Schleyer, president of the German Industrialists' Association, was kidnapped. The RAF, which claimed responsibility for this, demanded the release of all key RAF members from prison. As the federal government did not give in to their demand, four Palestinians of the Popular Front for the Liberation of Palestine (PFLP) increased pressure on Chancellor Schmidt by hijacking a Lufthansa jet, the 'Landshut', on 13 October. They rerouted it several times until it was stormed by a special anti-terrorist commando of the German border guards, the *Grenzschutzgruppe 9* (GSG 9), in Mogadishu early on 17 October. After they learned of the failed operation, Baader,

Ensslin, and several other RAF leaders committed suicide in their prison cells. Several days later, the dead body of Schleyer was found in Mulhouse.[12] The 'German Autumn' had come to an end. Despite the death of Schleyer, the successful release operation in Mogadishu and Schmidt's crisis management had drastically increased his popularity ratings, which were unmatched by his predecessors or successors.[13] The handling of the crisis and its success also helped to firmly establish Bonn's new anti-terrorism policy of not conceding to terrorist demands. The government had not given in to the terrorists, the *Rechtsstaat* had prevailed and the young democracy in West Germany passed its litmus test.

The year 1977 consequently marked the peak of terrorism in and against West Germany. Although the RAF continued to attack representatives of the state until the early 1990s, the intensity and violence of 1977 was never matched again. In 1992, the RAF declared a 'truce' and officially dissolved in 1998.[14] Germany's encounter with leftist terrorism had ended.[15]

As the above-mentioned examples show, terrorism in the 1970s, especially the variant that was committed by or directed against West Germans, was highly international in nature. German terrorist groups went abroad for training and committed their attacks against West German targets in foreign countries. Moreover, all terrorist groups occasionally cooperated with foreign actors, such as the PFLP, 'terrorists for hire', such as the infamous Carlos the Jackal, or – at least indirectly – with foreign countries, such as East Germany.[16] Because of this international dimension, the West German government soon realized that it could only successfully fight terrorism by striving for better multilateral cooperation. This was a consequence of two factors. First, West Germany's policy of not conceding to terrorist demands made the cooperation of foreign governments essential when it came to the solution of a terrorist crisis abroad. Besides, for the credible punishment of perpetrators and thus to discourage terrorists from new attacks, safe havens had to be abolished. Consequently, states had to be under legal obligations to assist each other to the best extent possible in their struggles against international terrorism. That was of particular importance when it came to Third World[17] countries that had either shown blatant support for Western terrorists or at least benign indifference to them. Second, Germany's Nazi past also influenced anti-terrorism policies. Because of Hitler's aggression and disrespect for other countries' sovereignty, the federal government had to be extremely cautious regarding any intervention of its police abroad – military interventions were practically impossible for constitutional reasons. They could only take place with the consent of the foreign government concerned.[18] As the commander of the GSG 9, Ulrich Wegener, put it: 'a solution à la Entebbe is not an option for us'.[19]

As far as West Germany's reactions to terrorism are concerned, two dimensions have to be examined. On the domestic level, the federal government had increased the competence of the federal police institutions. Moreover, several bills of anti-terrorism legislation had been passed.[20] Yet, on the international level, norms and obligations regarding the coop- eration of states against terrorists hardly existed. In the mid-1970s, West Germany therefore became an active supporter of anti-terrorism efforts at the UN to address this shortcoming. This chapter will look at those policies.

Bonn's anti-terrorism strategies at the UN

By the early 1970s, the UN had undergone a remarkable transformation and had witnessed a significant shift in power. While the emerging Western and Eastern blocs of the Cold War had had an absolute majority of votes in the late 1940s – and included the five members with veto power in the Security Council – the situation had changed over the following twenty years. In the course of decolonization, more countries in Africa and Asia became independent from their former mother countries and attempted to organize themselves as a new force globally. This was also reflected at the UN. In the 1970s, the Third World countries together had a two-thirds majority in the General Assembly. This generated self-confidence and they pushed increasingly more determinedly for their topics – most importantly decolonization and plans for a new international economic order – to be on the agenda of the world organization.[21] Western countries were anything but happy with these changes. President Richard Nixon found very drastic words to express his dissatisfaction with recent developments and referred to delegates from Third World countries as a 'bunch of apes'.[22] It seemed to contemporary observers that Western influence at – or control over – the UN was in decline.

It was against this backdrop that the two German states, the German Democratic Republic (GDR) and the FRG, were admitted to the world organization in the autumn of 1973. The membership of both Germanys was only made possible because the two states had finally agreed on estab- lishing basic relations between each other through the Basic Treaty of 1972, which ensured that neither the US nor the Soviet Union would veto their membership at the UN. Upon accession, both Germanys were eager to play prominent roles at the UN.

But both were not total newcomers. West Germany, for instance, had had an observer mission at the UN before 1973 and had paid very close atten- tion to the developments there prior to accession. Therefore, Bonn's diplomats had also noticed the growth in Third World power at the UN and were unhappy with this emerging '*Chaosmacht*' – or force of chaos – instru- mentalizing and paralyzing the UN at its liking.[23]

Those developments had an impact on the topics discussed at the UN. When it came to the issue of terrorism, stances differed significantly. To begin with, agreeing on a common definition was an impossible endeavour. For the West, a 'terrorist' was a person that committed politically motivated violence against a government or citizens of a state in order to force the government to concede to specific political demands. The perpetrator could be either a foreigner or a national of the home country. The Third World countries had a different understanding of what a 'terrorist' was. Since many of these countries achieved independence only because of violent acts of national liberation movements, they could hardly condemn political violence committed in that context. They also did not want to delegitimize movements that were still fighting for independence, for instance in Palestine and southern Africa. 'Terrorism' as the Third World understood the term, rather referred to governments depriving those movements of their right to self-determination.[24] Those governments – especially in Israel and South Africa – however, were close allies of the West. There were thus considerable differences as to the definition of 'terrorists'. To make matters even more complicated, the East also had a different understanding of a terrorist. For the communist states, a terrorist was rather a dissident or a defector. It was under these circumstances that West Germany had to pursue its anti-terrorism policies.

Failed attempts: the project of a comprehensive convention against international terrorism

In the aftermath of the attack by the Japanese Red Army on the Israeli airport of Lod in May 1972, and triggered by the Munich hostage crisis during the Olympics in September 1972, UN Secretary General Kurt Waldheim proposed to the General Assembly to add an urgent item to the agenda.[25] The delegates were to debate 'measures to prevent terrorism and other forms of violence which endanger or take innocent human lives or jeopardize fundamental freedoms'.[26] At the same time, the US government also submitted a proposal to the General Assembly to elaborate a 'Draft Convention on the Prevention and Punishment of Certain Acts of International Terrorism'.

Both suggestions, however, faced immediate objections from the Third World. To counter those alleged Western attempts to legitimize interventionism in the Third World, it pushed for amendments and changes in the text of the draft convention.[27] Rather than condemning international terrorism altogether, Third World countries wanted to insert exceptions for certain situations, in which terrorist means were used for a 'just cause', for instance by liberation movements. Holding the majority at the UN, the Third World countries succeeded in translating their demands into a draft resolution reiterating the right to self-determination and the legitimacy of the struggle for independence, which in this context could only be read as a justification for certain terrorist acts.[28] In addition, the Third World managed to have a clause inserted into the resolution, which condemned state terrorism exercised by racist, colonial, and alien regimes. An amendment was also adopted that called for an examination of the 'underlying causes' of terrorism.

Thus, in the course of several weeks, the US proposal had experienced a total reorientation: instead of banning terrorism, it could now be read as actually legitimising certain forms of it. This could only provoke the resistance of the West, which unanimously and unsuccessfully voted against General Assembly Resolution 3034 (XXVII) 'On Measures to Prevent International Terrorism' on 18 December 1972.[29] This frustrating experience and the emerging 'stone wall front' of the Third World led most Western states to agree with the US that anti-terrorism issues at the UN were 'sidelined indefinitely' and practically 'buried'.[30] On the basis of Resolution 3034, an ad hoc committee on international terrorism was established under the aegis of the Sixth – or legal – Committee of the General Assembly, which was to meet every other year.[31] However, the outcome of this committee was marginal. As the *New York Times* noted: 'Last year, the sum total of General Assembly action on the matter was to assign it to this year's agenda for consideration'.[32] Indeed, it appears that the only achievement of the committee throughout the 1970s was to keep itself in session and the issue of terrorism on the agenda.[33]

Although only an observer to the UN until late 1973, West Germany took a supportive and interested stance on the proposals by the US and Waldheim from the very beginning. West German diplomats also expressed their support for the projects at European Political Cooperation (EPC) meetings that debated UN issues.[34] Much like the Americans, the Germans were concerned about the 'deformation' of the US draft resolution and the Third World's stance on anti-terrorism initiatives.[35] Nevertheless, pragmatism prevailed and once the committee was established Bonn had to find a way of dealing with it. The Germans were not ready to leave the important field of terrorism entirely to the discretion of the Third World. Therefore, the FRG took an active interest and suggested to Waldheim that the committee deal with the elaboration of a convention that would strengthen international cooperation against terrorism.[36] At the same time though, the federal government was in a dilemma. Claiming the right to self-determination for the Germans in the GDR, Bonn could not simply ignore or dismiss the Third World attempts to give special consideration to this issue. West Germany thus paid some lip service to self-determination. But it also left no doubt about the fact that rather than engaging in highly philosophical debates about the definitions of terrorism or its roots, Bonn wanted the committee primarily to develop practical proposals as to how to fight it.

In the course of the debates in the committee in 1973, the West Germans – and their allies – came to realize that the probability of any feasible and substantial outcome of the committee was minimal. No results were likely anytime soon.[37] In late 1973, the AA became increasingly concerned about spillover effects from the deadlocked negotiations at the ad hoc committee on the parallel negotiations about a convention for the protection of diplomats against terrorist attacks.[38] Opinions were voiced in the Western camp

– and within the AA – whether it would not be better to avoid a renewal of the mandate of the ad hoc committee. Many perceived it as an instrument for Third World countries and questioned whether it still served any useful purpose for the West. Eventually though, the West Germans wanted to keep the committee in session as it would be a good stage on which Third World governments could appeal to their domestic audiences – without any serious damage. At the same time though, this would enable them to make silent concessions on other issues, such as the Diplomats Convention, or the Convention against the Taking of Hostages.[39] In Bonn's view, the ad hoc committee could be used as a tool to allow for more successful results in other anti-terrorism negotiations and should therefore be kept on the agenda. The AA lobbied for this policy among its allies and managed to convince them to keep the committee in session. The value of the committee for actual anti-terrorism results, however, was small for Bonn. Thus, the West German representative at the UN was instructed to keep a low profile at the committee.[40] This would remain West Germany's policy on the committee throughout the whole decade.[41] Given the circumstances, this was certainly the best strategy to pursue: it allowed Bonn not to expose itself on highly politicized and sensitive issues and to instead focus its energies on more feasible projects, such as the Diplomat's Convention and – most importantly – the Hostage Convention.

Owing to the fact that it was in deadlock, the ad hoc committee never managed to produce any feasible results. However, in its last session in 1979 it adopted a statement that, while upholding the special situation of struggles for national liberation, also for the first time condemned terrorism as such.[42] That was a small but remarkable achievement. It demonstrated that at the end of the 1970s, the radical positions of the early 1970s on terrorism had softened, that some consensus was possible, and that the international environment for anti-terrorism measures had improved.

The exception that proves the rule: the protection of diplomats

In light of the discouraging outcome of the ad hoc committee on terrorism, the Western countries realized that reaching a comprehensive solution to the problem of terrorism would not be feasible at the UN at the moment. Instead they decided to focus their energies on certain aspects of terrorism and shifted towards a sectoral approach.[43]

One of the problems that was becoming increasingly worrisome to the international community at large was the issue of terrorist attacks on diplomats.[44] Two of the hostage crises that gained a lot of media attention involved the FRG either directly or indirectly. In March 1970, the West German ambassador to Guatemala, Karl Count von Spreti was kidnapped by guerrillas who wanted to exchange him for twenty-two imprisoned rebels. Difficult negotiations between the Guatemalan government and the West Germans commenced, during which Bonn urged Guatemala to give in to the demands. On several occasions, Foreign Minister Walter Scheel and Chancellor Willy Brandt personally intervened. When word spread that Guatemala's government would not meet the demands, von Spreti was murdered. Upon learning of von Spreti's assassination, the German government was outraged and heavily criticized the Guatemalans' handling of the affair. The AA also set up an internal group to elaborate procedures to afford better protection to diplomats.[45]

The second important crisis that gained global public attention and was of some relevance to the FRG occurred in Khartoum in Sudan in March 1973. During a farewell reception at the Saudi embassy, several diplomats – among them Americans and Belgians – were taken hostage by six Palestinians. The West German ambassador Michael Ernst Jovy escaped this fate, as he had had to cancel his attendance on short notice. The terrorists demanded the release of prisoners in Jordan, Israel, and West Germany. However, as they failed to get a hold of Bonn's ambassador, they dropped the demand regarding the release of the RAF prisoners. As the governments concerned would not give in to the demands, the terrorists eventually killed the three Western diplomats in their hands.[46]

These two events demonstrated that diplomats had become the terrorists' targets of choice, and that those attacks were a serious concern for German diplomats, too. It is against the backdrop of these two crises that the negotiations at the UN about a Convention for the Protection of Diplomatic Agents took place.

At the UN, the issue of better protection for diplomats against terrorist attacks had already been on the agenda by the time of the Khartoum crisis and negotiations received a new impetus from this development. Because of the increasing numbers of kidnappings of diplomats, especially in Latin America, the General Assembly asked the International Law Commission (ILC) in December 1971 to elaborate a draft convention for the protection of diplomatic agents. Yet, the busy agenda of the ILC only allowed this topic to be addressed in mid-1972. By July, the ILC had adopted twelve draft articles and submitted them to the General Assembly for discussion.[47]

The draft convention was designed on the principle of *aut dedere aut iudicare* (extradite or prosecute), meaning that a country would either have to extradite perpetrators or put them on trial. The idea was that terrorists would no longer be able to escape punishment which would then – so the theory ran – discourage possible future attacks.[48] However, the major bone of contention was once again the issue of definition. Moreover, there was an amendment, introduced by Third World countries, to insert a clause exempting situations of national liberation from the scope of the convention. That was unacceptable to the West, as most kidnapping crises had taken place in circumstances which could be considered struggles for national liberation.[49]

When the FRG joined the UN in September 1973, the negotiations ran into a stalemate. Bonn had a significant interest in the negotiations and had followed them closely already prior to the accession to the UN. Now, as a member, it assumed a key role in the discussions and became one of the fifteen members of the drafting committee for the future convention.[50] As West German diplomats were in a prominent position on the target list of terrorists, Bonn's interest in the matter was understandable.

As for their strategy, the AA spent a considerable amount of energy on preventing spillover effects and negative consequences from the simultaneous debates at the ad hoc committee on terrorism. In the federal government's view, the ad hoc committee dealt with general issues pertaining to terrorism as a whole, while the drafting committee was only concerned with a small fraction – albeit an important one – of the problem of terrorism, namely, attacks on diplomats.[51] Bonn's active policy was quite successful. The West Germans were the only ones who were able to successfully insert a new clause into the convention during the negotiations, which obliges states on the territory of which an incident occurred to provide all available information to the state whose diplomats have become the victim of an attack.[52] This success demonstrates the importance that Bonn attached to the negotiations and to the Convention as such and indicated that it had already become an important actor in anti-terrorism efforts at the UN. However, the clause was also a consequence of Germany's recent experiences with terrorism against diplomats. In the case of Count von Spreti the Guatemalan government was not willing to share information with the West German government, which reduced the manoeuvring room for Bonn during the crisis. This experience explains West Germany's insistence on this obligation being included in the Convention text.

After difficult negotiations, the members of the committee finally managed to overcome the deadlock on the issue of national liberation movements. According to the compromise reached, such an exception would not be included in the text of the convention but would become an integral part of an accompanying resolution that would always have to be published with the convention.

Upon casting his vote in favour of the convention, the West German representative, like most of his Western colleagues, issued an 'explanation of vote' statement. In his speech, Bonn's man in New York stressed the FRG's 'peaceful interpretation of the right to self-determination'. He also underlined Bonn's understanding that '[the] prohibition of the use of force also applies as far as the implementation of the right to self-determination is concerned'.[53] With this statement, West Germany subtly pointed out that it would not consider acts committed by national liberation movements to be exempted from the scope of the convention. This understanding and the fact that the exception clause was not an integral – and therefore legally binding – element of the convention itself provided for enough ambiguity for Bonn to agree to it. As a matter of fact, the Germans even considered the convention an outright success of their own diplomacy and a milestone in the fight against international terrorism. While criticising the obstructive role that France had played in the negotiations, the AA highlighted the important contribution that West Germany had made to the successful adoption of an effective convention despite being a new member of the UN.[54]

Certainly, the Convention on the Prevention and Punishment of Crimes against Internationally Protected Persons, including Diplomatic Agents was an important achievement and milestone at the UN. However, it was also a special case. On the one hand, East and West had a common interest in such an instrument as Eastern diplomats also suffered at the hands of terrorists. On the other hand, many countries of the Third World were in favour of better protection for diplomats as well. As the events at Khartoum showed, their diplomats were not safe from attacks either. Besides, with many of these Third World countries maturing, leaving their revolutionary phase behind, they had an interest in functioning interstate relations without being disturbed by non-state actors such as terrorists. The speedy and successful adoption of the Diplomats Convention was hence an exceptional development and – as the West Germans had already realized themselves in 1973 – would not serve as a blueprint for future negotiations.[55]

Success against all odds: the issue of hostage-taking

In late December 1975, during a raid on a meeting of oil ministers of the Organization of Petroleum Exporting Countries (OPEC) in Vienna, terrorists led by the infamous Ilich Ramírez Sánchez – better known as 'Carlos the Jackal' – took about one hundred people hostage, among them oil ministers from several Arab countries. In the course of the negotiations between the Austrian government and the terrorists, the kidnappers were granted a plane to leave Austria with some of the hostages. After two additional days of negotiations, the hostages were finally released and the crisis ended in Algiers. As Austria did not ask for the extradition of the kidnappers, the Algerian authorities allowed the terrorists to leave for an unknown destination.[56]

At his holiday resort in Greece, German Chancellor Helmut Schmidt learned about the events in Vienna and immediately instructed Foreign Minister Hans-Dietrich Genscher to see if these events might have improved the environment for multilateral anti-terrorism negotiations.[57] The AA came to a positive assessment and considered this to be a window of opportunity. Encouraged by Schmidt's enquiry, the diplomats developed plans for an international convention that would have to focus on one aspect of terrorism that most countries would be keen to fight and on which consensus could thus be reached. It soon became evident that hostage-taking was such an aspect. Yet before launching its initiative at the UN officially, Bonn wanted to test the waters and conducted a survey of opinions with other governments – especially in the Third World – on this issue.[58] The results of the survey were mediocre: no clear support was evident but neither was there total rejection of the project. Despite this rather discouraging outcome, the AA was convinced that the momentum should be seized and decided to pursue its UN initiative regardless.[59] The belief was that many Third World countries would have been alienated by the recent terrorist attacks against them and hence support for terrorists would drop significantly. This would improve the chances for multilateral anti-terrorism projects and pave the way for a smooth adoption of a German convention proposal.[60]

However, the West Germans soon learned that they were quite alone in this enthusiasm. Already, during the EPC consultations in early 1976, it became clear that there would not be significant support from other European countries. Although most of the European Communities members welcomed the German plan, all of them expressed severe doubts as to its feasibility and some, such as France, were openly dismissive of it. There was a fear that it might just turn into another project that the Third World would exploit to legitimize acts committed by national liberation movements.[61] Nevertheless, optimism at the AA prevailed and an internal report concluded: 'But we do have a chance'.[62] The preparations therefore continued, although Bonn soon had to bury its initial intentions of submitting the project at the UN as a joint EC initiative.[63] West Germany's other important partner, the US, though, was much more supportive and encouraged Bonn to continue working on the project.[64]

Consequently, and encouraged by the Entebbe hijacking crisis in July 1976, Bonn was eager to pursue its first big initiative at the UN, and proceeded with the plans to call for the elaboration of a convention against the taking of hostages. Genscher officially announced the initiative during his speech to the General Assembly on 28 September 1976.[65] However, the Germans had to realize that the road to the convention was a stony one and at times it even appeared that the path led to a cul-de-sac. Problems centred around two issues in particular. One was the attempt by certain radical Third World states such as Algeria and Mali to link the issue of the convention with the debates going on in the ad hoc committee on terrorism. This, obviously, was not in the interest of the Germans, who did not want to see their project dragged into the general debates about origins, definitions, and possible justifications for terrorism. If both issues were connected, so the AA feared, the convention would never see the light of day as negotiations would go on *ad infinitum*.[66] The second issue was equally dangerous. As in the case of the Diplomatic Agents Convention, Third World countries once again insisted that exceptions should be made for national liberation movements and that state terrorism should explicitly be condemned. This again faced severe resistance from the West. The French in particular were hostile to anything that could remotely be interpreted as an exception clause for national liberation movements.[67] The US and Great Britain were also against these amendments. They feared that extending its scope to state terrorism would turn the convention into an instrument that could be used against friendly regimes in countries such as South Africa or Israel.[68] Consequently, Bonn's man in New York, Ambassador Rüdiger von Wechmar, had the delicate task of preventing a merger of the terrorism issue with the anti-hostage-taking project. He also had to find compromises that both Western allies and Third World countries could agree on. This seemed to be impossible and it appeared that the convention project would soon be buried by the General Assembly.[69]

Then, the situation improved slightly in early 1978 when first – and limited – success was achieved during a session of a small drafting committee in Geneva.[70] It took another year, however, for the real breakthrough to occur at another Geneva session. The compromise text alluded to the principle of self-determination in the preamble while Article 12 of the convention excluded acts committed in armed conflicts – including struggles for self-determination – from the scope of the convention.[71] Even a last-minute attempt by the Soviet Union to stop the compromise could not halt progress but only further isolated Soviet diplomats.[72] With this major bone of contention removed, some last remaining minor issues were resolved in the autumn of 1979 and the convention was finally adopted by the General Assembly in December 1979. Three years later it entered into force.

Despite the highly unfavourable environment, especially at the beginning of the negotiations, the convention was adopted. What explains this success of West Germany's project? To begin with, Bonn was very persistent about its project. It was the recently admitted country's first big initiative at the UN and, hence, a failure would have been a major blow to the FRG's reputation. Therefore, the West Germans used a great deal of political capital and lobbied hard to keep the issue on the agenda, even though they had no support from their European allies. Certainly, persistence was a key factor. Moreover, Bonn from the very beginning, tried to assemble as much support behind the initiative as possible, from all over the world, especially from smaller countries. As such, the perception of a Western initiative should be avoided. This, the AA thought, would then reduce Third World resistance to it. Besides this, West Germany wanted to be seen as an honest broker that was interested first and foremost in the humanitarian consequences of terrorism and not so much in the political dimensions of it. Bonn's diplomats highlighted the suffering that hostage situations would bring to the victims and emphasized that hostage-taking was prohibited in most national law codes. Furthermore, the Germans also managed to keep their group of sponsors together and thus provided a coordinated and coherent bargaining position. Lastly, Bonn's diplomat tried to resolve difficult issues in small groups that would not be under the scrutiny of public opinion so that compromises could more easily be achieved. All this together in connection with three-track diplomacy – German diplomats at the UN, in Bonn, and in the capitals of important countries were at several stages involved in the negotiations – accounted for the eventual success of the project.

However, to some extent, it was also a matter of luck. The intensifying Cold War, the official rejection of terrorist means by the PLO, as well as the decline in struggles for national liberation, facilitated the negotiations in the later part of the 1970s.[73] Moreover, at the same time, many 'new' Third World countries that had emerged from struggles of national liberation now were faced with terrorist threats as well. This made them more willing to collaborate with Western countries on international anti-terrorism instruments. By the late 1970s, the 'stone wall front' of the Third World showed some serious cracks.

Conclusion

In the 1970s, West Germany was a key player in the field of international anti-terrorism efforts at the UN. It not only participated in ongoing nego- tiations but also set the agenda by launching initiatives of its own. Despite being a newcomer to the UN, and against the backdrop of a highly unfriendly environment, Bonn's efforts and strategies to fight international terrorism were nevertheless a success.

Perhaps more important than the passing of the conventions, however, was the fact that Bonn kept the issue of international terrorism on the agenda of the UN. This policy contributed to an environment that was eventually conducive to better cooperation against international terrorism. While no consensus on defining or combating terrorism was possible in the early 1970s, the situation changed slightly towards the end of the decade. This paved the way for more conventions addressing aspects of international terrorism to be adopted by international organizations in the 1980s. In 1985, the General Assembly even passed a remarkable resolution that '[u]nequivocally condemns, as criminal, *all acts, methods and practices* of terrorism *wherever and by whomever committed*'.[74] This straightforward condemnation of all forms of terrorism independent of their circumstances was also a consequence of persistent West German anti-terrorism policies at the UN in the 1970s.

Certainly, the road there was a stony one. Resistance came not only from the Third World or the East but some of the staunchest objectors could also be found among Bonn's most important allies, such as France. The success- ful conclusion of anti-terrorism efforts at the UN was only possible with well balanced and careful diplomacy, a certain dose of persistence, a great deal of background negotiation, and a high level of coordination. West Germany managed to find the right mixture of all those ingredients.

Against all odds, the Germans indeed had the chance and courage to pursue their own initiative and they used it. It was a risky endeavour, one that could have easily turned into a major foreign policy disaster. However, a fortunate combination of changes in the international environment together with West Germany's skilful strategy allowed for a successful outcome. In the end, Bonn's success seems to confirm the saying that sometimes even in international politics, fortune favours the bold.

The UN anti-terrorism negotiations in the 1970s might also teach some lessons to diplomats who are still struggling to elaborate a comprehensive convention against terrorism. Still today, international terrorism is a serious concern to the international community. Rather than focusing on describing or defining the phenomenon as such, however, it might be once again more feasible – and useful – to address its consequences. The Terrorist Financing Convention of 1999, the 2005 Nuclear Terrorism Convention, and the 2010 New Civil Aviation Convention are all important instruments to deal with aspects of terrorism and are as such the continuation of UN anti-terrorism strategies developed in the 1970s. A sectoral approach rather than a general one seems to be a much more promising way to deal with terrorism, not just in the 1970s but also today.

Notes

1   Memorandum From the Acting Secretary of State (Ingersoll) to President Ford, Washington, February 18, 1975; US National Archives, RG 59, Central Foreign Policy Files, P750037–0744, Secret.

2   See for instance M. Dahlke, *Der Anschlag auf Olympia '72: Die Politischen Reaktionen auf den Internationalen Terrorismus in Deutschland*, Munich: Martin Meidenbauer Verlag, 2006; J. Hürter and G.E. Rusconi (eds), *Die Bleiernen Jahre. Staat und Terrorismus in der Bundesrepublik Deutschland und Italien 1969–1982*, Munich: Institut für Zeitgeschichte, Oldenbourg, 2010; M. März, *Die Machtprobe 1975: Wie RAF und Bewegung 2. Juni den Staat Erpressten*, Leipzig: Forum Verlag, 2007.

3   For the international character of '1968' see M. Klimke and J. Scharloth (eds), *1968 in Europe. A History of Protest and Activism, 1956–1977*, New York: Palgrave Macmillan, 2008; J. Suri, *Power and Protest. Global Revolution and the Rise of détente*, Cambridge, MA and London: Harvard University Press, 2003.

4   For more information on the RAF see for instance the two-volume edition by W. Kraushaar (ed.), *Die RAF und der Linke Terrorismus*, Hamburg: Hamburger Edition, 2006.

5   A. Kurth Cronin, *How Terrorism Ends. Understanding the Decline and Demise of Terrorist Campaigns*, Princeton and Oxford: Princeton University Press, 2009, p. 97.

6   For more information on this, see S. Aust, *Der Baader-Meinhof Komplex*, Hamburg: Hoffmann und Campe, 2008, 56; M. Dahlke, 'Nur Eingeschränkte Krisenbereitschaft. Die Staatliche Reaktion auf die Entführung des CDU-Politikers Peter Lorenz 1975', *Vierteljahrshefte für Zeitgeschichte*, 2007, vol. 55, pp. 641–78.

7   Helmut Schmidt quoted in M. Rupps, *Helmut Schmidt: Eine Politische Biographie*, Stuttgart: Hohenheim, 2002, 236 (my translation).

8   Schmidt cited in M. Schwelien, *Helmut Schmidt: Ein Leben für den Frieden*, Hamburg: Hoffmann und Campe, 2003, pp. 290–1 (my translation).

9   For more information on the Stockholm crisis, see M. März, *Die Machtprobe 1975: Wie RAF und Bewegung 2. Juni den Staat Erpressten*, Leipzig: Forum Verlag, 2007.

10   M. Rupps, *Helmut Schmidt: Eine Politische Biographie*, Stuttgart: Hohenheim, 2002, p. 241 (my translation).

11   Ibid. My translation.
12   *Dokumentation der Bundesregierung zur Entführung von Hanns Martin Schleyer: Ereignisse und Entscheidungen im Zusammenhang mit der Entführung von Hanns Martin Schleyer und der Lufthansa-Maschine "Landshut"*, ed. Bundespresseamt, Augsburg: Goldmann, 1977, pp. 133–80. For a detailed account of the odyssey of the 'Landshut' aircraft see T. Geiger, 'Die "Landshut" in Mogadischu. Das Außenpolitische Krisenmanagement der Bundesregierung Angesichts der Terroristischen Herausforderung 1977', *Vierteljahreshefte für Zeitgeschichte*, 2009, vol. 57, pp. 413–56.
13   M. Rupps, *Helmut Schmidt: Eine Politische Biographie*, Stuttgart: Hohenheim, 2002, p. 248.
14   A. Straßner, 'Die Dritte Generation der RAF. Terrorismus und Öffentlichkeit', in W. Kraushaar (ed.) *Die RAF. Entmythologisierung einer Terroristischen Organisation*, Bonn: Bundeszentrale für politische Bildung, 2008.
15   While the RAF was certainly the most infamous German terrorist group, the *Bewegung 2. Juni* and the *Revolutionäre Zellen* also committed attacks that claimed victims and contributed to the subjective feeling of insecurity in West Germany in the 1970s.
16   For the international links of German terrorist organizations see for instance C. Daase, 'Die RAF und der Internationale Terrorismus. Zur Transnationalen Kooperation Klandestiner Organisationen', in W. Kraushaar (ed.) *Die RAF: Entmythologisierung einer Terroristischen Organisation*, Bonn: Bundeszentrale für politische Bildung, 2008; T. Wunschik, 'Baader-Meinhof International?', *Aus Politik und Zeitgeschichte*, 2007, vol. 40–1, pp. 23–9.
17   The term 'Third World' will be used loosely in the context of this chapter, as it was by the AA in the 1970s. It basically referred to all countries outside of the Eastern or Western blocs. For more information on the Third World and the Cold War in general see O. Arne Westad, *The Global Cold War. Third World Interventions and the Making of Our Times*, Cambridge: Cambridge University Press, 2005.
18   See the assessment of the situation in a contemporary article: '"Kopf Runter, Wo Sind die Schweine?" Wie die Geiseln in Mogadischu Befreit Wurden,' *Der Spiegel*, no. 44 , 1977, p. 20.
19   Wegener as quoted in M. Schwelien, *Helmut Schmidt: Ein Leben für den Frieden*, Hamburg: Hoffmann und Campe, 2003, p. 305 (my translation).
20   For the domestic responses of the federal government see for instance the study by V. Mauer, 'Germany's Counterterrorism Policy,' in D. Zimmermann and A. Wenger (eds) *How States Fight Terrorism. Policy Dynamics in the West*, London: Boulder, 2007, p. 68; M. Petri, *Terrorismus und Staat. Versuch einer Definition des Terrorismusphänomens und Analyse zur Existenz einer Strategischen Konzeption Staatlicher Gegenmaßnahmen am Beispiel der Roten Armee Fraktion in der Bundesrepublik Deutschland*, Munich: Meidenbauer, 2007.
21   K. Seitz, 'Die Dominanz der Dritten Welt in den Vereinten Nationen', *Europa-Archiv*, 1973, vol. 28, pp. 403–4; L. Ziring, *The United Nations: International Organization and World Politics*, 4th ed., Belmont: Thomson Wadsworth, 2005, pp. 105–6.
22   Conversation between Nixon and Kissinger, Washington, February 3, 1973, US National Archives, Nixon Presidential Materials, White House Tapes, Oval Office, Conversation No. 840–12.
23   K. Seitz, 'Die Dritte Welt als Neuer Machtfaktor der Weltpolitik', *Europa-Archiv*, 1975, vol. 30, p. 220.

24 For an interesting assessment of this, see also Shaloma Gauthier, 'SWAPO, the United Nations, and the Struggle for National Liberation", Chapter 10 of this volume.

25 For more information on the Lod incident and its consequences for the UN see, for example, W.A. Farrell, *Blood and Rage. The Story of the Japanese Red Army*, Washington, DC: Lexington Books, 1990, pp. 129, 138–47; Y. Kuriyama, 'Terrorism at Tel Aviv Airport and A "New Left" Group in Japan', *Asian Survey*, 1973, vol. 13: 336; and, more recently, P. Romaniuk, *Multilateral Counter-Terrorism. The Global Politics of Cooperation and Contestation*, Oxford: Routledge, 2010, p. 37. Mathias Dahlke produced a very well-researched and interesting book on the Munich crisis, M. Dahlke, *Der Anschlag auf Olympia '72: Die Politischen Reaktionen auf den Internationalen Terrorismus in Deutschland*, Munich: Martin Meidenbauer Verlag, 2006.

26 G.M. Levitt, 'The International Legal Response to Terrorism. A Reevaluation', *University of Colorado Law Review*, 1989, vol. 60, pp. 536–7; A.D. Sofaer, 'Terrorism and the Law', *Foreign Affairs*, 1985–6, vol. 64, p. 903.

27 P. Romaniuk, *Multilateral Counter-Terrorism. The Global Politics of Cooperation and Contestation*, Oxford: Routledge, 2010, p. 39.

28 A.D. Sofaer, 'Terrorism and the Law', *Foreign Affairs*, 1985–6, vol. 64, p. 904.

29 For an assessment of the Resolution, see, for example, P. Romaniuk, *Multilateral Counter-Terrorism. The Global Politics of Cooperation and Contestation*, Oxford: Routledge, 2010, p. 40.

30 Action Memorandum from Hoffacker and Maw to Kissinger, Washington, December 29, 1973; US National Archives, RG 59, Central Files 1970–73, POL 23–8. Confidential; and Memorandum from Kissinger and Ehrlichman to Nixon, Washington, January 17, 1973; US National Archives, Nixon Presidential Materials, NSC Files, Box 310, Subject Files, Cabinet Committee on Terrorism, September 72–July 73, Confidential.

31 G.M. Levitt, 'The International Legal Response to Terrorism. A Reevaluation', *University of Colorado Law Review*, 1989, vol. 60: 537; Draft Report of the Ad Hoc Committee on international terrorism, UN GA document A/AC.160/L.3, 08.08.1973, B83 825, Politisches Archiv des Auswärtigen Amtes (PA); Airgram A–128 From the Department of State to All Diplomatic Posts, Washington, January 5, 1973; US National Archives, RG 59, Central Files 1970–73, UN 8 GA, Limited Official Use.

32 P. Grose, 'U.N Accord Sought on Hostage Problem', *New York Times*, 14 September 1976, p. 32.

33 A.D. Sofaer, 'Terrorism and the Law', *Foreign Affairs*, 1985–6, vol. 64, pp. 904–5.

34 See, for instance, Drahtbericht Beobachtermission bei den VN an das AA, 16.03.1973, ZA 121069, PA.

35 Protokoll: Bekämpfung des internationalen Terrorismus, 21.03.1973, ZA 121069, PA.

36 Memo: Sachstand attached to Memo Ref. 511 an das Ref. 230, 27.08.1973, B83 825, PA; Memo: Entwurf einer Antwortnote an den UN-Generalsekretär zur Resolution 3034 (27) betreffend Terrorismus, Übersetzung, 30.03.1973, ZA 121069, PA. This draft then became the official response of the German government.

37 Memo Referat 511 an die Gruppe 23, 05.06.1973, B83 824, PA; Memo Referat 511 an das Referat 230, 29.06.1973, ZA 121069, PA.

38 Memo Referat 502 an das Referat 511, 20.03.1973, ZA 121069, PA.
39 Drahtbericht Beobachtermission bei den VN an das AA, 14.08.1973, B83 825, PA; Drahtbericht Ständige Vertretung bei den VN an das AA, 11.10.1973, ZA 121069, PA.
40 Ibid.
41 Memo: Haltung der Bundesrepublik Deutschland, attached to Memo Ref. 511 an das Ref. 230, 15.08.1974, B83 825, PA; Brief Referat 511, AA, an den Bundesminister der Justiz, an dem Bundesminister des Inneren, 13.08.1975, B83 983, PA.
42 R.A. Friedlander, 'Terrorism and International Law: Recent Developments', *Rutgers Law Journal*, 1981–82, vol. 13, pp. 509–10; G.M. Levitt, 'The International Legal Response to Terrorism: A Reevaluation', *University of Colorado Law Review*, 1989, vol. 60, p. 538.
43 Memorandum from Rogers to Nixon, Washington, January 8, 1973; US National Archives, Nixon Presidential Materials, NSC Files, Box 310, Subject Files, Cabinet Committee on Terrorism, September 72–July 73, Confidential; Drahtbericht Beobachtermission bei den VN an das AA, 14.08.1973, B83 825, PA.
44 For an – incomplete – overview of crises involving diplomats see B.M. Jenkins, *Embassies under Siege: A Review of 48 Embassy Takeovers, 1971–1980*, Santa Monica: RAND, 1981.
45 See, for example, 'Bonn. Graf Spreti. Right or Wrong', *Der Spiegel*, no. 16, 13 April 1970; 'Kidnapped German Envoy Found Slain in Guatemala', *New York Times*, 6 April 1970.
46 'Arab Terrorists Give up in Sudan: Free 2 Hostages', *New York Times*, 4 March 1973; R.D. Lyons, 'US Ambassador to Sudan and His Aide Reported Seized by Guerrillas at Party', *The New York Times*, 2 March 1973. Drahtbericht Botschaft Karthoum an das AA, 01.03.1973, B83 824, PA; Drahtbericht Botschaft Karthoum an das AA, 02.03.1973, B83 824, PA; Brief der Botschaft Khartoum an das AA, 08.03.1973 (Ber. Nr. 197), B83 824, PA.
47 A.B. Green, 'Convention on the Prevention and Punishment of Crimes against Diplomatic Agents and Other Internationally Protected Persons: An Analysis', *Virginia Journal of International Law*, 1973–4, vol. 14, pp. 704–6.
48 Sir M. Wood, 'Convention on the Prevention and Punishment of Crimes against Internationally Protected Persons, Including Diplomatic Agents, New York, 14 December 1973', *United Nations Audiovisual Library of International Law* (2008). Online [http://untreaty.un.org/cod/avl/ha/cppcipp/cppcipp.html] (accessed 8 August 2012).
49 A.B. Green, 'Convention on the Prevention and Punishment of Crimes against Diplomatic Agents and Other Internationally Protected Persons: An Analysis', *Virginia Journal of International Law*, 1973–4, vol. 14, pp. 710–14.
50 Memo: TOP Konventionsentwurf zur Verhütung und Ahndung von Verbrechen gegen Diplomaten und andere unter Schutz stehende Personen, attached to Memo Ref 502 an das Ref. 230, 27.08.1973, ZA 113974, PA; M.C. Wood, 'The Convention on the Prevention and Punishment of Crimes against Internationally Protected Persons, Including Diplomatic Agents', *International and Comparative Law Quarterly*, 1974, vol. 23, p. 794.
51 Memo Referat 502 an das Referat 511, 20.03.1973, ZA 121069, PA.
52 Memo Abteilung 5 dem Herrn Staatssekretär, 28.12.1973, ZA 113974, PA.

53 Anlage 1 attached to Memo Abteilung 5 dem Herrn Staatssekretär, 28.12.1973, ZA 113974, PA.

54 Memo Abteilung 5 dem Herrn Staatssekretär, 28.12.1973, ZA 113974, PA.

55 Brief Referat 511, AA, an den Bundesminister der Justiz, an dem Bundesminister des Inneren, 13.08.1975, B83 983, PA.

56 'Curtain Descends in Algiers on OPEC Terrorists' Fate', *New York Times*, 24 December 1975; R.D. McFadden, 'Terrorist Group and Oil Officials Flown to Mideast', *New York Times*, 23 December 1975; 'Terrorists Who Raided OPEC Reported to Leave Algeria,' *New York Times*, 31 December 1975.

57 Schreiben des Bundeskanzleramts an Staatssekretär Gehlhoff, 06.01.1976, ZA 121070, PA.

58 Vermerk: Initiative der Bundesrepublik Deutschland auf dem Gebiet der Bekämpfung des Terrorismus, 08.01.1976, ZA 121070, PA.

59 Memo Unterabteilung 23 an den Herrn Bundesminister, 29.01.1976, ZA 121074, PA.

60 Referat 230, Vermerk: Maßnahmen gegen den internationalen Terrorismus, 09.01.1976, ZA 121070, PA; Runderlass an die deutschen Auslandsvertretungen, 12.01.1976, ZA 121070, PA.

61 Letter Deutsche Botschaft Paris an das AA, 17.02.1976, ZA 121071, PA; Note: Réunion du Groupe d'expert Nations Unies le 11 février à Luxembourg. Note d'appui sur le terrorisme international, no date, probably 11 or 12 February 1976, ZA 121074, PA; Vermerk Referat 230: Außenpolitischer Meinungsaustausch über Themen 31. GV der VN in der 259. Sitzung des KMB vom 23.6.1976, 25.06.1976, B83 676, PA.

62 Memo Unterabteilung 23 an den Bundesminister, 13.08.1976, B83 676, PA.

63 Vermerk Unterabteilung 23 an den Herrn Minister, 06.07.1976, B83 676, PA (my translation).

64 Drahtbericht Botschaft Washington an das AA, 15.01.1976, ZA 121071, PA; Telegram 220772 From the Department of State to All Diplomatic Posts, September 6, 1976, US National Archives, RG 59, Central Foreign Policy Files, Confidential, Priority.

65 Memo Referat 230, 22.07.1976, B83 676, PA; The letter is attached to Memo Unterabteilung 23 an den Bundesminister, 19.08.1976, B83 676, PA; 'Address by Hans-Dietrich Genscher to the General Assembly of the United Nations 7th Session, 28 September 1976,' in *Assemblé Générale, 31er Session 1976–1977, Séances Plénières 1–4*, ed. Nations Unis (1976), 88–9.

66 Memo Abteilung 2 an den Bundesminister, 28.10.1976, B83 983, PA.

67 A good explanation of why the French took this position is given in N. Powell, 'The 'Claustre Affair': A Hostage Crisis, France, and Civil War in Chad, 1974–77', Chapter 11 of this volume. The French were victims of hostage crises by alleged national liberation movements in Africa at the time.

68 Runderlass, 12.01.1976, ZA 121072, PA; Letter Ständige Vertretung bei den VN an das AA, 26.01.1977, B83 986, PA.

69 Vermerk: Einige Element für eine Erklärung im 6. Ausschuss für den Fall, dass wir unseren Res.E. zurückziehen, 03.12.1976, ZA 121077, PA.

70 Drahtbericht Ständige Vertretung bei den VN (Genf) an das AA, 24.02.1978, ZA 121078, PA; Ortex nr. 18, 03.03.1978, ZA 121078, PA.

71 At the time, to Western diplomats, this was not a problem as negotiations were going on about the Additional Protocols to the Geneva Conventions

prohibiting hostage-taking not only in cases of conventional interstate war but also in situations of civil war. For an assessment of the legal implications of the compromise see W.D. Verwey, 'The International Hostages Convention and National Liberation Movements', *American Journal of International Law*, 1981, vol. 75, pp. 71–8, 84–9.

72 Drahtbericht Ständige Vertretung bei den VN (Genf) an das AA, 15.02.1979, ZA 121080, PA; Memo D 5 an das Ref. 511, 20.02.1979, ZA 121080, PA.

73 For the end of superpower détente in the late 1970s, see for instance O. Njølstad, 'The Collapse of Superpower Détente, 1975–1980', in M.P. Leffler and O. Arne Westad (eds) *The Cambridge History of the Cold War: Endings*, Cambridge: Cambridge University Press, 2010. For the PLO's changed policy on terrorism see for instance J.F. Clarity, 'Terrorists' Techniques Improve, and So Do Efforts to Block Them', *New York Times*, 23 July 1976, p. 2.

74 GA Res. 40/61 of 9 December 1985. Emphasis added.

5 The absent terrorism

Leftist political violence and the French state, 1968–74

Markus Lammert

Introduction

In the spring of 1968, France seemed on the verge of revolution. The sudden outbreak of violent student riots and a massive general strike paralyzed the government and were ultimately at the origin of president de Gaulle's departure in 1969. 'May 68' rapidly became the symbol of a global youth revolt that profoundly changed western society.[1] However, the events of May ended as quickly as they had begun and the country was largely spared from the violent legacy of 1968 with which many other Western countries had to deal. In light of left-wing terrorism in West Germany and Italy, French scholars even speak of a 'French exception'.[2]

The relatively peaceful outcome of the French post-1968 period obscures the fact that there was indeed an intense and sometimes violent struggle between far-left groups and the French state. In the aftermath of May 1968, a multitude of so-called revolutionary groups emerged. They claimed responsibility for, and carried out hundreds of, guerrilla-style attacks. The reaction of the French authorities to these groups was considered excessive by many in the French public. In October 1970, the French weekly *Le Nouvel Observateur* wrote: 'ID Checks, police custody, beatings, the Court of State Security, verdicts whose severity shock even the supporters of a policy of "law and order". France finally awakes when faced with the escalation of the police violence.'[3] The German weekly *Der Spiegel* noted, 'Revenge for 1968! French policemen beat and torture'.[4] Jean-Paul Sartre stated, 'The state is not yet fascist, but the police already is'.[5]

While the ultimate abdication of the 'terrorist temptation' within the leftist movement 'remains somewhat of a historical quandary',[6] this article will try to shed light on the French response to the challenge posed by the revolutionary groups and its effects on French society in the 1970s. In order to do so, I will first summarize the policy field of internal security in France following the events of May 1968. I will then examine three aspects of the conflict between the state and the leftists: the theatrical dimension of political violence, the expansion of the rule of law, and, finally, the boom of civil rights and liberties in 1970s France.

Policies of public order in the aftermath of May 1968

May 1968 shaped French perceptions of threats to public order. The events of that spring began with protests by students and far-left groups at the University of Nanterre. The harsh reaction of the police led to solidarity demonstrations in Paris. Ten of thousands of students marched in the streets. Protesters constructed barricades and started street fights. Two-thirds of all French workers went on strike. For almost two weeks, the government effectively lost control over the country. Only at the end of the month were General de Gaulle and Prime Minister Georges Pompidou able to take back the reins.[7]

Restoring public order

On 30 May, De Gaulle ordered workers to go back to work and announced a snap election for the following month.[8] In lieu of Christian Fouchet, who had been unable to cope with the upheaval, he appointed Raymond Marcellin as the new Minister of the Interior.[9] To insiders, Marcellin was known as an energetic law-and-order politician who had successfully crushed violent miner strikes in 1948.[10] His loyal services found the approval of both General de Gaulle and his successor Georges Pompidou. Until his dismissal in 1974, Marcellin played a key role in the repression of leftist unrest.

The new Interior Minister cracked down hard on the leftists. On 12 June, Marcellin announced a ban on all demonstrations sponsored by revolutionary groups, the clearing of all still-occupied buildings, and the expulsion of foreigners involved in the events of May (about two hundred and fifty were expelled).[11] In addition, the Council of Ministers ordered the formal dissolution of eleven leftist groups suspected of being the instigators of the May upheavals. Among others, the Trotskyist *Jeunesse communiste révolutionnaire*, the Maoist *Union des jeunesses communistes marxistes-léninistes*, and the *Mouvement du 22 mars* led by Daniel Cohn-Bendit were proscribed.[12]

In his campaign for the June elections, de Gaulle used the threat of a Communist coup and called upon the French to choose between legitimate government and revolutionary anarchy. The overwhelming victory of the conservatives in the elections lent legitimacy to the governmental measures and marked the end of the first phase of the restoration of public order.[13]

Towards a civil war?

Many in the new radical left that emerged in May 1968 saw the events of May as the precursor of a revolution. Despite governmental repression, the leftist movement regrouped. In autumn 1968, Maoist activists of the banned *Union des jeunesses communistes marxistes-léninistes* formed the *Gauche prolétarienne* (GP) under the leadership of Benny Lévy. In the subsequent months, they welcomed student leaders of the May events such as Alain Geismar and Serge July into their group. The GP became the largest, most violent, and most famous of the French revolutionary groups.[14] The group received special attention through its proximity to important intellectuals such as Jean-Paul Sartre.[15]

The leaders of the GP were convinced that France was on the verge of a 'new fascism'.[16] They pursued a strategy of pushing spontaneous social protest to armed conflict and hoped to provoke a revolution via a civil war. GP members entered factories and tried to organize wildcat strikes.[17] Their clandestine military wing carried out sensational guerrilla and Robin Hood style attacks: in February 1970, GP members stole thousands of *Métro* tickets and distributed them to passengers. Three months later, they pillaged a luxury shop and, the next day, gave the goods to immigrant crowds in the suburbs.[18]

In some cases, the GP came dangerously close to the outright terrorism of the German *Rote Armee Fraktion* (RAF) or the Italian *Brigate Rosse*: in the fall of 1970, activists kidnapped Michel de Grailly, a member of the National Assembly. In May 1971, they staged a bomb attack against the far-right journal *Minute*, and, in March 1972, in reprisal to the murder of GP member Pierre Overney, they kidnapped Renault executive Robert Nogrette. However, the kidnappings ended with the release of the victims and the GP took care to avoid lethal violence.[19] In 1973, the GP leaders decided to dissolve the group because they feared its final step towards terrorism.[20] In total, French radical leftists carried out three hundred and twenty-nine acts of political violence from 1968 to 1974.[21] Political murder or a systematic clandestine guerrilla fight remained absent.

The priority of public order

The fear of a second May 1968 made the 'maintenance of public order' and the repression of revolutionary groups an absolute priority for the Ministry of the Interior. In his first speech to Parliament, the new Interior Minister spoke exclusively about questions of public security and analyzed in detail the events of May.[22] For 1969, Raymond Marcellin announced an increase of fifteen per cent of the police budget. The funds went almost entirely to the riot police – the *Compagnies républicaines de sécurité* (CRS).[23] During his time in office, Marcellin hired eighteen thousand new police officers (from 1961 to 1968 there had been only one thousand new hires).[24] His obsession with political violence provoked criticism even within the ranks of the Gaullist party. Members of the Parliament complained about the neglect of local urban police forces in favour of the national riot police.[25]

Immediately after his appointment, Marcellin established task forces and working groups to improve riot control.[26] A series of new methods for the dispersion of demonstrators were introduced. Henceforward, police agents took part in the demonstrations to quickly arrest troublemakers.

The CRS were equipped with protective coveralls and helmets with visors. Vehicles designed for barricade clearances completed the police car pool.[27] The improved equipment facilitated a more defensive approach to policing riots. The lessons learned in 1968 thus had important consequences in the long run: following 1968, demonstrations in France became less violent.[28]

Likewise, the Minister introduced new structures for the surveillance and prosecution of far-left activists. All police investigations against leftist extremists were centralized in a special police office – the *6e Bureau de la Direction centrale de la police judiciaire.*[29] In June 1968, Marcellin reactivated the *Bureau de liaison*, a liaison office that had been responsible for the coordination of all anti-terrorist services during the Algerian war.[30] Similarly, new departments within the intelligence services were established. A special anti-terrorist unit under Jacques Harstrich, who had previously fought against the right-wing terrorists of the OAS,[31] now surveyed and investigated leftists:

> With the techniques they had brought to perfection during the Algerian War and in the fight against the OAS – tailing, surveillance, postal interception, phone tapping, clandestine and illegal searching, bugging of apartments, infiltration, manipulation – the *Brigades opérationelles* worked wonders against the closed and suspicious far-left groups.[32]

At the beginning of the 1970s, over two hundred undercover agents and paid informants worked in the far-left milieu.[33] Shortly after the GP was banned in May 1970, Harstrich arrested GP leader Alain Geismar in the latter's Parisian hideout.[34] In the following months, several hundred leftist activists were imprisoned.[35]

Leftist violence and the state: interactions and effects

The theatrical dimension of political violence

Despite its explosive and politically destabilizing character, May 1968 had been 'curiously peaceful by the standards of revolutionary turbulence elsewhere, or in France's own past'.[36] Thanks to the moderation of the Paris police forces under the sympathetic Maurice Grimaud, no students were killed.[37] Above all, the protesters had held back in the first place: the students mimicked previous revolutions, rather than proceeding themselves. This largely symbolic or even 'playful' nature of the May uprisings was emphasized even while the events took place,[38] the best example being the barricades in the *Quartier Latin*. With no actual military use, they were mainly a historical reference to the many uprisings of the people of Paris in the eighteenth and nineteenth centuries.[39]

A similar symbolic dimension can be discerned in the challenge of the French state by far-left extremists in the early 1970s. There was a huge discrepancy between the rhetoric of violence and the largely non-violent course of the conflict. For both, the leftist radicals and the authorities, the patterns developed in May 1968 shaped actions in subsequent years.

French researcher Isabelle Sommier has outlined the 'theatrical' character of groups such as the GP and the gap between their violent revolutionary talk and their actions.[40] In their manifesto, *Vers la guerre civile* – 'Towards a civil war' – GP members called for an armed uprising against the 'class enemies'.[41] By equating the French state with fascism, they likened their 'revolutionary struggle' with the one of the *Résistance* – the French resistance movement against the Nazi occupation regime.[42] Accordingly, their clandestine guerrilla group called itself the *Nouvelle résistance populaire*. In its periodical, *La cause du people*, the GP encouraged people to kill 'fascist policemen' and 'capitalist managers'.[43] However, actual violence was mostly restrained to demonstrations and street fights with the police after which some demonstrators as well as police officers would end up in hospital.[44] In their guerrilla style actions – and in a blatant contrast to the terrorists of the RAF – the GP always took care not to seriously injure their adversaries.

Most of the authors dealing with the post-1968 period have overlooked the fact that the reaction of the French government remained largely symbolic as well.[45] While the Minister of the Interior publicly dramatized the actions of the leftists, actual state repression remained moderate. Raymond Marcellin called the far-left groups 'enemies of democracy' and 'subversive' threats to the public order.[46] As early as 1968, the ministry published a report on the 'Goals and Methods of the Revolutionary Groups on the Basis of Their Pamphlets and Journals'.[47] In 1969, Marcellin released an extended version entitled 'Public Order and the Revolutionary Groups'. According to the report, these groups had played a major role in the May events and were still planning the 'overthrow of the government by force and the destruction of Republican and democratic institutions'.[48] Marcellin saw the French leftists as part of an 'international conspiracy' headquartered in Cuba and directed against all western democracies.[49]

However, just like the writings of the leftists he described, Marcellin's analysis was barely connected to actual political crimes and violence. The reports relied exclusively on self-portrayals and statements.[50] In taking the rhetoric of the revolutionary groups seriously, the government mirrored the actions of the leftists. To their rhetorical radicalization, the state answered with a demonization, which remained mostly rhetorical as well.[51]

French researcher Michelle Zancarini-Fournel has shown that this demonization was not limited to the top of the administration. Police files and bulletins of the intelligence services reflect the language of the Interior Minister. Prefects noted every 'revolutionary agitation' in their province and the intelligence services tried to find evidence of an international conspiracy suspected of financing terrorist actions in France. Only after Marcellin's departure in 1974 did the language of the reports change.[52]

In the aftermath of May 1968, the Minister of the Interior copied the behavioural patterns of the leftists: the ritualized calls for violence of the revolutionary groups provoked their ritualized demonization by the authorities. While the rhetoric on both sides created the impression of a 'country in civil war',[53] the actual response of the French State was rather reasonable.

The Expansion of the rule of law

The way in which France dealt with the major political crisis of 1968 and leftist extremism in the subsequent years can indeed be read as an expansion of the rule of law. While, owing to Raymond Marcellin's law-and-order rhetoric, many contemporary observers feared a fascisization of the Gaullist regime, the overall reaction of the French state was in fact a sign of the stabilization of democracy in post-1945 France.

For a proper understanding of the French response to leftist political violence after 1968, we need to briefly discuss the French experience of terrorism and counter-terrorism during the Algerian War.[54] From 1954 to 1962, France had to deal with both terrorist attacks from the Algerian *Front de libération nationale* (FLN) and the right-wing activists of the French *Organisation de l'armée secrète* (OAS).[55] In Algeria, France led a 'war on terror', including a massive military campaign, systematic torture, and hundreds of thousands of deaths.[56] In the French mainland, too, exceptional measures were taken. With a series of 'emergency' and 'special powers' laws, parliament allowed the internment of terrorist suspects in camps and other exceptional sanctions against the rebels.[57] State violence against Algerians was a permanent feature of the war, the most striking example being the Paris massacre of October 1961, when French police attacked a peaceful pro-FLN demonstration and killed several dozen demonstrators.[58] In 1958, General de Gaulle established a new constitution, allowing the president to govern without parliamentary control in times of 'grave and imminent danger'.[59] In 1963, a special half-military Court of State Security (*Cour de Sûreté de l'État*) was set up to sentence the OAS terrorists who had attempted to kill de Gaulle.[60] The Court was charged with all future offences involving state security and became a permanent anti-terrorist jurisdiction with especially severe regulations: the government decided whether a prosecution was opened and maximum police custody was extended from forty-eight hours to ten days.[61]

In the aftermath of 1968, these far-reaching instruments of repression were not, or only very carefully, applied. At no point, did the government declare a 'state of emergency' or a 'state of siege'. With Marcellin's campaign to re-establish public order, police repression indeed increased massively, but police forces only occasionally overstepped legal boundaries.[62] The authorities privileged the infiltration of extremist groups over random all-out arrests.[63] The newly equipped riot police also pursued a rather defensive approach.[64] The Court of State Security, which, from 1963 to 1968, had convicted over two thousand six hundred people to often long-term prison sentences, remained almost inactive: from 1969 to 1975, the judges ruled in only eighty-five cases.[65] The absolute majority of the one thousand and thirty-five leftists sentenced to prison for crimes related to political activity were judged by civilian courts.[66] This was also true for the first trial of GP leader Alain Geismar who, in 1970, was found guilty for 'incitation to public unrest' and convicted to 18 months in prison – a sentence who's 'severity' initiated a broad protest campaign.[67] Rather than bearing the sign of a new fascism *à la française*, French law enforcement after 1968 thus was evidence of the renunciation of the logic of war.

The legal response to the activities of the revolutionary groups reveals an actual expansion of the rule of law. In June 1970, the government proposed a bill 'to combat specific new forms of criminality'.[68] The *loi anticasseur* ('Anti-Rioter Act') – was directed against the GP and other far-left groups. It aimed at the 'maintenance of public peace and the punishment of those who try to disturb it with violent actions'.[69] The new law held that anyone who took part in a demonstration – organizers as well as participants – could be held responsible for the results of any violent act or assault that occurred during the demonstration.[70] It thereby introduced collective punishment to the criminal code. The bill kicked off a wave of protest that widely surpassed the radical left.[71] After a long debate, the National Assembly and the Senate finally adopted the *loi anticasseur* but the committees of both chambers substantially weakened the draft before its passage: Parliament limited the law's validity to those demonstrators who deliberately refused to leave the demonstration after the outbreak of violence.[72] Furthermore, the MPs demanded a 'cautious application' of the law.[73]

Despite these corrections, the *loi anticasseur* remained a symbol of arbitrary repression among the political left throughout the 1970s.[74] Nevertheless, the parliamentary process, including a partial opposition of the Gaullist majority to the government, shows that the constitutional separation of powers worked – even when faced with leftist extremism. The parliament not only erased the strongest provisions of the government's proposal, it also served as a catalyst for public debate.

One year later, the Interior Minister failed with another legal project – a modification of the law of associations designed to prevent the reforming of already banned groups under a new name.[75] Like the *loi anticasseur*, it aimed at more effective repression of revolutionary groups. After the GP was banned in May 1970, intellectuals and GP-ists had launched a 'circle of friends' of *La cause du peuple*, which, in the eyes of Raymond Marcellin, was just a manner to circumvent the law.[76] The opposition parties violently opposed this new proposal. They were joined by many MPs of the conservative party and much of the media. Critics claimed that the law violated the principles of the constitution because it allowed a pre-emptive ban of organizations on the grounds of mere suspicions. While the Senate vetoed the draft, it eventually was adopted in the National Assembly in a night session.[77]

However, this time, the Constitutional Council – by applying the Human Rights Declaration of 1789 and the preamble of the 1946 Constitution – declared the law unconstitutional.[78] This decision is considered a turning point in French constitutional history, as for the first time since the founding of the Fifth Republic in 1958, the Council opposed an initiative of the powerful French executive.[79] The failure of the ministerial bill shows that the constitutional state not only proved its stability but that the rule of law was even strengthened in the conflict with the leftists. By including the Human Rights Declaration and the preamble of the Constitution to the 'constitutional block', the judges considerably broadened their jurisdictional competences.[80] The new autonomy of the Constitutional Council created a new equilibrium in the balance of powers and thereby completed the French political system.

The decision also marked a turning point in the policies of public order after 1968. In setting boundaries to the actions of the Interior Minister, the Constitutional Council reacted to a shift in public opinion. Since 1970 the fear of unrest had become less prevalent. Along with it, the acceptance of police repression noticeably diminished.

The boom of civil rights and liberties in 1970s France

One of the most significant outcomes of the conflict between far-left groups and the French state was a new emphasis on civil rights in the public sphere. Debates on liberties, law, and human rights dominated French political culture throughout the 1970s.[81]

It was crucial for the emergence of this discourse that police actions against far-left groups were perceived as exaggerated. Already, in May 1968, police brutality had proved to be particularly effective in creating solidarity for the protesters. In Raymond Marcellin's account of the events, this rather spontaneous reaction appeared as the result of a strategy of 'psychological warfare': after calling a demonstration, the revolutionary groups would deliberately provoke the police forces and then 'systematically spread lies' about state violence to mobilize bystanders and the public for their revolutionary goals.[82]

Even though the great majority of the French – after initially sympathizing with the students – disapproved of the far-left's violent actions, state repression became a key issue in public debates in the long run. The anti-repression campaigns of the leftists initiated a movement that ultimately affected the entire nation and served to initiate major changes within French society.

Firstly, far-left groups focused on anti-repression and civil rights out of mere necessity. With the state's repression sending more and more activists to jail, public support for the incarcerated 'comrades' became essential. In 1970, with the help of Jean-Paul Sartre, Maoist activists established the prisoner's aid organization *Secours rouge*.[83] In 1971, incarcerated members of the GP initiated a hunger strike that was widely publicized and led to the founding of Michel Foucault's *Groupe d'information sur les prisons*.[84]

Secondly, intellectuals such as Sartre and Foucault played a key role as amplifiers of the anti-repression campaigns. Their interventions elicited public notice of the causes raised by the far-left.[85] Moreover, after several cases of police violence against critical journalists, the national press took the side of the leftists and started its own campaign against police brutality.[86]

Finally, the moderate left-wing parties integrated the protests against repression in their political programmes. The *programme commun* of both the Socialist Party and the Communists highlighted issues of civil rights and liberties:

> Since 1958, year after year, the present regime has put in place a wide range of repressive laws that put at risk democracy and individual liberty. France has to preserve and develop its democratic traditions. All the laws affecting civil rights must be abolished; laws that protect these rights have to be established.[87]

Throughout the 1970s, liberalization remained a crucial issue in the electoral campaigns of the political left.[88] Consequently, the first measures of the new socialist government under François Mitterrand in 1981 included the dissolution of the Court of State Security and the deletion of the *loi anticasseurs* from the criminal code.[89]

The anti-repression campaigns of the early 1970s initiated and amplified a strong demand for liberalization and the extension of the rule of law. In France, liberty prevailed in debates on 'Security versus Liberty'. Ultimately, the new discourse also affected the conservative majority and the government. In 1974, future President Giscard d'Estaing campaigned for a 'progressive liberalism' and integrated many of the left-wing ideas in his government programme.[90]

Conclusion

What were the specific characteristics of the French response to leftist political violence in the late 1960s and early 1970s? First, the formative role of the experiences of the May Uprisings of 1968: the newly appointed Interior Minister concentrated almost exclusively on the maintenance of public order. The budget and work force of the security forces were massively increased; in addition, new material and modern police techniques were

The absent terrorism 95

introduced. Only Raymond Marcellin's resignation in 1974 marked a new orientation of the security strategy.

The French state responded quickly to the challenge posed by the revolutionary groups. The most important far-left groups were already banned in the summer of 1968. The Interior Ministry responded to the rhetoric of the leftists in the same vein and created a picture of a state in civil war. However, it became clear that France was not an authoritarian police state but rather a stable democracy, which – considering the rather low level of violence – even expanded the guarantees of individual rights during the conflict.

The societal countermovement also demonstrated its muscle early on, and, especially with its call for civil rights and freedom, its effects proved sustainable. The existence of a rising left-wing opposition lent the theme of liberty an important presence in the French public debate.

Notes

1   On the international dimension of 1968, see M. Klimke, J. Pekelder and J. Scharloth (eds), *Between Prague Spring and French May: Opposition and Revolt in Europe, 1960–1980*, New York: Berghahn Books, 2011; Ph. Gassert and M. Klimke (eds), *1968: Memories and Legacies of a Global Revolt*, GHI Bulletin Supplement, Washington, DC: German Historical Institute, 2009.
2   See, for example, M. Zancarini-Fournel, 'Récit', in P. Artières and M. Zancarini-Fournel (eds) *Les années 68. Une histoire collective 1962–1981*, Paris: La Découverte, 2008, p. 428.
3   *Le Nouvel Observateur*, 19 October 1970, p. 58.
4   *Der Spiegel*, 12 July 1971, p. 80.
5   *Der Spiegel*, 12 July 1971, p. 80.
6   J. Bourg, *From Revolution to Ethics: May 1968 and Contemporary French Thought*, Montreal: McGill-Queen's University Press, 2007, p. 57. For an account of the decision-making process of the GP leaders, see A. Geismar, *L'engrenage terroriste*, Paris: Fayard, 1981; F. Furet, A. Liniers and Ph. Raynaud, *Terrorisme et démocratie*, Paris: Fayard, 1985.
7   For an overview see M. Seidman, *The Imaginary Revolution: Parisian Students and Workers in 1968*, New York: Berghahn Books, 2004; B. Gobille, *Mai 68*, Paris: La Découverte, 2008.
8   B. Gobille, *Mai 68*, Paris: La Découverte, 2008, p. 97.
9   De Gaulle received Marcellin with the words: 'Finally, the real Fouché' – a reference to the (in)famous Minister of Police under Napoleon, Joseph Fouché. F. Zamponi, 'Raymond Marcellin, le Fouché breton', in R. Faligot and J. Guisnel (eds) *Histoire secrète de la Ve République*, Paris: La Découverte, 2006, pp. 405–7.
10 On Marcellin see S. Dépit, *Raymond Marcellin et le spectre de la répression policière dans la France de l'après-mai 1968 (1968–1974)*, unpublished Masters thesis, Institut d'Études Politiques Paris, 2007.
11 R. Marcellin, *L'ordre public et les groupes révolutionnaires*, Paris: Plon, 1969, pp. 53–8.
12 S. Dépit, *Raymond Marcellin et le spectre de la répression policière dans la France de*

l'après-mai 1968 (1968–1974), unpublished Masters thesis, Institut d'Études Politiques Paris, 2007, p. 44.

13   B. Gobille, *Mai 68*, Paris: La Découverte, 2008, pp. 86–100.

14   See Ch. Bourseiller, *Les maoïstes. La folle histoire des gardes rouges français*, Paris: Points, 2008.

15   On Sartre's role in the Maoist movement see R. Wolin, *The Wind from the East. French Intellectuals, the Cultural Revolution and the Legacy of the 1960s*, Princeton and Oxford: Princeton University Press, 2010, pp. 179–232.

16   See, for example, A. Glucksmann, 'Fascismes: l'ancien et le nouveau', *Les Temps Modernes* 1972, vol. 310bis, 266–334. See also J.-P. Le Goff, *Mai 68. L'héritage impossible*, Paris: La Découverte, 1998, pp. 189–203.

17   See, for example, M. Dressen, *Les établis, la chaîne et le syndicat. Évolution des pratiques, mythes et croyances d'une population d'établis maoïstes, 1968–1982. Monographie d'une usine lyonnaise*, Paris: L'Harmattan, 2000.

18   I. Sommier, *La violence politique et son deuil. L'après 68 en France et en Italie*, Rennes: Presses Universitaires de Rennes, 2008, p. 94.

19   See H. Hamon and P. Rotman, *Génération, vol. 2: Les années de poudre*, Paris: Éditions du Seuil, 1988, pp. 274–8, 393–422.

20   Ch. Bourseiller, *Les maoïstes. La folle histoire des gardes rouges français*, Paris: Points, 2008, pp. 330–4.

21   I. Sommier, *La violence politique et son deuil. L'après 68 en France et en Italie*, Rennes: Presses Universitaires de Rennes, 2008, p. 96.

22   *Journal Officiel de la République Française* (JORF)/Assemblée Nationale, Débats parlementaires, 2e séance du 14 novembre 1968, pp. 4004–9.

23   Ibid.

24   See JORF/Assemblée Nationale, Avis présenté au nom de la commission des lois constitutionnelles, de la législation et de l'administration générale de la République sur le projet de loi de finances pour 1969, annexe 394 à la 1e session ordinaire de 1968–1969, p. 773; M. Aubouin, A. Teyssier and J. Tulard, *Histoire et dictionnaire de la police du Moyen-Âge à nos jours*, Paris: Laffont, 2005, pp. 492–3.

25   See, for example, JORF/Assemblée Nationale, Avis présenté au nom de la commission des lois constitutionnelles, de la législation et de l'administration générale de la République sur le projet de loi de finances pour 1970, annexe no 840 à la 1e session ordinaire de 1969–1970, p. 836.

26   See F. Jobard, 'Ce que Mai fit à la police', in Artières/Zancarini-Fournel, *68. Une histoire collective*, Paris: La Découverte, 2008, pp. 577–82.

27   P. Bruneteaux, *Maintenir l'ordre. Les transformation de la violence d'État en régime démocratique*, Paris: Presses de Sciences Po, 1996, pp. 205–9.

28   J.-M. Berlière and R. Lévy, *Histoire des polices en France. De l'ancien régime à nos jours*, Paris: Nouveau Monde éditions, 2011, p. 241.

29   S. Dépit, *Raymond Marcellin et le spectre de la répression policière dans la France de l'après-mai 1968 (1968–1974)*, unpublished Masters thesis, Institut d'Études Politiques Paris, 2007, p. 81.

30   S. Dépit, *Raymond Marcellin et le spectre de la répression policière dans la France de l'après-mai 1968 (1968–1974)*, unpublished Masters thesis, Institut d'Études Politiques Paris, 2007, p. 81.

31   In the final stages of the Algerian war of independence the French right-wing *Organisation de l'Armée Secrète* (OAS) launched a terror campaign to stop the peace process and keep Algeria a part of France. See R. Kauffer, *OAS. Histoire*

d'une guerre franco-française, Paris: Éditions du Seuil, 2002.

32   J.-M. Berlière and R. Lévy, *Histoire des polices en France. De l'ancien régime à nos jours*, Paris: Nouveau Monde éditions, 2011, p. 321. See also J. Harstrich, *20 ans de police politique*, Paris: Calmann-Lévy, 1991, pp. 155–90.

33   J.-P. Brunet, *La Police de l'ombre. Indicateurs et provocateurs dans la France contemporaine*, Paris: Éditions du Seuil, 1990, p. 332.

34   J. Harstrich, *20 ans de police politique*, Paris: Calmann-Lévy, 1991, pp. 172–81.

35   J. Bourg, *From Revolution to Ethics: May 1968 and Contemporary French Thought*, Montreal: McGill-Queen's University Press, 2007, p. 68.

36   T. Judt, *Postwar: A History of Europe Since 1945*, New York: Penguin Books, 2005, p. 412.

37   See M. Grimaud, *En mai, fais ce qu'il te plaît*, Paris: Stock, 1977.

38   See, for example, R. Aron, *La Révolution introuvable. Réflexions sur les événements de mai*, Paris: Fayard, 1968.

39   I. Gilcher-Holtey, „*Die Phantasie an die Macht". Mai 68 in Frankreich*, Frankfurt am Main: Suhrkamp, 1995, pp. 232–58.

40   I. Sommier, *La violence politique et son deuil. L'après 68 en France et en Italie*, Rennes: Presses Universitaires de Rennes, 2008, pp. 89–97.

41   A. Geismar, S. July and E. Morane, *Vers la guerre civile*, Paris: Éditions et publications primaires, 1969.

42   J.-P. Le Goff, *Mai 68. L'héritage impossible*, Paris: La Découverte, 1998, pp. 186–8.

43   'Interview de la Nouvelle Résistance Populaire', *La Cause du peuple – J'accuse*, 1 August 1971, p. 4.

44   I. Sommier, *La violence politique et son deuil. L'après 68 en France et en Italie*, Rennes: Presses Universitaires de Rennes, 2008, pp. 77–81.

45   See, for example, K. Ross, *May '68 and Its Afterlives*, Chicago: University of Chicago Press, 2002.

46   JORF/Assemblée Nationale, *Débats parlementaires*, 2e séance du 14 novembre 1968, pp. 4404, 4409.

47   Ministère de l'intérieur, *Objectifs et méthodes des mouvements révolutionnaires d'après leurs tracts et journaux*, Paris, 1968.

48   R. Marcellin, *L'ordre public et les groupes révolutionnaires*, Paris: Plon, 1969, p. 8.

49   JORF/Assemblée Nationale, *Débats parlementaires*, 2e séance du 14 novembre 1968, p. 4007 f.

50   R. Marcellin, *L'ordre public et les groupes révolutionnaires*, Paris: Plon, 1969, p. 14.

51   For a different interpretation, see J. Bourg, *From Revolution to Ethics: May 1968 and Contemporary French Thought*, Montreal: McGill-Queen's University Press, 2007, pp. 61–7.

52   M. Zancarini-Fournel, *Le moment 68. Une histoire contestée*, Paris: Éditions du Seuil, 2008, p. 107.

53   Ibid.

54   For an overview of the history of the Algerian war, see B. Stora, *Histoire de la guerre d'Algérie 1954–1962*, Paris: La Découverte, 2006; S. Thénault, *Histoire de la guerre d'indépendance algérienne*, Paris: Flammarion, 2005.

55   G. Pervillé, 'Le terrorisme urbain dans la guerre d'Algérie', in J.-Ch. Jauffret and M. Vaïsse (eds) *Militaires et guérilla dans la guerre d'Algérie*, Bruxelles: Editions Complexes, 2001, pp. 447–68.

56   R. Branche, 'The French State Faced With the Algerian Nationalists (1954–1962):

98   *Markus Lammert*

A War Against Terrorism?', in S. Cohen (ed.) *Democracies at War Against Terrorism. A Comparative Perspective*, Paris: Palgrave Macmillan, 2008, pp. 59–76.

57   See A. Heymann, *Les libertés publiques et la guerre d'Algérie*, Paris: Pichon et Durand-Auzias, 1972.

58   See J. House and N. Macmaster, *Paris 1961: Algerians, State Terror, and Memory*, Oxford: Oxford University Press, 2006.

59   Constitution de la République Française, Art. 16.

60   JORF, Loi no 63-22 modifiant et complétant le Code de procédure pénale en vue de la répression des crimes et délits contre la sûreté de l'État, 16 January 1963, pp. 24–9.

61   Ibid.

62   For a detailed account of police violence in the post-1968 era, see M. Rajsfus, *Mai 68. Sous les pavés, la répression (mai 1968 – mars 1974)*, Paris: le cherche midi éditeur, 1998.

63   For an insight in the surveillance and infiltration of the GP, see S. Savoie, *RG. La traque d'Action Directe*, Paris: Nouveau Monde éditions, 2011, pp. 35–40.

64   P. Bruneteaux, *Maintenir l'ordre. Les transformation de la violence d'État en régime démocratique*, Paris: Presses de Sciences Po, 1996, pp. 198–227.

65   J. Ficet, *Indépendance et dépendances de la justice. Le concept d'indépendance de la justice comme enjeu de luttes politiques en France, 1954–1986*, unpublished PhD thesis, Institut d'Études Politiques Paris, 2005, pp. 202–3.

66   A. Monchablon, 'Maoïsme', in J.-F. Sirinelli (ed.) *Dictionnaire historique de la vie politique française au XXe siècle*, Paris: Presses Universitaires de France, 1995, p. 744.

67   See *Minutes du Procès d'Alain Geismar. Préface de Jean-Paul Sartre*, Paris: Éditions Hallier, 1970. A few weeks later, the *Cour de Sûreté de l'État* confirmed this decision. See M. Rajsfus, *Mai 68. Sous les pavés, la répression (mai 1968 – mars 1974)*, Paris: le cherche midi éditeur, 1998, p. 68.

68   JORF, Loi no 70-480 du 8 juin 1970, tendant à réprimer certaines formes nouvelles de délinquance, 9 July 1970, p. 5324.

69   Assemblée Nationale, Projet de loi tendant à réprimer certaines formes nouvelles de délinquance, no 1072, 14 April 1970, p. 5.

70   JORF, Loi no 70-480 du 8 juin 1970, tendant à réprimer certaines formes nouvelles de délinquance, 9 July 1970, p. 5324.

71   See, for example, R. Badinter and D. Bredin, 'L'escalade', *Le Monde*, 29 April 1970.

72   JORF, Loi no 70-480 du 8 juin 1970, tendant à réprimer certaines formes nouvelles de délinquance, 9 July 1970, p. 5324.

73   The application of the *loi anticasseur* seems to have been indeed relatively 'cautious': 18 convictions in 1970; 56 convictions in 1971, mostly against GP members. See S. Dépit, *Raymond Marcellin et le spectre de la répression policière dans la France de l'après-mai 1968 (1968–1974)*, unpublished Masters thesis, Institut d'Études Politiques Paris, 2007, p. 115.

74   E. Agrikoliansky, 'La gauche, le libéralisme politique et les droits de l'homme', in J.-J. Becker and G. Candar (eds) *Histoire des gauches en France, Vol. 2: XXème siècle: à l'épreuve de l'histoire*, Paris: La Découverte, 2005, p. 537.

75   'Loi, délibérée par l'Assemblée nationale et le Sénat et adoptée par l'Assemblée nationale, complétant les dispositions des articles 5 et 7 de la loi du 1er juillet 1901 relative au contrat d'association', in La Documentation Française, *Les grands textes juridiques sur les associations*. Online

[http://www.ladocumentationfrancaise.fr/dossiers/centenaire-loi-associations/documents.shtml] (accessed 12 August 2012).

76 See M. Rajsfus, *Mai 68. Sous les pavés, la répression (mai 1968 – mars 1974)*, Paris: le cherche midi éditeur, 1998, p. 205.

77 Ibid.

78 JORF, Conseil Constitutionnel, Décision no 71-44 DC du 16 juillet 1971, 18 July 1971, p. 7114.

79 See, for example, J. Chevallier, *L'État de droit*, Paris: Montchrestien E.J.A, 1994, pp. 91–6.

80 G. Lebreton, *Libertés publiques et droits de l'Homme*, Paris: Éditions Dalloz, 2009, p. 100.

81 On the global rise of the human rights discourse in the 1970s, see S. Moyn, *The Last Utopia: Human Rights in History*, Cambridge, MA and London: The Belknap Press of Harvard University, 2010. See also M. Lammert, 'Die französische Linke, der Terrorismus und der „repressive Staat" in der Bundesrepublik in den 1970er Jahren', *Vierteljahrshefte für Zeitgeschichte*, 2011, vol. 59, pp. 533–60.

82 R. Marcellin, *L'ordre public et les groupes révolutionnaires*, Paris: Plon, 1969, p. 33.

83 Ch. Bourseiller, *Les maoïstes. La folle histoire des gardes rouges français*, Paris: Points, 2008, pp. 279–81.

84 See J. Bourg, *From Revolution to Ethics: May 1968 and Contemporary French Thought*, Montreal: McGill-Queen's University Press, 2007, pp. 68–102.

85 The support of important intellectuals helped keep the far-left away from terrorism by maintaining a 'dialogue' between radical activists and the moderate mainstream left. See, for example, J. Requate and Ph. Zessin, 'Comment sortir du 'terrorisme'? La violence politique et les conditions de sa disparition en France et en République Fédérale d'Allemagne en comparaison. 1970 – années 1990', *European Review of History*, 2007, vol. 14, pp. 423–45; D. Paas, 'Frankreich: Der integrierte Linksradikalismus', in Henner Hess (ed.) *Angriff auf das Herz des Staates. Soziale Entwicklung und Terrorismus*, Frankfurt am Main: Suhrkamp, 1988, 169–278. See also M. S. Christofferson, *French Intellectuals Against The Left. The Antitotalitarian Moment of the 1970s*, New York: Berghahn Books, 2004.

86 The press campaign started in May 1971 when the journalist Alain Jaubert was beaten in a police car. See H. Hamon and P. Rotman, Génération, vol. 2: Les années de poudre, Paris: Éditions du Seuil, 1988, pp. 341–61.

87 'Programme commun', *Bulletin Socialiste. Organe d'information du Parti Socialiste*, Supplément, juin 1972, p. 11.

88 See E. Agrikoliansky, 'La gauche, le libéralisme politique et les droits de l'homme', in J.-J. Becker and G. Candar (eds) *Histoire des gauches en France, Vol. 2: XXème siècle: à l'épreuve de l'histoire*, Paris: La Découverte, 2005, pp. 524–41.

89 JORF, Loi no 81-737 portant suppression de la Cour de sûreté de l'État, 5 August 1981, p. 2142; JORF, Loi no 81-1134 modifiant l'article 108 du code pénal et abrogeant les articles 184, alinéa 3, et 314 du même code, 24 December 1981, p. 3499.

90 See, for example, S. Berstein and J.-F. Sirinelli (eds), *Les années Giscard. Les réformes de société 1974–1981*, Paris: Armand Collin, 2007.

6 The success of Italian anti-terrorism policy

Tobias Hof

Introduction

On 12 December 1969, a bomb exploded in the *Banca Nazionale dell'Agricultura* at the Piazza Fontana in Milan, killing seventeen people and injuring over eighty. It was the peak of a wave of right-wing terrorist attacks that had begun in the spring of 1969. The bombing is also commonly regarded as the beginning of the Italian *anni di piombo* (years of lead) which lasted for almost twenty years. During the five years after the Piazza Fontana attack, terrorism in Italy was overwhelmingly a right-wing phenomenon, culminating in the Brescia and *Italicus* bombings of 1974. Terrorism then dropped to a temporary low in 1975, only to increase again rapidly and more heavily with its peak in 1978, when former Prime Minister Aldo Moro was kidnapped and killed. Contrary to the years before 1975, however, terrorism in Italy was now dominated by left-wing groups. Between 1969 and 1982 Italy suffered over 8,800 terrorist attacks that left three hundred and fifty-one dead and seven hundred and sixty-eight injured.[1]

In this period, Italy faced a greater terrorist threat from left- and right-wing terrorist groups than any other Western democracy. How was it possible for a state such as Italy, traditionally considered weak and corrupt, to defeat left- and right-wing terrorism? In this chapter, I focus on the one law which was – and still is – regarded as the most successful Italian anti-terrorism law, namely the 'Measures in Defence of the Constitutional Order' of May 1982.[2] These new regulations for principal witnesses quickly became known as the law on the repentant terrorist, the so called *pentiti*.[3]

In the first part, I give an overview of the development of repentant regulations within Italian anti-terrorism legislation between 1969 and 1982. In the second part, I examine the content of the *Legge Pentiti* and discuss its impact. What were the most important articles? Was it really as successful and undisputed as generally assumed? In the conclusion, I further consider the question of whether the implementation of a law similar to the *Legge Pentiti* would really be a useful addition to today's anti-terrorist policies, as some scholars have recently suggested.[4]

The development of repentant legislation (1969–82)

Despite rising criminal and terrorist activities in the late 1960s and early 1970s, the Italian parliament did not suspend the necessary liberalization process of the Penal Codes, which originated in the Fascist era. It was not until October 1974 that the government responded to the new crisis of public order by enacting the law 'New norms against criminality'. It was commonly known as the *Legge Bartolomei*, named after the senator of the Christian Democratic Party, Giuseppe Bartolomei. It granted kidnappers who released their hostages unharmed reduced prison sentences. Until recently, the law escaped the attention of scholars of Italian anti-terrorism legislation because it was not exclusively directed against terrorism. In fact, it was part of a wider strategy to repress all kinds of crime and violence.[5] However, the legislation process was heavily affected by the abduction of state attorney Mario Sossi in April 1974: members of the left-wing terrorist group, the Red Brigades, kidnapped Sossi and held him hostage for over a month. The kidnapping was the beginning of the Red Brigades' 'attack on the heart of the state', who had before directed their actions only against employers of the big firms in Northern Italy.[6] When the abduction took place, parliament was still debating the draft of the *Legge Bartolomei*, which the government had proposed as early as November 1973. Yet an enactment failed because of the joint opposition of Socialists and Communists. It was finally the kidnapping of Sossi that convinced politicians of all parties, who were deeply shocked by the helplessness of the security forces, that a serious discussion of the draft should begin.[7]

When the Red Brigades kidnapped Aldo Moro in March 1978 and killed him two months later, politicians' and the public's demands for a severe anti-terrorism policy grew stronger. The Italian state responded with the modernization and reorganization of the security forces, the foundation of a special anti-terrorist unit under the command of Carabinieri-General Carlos Alberto Dalla Chiesa,[8] and the enactment of repressive legislation such as the *Legge Moro* of March 1978 ('Penal Norms and Penal Procedures Norms for the Prevention and Repression of Serious Crimes') and the *Legge Cossiga* of December 1979 ('Urgent Measures for the Defence of the Democratic and Public Order'). The *Legge Moro* created the offence of 'kidnapping for terrorist or subversive aims', with prison sentences ranging from twenty-five years to life imprisonment. Furthermore, restrictions on tapping telephones were scaled back and the obligation to report new tenants was introduced. The *Legge Cossiga*, named after the Christian Democratic Prime Minister at that time, Francesco Cossiga, increased the sentences for politically motivated violent offences by introducing 'terrorist organizations' and 'crimes for terrorist aims' as aggregating factors in the sentencing decisions.

However, conciliatory approaches and the idea of encouraging terrorists to collaborate with the public authorities were not entirely replaced. The notion that success against terrorism could not be achieved only with repressive measures still prevailed among politicians.[9] Thus, the *Legge Moro* also offered reduced sentences to terrorists who broke with their organizations and helped to ensure that hostages were released unharmed.[10] This provision was inspired by the above-mentioned *Legge Bartolomei* of 1974. Article one of the *Legge Cossiga* granted reduced prison sentences for every terrorist who cooperated with the police.[11]

As early as December 1979 terrorists began to come forth and provide information to the authorities. Many terrorists, who were caught by the security forces and also felt that the time for revolution was over, began to collaborate with the police on the basis of the *Legge Cossiga*. The testimony of the former head of the Red Brigades' cell in Turin, Patrizio Peci, alone led to the arrest of 85 suspected terrorists.[12] The *Legge Moro* and above all the *Legge Cossiga* symbolized the transition from merely repressive to compensatory anti-terrorism legislation. Its efficiency originated from dialectic between drastically increased sentences and mitigation. It seemed that the tide had turned in favour of the state authorities. In the spring of 1980, the German weekly *Der Spiegel* quoted a delighted Ugo Pecchioli, the person responsible for public order issues within the Communist Party: 'The terrorist-fishes', he said referring to Mao Zedong's famous dictum of guerrilla warfare, 'have less and less water to swim in'.[13]

The terrorists tried to fight back: in January 1979, the trade unionist Guido Rosa was killed. He had testified against members of the Red Brigades, who worked with him at the same factory. On 10 June 1981, the Red Brigades kidnapped Patrizio Peci's brother, Roberto, and killed him two months later. They filmed the execution and – for the first time – sent a copy of the tape to the TV station RAI. The aim of the terrorists was to frighten potential traitors, which they tried to achieve by nationwide media coverage.[14] Yet these acts of revenge backfired: they deepened the already existing gap between terrorists and extremist groups, thus antagonizing the only social environment from where new recruits would come.[15]

The Legge Pentiti of May 1982

The pressure from the authorities and the public outrage after the killing of Roberto Peci prompted the government to elaborate new means to widen Article 4 of the *Legge Cossiga*. The republican Prime Minister of the time, Giovanni Spadolini, presented the new plans to his cabinet colleagues on 28 August 1981.[16] Spadolini focused especially on two provisions: first, sympathizers would get no sentence at all if they stopped to support terrorists and dissociated themselves from the terrorist scene. Second, terrorists who committed severe crimes would get reduced sentences if they cooperated with the public authorities. Thus, the Prime Minister hoped to deprive terrorist groups of the support they still enjoyed in the extreme left-wing milieu. Furthermore, he wanted to encourage other terrorists to help the authorities. At first, Spadolini intended these measures to run for two years. However, in the end, the cabinet decided against a fixed time limit. Ministers feared that two years might not be sufficient to defeat terrorism.[17]

During the cabinet meeting, the Minister of Justice, Clelio Darida, and the Minister of the Interior, Virginio Rognoni – both members of the Christian Democratic Party – supported Spadolini's plans uncondition-ally.[18] Only the Minister of the Merchant Navy, Calogero Antonio Mannino, also a member of the Christian Democrats, had second thoughts. He feared that the Italian public might get the impression that success against terror-ism would mainly depend on the testimonies of former enemies of the state – assuming, of course, their willingness to cooperate with the public author-ities.[19] Furthermore, he complained that the judges would get a disproportionate degree of leeway in their scope of judgment evaluation.[20] Finally, Rognoni was able to dispel Mannino's concerns and the entire cabinet agreed to the prime minister's plans.[21]

The new government draft was presented to the Senate on 12 September 1981. It caused a lively discussion in both the parliament and the Italian public. The strongest opposition came from extreme right- and left-wing political parties, as well as other organizations.[22] Politicians of the extreme left rejected the ideas altogether. They complained that only high-ranking terrorists would profit from the new regulations because only they were in a position to provide the desired information to the authorities.[23] Furthermore, the intended law would introduce a 'dual penal law' in Italy, since only individuals accused of having committed a crime of a terrorist nature could benefit from the planned sentence reductions. Hence, some politicians like senator and former President of the Constitutional Court, Giuseppe Branca, demanded that the new regulations should also be extended to members of organized crime.[24] Marco Boato, member of the Radical Party, denounced the 'perverse impact' of the governments' plans altogether: he claimed that Article 4 of the *Legge Cossiga* had not only not brought the desired success but had rather led to an escalation of violence. To support his claim he referred to the case of the Peci brothers.[25] Furthermore, his party colleagues condemned as morally wrong that the state advocated denunciation. The Italian Minister of the Interior, Rognoni, tried to defend the government's draft against these accusations. He said that a different notion about morality was the reason for the differ-ent evaluation of the law and the strong criticism: in his opinion, the highest moral virtues were freedom and the life of every single citizen. Every terrorist who did not cooperate with the public authorities would violate these virtues.[26]

Right-wing politicians also objected to the government's plans. In their opinion it was not possible to be a member of a terrorist organization with-out committing any crime at all. Furthermore, they argued that a judge would not be fully able to assess the truth and the value of the testimony of a terrorist trying to save his skin. According to them, the plans of the government were perfunctory, not exactly sophisticated, and would even violate the principles of penal law.[27] Right-wing politicians thus understood the intended law as further proof of the confusion and helplessness of a government that was entirely clueless about how to fight terrorism.[28] For the neo-fascists, the initiative of the government symbolized nothing more than an obvious defeat of the state.[29]

Even though politicians who belonged to the parties of the *arco costi-tuzionale* did not agree on every article, they totally supported the basic idea behind the government's plans. They all believed that it was of the utmost importance to further the isolation of terrorist groups from society. For the Republican Vitale Robaldo, the Italian state had two possible ways to achieve this goal: the state could either – like an authoritarian state – criminalize political disagreement and sanction it with severe punishment, or it could utilize all possibilities that were offered by the Italian Constitution to make it easier for terrorists to abandon their organiza-tions.[30] Robaldo intended to stress the uniqueness and the constitutionality of the planned measures. However, the previous anti-terrorism policy of the Italian state was primarily based on repression and a criminalization of political dissent – thus, Robaldo accidently compared the Italian state with an authoritarian state.

Due to all these different opinions, the members of Parliament decided against the government's draft as a basis for any further discussion. Instead, they agreed to formulate a new text. This second draft was discussed several times in the Senate and in the Chamber of Deputies, which subjected it to a number of changes. It took nearly nine months until the law 'Measures in Defence of the Constitutional Order', consisting of thirteen articles, was finally enacted on 29 May 1982.[31] In the following paragraphs, I take a closer look at the most important articles and their controversial provisions.

Article 1 stated that terrorists would receive no sentence at all, if they abandoned their former group, renounced violence as means of political struggle, and had committed only one of the following crimes:

- formation, organization, conducting, or participating in a 'subversive' (Art. 270 CP) or 'terrorist organization' (Art. 270-bis CP);
- formation of or participation in an 'armed group' (Art. 306 CP);
- acquiescence of a 'political conspiracy' (Art. 304 CP); or the
- formation of groups with the aim of political conspiracy (Art. 305 CP).[32]

Already, in October 1981, the Minister of the Interior, Rognoni, had told his German colleague Gerhart Baum about these ideas: 'Everyone', he said, 'who took part in or supported an armed organization or possessed a weapon but has voluntarily abandoned his illegal actions should receive no sentence at all'.[33] The Communists, however, wanted two preconditions to be fulfilled before the terrorist would be able to benefit from this clause. First, terrorists were to tell the public authorities everything regarding their own crimes. Second, they should be obliged to give further information about the organization, plans, and members of their former group. Only then it would be guaranteed that a terrorist sincerely repented his crimes and that his information would truly help to defend democracy.[34] These demands were, however, rejected by the other parties of the *arco costituzionale*. In their opinion, Article 1 in its original form offered the only way for former sympathizers to re-enter society and to put an end to the circle of violence, as well as to the 'years of lead'.[35]

Articles 2 and 3 dealt with all of the cases in which a terrorist was accused of having committed further crimes that were not listed in Article 1. If a terrorist abandoned his former group and helped to resolve his crimes, a life sentence could be reduced to between fifteen and twenty-one years of imprisonment. Other prison sentences were reduced up to one-third, with a maximum of fifteen years.[36] If a terrorist furnished further information to the public authorities to help them in their fight against terrorism, a life sentence would be reduced to between ten and twelve years of imprisonment. All other sentences were simply divided in half. Should a terrorist provide information that turned out to be of exceptional value for the investigations, the original sentence could even be cut down to one-third of the original sentence.[37]

Another controversial issue was the exact moment when a terrorist should begin to cooperate with the public authorities. The Communists wanted to grant a sentence reduction only if the terrorist dissociated himself out of a personal conviction. Therefore, they demanded to oblige terrorists to show their willingness to cooperate with the authorities before the criminal proceeding was initiated.[38] They complained that the government would allow terrorists to confess even after the hearings had started. This would only insult the victims of terrorism and their relatives.[39] In their struggle to modify this provision, the Communists were supported by the *Magistratura Democratica*, a leftist organization of lawyers. The lawyers argued that such a regulation could cause terrorists to take a mere opportunistic position, simply trying to cut down their sentences. Thus, nobody would be able to trust their testimonies.[40] Furthermore, both the Communists and the *Magistratura Democratica* criticized the extent of the sentence reduction the government had proposed. It would give judges a 'power to grant mercy' that should only rest with the President. In their opinion, the new plan would be in 'schizophrenic contrast' to the emergency legislation of 1978–79, which had constrained the power of judges.[41] In the end, however, their criticism did not lead to a modification of the original draft.

Articles 6 to 9 scaled back the regulations for granting bail and for being released on parole.[42] The previous prohibition to free terrorists prematurely was nullified. The judge could now release repentant terrorists after they had served half of their sentence. Aldo Rizzo, deputy of the left-wing party, *Sinistra Independente*, complained that these new regulations would build 'golden bridges' for terrorists. He feared that every means to execute control would be neglected. Therefore he proposed making it compulsory for every terrorist who had benefited from the new law to report to a police station regularly.[43] In the beginning, the government had even played with the idea of empowering the Minister of Justice to be able to influence the decision to grant bail and on being released on parole. Of course, these plans were highly controversial.[44] Politicians of all different parties – from the Radical Party to the right fringes of the Christian Democrats – rejected any interference of the executive with the judiciary. The I. Commission of the Senate, which was responsible for questions about the constitutionality of bills and laws, also expressed its doubts.[45] In the end, neither Rizzo nor the government succeeded in getting their plans enacted.[46]

Rognoni tried to justify all of these far-reaching measures: it was of the utmost importance – so he argued – for the state to get as much information about the terrorist phenomenon and terrorist groups as possible. The German Minister of the Interior, Baum, did not accept Rognoni's statement. In his opinion, these measures were not justifiable because the 'erosion of the rule of law is too great'.[47] The government in Rome, however, stuck to its plan and pointed to the success of Article 4 of the *Legge Cossiga* over and over again.[48]

The impact of the *Legge Pentiti*

As mentioned above, the *Legge Pentiti* is still regarded as the most successful anti-terrorism law enabling the Italian state to defeat terrorism.[49] Statistics seem to verify such a positive conclusion: on 31 August 1982, the authorities had already counted three hundred and eighty-five repentant terrorists.[50] The testimony of these *pentiti* led in turn to the arrest of over three thousand suspected terrorists. Despite these impressive figures, both the efficiency and the constitutionality of the penitence law must be assessed more carefully.

When the law came into effect in the spring of 1982, Italian terrorism was perhaps not totally defeated but reduced to a controllable entity – especially in comparison with the increase in organized crime. Many terrorists like Patrizio Peci had already cooperated with the authorities, before the *Legge Pentiti* was finally enacted.[51] It was above all Article 4 of the *Legge Cossiga* that had made cooperation with the state attractive. Also, erosions within terrorist groups played into the hands of the government. Therefore, these *pentiti* of the 'first generation' were far more responsible for the fragmentation and the later defeat of the terrorist organizations than the *pentiti* after May 1982. The importance of the *Legge Pentiti* can be found more in an indirect rather than in a direct fight against terrorism: it helped to hinder potential recruits from joining terrorist organizations and impeded the further radicalization of extremist groups. Yet the law was primarily effective against left-wing terrorism, since only a few right-wing terrorists repented their crimes. And, if they did, they did not really help the investigations. There are two main reasons to explain this difference. First, the numbers of left-wing terrorists and people who sympathized with their actions was higher. Second, right-wing organizations never experienced an internal ideological crisis like their left-wing counterparts.[52] Thus, one of the major reasons why left-wing terrorists began to cooperate with the authorities was missing.

Above all, the *Legge Pentiti* was a pragmatic way of exploiting the inner crisis of terrorist groups. It was inspired by a trade-off philosophy between state and terrorists.[53] Hence, the Italian state used a strategy, which was part of the political struggle since the founding of the Italian Republic, the so called *trasformismo*. The opponent should not only be defeated by means of repression and confrontation, but deals and compromises should be equally implemented to achieve the desired goals. Without this 'political and cultural predisposition which was shared by the political elite as well as the terrorists, this kind of trade-off would not have worked'.[54]

As could be seen, the Communists, in contrast to the Christian Democrats, were less inclined to grant excessive concessions to repentant terrorists. They pleaded for a more rigorous definition of the *pentiti* group, they tried to limit the sentence reduction, and wanted to establish an official control mechanism. After the peak of the terrorist challenge, the Communists were anxious to separate themselves from the left-wing terrorists by an even firmer anti-terrorism policy. Especially in the early and mid-1970s, they had been accused of promoting and supporting left-wing terrorism.

The Christian Democrats' empathy for the terrorists derived less from a concern for the 'lost children', as could be found among some politicians of the extreme left. Many children and relatives of prominent members of the Christian Democratic Party from the left-Catholic milieu were involved in terrorist activities. It was not until Marco Donat-Cattin, the son of one of the leading figures of the Christian Democrats, was arrested as a member of the terrorist group *Prima Linea* in December 1980 that the majority of the party began to support the repentance law.[55]

The time limit of 120 days is a further indication for the pragmatic 'realpolitik' of the government.[56] They wanted to get useable information as quickly as possible. This is another proof for the assumption that success in the fight against terrorism had a much higher priority than reconciliation with terrorists. The only exception was Article 1 of the *Legge Pentiti*. As already mentioned, it stated that suspected terrorists would get no sentence at all when they were simply members of a terrorist organization and had not committed any other terror-related crime. There was no need for them to cooperate with the authorities. Therefore, this article was the true novelty of the repentant law. It was precisely this provision which revealed a first step taken by the state towards reconciliation with the terrorists and the sympathizers of the extreme left.

The *Legge Pentiti* was also criticized as anti-constitutional. Not only extremist parties from the left and the right, but also people such as the President of the State, Sandro Pertini, had trouble with the proposition. They criticized, as has been shown, the rewarding of informers who betrayed their friends, the introduction of a 'dual penal law' in Italy, and doubted the truth of the terrorist's testimony.[57] Despite this 'perversion of jurisdiction', as Marco Boato called the law, the government was convinced that the law was successful and the only way to defeat terrorism. Therefore, it enacted a law-decree on 1 October 1982 to extend the duration of the *Legge Pentiti* for another 120 days.[58] The majority of the members of parliament agreed with the government's evaluation and approved the decree without any modification.[59] On 28 January 1983, the cabinet again discussed whether there should be another extension. In the end, the ministers decided against it, because they still regarded the *Legge Pentiti* as an emergency law. Another extension – so they argued – would have nullified this character of the law.[60]

The *Legge Pentiti* was not only highly controversial in political circles, but was also regarded as such by the public. Even though the judges made a large effort to verify the testimonies given by terrorists by getting more information and evidence, they were not always able to disperse the public's impression of an arbitrary jurisdiction.[61] The terrorist Roberto Sandalo, for example, committed three murders, but was released after only two years. Michele Viscardi, also accused of three murders, got a five year sentence. Walter Sordi, who had evidently killed eight people, was released after four years. The greatest outrage, however, was caused by the judgment against Marco Barbone, a member of the left-wing terrorist group *Brigata XXVIII marzo*. On 28 May 1980, Barbone killed the popular journalist, Walter Tobagi. For that murder he was sentenced to eight years and nine months imprisonment.[62] However, the judge ordered parole, leading to Barbone's release when he had only served three years in prison. The neo-fascist party *Movimento Sociale Italiana* tried to exploit the public's outrage. They started a campaign to abolish Articles 6, 8, and 9 of the *Legge Pentiti*. Yet, their plans failed in parliament.[63]

Thus, the allegation that the *pentiti* were deified by the Italian population cannot be upheld:[64] forty-two per cent of those asked in a survey in December 1983 felt disrespect and derision for the *pentiti*. Only 6.7 per cent thought them laudable. In the same survey, only 24.3 per cent regarded the *Legge Pentiti* as a prudent law. More than 57.3 per cent even understood the law as a defeat of the state.[65] The widespread disapproval of the *pentiti* was due to the morally questionable deal between the state and the terrorists. Other plans, initiated by politicians from different parties as early as 1982, intended to reduce sentences for terrorists who merely dissociated themselves from their former groups and repented their past independently of the crimes they had committed. Unlike the *pentiti*, these former terrorists were not required to testify against other people. Therefore, dissociation was more of a way to reintegrate former terrorists into society than a counter-terrorism tool. This idea was not only supported by a broad segment of the population, but also by the Catholic Church. Over the years, the desire to end the circle of violence, to defuse the tense situation in the high-security prisons, and to finally bring the years of lead to an end grew stronger and stronger.[66] However, owing to the reluctance of the government and the opposition of the Communists, it was not before the spring of 1987 that this law 'Measures in Favour for People who Dissociate Themselves from Terrorism' was enacted.[67] Italy had struggled for nearly five years to get the law enacted, despite all the odds Italy was the first country which ever passed such a law.[68]

Conclusion

Might a law such as the *Legge Pentiti* be useful in the implementation of today's anti-terrorist policies? The key to the success of the Italian anti-terrorism policy was a pragmatic and flexible double strategy and not just a single law as the *Legge Pentiti*. On the one hand, the repressive legislation facilitated police investigations and the work of the special units of the *Carabinieri* and of the police.[69] On the other hand, a former enemy of the state was not to be excluded from society: a terrorist willing to abandon his former group was not a judicial *persona non grata* despite the martial rhetoric politicians often used.[70] He did not stand outside the rule of law or society from a mere criminalistic point of view. This double strategy which constitutes the state's monopoly on the use of force as well as a conciliatory state – although it expects something in return – should be considered in the current discussion on fighting terrorism. However, two very important factors that indicate why this kind of strategy worked in Italy in the late 1970s and 1980s, should always be considered. First, the traditional political game of *trasformismo* in Italy, the principle of 'give and take' instead of humbling an enemy who is facing defeat proved to be of great value in the strategy against terrorism. Second, Catholicism was deeply rooted within society and politics. This – so it seems – increased the willingness to forgive someone who showed penitence. It was particularly important that the Catholic Church provided a venue by which such repentant terrorists were able to re-enter society. 'This experience suggests', as Erica Chenoweth rightly concludes, 'that non-governmental organizations can be helpful in aiding the implementations of anti-terrorism policies'.[71]

Notes

1   L.B. Weinberg and W.L. Eubank, *The Rise and Fall of Italian Terrorism*, London: Westview Press, 1987, p. 106. For the problem of statistics regarding terrorist incidents in Italy, see R. Drake, 'The Red and the Black: Terrorism in Contemporary Italy', *International Political Science Review*, 1984, vol. 2, p. 279; D. Moss, *The Politics of Left-Wing Violence in Italy, 1969–85*, New York: St. Martin's Press, 1989, p. 21; S.M. Sobieck, *Democratic Responses to Revolutionary Terrorism: A Comparative Study of Great Britain, Italy and West Germany*, Phil. Diss. Claremont, pp. 225–7.

2   For a recent account of Italian anti-terrorism policy between 1969 and 1982, see T. Hof, *Staat und Terrorismus in Italien 1969–1982*, München: Oldenbourg, 2011.

3   Legge 29 maggio 1982, n. 304: Misure per la difesa dell'ordinamento costituzionale, in *Gazzetta Ufficiale*, 2 June 1982, n. 149, pp. 4024–6; Legge 29 novembre 1982, n. 882: Conversione in legge del decreto-legge 1 ottobre 1982, n. 695, concernente differimento del termine previsto dall'articolo 12 della legge 29 maggio 1982, n. 304, in *Gazzetta Ufficiale*, 1 December 1982, n. 330, p. 8655.

4   See, for example, E. Chenoweth, 'Italy and the Red Brigades: The Success of Repentance Policy', in J.J.F. Forest (ed.) *Countering Terrorism and Insurgency in the 21st Century. International Prospective, vol. 3: Lessons from the Fight against Terrorism*, London: Praeger Publisher, 2007, pp. 352–65.

5   See, for example, V. Grevi, 'Sistema penale e leggi dell'emergenza: la risposta legislative al terrorismo', in G. Pasquino (ed.) *La Prova delle armi*, Bologna: Il Mulino, 1984, pp. 17–76.

6   For an account of Sossi's kidnapping, see A. Franceschini and G. Fassanella, *Che cosa sono le BR: le radici, la nascita, la storia, il presente*, Mailand: Rizzoli, 2004, pp. 133–45; M. Sossi, *Nella prigione delle BR*, Mailand: Cigra, 1979. For an account of the history of the Red Brigades, see G.C. Caselli and D. Della Porta, 'The History of the Red Brigades: Organizational Structure and Strategies of Action (1970–82)', in R. Catanzaro (ed.) *The Red Brigades and Left-Wing Terrorism in Italy*, New York: St. Martin's Press, 1991, pp. 70–114; T. Hof, 'Vom italienischen "Robin Hood" zum "Staatsfeind Nr. 1". Die Entwicklung der linksterroristischen Gruppe Brigate Rosse', in M. Gehler and M. Guiotto (eds) *Italien, Österreich und die Bundesrepublik Deutschland in Europa. Ein Dreiecksverhältnis in seinen wechselseitigen Beziehungen und Wahrnehmungen von 1945/49 bis zur Gegenwart*, Wien Köln Weimar: Böhlau Verlag, 2011, pp. 405–27.

7   Legge 14 ottobre 1974, n. 497: Nuove norme contro la criminalità, in *Gazzetta Ufficiale*, 22 October 1974, pp. 7225–7.

8   For a recent account of the anti-terrorist unit of Dalla Chiesa, see V. Satta, 'Die Polizei und der Terrorismus in Italien', in J. Hürter and G.E. Rusconi (eds) *Die bleiernen Jahre. Staat und Terrorismus in der Bundesrepublik Deutschland und Italien 1969–1982*, München: Oldenbourg, 2010 (= Zeitgeschichte im Gespräch, 9), pp. 43–52.

9   For the anti-terrorism strategy especially in the years 1976–77, see T. Hof, *Staat und Terrorismus in Italien 1969–1982*, München: Oldenbourg, 2011, pp. 160–208.

10 Legge 18 maggio 1978, n. 191: Conversione in legge del decreto-legge 21 marzo 1978 n. 59, concernente norme penali e processuali per la prevenzione e la repressione di gravi reati.

11 Legge 6 febbraio 1980, n. 15: Conversione in legge, con modificazioni, del decreto-legge 15 dicembre 1979, n. 625, concernente misure urgente per la tutela dell'ordine democratica e della sicurezza pubblica, in *Gazzetta Ufficiale*, 7 February 1980, n. 37, pp. 1023–5.

12 Hearing of Dalla Chiesa, 23 February 1982, in: Commissione parlamentare d'inchiesta sulla strage di via Fani e sul sequestro e l'assassinio di Aldo Moro e sul terrorismo in Italia, in Atti Parlamentari: Camera dei Deputati, Senato della Repubblica, VIII Leg, Doc. XXIII, n. 5 (hereafter Commissione Moro), vol. IX, p. 235.

13 *Der Spiegel*, Italien. Laus im Baum: Ist der Sohn des christdemokratischen Vize-Chefs Donat-Cattin ein Terrorist, 19 May 1980, p. 168.

14 G. Guidelli, *Operazione Peci. Storia di un sequestro mediatico*, Urbino: Quatro venti, 2005, p. 60. Also, see *Der Spiegel*, Italien: Wandelnder Leichnam, 22 June 1981, p. 125; R. Drake, *The Revolutionary Mystique and Terrorism in Contemporary Italy*, Bloomington: Indiana University Press, p. 163.

15 T. Hof, *Staat und Terrorismus in Italien 1969–1982*, München: Oldenbourg, 2011, pp. 340–2.

16 Verbale della Riunione del Consiglio dei Ministri del 28 agosto 1981, in Archivio Centrale dello Stato, Presidenza del Consiglio dei Ministri, Verbali del Consiglio dei Ministri, 1981, 3 July 1981 – 29 December 1981, p. 1.

17 Verbale della Riunione del Consiglio dei Ministri del 28 agosto 1981, in Archivio Centrale dello Stato, Presidenza del Consiglio dei Ministri, Verbali del Consiglio dei Ministri, 1981, 3 July 1981 – 29 December 1981, pp. 2–3, 5.

18 Ibid., p. 4.

19 The possible public reaction towards the new regulations was also part of the parliamentary discussion. See, for example, Senato, VIII, Leg., Giunte, 10 March 1982, p. 9; Senato, VIII Leg., Giunte, 16 March 1982, p. 3; Senato, VIII Leg., Giunte, 23 March 1982, p. 7.

20 Verbale della Riunione del Consiglio dei Ministri del 28 agosto 1981, in: Archivio Centrale dello Stato, Presidenza del Consiglio dei Ministri, Verbali del Consiglio dei Ministri, 1981, 3 July 1981 – 29 December 1981, p. 4.

21 Ibid., p. 5. The protocol gives no clue about the arguments Rognoni used to convince the critics within the Cabinet. However, during an interview with his German counterpart, Gerhart Baum, he rejected all of these arguments as pure demagogy. He only pointed out that, at the same time, the police forces were modernized. Vgl. *Der Spiegel*, 'Der Staat darf nicht unversöhnlich sein'. Bundesinnenminister Baum und Italiens Innenminister Rognoni über neue Wege der Terrorismusbekämpfung, 19 October 1981, p. 128.

22 Even President Sandro Pertini was one of the critics. Vgl. M. von Tangen Page, *Prisons, Peace and Terrorism. Penal Policy in the Reduction of Political Violence in Northern Ireland*, London and New York: MacMillan 1998, p. 110.

23 Senato, VIII Leg., Assemblea, 20 January 1982, p. 18929.

24 Camera, VIII Leg., Discussioni, 24 February 1982, p. 41308; Senato, VIII Leg., Assemblea, 14.1982, p. 21097. Also, see Camera, VIII Leg., Discussioni, 23 February 1982, p. 41256.

25 Camera, VIII Leg., Discussioni, 24 February 1982, p. 41333.

26 *Der Spiegel*, 'Der Staat darf nicht unversöhnlich sein'. Bundesinnenminister Baum und Italiens Innenminister Rognoni über neue Wege der Terrorismusbekämpfung, 19 October 1981, p. 122.

27   Senato, VIII Leg., Documenti, Relazione di minoranza della II Commissione Permanente (Giustizia), 18 January 1982, n. 1412, 1549, 1562-A-bis, p. 12.
28   Ibid., p. 8.
29   Camera, VIII Leg., Discussioni, 2 March 1982, p. 41585.
30   Camera, VIII Leg., Discussioni, 23 February 1982, p. 41233.
31   Legge 29 maggio 1982, n. 304: Misure per la difesa dell'ordinamento costituzionale, in *Gazzetta Ufficiale*, 2 June 1982, n. 149, pp. 4024–6.
32   Ibid., Art. 1.
33   *Der Spiegel*, 'Der Staat darf nicht unversöhnlich sein'. Bundesinnenminister Baum und Italiens Innenminister Rognoni über neue Wege der Terrorismusbekämpfung, 19 October 1981, p. 117.
34   Camera, VIII Leg., Discussioni, 24 February 1982, p. 41319.
35   Senato, VIII Leg., Giunte, 13 January 1982, p. 5; also, see Senato, VIII Leg., Documenti, Relazione della IIa Commissione Permanente (Giustizia), n. 1412, 1549, 1562-A, p. 2; Senato, VIII Leg., Assemblea, 20. January 1982, p. 18912 and p. 18915.
36   Legge 29 maggio 1982, n. 304: Misure per la difesa dell'ordinamento costituzionale, in *Gazzetta Ufficiale*, 2 June 1982, n. 149, p. 4024–6, Art. 2.
37   Ibid., Art. 3.
38   Senato, VIII Leg., Assemblea, 28 January 1982, p. 19357.
39   Senato, VIII Leg., Documenti, Disegno di Legge, 30 April 1981, n. 1412: Misure penali, processuali e penitenziarie relative al terrorismo e all'eversione dell'ordine democratico, p. 4.
40   Osservazioni formulate dal Comitato esecutivo di Magistratura Democratica sul disegno di legge governativo 28 agosto 1982 (n. 1562), 24.10.1982, in M. Laudi, *I casi di non punibilità dei terroristi 'pentiti'*, Mailand: Giuffrè, 1983 (= La Legislazione dell'emergenza, vol. 12), pp. 185–6, here p. 186.
41   Osservazioni formulate dal Comitato esecutivo di Magistratura Democratica sul disegno di legge governativo 28 agosto 1982 (n. 1562), 24 October 1982, in: M. Maddalena, *Le circostanze attenuanti per I terroristi 'pentiti'*, Mailand: Giuffrè, 1984 (= La Legislazione dell'emergenza, vol. 13), pp. 194–5, here p. 195.
42   Senato, VIII Leg., Documenti, Disegno di Legge, 12 September 1981, n. 1562: Misure per la difesa dell'ordinamento costituzionale, Arts. 6–9.
43   Camera, VIII Leg., Discussioni, 24 February 1982, p. 41309.
44   Ibid., p. 8.
45   See, for example, the statements of Marco Boato, Francesco Lodas, and Nicola Vernolas: Camera, VIII Leg., Bollettino, 11 February 1982, pp. 6–8; Osservazioni formulate dal Comitato esecutivo di Magistratura Democratica sul disegno di legge governativo, in M. Laudi, *I casi di non punibilità dei terroristi 'pentiti'*, Mailand: Giuffrè, 1983 (= La Legislazione dell'emergenza, vol. 12), p. 113; Parere della Ia Commissione Permanente, 11 March 1982, in Senato, VIII Leg., Documenti, Relazione della IIa Commissione Permanente (Giustizia), n. 1412, 1549, 1562-A, p. 3.
46   Senato, VIII Leg., Documenti, Disegno di Legge, 12 September 1981, n. 1562: Misure per la difesa dell'ordinamento costituzionale, Arts. 6 and 8.
47   *Der Spiegel*, 'Der Staat darf nicht unversöhnlich sein'. Bundesinnenminister Baum und Italiens Innenminister Rognoni über neue Wege der Terrorismusbekämpfung, 19 October 1981, p. 119.
48   Camera, VIII Leg., Discussioni, 23 February 1982, p. 41233.

49 V. Rognoni, *Intervista sul terrorismo,* Bari Rom: Laterza 1989, p. 97.
50 Servizio per le informazioni e la sicurezza democratica (SISDE): Elenco dei terroristi pentiti in data 31 agosto 1982, in Commissione Moro, vol. XXVIII, pp. 159–531, here pp. 161–73.
51 D. Moss, *Italian Political Violence 1969–1988. The Making and Unmaking of Meanings,* United Nations Research Institute for Social Development Discussion Paper 41, 1993, p. 37.
52 R. Minna, 'Il terrorismo di destra', in D. della Porta (ed.) *Terrorismi in Italia,* Bologna: Il Mulino, 1990, p. 25.
53 Senato, VIII Leg., Giunte, 28 October 1981, p. 3; K.-P. Fritzsche, *Die politische Kultur Italiens,* Frankfurt am Main/New York: Campus-Verlag, 1987, p. 216; A. Jamieson, 'Counter-Terrorism in Europe: Implications of 1992. The Italian Experience', *Conflict Studies,* 1991, vol. 238, p. 17.
54 K.-P. Fritzsche, *Die politische Kultur Italiens,* Frankfurt am Main/New York: Campus-Verlag, 1987, p. 217.
55 On 29 January 1979, Marco Donat-Cattin and Sergio Segio killed state attorney Emilio Alessandrini. Donat-Cattin was able to escape to France before the police could arrest him. Prime Minister Francesco Cossiga and his party colleague and father of the terrorist, Carlo Donat-Cattin, were accused of helping him to flee into exile. However, the Donat-Cattin case was not an isolated incident. The son of Emilio Taviani, Minister for the Interior between 1962–68 and 1973–74, also sympathized with terrorist groups.
56 *L'Espresso,* Pentitocrazia, 13 September 1981, p. 4; *L'Espresso,* Pentitevi e diventeremo amici, 13 September 1981, p. 4–8.
57 R. Drake, *The Revolutionary Mystique and Terrorism in Contemporary Italy,* Bloomington: Indiana University Press, p. 282.
58 Decreto-legge, 1 ottobre 1982, n. 695: Differimento del termine previsto dall'articolo 12 della legge 29 magio 1982, n. 304, Art. 1, in *Gazzetta Ufficiale,* 2 October 1982, n. 272, pp. 7136–7.
59 See, for example, Camera, VIII Leg., Discussioni, 10 November 1982, p. 53889 and pp. 53897–8; Senato, VIII Leg., Giunte, 24 November 1982, pp. 4–5.
60 Verbale della Riunione del Consiglio dei Ministri del 28 gennaio 1983, in Archivio Centrale dello Stato, Presidenza del Consiglio dei Ministri, Verbali del Consiglio dei Ministri, 1983, 12 December 1982 – 30 July 1983, p. 4.
61 D. Moss, *The Politics of Left-Wing Violence in Italy, 1969–85,* New York: St. Martin's Press, 1989, pp. 223–4.
62 Ibid., p. 173.
63 *L'Espresso,* Delitto senza castigo, 11 December 1983, pp. 6–8; Rognoni, *Intervista sul terrorismo,* Bari Rom: Laterza 1989, p. 107.
64 See C. di Iesi, 'Appunti in margine al fenomeno del pentitismo', *La Giustizia Penale,* 1986, vol. I, p. 62.
65 K.-P. Fritzsche, *Die politische Kultur Italiens,* Frankfurt am Main/New York: Campus-Verlag, 1987, pp. 218–9.
66 For the connection between the law 'Measures in Favor for People who Dissociate Themselves from Terrorism' and the situation in the prisons, see C.G. De Vito, *Camosci e girachiavi. Storia del carcere in Italia 1943–2007,* Bari: Editori Laterza, 2009, pp. 107–14.
67 Legge 18 febbraio 1987, n. 34: Misure a favore di chi si dissocia dal terrorismo, in *Gazzetta Ufficiale,* 21 February 1987, n. 43.

68 T. Hof, *Staat und Terrorismus in Italien 1969–1982*, München: Oldenbourg, 2011, pp. 297–303.

69 Ibid., pp.141–51 and 242–9.

70 Ibid., pp. 73–105.

71 E. Chenoweth, 'Italy and the Red Brigades: The Success of Repentance Policy', in J.J.F. Forest (ed.) *Countering Terrorism and Insurgency in the 21st Century. International Prospective, vol. 3: Lessons from the Fight against Terrorism*, London: Praeger Publisher, 2007, p. 362.

7 Quid pro quo

State sponsorship of terrorism in the Cold War

Thomas Riegler

Introduction

1970s and 1980s terrorism is very different from contemporary political violence: whereas radical Islamic terrorists today form a web of decentralized local actors without clear hierarchies, who are linked together by the internet, the 'old terrorism' of the Cold War era was a group phenomenon, with clear structures, and primarily secular by nature. One of the foremost characteristics of organizations, led by Abu Nidal or 'Carlos', was that the terrorists received substantial assistance from state actors. The main sponsors, Soviet satellites in the Middle East and the Eastern Bloc, not only tolerated the presence of terrorists on their soil, but provided them with training, weapons, explosives, and safe passage. The enlisted groups and organizations were then used to conduct surrogate operations against rival states, internal enemies, or dissidents. Whereas the relationship between sponsors and terrorists has often been described in the form of top-down control, this contribution instead suggests more of a balanced mode of quid pro quo collaboration among the two parties.

To explore the connection between states and terrorists further, a case study is presented by drawing on primary sources from the Foundation Bruno Kreisky Archive (StBKA, Vienna) and the Federal Commissioner for the Stasi Archives (BStU, Berlin): the confrontation between Austria and the Abu Nidal group, which was then supported by Syria. Since Austria played a key role in promoting the Palestine Liberation Organization (PLO) as a political force in the late 1970s, it became a target for Palestinian hardliners, who opposed any compromise with Israel. By attacking Austria in 1981 and 1985, Abu Nidal served his own ideological agenda, but also satisfied the political interests of his sponsor in the Middle Eastern power game – which makes this case a telling example for the described pragmatic cooperation between host and client.

State-sponsored terrorism and the Cold War

In 2010, Corinna Ponto, the daughter of a prominent victim of the Red Army Faction (RAF), published a critical article in a major German newspaper. Therein she criticized the 'mythologization' of prominent RAF members as popular culture 'icons', while the history and background of German left-wing terrorism still remain largely unexplored:

> The actions of the RAF were systematic, as well as supported by a system. [...] This system directed the attack against the system of the free and democratic constitutional state by eliminating certain important officials of that system. And the system behind it was composed of financiers and agents and principals, whose long arms we still, even after forty years, do not know exactly.[1]

Ponto, who had researched her father's death in the files of the East German Ministry for State Security (MfS), described the process as being caught up in a 'murky and frightening web.

Indeed, many aspects and mechanisms of 1970s and 1980s terrorism are still largely unknown to the greater public, since the media and historical research tend to personalize political violence, while neglecting vital structural aspects such as financing, training, and sheltering. Ponto's conclusion was that Cold War terrorism had a Janus face – on the one side the known protagonists, on the other side intelligence agencies and the secret policies, whose exact influence on the events is still a matter of dispute.[2]

With regard to the RAF, the terrorist attacks orchestrated by its 'third generation' against prominent Western German officials during the 1980s and early 1990s remain unsolved until today. No culprit has ever been charged with those crimes that stunned investigators with the level of their sophistication.[3] The military and deadly precision of the 'third generation' fed suspicions that the RAF had gotten a helping hand – in the form of assistance and training by MfS special forces, who wanted to target its 'main enemy' by using terrorist surrogates. Yet, so far, the evidence for active involvement of the MfS in RAF terrorism is inconclusive.

The still mysterious 'third generation' is a telling example of the gaps in the public debate on Cold War terrorism. In Germany, the discourse concentrates mainly on the origins of the RAF, the student revolt of 1968, and the post-war generational conflict, while neglecting the later years, when terrorism became a sort of secondary front in the overall struggle between the East and West. According to German historian Wolfgang Kraushaar, waging terrorist proxy wars could have been an advantage for both East and West to deliver destabilizing 'pin prick attacks', while conventional warfare was not an option in the nuclear age.[4]

While the specific background of these proceedings remains vague, the notion that terrorism indeed played a major part in the Cold War confrontation is not new. Starting with the 1979 Jerusalem conference of the 'Jonathan Institute to Fight Terrorism', the Soviet Union was publically accused of sponsoring terrorism. Fitting the political imperative of the Reagan administration's confrontational policies, Moscow was described as the centre of terrorist activity worldwide, with every major group sponsored and forming a subversive proxy force to undermine Western democracies.[5] Most influential in the promotion of this threat was 'the Terror Network' (1981) by Claire Sterling, an American correspondent living in Italy. Her main thesis was that Moscow had infiltrated every major left-wing group, including the Palestinian factions, and turned them against Western targets. A Central Intelligence Agency (CIA) research team later found out that 'the Terror Network' contained some 'black information', which had been circulated by the intelligence service itself.[6] But US officials nevertheless used the book to send their message: Foreign Secretary Alexander Haig presented 'the Terror Network' at his first press conference to accuse the Soviet Union of state sponsorship of terrorism.[7] Unofficially, the US intelligence community had reached a more sober assessment on the subject in 1981 – with regard to the links between Moscow and Middle Eastern groups the National Intelligence Estimate (NIE) stated:

> The Soviets provide assistance, including training and weapons support, to states and organizations which they know conduct or support terrorist activities. The Soviets themselves do not direct these groups, however they encourage specific terrorist operations. In some cases, they have advised their friends and allies against the use of such tactics, although they have acquiesced in their use.[8]

Since this early discourse was swayed by ideology and lacked a neutral fact oriented basis, it took the fall of the Iron Curtain (1989) for the nature of the nexus between the Soviet Union and international terrorism to become more apparent. While Moscow had not been the source of all terrorist evil, as described by Sterling, it was certainly no innocent bystander. The Soviets had supplied arms not only to Third-World 'national liberation movements' in Asia, Africa, and Latin America, but also to terrorist groups in the Middle East and in Northern Ireland. Substantial as it was, this supporting role did not amount to total control as Sterling and other experts had suggested. According to historian Timothy Naftali, these relationships, 'while significant, were limited and represented assistance to autonomous movements. These groups did not become extensions of Soviet foreign policy.'[9]

An often-cited example for the relationship between the KGB and terrorist allies is Wadi Haddad, founder of the Popular Front for the Liberation of Palestine (PLPF) external operations department and 'godfather' of international terrorism. According to Vasili Mitrokhin, a senior KGB defector, Haddad had been recruited by the KGB under the codename 'NATIONALIST' in 1970.[10] KGB chief, Yuri Andropow, reported to prime minister Leonid Brezhnev:

> W. Haddad turned to us with a request of help for his organisation in the acquisition of certain kinds of special technical means necessary

for carrying out specific terrorist operations. The nature of our relations with W. Haddad allows us to exercise partial control over the PFLP External Operations Department and influence it in the interests of the Soviet Union, as well as to carry out actions in the interests of the Soviet Union through W. Haddad's organisation under necessary secrecy.[11]

Another file from 1975 delineates the operational support that Haddad received: via secret transfer in the neutral waters of the Gulf of Aden, the KGB handed him a batch of foreign made weapons and munitions (fifty-eight sub-machine guns, fifty pistols, including ten equipped with silencers, and thirty-four thousand rounds of ammunition).[12] In the same year, the KGB funded Haddad's organization with US$30,000.[13] Alexander Bodarenko, a former official of the Soviet Ministry of Foreign Affairs, confirmed in a 2007 German TV programme that Haddad's group had indeed been employed by the KGB: 'This organisation was not subordinate to us. It decided alone. It was not very easy for us to get them to the desired results.' As former PLFP spokesman Bassam Abu Sharif explained further, it was cooperation among equals: 'Andropow was really keen to use Wadi's skill, but Wadi was generally opposed to be the tool of anyone'.[14]

There is little other evidence for such direct connections between Moscow and international terrorism, but the relationship of the West with terrorist actors is even harder to determine. While it is important not to equate the actions of the superpowers and their allies, this aspect should not be neglected. It is well established that the US checked the Soviet Union's assistance for Third-World national liberation movements by aiding 'freedom fighters' in Angola, Afghanistan, and Nicaragua. In the latter country, CIA directed mercenaries and contract agents carried out at least twenty-one sabotage attacks on economic targets between 1983 and 1984 in order to topple the left-wing government.[15]

One of the best known examples for Western links to terrorism is the secret NATO stay-behind network, commonly known under the Italian codename 'Gladio'. Originally designed as a guerrilla force in case of a Warsaw Pact invasion, it was also used internally in some NATO member states to prevent communist parties from coming to power. The stay-behind networks supported coup d'états in Greece and Turkey, as well as the suppression of political opposition in Portugal and Spain. In Italy, sporadic acts of right-wing terrorism were used to create tense political situations, in which the electorate rallied behind the status quo.[16]

Clandestine operations of Western intelligence services included the infiltration of terrorist groups. This was an efficient mean for combating political violence, but it produced some controversial results: several investigations have unearthed evidence that during the 1980s, British intelligence services had colluded with Loyalist death squads to 'turn the screw' on the Provisional IRA.[17] In Turkey, special forces engaged in a dirty war against the Kurdish PKK with widespread use of torture and tactics like 'disappearing' victims.[18] More and more information suggests that the Red Brigades in Italy had been penetrated, which allowed some degree of control over their operations.[19] Little is known about the secret struggle of the West German authorities against left-wing terrorism. But it is evident that, from the beginning, agent provocateurs were involved in arming the radical fringes of the 1968 student movement.[20] On one occasion in 1978, the domestic intelligence service went so far as to fake the liberation attempt of an RAF member by blowing a hole into the prison wall.[21]

Examples like these demonstrate that Western counter-terrorism had its dark side and that the fear of terrorism was sometimes manipulated to sustain political stability. However, according to the available records, the Eastern Bloc's involvement with terrorism was by far more substantial and directly aimed against the West. This is clarified in the following section by quoting from relating files from the archive of the German Democratic Republic's (GDR) Ministry for State Security and declassified CIA sources.

Sponsoring terrorism: the role of Middle Eastern governments and Eastern bloc countries

Soviet satellites in Eastern Europe and allied regimes in other regions engaged in substantial dealings with terrorists. This was especially true in the Middle East, where all major Arab groups were affiliated either with Libya, Syria, Iraq, or South Yemen (theocratic Iran was the main sponsor for Shiite extremists, mostly during the civil war in Lebanon in the 1980s and against American targets in the Arab peninsula in the 1990s). The governments had various reasons for the employment of terrorists. Mostly, they were used as surrogates to target regional rivals. For example, Syria and Iraq used terrorists to strike against each other's officials and facilities. From 1983 until 1985, Jordan was attacked several times by forces sent out by Syrian president Hafez al-Assad to punish the government in Amman for its support of the Islamist opposition against his rule.[22]

Another major reason was to have a covert capability ready to use against internal threats posed by dissidents and exiles. Between 1980 and 1985, the Libyan government alone engaged in more than thirty assassination attempts outside of its borders.[23] Sponsorship of terrorism was also an important means of undermining Western policies in the Middle East, to destabilize pro-Western governments and moderate Arab regimes, to weaken Israeli security, and to derail peace initiatives between Israel and the Palestinians. In effect, sponsors had various advantages to gain: plausible deniability, the possibility to project power despite little geopolitical significance, and the enhancement of their image as fighters for the cause of the 'oppressed'.[24] There is also no doubt that using terrorists bore considerable risks such as provoking retaliatory attacks or a tarnished international reputation in case of these secret policies becoming public.

The terrorists, on the other hand, profited from access to training facilities, weapons, explosive devices, passports, intelligence, ideological promotion, money, or safe havens. Despite considerable tensions, such relationships proved mutually beneficial. Yet when interests no longer coincided, there were frequent and rapid shifts of allegiance. Abu Nidal, for example, relocated his organization three times: from Baghdad to Damascus and then on to Tripoli. From time to time, economic sanctions, diplomatic expulsions, and demarches, counter-terrorism measures, and regional political developments caused states to lower their profiles and become more discreet. In such situations, terrorist allies became a liability and were soon divested of protection.[25] How strained and difficult relations could prove is apparent from a 1989 CIA report on the terrorist connections of Libya's leader Muammar al Qadhafi:

> The Libyan leader's influence with these groups – based primarily on his ability to provide them support – is not always sufficient to solicit attacks. Qadhafi's ability to do so is circumscribed to some extent by a desire on the part of his clients to protect their independence, by differences in political agendas, and by different views on how to achieve shared goals, as well as by the Libyan leader's mercurial temperament and repudiation as an unreliable patron.[26]

Eastern European nations had their own reasons for their approach to terrorism: the GDR, Hungary, Czechoslovakia, Poland, Bulgaria, Yugoslavia, and Romania tolerated the presence of terrorist groups on their territory. They had direct ties to several Middle Eastern organizations, among them the Abu Nidal Group, the PLFP, and the Carlos Group. Moscow certainly knew about these arrangements and 'presumably acquiesced'.[27] Western European groups benefited only to some degree. According to Czech investigators, members of the Italian Red Brigades who were involved in the kidnapping of Aldo Moro (1978) had been trained in a military installation in Karlsbad.[28] Czechoslovakia functioned also as the key supplier of the plastic explosive Semtex. The main purchaser was Libya, which transferred large amounts to its Palestinian clients, which in turn provided other groups with the material.[29] Most notably, from 1980 onwards, the GDR sheltered ten 'retirees' of the second generation of the RAF. This 'drop out' programme aroused interest on the part of the active members. From 1980 until 1982, members of the RAF were trained in the use of rocket launchers, obviously in connection with the attack on NATO's commander Frederick Kroesen on 15 September 1981. However, it has not been possible to determine whether this training session occurred before or after the failed assassination attempt.[30] The suspected, but unproven involvement of the MfS in RAF-'third generation' terrorism has already been mentioned.

Only in some cases did Socialist countries directly employ the services of terrorists. In 1981, Romania's dictator Ceausescu ordered a strike by the

Carlos Group to 'silence' the Romanian branch of Radio Free Europe in Munich (a gross operational error was committed by detonating the fifteen-kilo bomb in front of the Czech section of the building).[31] Mostly, the value of the terror connection paid off in an indirect form: the host gained access to valuable intelligence, Western weapons and technology, while the client benefited from safe haven, training, and easy transit into Socialist countries and Western Europe. A major motif for the Eastern bloc was to keep its territory safe from possible security risks. The danger of possible retaliatory attacks by terrorists in case of an active approach against them was taken very seriously.[32] Another priority was to ensure that Socialist countries would not be implicated in case of terrorist attacks in Western Europe. But, while the secret services had detailed knowledge about planned strikes, sometimes nothing was done to stop the perpetrators. In 1983, an MfS officer returned confiscated explosives, which were then used to commit a bomb attack against the Maison de France in West Berlin. In the case of the La Belle bombing (1986), the MfS knew at least five days ahead that Libyan agents would possibly target the discotheque, but no warning was given.[33]

This is hardly surprising, since the destabilization of the West by terrorism was in the interest of the Eastern Bloc. It provided the Socialist countries with a means of inciting or exploiting violent conflict on a regional as well as global scale, with small risk of US retaliation or direct military confrontation. But some red lines were observed: when Palestinian terrorists hijacked a Lufthansa jet in 1977, the Soviet Union and the GDR pressured its ally South Yemen to prohibit the landing and thereby foiled the original plan of the terrorists.[34] On another occasion, Bulgaria allowed the arrest of several left-wing terrorists by German police on its territory in 1978.[35] In the same year, Yugoslavian authorities detained four RAF members in Zagreb, but released them after receiving threats from a Palestinian group.[36] 'Carlos', whose presence became an open secret for Western intelligence agencies and thereby compromised his hosts, was eventually kicked out: in 1984, he was banned from the GDR and Hungary, in 1985 Czechoslovakia served its ties with his organization.[37] Obviously, terrorist plotting against the West was tolerated within certain limits, on the condition that it would not cause a major disruption in superpower relations. But, as Markus Wolf, head of the foreign intelligence division of the MfS, wrote in his memoirs, his superior, Minister for State Security Erich Mielke, did consider a supportive role for terrorist organizations in the event of war: 'his theory seemed to be that the terrorists we befriended or, as in the case of the Red Army Faction, sheltered, could be used as behind-the-lines guerrilla forces for sabotage against the West'.[38]

In contrast to these frank words, during the Cold War, the reasons for this uneasy but extensive cooperation with terrorists were often dressed up in terms of ideology. An undated document about a meeting between representatives of the MfS and members of the Palestinian PLFP stated:

The socialist GDR supports, in accordance with its possibilities, national liberation movements all over the world, and stands in solidarity at the side of the Palestinian people in their fight for assertion of their legitimate rights. The support of the Palestinian resistance is in line with the foreign policy activities of the GDR. It is an expression of active peace policy, proletarian internationalism and anti-imperialistic solidarity of the GDR with the national liberation movements.[39]

According to historian, John O. Koehler, Minister of State Security Mielke never used the word 'terrorism' when discussing the assistance for Arab groups organized by his subordinates:

The gist of the Stasi chief's talk was that the question of whether capitalism or socialism would achieve world supremacy would be decided in the Third World. Mielke described the Arab world as especially critical to the outcome of this epic struggle, and said that 'whoever controls the intelligence organizations of those countries will contribute decisively in the battle against imperialism'.[40]

Mielke's subordinate, Wolf, was closely involved in the implementation of this policy. In his memoirs, he described how his department established close contacts with the PLO's security branch soon after Arafat had visited the GDR in 1972. The PLO abandoned international terrorism in 1974, yet its operational capabilities profited from the assistance granted by the MfS:

In return for our aid and training, we hoped to get access to PLO information on American security, global strategy, and weaponry... Our service had little information to give the PLO in exchange... We did, however, give instruction. My senior officers were called in to give lectures on intelligence gathering and encoding and decoding, and to pass our experience of counterespionage techniques to Palestinian visitors. We of course guessed that this information might pass to terrorist commandos against Israel or their trainers.[41]

This 'trickle-down effect' indeed did occur: from the early 1970s, especially the Palestinian groups were at the forefront of international cooperation among left-wing groups and movements. Wadi Haddad's PLFP, who as mentioned received Soviet arms, had built extensive links with West German groups such as the RAF or the Revolutionary Cells, the Japanese Red Army, as well as with Basque and Irish separatists. Haddad provided his allies with training, hideouts, finances, and weapons – in return, for example, he enlisted West German and Japanese terrorists in his own operations on several occasions.[42] In early October 1978, even the PLO's own security service hosted a meeting of nine European, Latin American, and Japanese terror groups in a Yugoslav border town.[43] So, when considering state sponsorship of terrorism, one has to include the active exchange among the groups themselves, which, of course, had been enabled beforehand, as the case of Wadi Haddad and his KGB connections exemplifies.

Owing to its key role in the whole process, the GDR became, in fact, a major basis for international terrorism. This is evident from a report that Major General Werner Irmler sent to Mielke in 1979. The document, where details of the activities of terrorists residing in the GDR were stated, was so sensitive that it was labelled 'only for personal information, return is requested'. Besides Mielke only seven other high-ranking officials got to read the material before it was discussed in a Politburo meeting chaired by Erich Honecker.[44] A key passage reads:

> According to inside information, partly politically indeterminable forces of the Palestine national liberation movement, in alliance with anarcho-terrorist groups from Western countries are increasingly undertaking efforts to use the territory of the GDR as a logistical base and starting point for the execution of terrorist acts in Western Europe. The generous solidarity of the GDR with national liberation movements of the Arab people is seen as favourable for the planning and preparation of operations by these forces. The communication possibilities of the capital of the GDR are also taken into account.[45]

The report also details the agenda of terrorist groups such as the Organization of International Revolutionaries, led by Ilich Ramirez Sanchez, aka 'Carlos the Jackal', on East German soil:

> Establishment of logistic bases in the capital of the GDR with involvement of GDR citizens; Arrangement of conspiratorial gatherings and meetings between citizens of various Arab states; Acceleration of travel activities of liaisons of the 'Carlos' group into the FGR (Federal German Republic) and other Western European countries as well as to West Berlin; Efforts for the acquisition of weapons, explosives, funds, and information; Agreements for an expansion of a conspirative 'revolutionary department'; Inspiring violent acts of the armed struggle as well as single actions, terrorist attacks and so on against the imperialistic policy of the US, the Zionists, and the clique around Sadat; Activating contacts to anarcho-terroristic forces in the FGR/West Berlin; Intentions to create operation centres in the SAR (Syrian Arabic Republic) via the capital of the GDR with involvement of the embassies of the USSR and the GDR in Syria.[46]

By providing such possibilities, countries like the GDR enabled comparatively small terrorists organizations like the one led by 'Carlos' to function in a way that served their own strategic interests.[47]

Another exemplary case is the ventures of the Palestinian terrorist Abu Nidal in Eastern Europe. Like 'Carlos', he served a number of different Arab regimes and also had a strong presence behind the Iron Curtain. In 1987, the MfS explored the relations of Abu Nidal's organization (also known as 'Fatah-RC') – in regard to the links with the Soviet Union, the report specified:

> For years the group has maintained unofficial contacts with the SU (Soviet Union), especially through the military attaché of the embassy in Damascus. Because of increasing pro-Soviet leanings of the group, these contacts have been intensified since 1984. Since then, the 'Fatah-RC' accepts special requests to acquire military equipment . . . Stable contacts to leading staff of the KGB headquarter are said to exist. Meetings take place in Warsaw, Sofia, Damascus and Tripoli. In these meetings, the current KGB residents are said to take part. Regular consultations are held with the second secretary of the USSR embassy in Tripoli.[48]

According to another document from 1986, the Abu Nidal group offered specific 'services' in order to establish its secret contacts:

> Providing political and military information about American military-political advance into Arab countries, Turkey, and Greece; acquisition of information, documentation, and blueprints of Western special and military equipment subject to the embargo; preparation of information on the structure and activities of the secret services of the US, England, France and others against Arab countries and the Arab national freedom movement, etc.; influencing other like-minded organisations to refrain from terrorist operations on the territory of socialist countries and against their representations in foreign countries.[49]

After his expulsion from Iraq to Syria in 1983, Abu Nidal indeed formed ties with Poland and the GDR, and in turn received intelligence and sabotage training. In 1984–85, the MfS organized three courses lasting several weeks for forty-one Abu Nidal cadres in East Berlin. Among the instructors were members of the Arbeitsgruppe des Minister (AGM) – the special forces of the MfS, who were experts in sabotage and behind enemy lines fighting techniques.[50] To fund his terrorist activities, Abu Nidal formed several export and import businesses. As the files of the MfS show, the secret services not only had detailed knowledge about those dealings, but tolerated it on their turf: Zibado Foreign Trade Consultants, a firm controlled by Abu Nidal, was based in the International Trade Center in East Berlin. It was active until at least the end of 1988. According to news reports, Zibado and its parent company SAS (operating from Warsaw), made an annual profit of 80 million dollars, mainly by selling Eastern European arms to Iran, Iraq, Libya, or the PLO.[51]

Case study: Austria as a victim of state-sponsored terrorism

The following section consists of a case study to clarify the nature of Cold War state-sponsored terrorism in detail: Abu Nidal attacked Austria on three occasions in 1981 and 1985. The terrorist offensive was exceptional in regard to the republic's history of political violence. The country had been relatively spared from terrorism because of the nature of its post-war system, which had been devised to provide maximum stability. Thus, to a large extent, terrorism was the work of foreign elements operating on Austrian soil and it was Palestinian terrorism that formed the single most virulent brand.[52]

The major reason for these terrorist strikes was Austria's active role in the Middle Eastern conflict, exemplified by the personal diplomacy of Chancellor Bruno Kreisky (1911–1990, in office: 1970–83). He argued strongly that terrorism could only be tackled if its root causes were addressed. In order to fight terror, the grievances causing it had to be removed as a form of prevention. To achieve this result, a legitimate political representation of the Palestinian cause had to be fostered, thereby rendering the rampant 'armed struggle' obsolete. Therefore Kreisky contributed to the international legitimization of the PLO and its chairman, Arafat. For example, in 1979, Kreisky hosted a widely reported meeting between Arafat and Willy Brandt, then chairman of the Socialist International (SI).[53]

The most important aim of Kreisky's preventive policy was, of course, security for Austria itself. The country's function as a transit point for Jewish emigration from the Eastern Bloc to Israel practically involved it in the Middle Eastern conflict. In 1981, Kreisky argued that because of his good relations with the PLO, Austria had been more or less spared by attacks in the past – despite the fact that extremist groups had a strong motive to attack and disrupt the transfer of Soviet Jews. In 1973, two Arab gunmen had entered a train with Jewish émigrés and took three people hostage. After long hours of negotiation, Kreisky granted them a plane to fly out of the country, leaving their hostages behind. Furthermore, restrictions were imposed on the transfer of Russian Jews by closing down a camp operated by the Jewish Agency. This move drew angry protests from Israel and throughout the West, but served its purpose of deflecting attention from the continuing emigration process. No further attacks against it occurred.[54]

But it was not possible to keep terrorism entirely away from Austria. The famous hostage-taking of the Organization of Petroleum Exporting Countries (OPEC) ministers in 1975 had nothing to do with Austrian politics. The operation aimed to blackmail a ransom to arm the Palestinian resistance in Lebanon and according to some testimony, it was specifically 'ordered' by Qadhafi to increase the pressure for a higher oil price (which makes the OPEC hostage-taking a showcase for state-sponsored terrorism).

In 1981, Heinz Nittel, a high-ranking Viennese city official and Jewish representative, was murdered. A few months afterwards, the Viennese synagogue was assaulted by two Arab gunmen who killed two worshippers and wounded twenty-two others. The worst attack took place on 27 December 1985: three terrorists attacked the El Al counter at Vienna airport with grenades and assault rifles. Three bystanders were killed and thirty-nine wounded.

As mentioned, Abu Nidal was responsible for all three plots. Besides Austria, he also targeted other Western European countries with pro-Palestinian leanings and who supported the PLO. From 1969 until 1974, Abu Nidal himself had been a high-ranking PLO representative in Sudan and Iraq. But soon he became a focal point for the 'rejectionists', a coalition formed by radical Palestinian factions that were aiming to undermine Yasser Arafat's claim to PLO leadership and faithful to the original programme that had elevated armed struggle to 'the one and only way to liberate Palestine'. With Arafat's famous 'gun and olive branch' speech in front of the United Nations (1974) that marked the beginning of the political transformation of the PLO, the split was final. From then on, Abu Nidal waged a merciless shadow war against moderates within the PLO and had its most active proponents assassinated.[55]

This struggle also had an international front, since Abu Nidal wanted to weaken Arafat by undercutting supporters in the West. This effort was in line with the interests of his sponsors. In the beginning, Abu Nidal had been allied to Iraq, which used his organization to target both Jordan and Syria. In 1983, he was able to establish offices in Damascus, despite the fact that his group had tried to kill high-ranking officials only years before. Commissioning Abu Nidal offered president Hafez al-Assad and his intelligence services certain advantages. Starting in the late 1970s, Assad pursued a regional strategy to become the dominant strongman in the Levant area and achieve a 'comprehensive strategic balance' with Israel.[56] To achieve this goal, Assad was eager to control 'all the Arab variables in the battle against Israel', as political analyst Patrick Seale put it. The Syrian President therefore strove to keep the PLO under his influence, to force neighbours like Jordan from making separate settlements with Israel, and deter interferences from the outside.[57]

By engaging in the dynamics of the Middle Eastern conflict and by supporting Arafat and the moderates inside the PLO, Kreisky had antagonized both the radicals and their sponsors, who, in turn, targeted Austria. On 24 September 1981, only weeks after the attack on the Viennese synagogue, the CIA reported: 'Syrians are encouraging Fatah dissident Abu Nidal to stage terrorist operations to discredit Arafat and undermine his policy of limiting such operations to Israel and the Israeli-occupied territories…They are determined to bring the PLO under Syrian control'.[58] So, when MfS-handlers questioned a source in 1981 about Abu Nidal's motive for assassinating Heinz Nittel, the informant pointed to the 'relatively stable links' between Arafat and Kreisky for a solution to the 'Middle Eastern problem'. The source continued to explain:

> Since Abu Nidal is against a political settlement of the Palestinian problem, he obviously wanted to demonstrate to Arafat that by murdering Heinz Nittel, his group would not stand idle when compromises with the US or other imperialistic nations are made.[59]

Another MfS-report from the same year stressed Syria's role behind the scene:

> It is said that Syria is not interested in a solution of the Palestine problem or in the conclusion of a peace treaty should it not have a leading role. For this reason, Abu Nidal is supported by Syria. The murder of Nittel is described as a warning for Kreisky to abandon his mediator role between Israel and the PLO.[60]

But Abu Nidal also had his own reason for targeting Austria: in the wake of the attacks of 1981, three members of his organization had been arrested, among them a high-ranking 'officer'. The group wanted to liberate him at all costs. It was Kreisky himself who authorized secret negotiations on the prisoner's fate in 1982. When those talks stalled, the terrorists subsequently attacked the Vienna airport in 1985. 'Abu Nidal is known to retaliate against those governments that imprison his members', a CIA paper concluded only days after the assault and emphasized: 'Both Italy and Austria are now holding three group members each. Senior officials of the Abu Nidal group last week held discussions with Austrian officials about the early release of its prisoners'.[61] Kreisky had already left office in 1983, but less than two weeks before the terrorist strike, he had tried to defuse the growing danger by utilizing his personal contact with Libyan leader Qadhafi. A trusted official was sent on a last minute mission to Tripoli to appeal to Qadhafi to discourage Abu Nidal from threatening Austria. The Libyan leader agreed to do just that, but eleven days later the attack nevertheless did take place. Afterwards Kreisky received an apology – the Libyans had been unable to contact the terrorists, who operated out of a military base in Syrian controlled Lebanon, in time.[62]

In order to prevent further bloodshed, a deal was struck. In 1988, the chief of the Austrian state police secretly met with an Abu Nidal representative at Orly airport in Paris. It was agreed that the group would not target Austria again. In return, their emissaries were allowed to visit the imprisoned 'officer' and to occupy an apartment in Vienna. By allowing such a presence in the capital, the Austrian authorities managed to postpone the pressing issue of an early release of the prisoner. He was a free man by 1995, after serving two-thirds of his jail term. At that time, the base in Vienna no longer existed – aided by a foreign intelligence service, it had kept operating under surveillance until 1993. Despite the high risks involved, there was no further act of Palestinian terrorism in Austria. By that time, Kreisky's successors had already abandoned the former highly visible role in international affairs and instead concentrated on joining the European Union. In part, this was also a result of the public's growing concern about terrorism after the wave of attacks in the early 1980s.[63]

To sum up, the example of Palestinian terrorism in Austria demonstrates the complicated nature of state-sponsored terrorism. The country got into the cross-hairs because of its prominent role in the early stages of the political transformation of the PLO. For different reasons, this drew the ire of both Syria and Abu Nidal – the latter responded with acts of terrorism that were in part funded and supported by Assad's intelligence services. In addition to the shared interest of disrupting Austrian policies in the Middle East and weakening Arafat, Abu Nidal also pursued his own goals, and by keeping up the pressure even reached a form of understanding with the Austrian authorities.

Conclusion

In 2010, Olivier Assayas presented his epic film *Carlos*, a biography of Ilich Ramirez Sanchez. According to the director, a key element in the film was the depiction of Cold War terrorism as a form of dirty warfare orchestrated and commissioned by states: 'Terrorism is about one state sending a message to another. Usually you never know who is sending a message to whom, it only surfaces years later'.[64] Assayas may have neglected the role of political and social preconditions for terrorism, but his main thesis is correct: without state support and international cooperation among the groups themselves, 1970s and 1980s terrorists would most certainly not have been as effective and operational as they were.

Compared with contemporary political violence, terrorists like 'Carlos' or Abu Nidal seem to belong to a different age. Back then, terrorist groups were thoroughly militarily organized, operated out of fixed bases, and had a chain of command with one almighty leader at the top. Contemporary radical Islamist terrorism does not need state sponsors any more. On the contrary, it flourishes in failed states, is mainly funded by private individuals, and constitutes a highly flexible network with flat hierarchies. No matter how confusing and destructive Cold War terrorism proved to be, it served political aims and interests. Radical Islamist terrorists, on the other hand, do not pursue a similar clear agenda. The death toll also differs. Spectacular suicide attacks began to set in during Lebanon's civil war during the early 1980s, but remained exceptional. Mainly, the violence inflicted by Cold War terrorists was limited and applied in close relation to the desired results. Today's terrorism targets the public at large for maximum impact, while the perpetrators are no longer constrained by the risk of alienating supporters or sponsors.

The main difference is that the 'old terrorism' cannot be separated from the general framework of the Cold War. The conflict between East and West contributed greatly to the surge in terrorist activity during the 1970s and 1980s. The superpower rivalry provided ample opportunity for terrorist surrogates – they benefited from financial and logistical support, as well as training and other resources. As a quid pro quo, the terrorists served the strategic agenda of their sponsors, but they were not simple heelers. They also pursued their own objectives and kept their independence, trying to make the most out of these partnerships of convenience. The hosts were prepared to drop their uncertain allies at any moment – as long as they functioned according to foreign and internal policy priorities. Similarly, the terrorists proved to be an unreliable lot, always looking for new possibilities and alliances.

Finally, the example of Palestinian terrorism against Austria has shown in detail that terrorism was a form of secret policy during the Cold War, a coercive diplomacy by dirty means. The long list of bloody events can not be understood properly if the hidden political aspects are not taken into account. On the whole, there is need for further research into this grey area, so that the memory of Cold War terrorism incorporates the critical structures facilitating and sustaining the 'years of lead'.

Notes

1   C. Ponto, 'Es war ein System, kein Komplex', *Frankfurter Allgemeine Zeitung*, 23 May 2010.
2   Ibid.
3   D. Crawford, 'The murder of a CEO', *The Wall Street Journal*, 15 September 2007.
4   W. Kraushaar, 'Zur Topologie des RAF-Terrorismus', in W. Kraushaar (ed.) *Die RAF und der linke Terrorismus*, vol. 1, Hamburg: Hamburger Edition, 2006, pp. 13–61.
5   I. Molloy, *Rolling Back Revolution. The Emergence of Low Intensity Conflict*, London: Pluto Press, 2001, p. 80
6   B. Woodward, *Veil: The Secret Wars of the CIA 1981–1987*, New York: Simon & Schuster, 1987, pp. 124–9.
7   D. Martin and J. Walcott, *Best Laid Plans. The Inside Story of America's War Against Terrorism*, New York: Harpers and Row, 1988, pp. 48–9.
8   'Soviet Support for International Terrorism and Revolutionary Violence', Special National Intelligence Estimate, 27 May 1981, Online [http://www.foia.cia.gov/docs/DOC_0000272980/DOC_0000272980.pdf] (accessed 15 June 2011).
9   T. Naftali, *Blindspot. The Secret History of American Counterterrorism*, New York: Basic Books, 2005, p. 16.
10 C. Andrew and W. Mitrochin, *Das Schwarzbuch des KGB. Moskaus Kampf gegen den Westen*, Berlin: Propyläen Verlag, 1999, p. 472.
11 'Moscow's Gold: Soviet Financing of Global Subversion', *National Observer*, No. 40, Autumn 1999, Online [www.nationalobserver.net/1999_autumn_campbell.htm] (accessed 20 March 2011).

12   Ibid.
13   C. Andrew and W. Mitrochin, *Das Schwarzbuch des KGB 2. Moskaus Geheimoperationen im Kalten Krieg*, Berlin: Propyläen Verlag, 2006, p. 370.
14   ‚Das Wunder von Mogadishu‘, TV-Documentary, ZDF, 4 September 2007.
15   I. Molloy, *Rolling Back Revolution. The Emergence of Low Intensity Conflict*, London: Pluto Press, 2001, p. 119.
16   D. Ganser, *NATO's Secret Armies. Operation Gladio and Terrorism in Western Europe*, London: Frank Cass, 2004, pp. 1–2.
17   Ibid., pp. 239–44.
18   M. Ingram and G. Harkin, *Stakeknife. Britain's Secret Armies in Ireland*, Dublin: O'Brien Press Ltd, 2004, pp. 209–10.
19   M. Wunderle, 'Die Roten Brigaden', in W. Kraushaar (ed.) *Die RAF und der linke Terrorismus*, Vol. 2, Hamburg: Hamburger Edition, 2006, pp. 782–808.
20   R. Igel, 'Linksterrorismus fremdgesteuert? Die Kooperation von RAF, Roten Brigaden, CIA und KGB', *Blätter für deutsche und internationale Politik*, 2007, vol. 10: 1221–35.
21   'Rote Ohren', *Der Spiegel* 18, 1986, pp. 24–5.
22   P. Seale, *Abu Nidal – Der Händler des Todes. Die Wahrheit über den palästinensischen Terror*, München: C. Bertelsmann, 1992, pp. 159–62.
23   'The Record of Libyan-Sponsored Assassination Attempts 1980–85', *Terrorism Review*, May 1985, vol. 20, Online [http://www.foia.cia.gov/docs/ DOC_0000256583/DOC_0000256583.pdf] (accessed 20 May 2011).
24   'Syrian Support for Terrorism – 1985', *Terrorism Review* 13 January 1986, Online [http://www.foia.cia.gov/docs/DOC_0000258586/DOC_0000258586.pdf] (accessed 20 May 2011).
25   'Focus: State Support for Terrorism', *Terrorism Review*, 6 October 1988, Online [http://www.foia.cia.gov/docs/DOC_0000258684/DOC_0000258684.pdf] (accessed 18 May 2011).
26   'Libya: Reviewing Terrorist Capabilities', April 1989, Online [http://www.foia.cia.gov/docs/DOC_0000259675/DOC_0000259675.pdf] (accessed 18 May 2011).
27   'National Intelligence Estimate: The Soviet Bloc in International Terrorism and Revolutionary Violence', August 1986, Online [http://www.foia.cia.gov/ docs/DOC_0000518060/DOC_0000518060.pdf] (accessed 13 March 2011).
28   'CSSR-Geheimdienst half offenbar Roten Brigaden', *Austria Presse Agentur*, 22 January 2010.
29   W. Kraushaar, 'Zur Topologie des RAF-Terrorismus‘, in W. Kraushaar (ed.) *Die RAF und der linke Terrorismus*, vol. 1, Hamburg: Hamburger Edition, 2006, p. 51.
30   J.-H. Schulz, 'Die Beziehungen zwischen der Roten Armee Fraktion (RAF) und dem Ministerium für Staatssicherheit (MfS) in der DDR', *Zeitgeschichte-online*, 2007, Online [http://www.zeitgeschichte-online.de/site/40208732/ default.aspx] (accessed 18 May 2011).
31   O. Schröm, *Im Schatten des Schakals. Carlos und die Wegbereiter des internationalen Terrorismus*, Berlin: Ch.Links, 2002, p. 218–19.
32   J. Koehler, *Stasi. The Untold Story Of The East German Secret Police*, Boulder: Westview Press, 1999, p. 371.
33   'Neues vom Derwisch', *Der Spiegel* 43, 1996, pp. 28–9.
34   S. Aust, *Der Baader Meinhof Komplex*, Hamburg: Hoffmann und Campe, 2008, p. 803.

35 B. Woodward, *Veil: The Secret Wars of the CIA 1981–1987*, New York: Simon & Schuster, 1987, p. 156.
36 'Eine perverse Kombination', in *Der Spiegel* 25, 1990, pp. 97–103.
37 J. Follain, *Jackal. The Complete Story of the Legendary Terrorist Carlos the Jackal*, New York: Arcade Publishing, 1998, p. 184.
38 M. Wolf and A. McElvoy, *Man Without A Face. The Autobiography of Communism's Greatest Spymaster*, New York: Times Books, 1997, p. 275.
39 'Internationaler Terrorismus', BStU, MfS – HA XXII Nr. 5537/3 [Translated by Th.R.].
40 J. Koehler, *Stasi. The Untold Story Of The East German Secret Police*, Boulder: Westview Press, 1999, p. 361.
41 M. Wolf and A. McElvoy, *Man Without A Face. The Autobiography of Communism's Greatest Spymaster*, New York: Times Books, 1997, pp. 269–70.
42 T. Skelton-Robinson, 'Im Netz verheddert. Die Beziehungen des bundesdeutschen Linksterrorismus zur Volksfront für die Befreiung Palästinas (1969–1980)', in W. Kraushaar (ed.) *Die RAF und der linke Terrorismus*, Vol. 2, Hamburg: Hamburger Edition, 2006, pp. 828–904.
43 XV/3031/78, BStU MfS – HA XXII, Nr. 18613 [Translated by Th.R.].
44 J. Follain, *Jackal. The Complete Story of the Legendary Terrorist Carlos the Jackal*, New York: Arcade Publishing, 1998, p. 119.
45 'Information über Aktivitäten von Vertretern der palästinensischen Befreiungsbewegung in Verbindung mit internationalen Terroristen zur Einbeziehung der DDR bei der Vorbereitung von Gewaltakten in Ländern Westeuropas', 8 May 1979, BStU, MfS, Z 3021 [Translated by Th.R.].
46 Ibid.
47 J. Follain, *Jackal. The Complete Story of the Legendary Terrorist Carlos the Jackal*, New York: Arcade Publishing, 1998, p. 121.
48 'Bericht zum Stand der Bearbeitung des OV 'Händler', Reg.-Nr. MfS XV/3690/82', 26 January 1987, BStU, MfS XV/3690/82 'Händler', 7116/91, Bd. 1 [Translated by Th.R.].
49 'Information über die Organisation Fatah-Revolutionsrat (Fatah-RR)', February 1986, BStU, MfS XV/3690/82 'Händler', 7116/91, Vol. 1 [Translated by Th.R.]
50 'Vermerk zu den stattgefundenen Lehrgängen mit der ‚Händler'-Organisation auf dem Territorium der DDR', in: BStU, XV 3690/82 'Händler', 7116/91 [Translated by Th.R.].
51 'Deal hinterm Bahnhof', *Der Spiegel* 41, 1991, pp. 152–54.
52 T. Riegler, *Im Fadenkreuz: Österreich und der Nahostterrorismus 1973–1985*, Wien: Vienna University Press, 2010, pp. 30–3.
53 H. Embacher and M. Reiter, *Gratwanderungen. Die Beziehungen zwischen Österreich und Israel im Schatten der Vergangenheit*, Wien: Picus, 1998, p. 161.
54 T. Riegler, *Im Fadenkreuz: Österreich und der Nahostterrorismus 1973–1985*, Wien: Vienna University Press, 2010, pp. 451–4.
55 K.B. Nasr, *Arab and Israeli Terrorism*, Jefferson: McFarland & Co., 1997, p. 143.
56 P. Seale, *Asad. The Struggle for the Middle East*, Los Angeles: University of California Press, 1989, pp. 345–6.
57 Ibid., p. 462.
58 'Syria-PLO: Reining in Arafat', 24 September 1981, Online [http://www.foia.cia.gov/docs/DOC_0000459239/DOC_0000459239.pdf] (accessed 19 March 2011).

59 ‚Erschießung der österreichischen Bürgers NITTEL‘, 1 July 1981, BStU, MfS –
    HA XXII Nr. 16762 [Translated by Th.R.].
60 'Information über Abu Nidal und seine Gruppe', 29 October 1981, BStU, MfS
    XV 3690/82 71116/91, Bd. 1. [Translated by Th.R.]
61 'National   Intelligence   Daily',   28   December   1985,   Online
    [http://www.foia.cia.gov/docs/DOC_0000637389/DOC_0000637389.pdf]
    (accessed10 March 2011).
62 T. Riegler, *Im Fadenkreuz: Österreich und der Nahostterrorismus 1973–1985*, Wien:
    Vienna University Press, 2010, pp. 454–7.
63 Ibid., pp. 292–3.
64 'I won't be doing Bin Laden, I've done Carlos!' French director, *rt.com*, 14
    December 2010, Online [http://rt.com/art-and-culture/news/carlos-terror-
    ism-assayas-laden/] (accessed 15 January 2011).

8 The hijacking of TWA-847

A strategic analysis

Richard C. Thornton

Introduction

The hijacking of flight TWA-847, on 14 June 1985, created a crisis of the first order for the Reagan administration and had a dramatic impact on future policy. An analysis of the event, including the administration's approach and the actions and motives of the sponsors and participants, offers important lessons for possible crisis-situation negotiators today.

The event seemed straightforward enough. Two Lebanese men hijacked the airliner after it left Athens headed for Rome and forced Captain John Testrake to divert from his scheduled destination to Beirut. From Beirut, they flew to Algiers, then back to Beirut. From Beirut they flew to Algiers a second time, then finally back to Beirut where a prolonged negotiation spanning over two weeks took place. The crisis was resolved by a swap of the passengers for over seven hundred Israeli-held prisoners.

The conventional wisdom, expressed in the works of Wills, Martin and Wolcott, and Woodward, holds that the hijack was sponsored by Syria and Iran and carried out by Iran's surrogate in Lebanon, Hezbollah.[1] These authors saw no motive beyond the use of a terrorist act to gain the release of incarcerated comrades. A close look at events, however, makes clear that these assumptions were incorrect and yields a much different interpretation of the hijacking as a supremely political act and offers lessons to those who might face a similar situation today.

A reconstruction of the crisis will demonstrate that Moscow and Qadaffi, not Syria and Iran, were the sponsors of the hijacking, and Imad Mugniyeh, not Hezbollah, was the perpetrator. In fact, Hafez Assad of Syria and Ayatollah Rafsanjani of Iran played critical roles in resolving the crisis both directly and through their surrogates in Lebanon, the Amal and Hezbollah.

A strategic perspective is an essential starting point. The fall of the shah and the resulting Iran–Iraq war offered Moscow an historic opportunity to draw Iran into its orbit. But the great opportunity appeared to be fleeting as President Reagan, starting his second term, expressly sought to re-establish relations with Iran. Moreover, Iran was receptive, hoping to acquire the weapons necessary to defend against Moscow's surrogate Saddam Hussein. I postulate, therefore, that the Soviets were desperate to prevent a rapprochement between Washington and Tehran.[2]

The Soviets no doubt adopted a panoply of measures in the hopes of preventing United States–Iranian rapprochement; for our purposes here, I will focus only on the plan to hijack an American airliner filled with American passengers and place the blame on Iran. Iranian complicity would act as a barrier to rapprochement.

The Soviets approached Qadaffi, one of their prime collaborators supporting global terrorism, crafting the hijack plan in a way that would also serve his interests. In the spring of 1985, as expressed in National Security Decision Directive 168, dated 30 April, the Reagan administration had decided to isolate Qadaffi and strengthen relations with his neighbours, Algeria, Tunisia, and Morocco.[3] Upgrading relations with Algeria was the centrepiece of this policy. Qadaffi therefore had an interest in disrupting US efforts to bring about a rapprochement with Algeria, in particular, to keep alive the prospects of his own long-term plan for union with that country.

Hijacking an American aircraft and flying it to Algiers offered Qadaffi an opportunity to engage Algeria and turn it away from the US. An added benefit lay in offering to swap the passengers for prisoners held in Israel, some of whom were Palestinians. Qadaffi supported the Palestine Liberation Organization (PLO) in a proxy struggle against Assad's Amal for control of Beirut. The release of Palestinian prisoners would strengthen the PLO in that struggle.

Qadaffi, in turn, contracted the task of seizing the airliner to arch terrorist Imad Mugniyeh, who also had an interest. Not only had Mugniyeh been on a terrorist rampage, highlighted by the October 1983 bombings of the Marine barracks and the French legation in Beirut, his brother-in-law, Mustafa Badreddine, was one of the Dawa seventeen imprisoned by Kuwait for terrorist acts against American and French embassies there the following month. Finally, his younger brother was killed in a US-sponsored, Lebanese government attempt to kill Sheik Fadlallah, the 'spiritual mentor' of Hezbollah, in March 1985.[4] So, for reasons of revenge and the possibility of gaining the freedom of his brother-in-law, Mugniyeh accepted this contract.

The Reagan leadership was not only divided in its policy approach to the crisis, but it also proceeded initially on the assumptions that Syria and Iran were the responsible parties. It was not until intelligence demonstrated otherwise that a successful way forward became possible. Even then, it was only late in the crisis that administration leaders began to understand that the hijackers were operating as free agents and were not under the control of Syria, Iran, or Hezbollah. Indeed, it is not clear that American intelligence identified Mugniyeh himself until after the crisis was over.

The analysis of events

After commandeering the plane, the hijackers demanded that Captain Testrake fly to Algiers, but, as there was insufficient fuel to reach Algiers, they chose to fly to Beirut for 'fuel only'.[5] On arrival at Beirut, the hijackers demanded the cooperation of Amal, the group that controlled Beirut and the airport, but no Amal leader would speak with them. At the same time, they spewed out a number of demands ranging from 'world' condemnation of the US and Israel to release of jailed Arabs all over Europe. Their main specific demands were for the release of the Kuwait seventeen and over seven hundred prisoners held by Israel in Atlit prison.

After refuelling, the aircraft was overweight with a full load of one hundred and fifty-three passengers and crew, including one hundred and four Americans. Captain Testrake persuaded the hijackers to release seventeen women and two children to lighten the load. At that point, after an hour and a half on the ground, the plane took off for Algiers, eighteen hundred miles away.

The initial US response to the hijacking was understandably disjointed and based on fragmentary information. The assumption was that Iran and Syria were the instigators of the event, which was carried out by Iran's Lebanon surrogate, Hezbollah. British intelligence sources supported that assumption.[6] Thus, when the plane landed in Beirut, Reagan sent the first of several cables to Hafez Assad requesting his assistance. When the plane took off and headed for Algiers, he also communicated with President Chadli Benjadid, requesting that he permit the plane to land but detain it and attempt to persuade the hijackers to surrender.

Arriving in Algiers, airport security surrounded the plane while government officials engaged the hijackers in a four hour discussion. The hijackers agreed to release twenty-one more passengers for 'humanitarian reasons', but threatened to kill the others if an attempt were made to assault the plane. In the course of their discussions, the hijackers reduced all of their demands to one: that Israel release the seven hundred and sixty-six prisoners being held in Atlit prison, in return for the release of the remaining passengers.[7]

During their talks, the Algerian authorities ignored the hijackers' demands for fuel until it became clear from the cries transmitted over the cockpit radio that they were beating several of the passengers. They singled out for harsh treatment US Navy diver, Robert Stethem and US Army reservist Kurt Carlson. After a tense standoff, the airport authorities permitted the plane to be refuelled and take off.[8]

Once airborne, the hijackers ordered Captain Testrake to return to Beirut. To him, this meant that 'the hijackers didn't really have a game plan. They'd known what to do to get this far – but not what to do afterward'.[9] Indeed, getting to Algiers had been their objective, but, having failed to accomplish their unspecified purpose once they got there, they were now on the way back to Beirut to determine their next course of action.

Arriving in Beirut at a little past two in the morning of 15 June, only the threat to crash-land the plane on the runway persuaded tower control to grant permission to land. Once again, the hijackers demanded that Amal join in the hijacking, which was refused. They also demanded that the Greek government free their third accomplice, who had been bumped from the overbooked flight to Rome and apprehended.[10] (The three hijackers were later identified as Mohamad al Hamadi, Hasan Izz al Din, and Ali Atwa.)

The hijackers threatened to kill eight Greek passengers aboard the airliner unless the Greek government immediately released Atwa. The Papandreou government agreed. Demanding fuel, and screaming through the intercom that they meant business, the hijackers dragged a barely conscious seaman Stethem to the doorway, shot him in the head, and dumped his body onto the tarmac. Tower control immediately directed Testrake to the refuelling area.

As the plane was being refuelled, a dozen gunmen charged onto the plane. Reportedly, members of Hezbollah, or Islamic *Jihad*, their true 'affiliation' was unknown. The leader of the group identified himself simply as *Jihad*, but, after the fact, it was learned that he was Imad Mugniyeh, the arch terrorist who had planned the hijack. Throughout the crisis his identity remained unknown and his relationship to the various terrorist groups in the area was in dispute.[11]

Imad Mugniyeh assumed direct command of the hijack operation from the moment he boarded the aircraft, making two decisions. The first was to go back to Algiers and attempt to fulfil the original plan; the second was to take out insurance against any rescue attempt. (Word had gotten out that the US had dispatched rescue teams, including a Delta Force team, to the region.) Mugniyeh selected a dozen passengers, split them into two groups, and hid them in West Beirut. In fact, he would hold on to one of these, a group of four men, until the very last moment of the crisis.

Algiers redux

Taking off at daybreak, 15 June, while en route to Algiers, the hijackers radioed Athens to send their accomplice, Ali Atwa, to join them, in return for which they would release several Greek passengers. The Greek government immediately complied, flying Atwa to Algiers that afternoon, where he was permitted to join the gunmen on the plane. Algerian negotiators persuaded Mugniyeh to release not only the Greek passengers, but also all of the women, children, and flight attendants – fifty-five in all. Left aboard the plane were fofrty-four men and the three-man crew.

The Reagan administration was split over its approach to the crisis. The president was inclined to negotiate a swap of Israeli prisoners for the passengers, while Secretary of State Shultz wanted to send in a rescue force. He sought to persuade the Algerian government to hold the plane and bring the crisis to an end there in Algiers. However, failing a negotiated settlement, he clung to the hope that they would agree 'at some point to let our shooters...take over the plane'.[12]

The Algerian government, while cooperative, would not countenance the US use of force on its soil. Furthermore, the Algerians believed that 'they could probably persuade the hijackers to release the passengers, if the United States could guarantee that Israel would release the Atlit prisoners'.[13] Although President Reagan was willing to accept this approach, and discrete discussions were held with the Israelis, Shultz strongly opposed a 'swap', insisting that American policy was not to make deals with terrorists, nor encourage others to do so.[14]

By early Sunday morning, the 16th, the hijackers had spent over twenty-four hours on the ground in Algiers, negotiating with no result. Concerned about an attack on the plane, Mugniyeh decided to leave. Algerian leaders, meanwhile, hearing that Delta Force was on its way and concerned that the US would attack the plane despite its objections, decided to permit the plane to refuel and depart.[15]

Airborne once again, Mugniyeh wanted Testrake to fly to Aden. But, when the captain pointed out that there would have to be a refuelling stop along the way, probably in Cairo, Mugniyeh replied: 'Okay, we will fly back to Beirut for fuel. Then we will go somewhere else'. To Captain Testrake 'it was obvious to all of us that the hijackers were fresh out of ideas and were just fumbling about without a real plan of attack'.[16] In desperation, they sought permission to go to Tehran, but 'the Iranian government announced that it would not allow the plane to land on its territory'.[17]

Intelligence discovery

While the plane was en route to Beirut, American intelligence produced surprising information that would have a direct bearing on the developing crisis. Reports based on 'hard intelligence' concluded, 'two senior officials of the Greek government of Andreous Papandreou [were] implicated, though perhaps indirectly, in the hijacking'. The two officials were Costas Naliotes, an aide to the prime minister, and Agamemnon Kostosgeorges, the Minister of Interior. Both were known 'supporters and protectors of international terrorism in Greece', and had been the 'focus of administration criticism...for quite some time'.[18]

American intelligence surmised that the weapons used by the hijackers 'were positioned aboard the TWA Boeing 727 while it was being serviced during its stopover in Athens, allowing the hijackers to bypass the airport's metal detectors and other security equipment'. A member of the service crew, probably one of the cleaning crew, hid the weapons' package in one of the lavatories on the aircraft.

One of the passengers, Peter Hill, a Chicago tour operator, offered corroboration of this thesis. Hill was sitting in the back row of the plane next to the two hijackers. Before takeoff, one of them pushed his way into the lavatory, refusing to keep seated as requested by the cabin attendant. Hill 'heard "a tremendous crash, a smashing of glass"'. Shortly afterwards, the man 'returned to his seat... and began whispering to his companion'.[19]

Perhaps more importantly, intelligence implicated Muamar Qadaffi in the hijacking. Qadaffi had contributed 'large sums of money' to Papandreou's 1981 election and had paid the resettlement costs for those Palestinian refugees in Greece, who had been driven from Lebanon during Israel's 1982 war. 'Libya', the report concluded, 'had a certain ability to collect favours from the Greek government'. One of these 'favours' was for the government to look the other way on 'terrorist operations occurring within Greece, but not directed against that country'.[20]

The evidence offered an explanation of the mechanics of the plot, but not its motives. Qadaffi had called in a favour from the Greek government to allow one of the cleaning crew to place weapons on the aircraft, which would enable Mugniyeh's men to hijack the plane. The only clear motive was to fly to Algiers.

This same evidence tended to exonerate both Syria and Iran. Hafez Assad's surrogate in Beirut, Amal, had consistently refused to cooperate with the hijackers, except under duress. Iran's role was as yet unclear, but it seemed unlikely that the Iranians would sponsor an action that would directly contradict their persistent attempts to establish an arms relationship with the US.

Based on this intelligence, Reagan sent a letter to Assad on 16 June, while the plane was heading for Beirut for the third time, proposing to have Nabbi Berri, leader of Amal, take control of the situation. As Shultz observed: 'we asked [Assad] to work on Berri to try to end the crisis'.[21] Up to this point, Berri had determinedly stayed out of it, twice attempting to prevent the plane from landing in Beirut and refusing even to talk with the hijackers.

Reagan most assuredly told Assad that he suspected Qadaffi was the perpetrator and that the Syrian leader had nothing to gain from supporting him. (Qadaffi was supporting the PLO in its struggle with Amal for control of Beirut.) To prevent the crisis from exploding and thus engulfing Syria, too, the president urged that Berri take control of the passengers when the plane landed. Assad promptly cabled his agreement.[22]

Shultz, however, persisted in an attempt to use force to seize the plane. He suggested that Captain Testrake fake engine failure and land at Larnaca, Cyprus, where a rescue could be attempted. Weinberger and the Joint Chiefs of Staff (JCS) disagreed. JCS Chairman John Vessey declared that 'the prospect for a successful rescue mission was virtually nonexistent'. In his view, the 'only safe way [was] to talk them out'.[23]

Testrake and his fellow crewmembers wanted no part of a rescue attempt, which they recognized would only mean the probable deaths of many passengers, terrorists, and crew. Faking engine failure appealed to them, however. Therefore, Captain Testrake, disregarding the suggestion of landing at Larnaca, proceeded instead to Beirut where he shut down the engines on arrival and insured that the plane could not fly anywhere else. Testrake, in short, had neatly put an end to any schemes Mugniyeh might have had to fly on from Beirut, or the US might have had to attempt a rescue by force. The hijack problem, in short, would be resolved diplomatically in Beirut.[24]

Assad's man Berri takes charge

As flight TWA-847 came rolling to a stop on the runway, 'contingents from the Amal militia were arriving at the airport'.[25] This, it would shortly become clear, was the first step in Assad's decision to take control of the hijacking away from Mugniyeh, but it would not be easy or clean-cut. Amal's chief, Nabbi Berri, would be Assad's agent in this effort. His first objective was to surround the hijackers with his men, but also position them for a defence against a possible rescue attempt by the US, or reinforcement of Mugniyeh by other terrorist groups, like Hezbollah, or Islamic *Jihad*.

According to observers, 'several jeeps loaded with Amal militiamen pulled up to the plane'. After some heated discussion the hijackers agreed to send a representative from the group 'to meet with Mr. Berri, the Amal leader, at his home'. The hijackers promised no harm would come to the passengers while the talks with Mr. Berri proceeded, but reiterated their threat to blow up the plane if their demand for the release of the Israeli-held detainees was not met.[26]

The upshot of their negotiation was a division of the spoils. Berri took control of the remaining passengers and dispersed them in small groups in West Beirut hideouts, while Mugniyeh retained control of the plane, the crew, and one of the two groups he had taken off the plane earlier as insurance. With Berri in control of most of the passengers, the focus of the crisis shifted to a swap of passengers for Israeli-held prisoners.[27]

The problem was, however, that the Israeli government seemed to want no part of the crisis. Against the backdrop of large-scale demonstrations in Tel Aviv opposing a recent government decision to swap over one thousand Lebanese detainees for three Israeli soldiers, protestors demanded that the government hold on to the Atlit prisoners.

Official government spokesmen sent contradictory signals. One said that Israel would not agree to any 'exchange' of prisoners for passengers. Another told reporters that while the government would meet with Red Cross representatives, 'the Americans will have to crawl on all fours before we even discuss' releasing the Lebanese detainees. A third spokesman said that Israel 'would consider a formal US request to swap the prisoners for the passengers'.[28]

Parsing these statements went to the heart of the coalition government then in power in Israel, the 'marriage of inconvenience', as one commentator described it.[29] The author of the no exchange line was obviously Deputy Prime Minister Yitzhak Shamir, whose visceral hated for the US was well known. Defence Minister Rabin, who was only slightly less antagonistic, was willing to discuss a swap if the 'Americans' crawled on all fours for it. And Prime Minister Shimon Peres was the obvious author of what became the official line: that the government would consider an exchange, 'if' Washington requested it.

Secretary Shultz interpreted Peres' demand that Washington make a formal request for a swap as 'putting the responsibility on us'. He professed to worry that 'if people were killed, we couldn't say it was because of Israel's refusal to swap prisoners for hostages'.[30] This, from a secretary of state who had no compunctions whatsoever about using deadly force to storm the plane. In reality, the split in Israel's coalition dictated a passive approach. The important point was that Peres had offered Washington an opportunity to bring the Israelis in, without responding to terrorist demands.

Shultz's interpretation also masked a complex situation in Washington in which President Reagan, as before, was eager to end the crisis with a swap, but Shultz wanted to protract it with no swap and no explicit deal with Israel. Fortuitously, thirty-two passengers aboard the plane signed a statement imploring the president 'not to take any direct military action', and urging a negotiated exchange of passengers for prisoners. Their plea strengthened Reagan's hand.[31]

Staking out negotiating positions

With Nabbi Berrri in charge the hijack turned into a quasi-diplomatic hostage negotiation. Berri's prominence was somewhat comforting to the American people, who were being treated to full television coverage of the event, because he had lived in the US and had family who still lived there. Indeed, he still held a green card.[32] However, when National Security Council head, Robert McFarlane, attempted to portray Berri as the key player, the Amal leader maintained that the crisis was still an 'American problem'. If Washington failed to pressure Israel to release the detainees, he would 'wash his hands' of the passengers and return them to the hijackers 'to do with them as they pleased'.[33]

Washington, too, refused to be pigeonholed. A White House statement intoned: 'we do not make concessions and we don't encourage others to make concessions'. The hijack crisis had 'effectively blocked Israel from proceeding with plans to release its Shiite prisoners'. If it is resolved, 'it might be possible the Israelis would proceed on the schedule they'd previously announced'.[34]

On Tuesday, the 18th, as Berri was releasing the remaining six Greek passengers as a friendly gesture to the Greek government for having released Ali Atwa, Assad was replying to Reagan's earlier letter. He now wanted to know whether the president would 'exert efforts' on Israel to release the detainees and 'make public' the fact that holding them was a violation of the Geneva Convention.[35]

Reagan was receptive. White House spokesman, Larry Speakes, said that the US 'would like Israel' to 'go ahead and make the release' of the detainees. Shultz, however, was furious. He knew that Speakes had not spoken out on his own authority and that it was the president who had authorized his statement. Shultz went to the president and demanded that he have the 'action'. All questions, he insisted, 'were to be referred to the State Department'.[36]

The president relented, issuing a statement reiterating the 'no concessions' line and sent a message to Assad insisting that the hijackers were the ones 'blocking the release of the prisoners held by Israel'.[37] Nevertheless, he privately passed word to the Israelis that they were 'allowed' to make the exchange of detainees for passengers.[38]

The president's message apparently was part of a plan to use the Red Cross as an intermediary, relieving both Washington and Tel Aviv of the onus of making concessions to terrorist demands. But the Israelis rejected the ploy. An Israeli spokesman declared that while the government was willing to meet with the Red Cross, they 'are not a party to it. We deal with the US', insisting on an American 'request'.[39]

With no alternatives in sight, at the Tuesday night press conference, the president reaffirmed the no concessions line. While demanding that the passengers be released forthwith, however, he also made public, as Assad had requested, US opposition to Israel's detention of prisoners as a 'violation of the Geneva accords'. On the other hand, he said, Washington would not 'interfere' with Israel's decision on whether or not to release the prisoners. There was no 'linkage' with the passengers.[40]

A step forward on the passenger issue contrasted with the seeming lack of progress with the Israelis on the detainees. The Algerian government, in contact with Berri, reported that he was willing to release the passengers, if the US could provide a 'silent but firm guarantee' that the Israelis would release their prisoners by a 'date certain'. Reagan thought this a promising development and wanted to call Berri and then 'work on the Israelis, but not as a quid pro quo'. Shultz and McFarlane, however, urged caution. Shultz wanted nothing 'in writing' that could be construed as collusion in brokering a deal.[41]

The approach decided upon was a leak through the *New York Times*. Bernard Gwertzman, quoting unidentified sources, said that Israel had agreed to release all Shiite prisoners to the Red Cross 'within a few hours' of the release of the passengers.[42] Although Shultz professed innocence that 'we had deliberately leaked this news' to pressure the Israelis, the report had the desired effect. The Israeli government at last agreed to the piecemeal release of the detainees once the passengers had been released.[43]

At the same time, the question of who the detainees were came into focus. The Israeli defence ministry announced that 'of the seven hundred and sixty-six detainees still in Atlit, five hundred and seventy are Shiite Moslems, one hundred and forty-seven are Palestinians and forty-nine others are Druze, Christians, and Sunni Moslems'.[44] Algerian negotiators, continuing their discrete behind-the-scenes role, 'could not imagine that [Berri] ... would knowingly seek to secure the release of Palestinians', with whom they were in deadly conflict.[45]

Putting the pieces together

Meanwhile, progress was also occurring on the hostage-passenger front. On Wednesday, the 19th, Assad abruptly made an unannounced trip to Moscow to meet with Gorbachev, a subtle sign that the crisis was entering the endgame. Gorbachev reportedly told him to make sure that the passengers were unharmed. On the same day, the government of Iran sent a message to Washington offering, 'to do as much as it could to end the TWA crisis'.[46] These actions were positive signs, but still did not rule out the possibility that Syria or Iran were parties to the crisis.

Word from US ambassador to Lebanon, Reggie Bartholomew, strengthened the presumption that they were not, but raised other questions. He reported that Berri was having success in persuading the hijackers to give up, except for an 'inner group of terrorists ... not under anyone's control, not Iran's and not Hezbollah's'. And, it should be noted, not under Syria's control either. Shultz correctly surmised that some of this 'inner group' was 'related by family to the Dawa prisoners held by Kuwait', but he did not know by whom they were led. It is now known that the leader was Imad Mugniyeh, whose group was 'not under anyone's control'.[47]

Two days after Assad had flown to Moscow, on 21 June, Ayatollah Rafsanjani travelled to Tripoli, ostensibly on an arms-purchasing trip, but also bringing Qadaffi into the picture for the first time. From there he flew to Damascus on the 24th for a meeting with Assad, who had returned from Moscow, and other principals.

Gathering in Damascus were also Sheik Fadlallah and Nabbi Berri, leading to the hope that their meetings would bring an end to the crisis. Indeed, sensing that the meeting of the main leaders involved in this matter in one way or another would be decisive, the Reagan administration imposed a news blackout in Washington. As Martin and Walcott observed, this was 'a sure sign that the posturing had ended and the dealing had begun'.[48]

While Rafsanjani was still in Tripoli, on June 22, Shultz sent a message to Assad. He urged the Syrian leader to influence Berri to 'release the passengers and crew'. It was 'the continued detention of passengers, crew and aircraft [that] constitute[d] a specific impediment to Israel's publicly-expressed policy to release the Atlit prisoners'. Shultz also wanted Assad to urge Rafsanjani to exert his influence on 'those groups in Lebanon' holding not only the passengers, but also the 'American, British, and French kidnap victims' taken off the streets of Beirut during the past year.[49]

Although Secretary Shultz had expressed US interests to Assad, there is little doubt that the Syrian leader hosted the meeting on advice he had received from Gorbachev. Assad had control over Beirut and northern Lebanon by virtue of the extensive presence of Syrian military power and through his agent Nabbi Berri. But many terrorist groups flourished under his umbrella, including Hezbollah, Islamic *Jihad*, and Imad Mugniyeh that were not under Syrian control.

That was where Rafsanjani and Sheik Fadlallah came in. Rafsanjani held sway over Hezbollah, but not Islamic *Jihad*. And, as we have seen, Mugniyeh was 'not under anyone's control'. If anyone had an influence with Mugniyeh, it was Sheik Fadlallah, who had been something of a mentor to him earlier when he served as his bodyguard. Rafsanjani's meeting with Fadlallah thus gave their exchange a special significance. After their conclave, Rafsanjani held a press conference in which he declared Iran's innocence: 'had [Iran] known in advance about this kind of action [the hijacking], it would have acted to prevent it'.[50] The implication was that now that Iran did know, it was acting to resolve it.

The major absence from the gathering was Qadaffi. If American intelligence had been correct in identifying him as the facilitator, if not instigator, of the hijacking, his absence suggested that the others had decided to cut him out. Rafsanjani's public declaration that Iran would have 'prevented' the hijacking had Tehran known about in advance made plain that neither he, nor Assad, was working with Qadaffi. The larger purpose of the hijacking scheme had failed. The hijack had failed to implicate Iran and thereby block a rapprochement with Washington and the flights to Algiers had failed to prod Algeria into cooperation with Libya against the US.

The Libyan dictator, however, was quick to muddy the analytical waters. As soon as Rafsanjani left Tripoli and headed for Damascus, Libyan state radio declared that Libya and Iran had announced plans to 'promote "Islamic revolution" on a worldwide scale and to form an army to "liberate Palestine"'. Abdel Salam Jalloud, Qadaffi's second in command, levelled a direct challenge to Assad, saying 'Libya and Iran have decided to work together in order to reunite the Moslem and Palestinian forces in Lebanon'.[51]

The broadcast was a clever attempt to create bad blood between Rafsanjani and Assad. Qadaffi knew, as did everyone else, that at this moment Syrian-supported Amal forces were attempting to destroy Arafat's PLO in the battle for control of Beirut. Their reconciliation was hardly imminent, or likely. Moreover, Assad had 'given ample evidence ' that he would not 'tolerate intervention in Lebanon by any foreign state, be it Arab, or non-Arab'.[52]

End games

The unfolding of events is always much clearer in retrospect than it is at the time. Assad and Rafsanjani, if not also Gorbachev, had decided to bring the crisis to an end. At the same time, at a National Security Planning Group meeting on the 25th, the president had also decided to give events a push, by issuing what might be termed a soft ultimatum. A White House spokesman announced that if diplomatic efforts were not successful in freeing the passengers 'within the next few days', the president was considering using economic and military measures to shut down the Beirut airport and to blockade Lebanon.[53]

Reagan's announcement seemed to be directed to Assad, but it was Israel's Peres who responded first. Peres sent word to the president that a public request was no longer necessary. Israel would do 'whatever the United States wanted'. Peres' shift opened the door to an exchange of letters formalizing what would come to be known as the 'no deal deal', the agreement for Israel to release the Atlit detainees as soon as the TWA passengers were released.[54]

Nabbi Berri responded the next day, the 26th. Freeing one of the passengers for medical reasons, he offered to transfer the remaining thirty-nine to either the French or Swiss embassies in Beirut to be held 'in escrow' until the Atlit detainees were released. But he also demanded that the US pledge not to attack Lebanon once the passengers were released. The president dismissed the escrow idea, but directed the State Department to respond positively to the no-retaliation demand, which was not inconsistent with declared US policy toward Lebanon.[55] Unfortunately, the State Department procrastinated in releasing a statement, which delayed a settlement.

Assad also responded, cabling Reagan that progress was being made. In what appeared to be a veiled offer to cooperate with Israel, he asked: 'what if the hijackers were informed that Syria would guarantee the release of the Lebanese prisoners after the TWA passengers were freed?' Shultz, however, ignored the implied offer and simply replied: 'Syria may be confident in expecting the release of the Lebanese prisoners after the freeing of the passengers of TWA 847, without any linkage between the two subjects'.[56]

Believing that resolution of the crisis was 'imminent', the administration sought to link the seven hostages taken earlier by Mugniyeh, who, at this point was operating under the banner of Islamic *Jihad*, to a settlement of the airliner crisis. It was a long shot because the administration was still uncertain 'whether Islamic *Jihad* exist[ed] as a coherent organization, or [was] merely a shadowy coalition of extremist Shiites loosely affiliated with Iran ... [whose] radicalism contrasts with the more moderate policies of Mr. Berri's Amal faction'.[57] Nevertheless, the president was not willing to press this demand to the point of damaging prospects for the resolution of the TWA crisis.

At this delicate moment, Qadaffi deftly tossed yet another political hand grenade into the mix, which held the potential to blow apart any solution, or, at the very least, undercut Hafez Assad. The grenade was lobbed from an unexpected quarter – from Malta, by Qadaffi's new ally, the Prime Minister of Malta, Carmelo Bonnici. The two had signed a treaty of 'friendship and cooperation' the previous November, effectively incorporating Malta into the Soviet-Libyan sphere.[58]

On 28 June, a 'senior Maltese official' made an 'unsolicited' offer to Ambassador James Rentschler. He offered to contact and persuade Nabbi Berri to send the passengers to Israel. They could then appeal to the Israelis for their own release and the release of the Atlit detainees, an appeal which the Israelis could hardly refuse coming from Americans who had suffered seventeen days of captivity.[59]

An unsuspecting Rentschler thought the offer 'well meaning, but greatly muddled'. Unfortunately, it was more than that. If adopted, this 'Maltese option' would have cut Assad out completely, required the unlikely cooperation between Amal and Israel, turned Berri against Assad, disrupted US cooperation with Syria, and Syrian cooperation with Iran. Switching to the Maltese option would have been a mistake, but would have served Qadaffi's interests perfectly. Wisely, the US government avoided this pitfall.[60]

By the 29th, everything seemed to be in order. Passengers were assembled for the trip from Beirut to Damascus, and the US had dispatched a C-141 transport plane to collect them. At literally the last minute, it was discovered that the four hostages originally held out by Mugniyeh as insurance, were not among the assembled passengers. Mugniyeh refused to release them without an American public guarantee that there would be no retaliation against Lebanon. The State Department promptly issued a statement honouring Lebanese sovereignty.[61]

Still Mugniyeh held back. It was only after Assad's issuance of an ultimatum against Iran's Revolutionary Guards in the Baalbeck to 'release the hostages or get out of Lebanon', that the four remaining passengers were released at just after noon on the 30th and the entire group set out in a Red Cross convoy for Damascus.[62] Their ordeal was finally over.

Conclusions

It seems axiomatic that the conventional wisdom is almost always wrong. That is certainly true in the case of the hijacking of flight TWA-847. Far from Syria and Iran being the sponsors and Iran's surrogate in Lebanon, Hezbollah, being the perpetrator, as American leaders initially assumed, there were an entirely different cast of actors involved. These were Gorbachev, Qadaffi, and independent, arch-terrorist Imad Mugniyeh. Moreover, the hijacking was not originally devised to bring about a trade of Israeli-held prisoners for the passengers, but had much more grandiose aims.

The Russians were determined to prevent a rapprochement between the US and Iran, but Tehran's assistance in resolving the crisis thwarted that objective in this instance. Qadaffi was determined to prevent a rapprochement between the US and Algeria, but the Algerian behind-the-scenes role in support of the US was instrumental in effecting a negotiated solution. Finally, Mugniyeh was determined to bring about the release of his comrades held in Kuwait, in the first instance, including his brother-in-law, and other terrorists held in prison. Only he, still unidentified as the conflict ended, seemed to have achieved a partial victory, although his brother-in-law remained in prison.

Without an understanding of the big picture, grand strategy, and the interests, national as well as personal, of the various protagonists, no clear understanding of the event was possible. Moreover, the integration of intelligence gathered during the crisis proved to be essential in arriving at a correct analysis of the identities and motives of the protagonists and provided a realistic basis for a negotiated solution.

Notes

1   D. Wills, *The First War on Terrorism: Counter Terrorism Policy During the Reagan Administration*, New York: Rowman & Littlefield, 2003; D. Martin and J. Walcott, *Best Laid Plans: The Inside Story of America's War Against Terrorism*, New York: Touchstone, 1988; B. Woodward, *Veil: The Secret Wars of the CIA, 1981–1987*, New York: Simon & Shuster, 1987.

2   See R. Thornton, *The Reagan Revolution, III: Defeating the Soviet Challenge*, Vancouver: Trafford, 2009.

3   'US Policy Toward North Africa', *NSDD 168*, 30 April 1985, in C. Simpson, *National Security Directives of the Reagan & Bush Administrations*, Boulder: Westview, 1995, pp. 528–32.

4   See R. Bergman, *The Secret War With Iran*, New York: Free Press, 2007, pp. 72–4, for a full account of Mugniyeh's activities.

5   J. Testrake, *Triumph Over Terror, On Flight 847*, Eastbourne: Kingsway Publications, 1988, 70–1.

6   D. Wills, *The First War on Terrorism: Counter Terrorism Policy During the Reagan Administration*, New York: Rowman & Littlefield, 2003, p. 116.

7   J. Testrake, *Triumph Over Terror, On Flight 847*, Eastbourne: Kingsway Publications, 1988, p. 81.

8   D. Martin and J. Walcott, *Best Laid Plans: The Inside Story of America's War Against Terrorism*, New York: Touchstone, 1988, p. 163.

9   J. Testrake, *Triumph Over Terror, On Flight 847*, Eastbourne: Kingsway Publications, 1988, p. 81.

10   R. Bergman, *The Secret War With Iran*, New York: Free Press, 2007, p. 101, says that shortly after the hijacking Israel's intelligence chief in Athens went to the airport, discovered that one of the hijackers' tickets had not been used, and concluded that the third hijacker was still in the airport. With the support of the Greek police they paged Atwa and arrested him when he attempted to take the call.

11   C.R. Dickey, 'Hijackings: Tool of Terrorism', *Washington Post*, 16 June 1985, p. 18.

12 G. Shultz, *Turmoil and Triumph*, New York: Charles Scribner's, 1993, pp. 654–5.

13 D. Wills, *The First War on Terrorism: Counter Terrorism Policy During the Reagan Administration*, New York: Rowman & Littlefield, 2003, p. 97.

14 G. Shultz, *Turmoil and Triumph*, New York: Charles Scribner's, 1993, p. 656.

15 D. Martin and J. Walcott, *Best Laid Plans: The Inside Story of America's War Against Terrorism*, New York: Touchstone, 1988, p. 182.

16 J. Testrake, *Triumph Over Terror, On Flight 847*, Eastbourne: Kingsway Publications, 1988, p. 92.

17 S. Segev, *The Iranian Triangle: The Untold Story of Israel's Role in the Iran-Contra Affair*, New York: Free Press, 1988, p. 142.

18 T. Agres, 'Two Greek Officials Implicated in Hijack', *Washington Times*, 20 June 1985, p. 1.

19 D. Martin and J. Walcott, *Best Laid Plans: The Inside Story of America's War Against Terrorism*, New York: Touchstone, 1988, pp. 161–2.

20 T. Agres, 'Two Greek Officials Implicated in Hijack', *Washington Times*, 20 June 1985, p. 1.

21 G. Shultz, *Turmoil and Triumph*, New York: Charles Scribner's, 1993, p. 656.

22 D. Wills, *The First War on Terrorism: Counter Terrorism Policy During the Reagan Administration*, New York: Rowman & Littlefield, 2003, p. 101.

23 Ibid., p. 102; and D. Martin and J. Walcott, *Best Laid Plans: The Inside Story of America's War Against Terrorism*, New York: Touchstone, 1988, p. 185.

24 J. Testrake, *Triumph Over Terror, On Flight 847*, Eastbourne: Kingsway Publications, 1988, pp. 93, 97–8.

25 D. Wills, *The First War on Terrorism: Counter Terrorism Policy During the Reagan Administration*, New York: Rowman & Littlefield, 2003, p. 98.

26 J. Berger, 'Gunmen Negotiate As Hostages Plead For Reagan To Act', *New York Times*, 17 June 1985, p. 1.

27 A. Borowiec, 'Shi'ites Said Holding Hostages in West Beirut', *Washington Times*, 18 June 1985, p. 1.

28 D. Wills, *The First War on Terrorism: Counter Terrorism Policy During the Reagan Administration*, New York: Rowman & Littlefield, 2003, p. 98.

29 J. Kraft, 'Marriage of Inconvenience', *Washington Post*, 25 June 1985, p. 15.

30 G. Shultz, *Turmoil and Triumph*, New York: Charles Scribner's, 1993, pp. 655–6.

31 J. Berger, 'Gunmen Negotiate As Hostages Plead For Reagan To Act', *New York Times*, 17 June 1985, p. 1.

32 J. Randal, 'Crisis Go-Between: Berri, With Ties on Both Sides, Could Find Leadership Tested', *Washington Post*, 18 June 1985, p. 9.

33 B. Weinraub, 'Passengers Taken From Hijacked Jet, Lebanese Reports', *New York Times*, 18 June 1985, p. 1.

34 Ibid.

35 D. Wills, *The First War on Terrorism: Counter Terrorism Policy During the Reagan Administration*, New York: Rowman & Littlefield, 2003, pp. 107–8.

36 G. Shultz, *Turmoil and Triumph*, New York: Charles Scribner's, 1993, p. 658.

37 Ibid.

38 D. Wills, *The First War on Terrorism: Counter Terrorism Policy During the Reagan Administration*, New York: Rowman & Littlefield, 2003, p. 108.

39 E. Walsh, 'Israel Agrees to Red Cross Meeting', *Washington Post*, 19 June 1985, p. 1.

40   B. Weinraub, 'President Bars "Concessions"; Orders Antihijacking Steps; 3 More T.W.A. Hostages Freed', *New York Times*, 19 June 1985, p. 1.

41   D. Wills, *The First War on Terrorism: Counter Terrorism Policy During the Reagan Administration*, New York: Rowman & Littlefield, 2003, p. 110.

42   B. Gwertzman, 'US Warns Shiites About Becoming Global "Outcasts"', *New York Times*, 20 June 1985, p. 1.

43   G. Shultz, *Turmoil and Triumph*, New York: Charles Scribner's, 1993, pp. 660–1.

44   T. Friedman, 'Israel To Release 31 Prisoners Seized In Lebanon', *New York Times*, 24 June 1985, p. 1.

45   G. Shultz, *Turmoil and Triumph*, New York: Charles Scribner's, 1993, p. 663.

46   *Report of the President's Special Review Board*, Washington, D.C.; GPO, 1987, B-13.

47   G. Shultz, *Turmoil and Triumph*, New York: Charles Scribner's, 1993, p. 662 and M. Getler, 'Smaller Group Said to Include Military Persons', *Washington Post*, 21 June 1985, p. 1.

48   D. Martin and J. Walcott, *Best Laid Plans: The Inside Story of America's War Against Terrorism*, New York: Touchstone, 1988, p. 196.

49   D. Wills, *The First War on Terrorism: Counter Terrorism Policy During the Reagan Administration*, New York: Rowman & Littlefield, 2003, p. 118.

50   Ibid., pp. 119–20.

51   'Libya and Iran Pledge to "Liberate Palestine"', *Wall Street Journal*, 25 June 1985, p. 34.

52   Ibid.

53   D. Oberdorfer, 'Reagan's Shift Risks Forcing His Hand If Deadline Passes', *Washington Post*, 26 June 1985, p. 17.

54   D. Martin and J. Walcott, *Best Laid Plans: The Inside Story of America's War Against Terrorism*, New York: Touchstone, 1988, pp. 197–8.

55   B. Gwertzman, 'US Weighing Shiite Offer on Moving Hostages', *New York Times*, 27 June 1985, p. 1.

56   G. Shultz, *Turmoil and Triumph*, New York: Charles Scribner's, 1993, p. 664.

57   H. Trewhitt, 'US Says 7 Seized Earlier Must be Released as Well', *Baltimore Sun*, 28 June 1985, p. 1.

58   "The Libyan-Maltese Alliance," in J. Churba (ed.) *Focus on Libya: February 1984 to June 1989*, Washington, D.C.: Pemcon Publishers, 1989, pp. 89–92.

59   D. Wills, *The First War on Terrorism: Counter Terrorism Policy During the Reagan Administration*, New York: Rowman & Littlefield, 2003, p. 130.

60   G. Shultz, *Turmoil and Triumph*, New York: Charles Scribner's, 1993, p. 665, refers implicitly to this episode, noting that many 'diplomatic volunteers' had suddenly 'emerged from all over the landscape, offering to get involved in "the release"'.

61   D. Wills, *The First War on Terrorism: Counter Terrorism Policy During the Reagan Administration*, New York: Rowman & Littlefield, 2003, p. 132.

62   Ibid. and pp. 249–50, n.155; D. Martin and J. Walcott, *Best Laid Plans: The Inside Story of America's War Against Terrorism*, New York: Touchstone, 1988, p. 200, say the threat was to 'get out of the Bekaa Valley'.

Part III
Non-western experiences with terrorism

9 Bengal terrorism and the ambiguity of the Bengali Muslims

Rashed Uz Zaman

Introduction

One hundred years ago, in 1911, subjects of the British Empire in India were treated to the extraordinary spectacle of an imperial durbar at Delhi. On this occasion, the newly crowned King-Emperor George V and his Queen presented themselves to their Indian subjects. The solemn occasion was conducted in a befitting manner and imperial pomp and pageantry dazzled both guests and spectators alike.

While imperial splendour was at its best, it could not hide the fact that all was not well within the Raj. Indeed, even as the gala event was being acted out in Delhi, parts of India were in turmoil, none more so than Bengal, where a fierce anti-Raj agitation movement had convulsed the region since it was hived off in 1905 to create a separate province of Eastern Bengal and Assam.[1] However, what makes this period of Bengal's and, for that matter, the Indian Raj's history stand out is the emergence and development of a terrorism campaign which made a significant impact upon the history of India. It is interesting to note that, at the Delhi Durbar, the King-Emperor announced the revocation of the partition of Bengal, the main demand of the anti-Raj agitation.[2]

To propose that terrorist activities were solely responsible for undoing partition would be credulous, for traditional mass politics played a critical role in influencing the opinion of the rulers. Still, it can be argued that terrorism acted as a catalyst in bringing this change. Moreover, the terrorist movement did not come to an end with the revocation of the partition plan. Instead, it metastasized into a movement which continued to challenge British authority in India until the early 1930s. The various 'waves'[3] within the Indian terrorist movement convulsed the Indian people time and again and, at times, even added an international dimension to the issue of India's freedom.[4]

This chapter will focus on the impact terrorism had upon Bengali Muslims who, interestingly enough, made up the majority of the population in the province of East Bengal and Assam. For Bengali Muslims, the terrorist movement, which began in the early years of the twentieth century and continued for the next thirty years or so, presented a dilemma that has not yet been resolved nearly one hundred years later, although the history and geography of British India underwent drastic changes with the emergence of the independent states of India and Pakistan in 1947 and subsequently, the break-up of Pakistan and the birth of Bangladesh in 1971. Bengali Muslims were torn between the clarion call for freedom that was made by the terrorists but, at the same time, the very nature of the terrorist ideology did not make it possible for them to join the movement or lend it wholehearted support. This chapter is an attempt to trace this ambiguity.

The chapter is divided into the following parts: in the first section, a description is made of the various stages of the terrorist movement. In the second section, an attempt is made to understand the nature of this movement. The third section will focus upon Bengali Muslims and their ambiguity towards Bengal terrorism. Interestingly enough, during the existence of East Pakistan from 1947 to 1971, the same community embraced the heroes of Bengal's terrorist movement as members of their own. I discuss this duality in the final section of the chapter.

The waves of Indian terrorism

The terrorist movement in India was firmly entrenched only in Bengal. Terrorism, however, originated in Maharashtra in the Bombay Presidency. The Bombay outbreak is interesting, for it showed a pattern that subsequent outbreaks in Bengal also replicated. Descriptions of the various waves are provided below.

The first wave (1897–1910)

As the nineteenth century drew to a close, the Indian political scene was dominated by an Indian National Congress which was moderate in its aims and methods. This approach appeared futile to a new generation of Congress members who, from the mid-1890s, began to castigate the moderate approach of the party and called for a bolder approach espoused by leaders such as Bal Gangadhar Tilak.

Tilak (1844–1920) started his political career with G. K. Gokhale, a famous Congress leader. Tilak soon parted ways with the moderate ways of Gokhale and adopted an increasingly extreme position, opposing colonial rule in India and at the same time, celebrating the Hindu nation. In 1893, Tilak initiated the celebration of the birth of the popular elephant-headed god, Ganesh (or Ganapati). In 1895, Tilak went a step further and introduced a second annual festival, this time in honour of Shivaji, the Maratha ruler who fought against the Mughals and established a Maratha kingdom. These festivals were accompanied by ceremonies designed to highlight Hindu and national glory, and to focus attention upon the political issues of the day.

It was under such circumstances that the first act of terrorism in British India took place in the Bombay Presidency. On 22 June 1897, Damodar Chapekar, assisted by his brother Balkrishna Chapekar, assassinated Walter Rand, the Plague Commissioner, along with another British officer Lieutenant Ayerst. Apparently, the killings were designed as an act of terror to prevent the British authority from going ahead with the steps they had initiated to fight a bout of bubonic plague that had struck Pune. The Chapekar brothers were soon arrested, put on trial, and hanged in 1898. Tilak was suspected of having an indirect role in the affair. He was imprisoned for a few months and the incipient terrorist movement in Bombay came to an end.[5]

Even as the terrorist activities were coming to an end in Bombay, a far more radical and organized movement was emerging in Bengal. In 1902, a Bengali barrister, Pramatha Nath Mitra, along with Sister Nivedita (an Irish lady who became a disciple of the famed Indian religious figure Swami Vivekananda) and Jatindranath Banerji, a Bengali expatriate serving in the Indian state of Baroda's army, formed the Calcutta *Anushilan Samiti* – the progenitor of the two main groups of terrorists in Bengal, namely *Anushilan* and *Yugantar*.[6] The objective of the groups was to indulge in terrorism in the form of targeting government officials. This was deemed as a tactic whereby the colonial government would be paralyzed and eventually brought to its knees. Funding was to be obtained through extortion of money from the rich and affluent and robbing post offices soon became the norm and the concept of 'political dacoities' became a signature mark of the Bengal terrorists.[7]

The *Anushilan Samiti* soon attracted a large number of recruits and branches were established all over the province of Bengal. Still, the movement did not assume serious proportions before the partition of Bengal in 1905. It was this event and the resulting *Swadeshi* movement that made terror groups such as *Anushilan* and *Yugantar* popular.

The increase in the popularity of the terrorist groups in Bengal reached a crescendo when a group of young men coalesced around Aurobindo Ghose and his younger brother, Barindra Kumar Ghose. The Ghose brothers organized a hideout in the north Calcutta suburb of Maniktola where young men were trained in the use of arms and bombs were manufactured. Thus was born what one prominent historian has called 'the cult of the bomb' in Bengal.[8] Between 1906 and 1908, the young men of the Maniktola group carried out a series of bomb attacks against high government officials. A botched assassination led the government to arrest the brothers and the first wave of Indian terrorism came to an end.[9]

The second wave (1911–18)

With the break-up of the Maniktola secret society, the small group who had gathered around the Ghose brothers faded into history. The revocation of the partition of Bengal that was announced in 1911 removed the rationale of the *Swadeshi* movement. However, this did not put an end to terrorist activities.

During the years 1911 to 1918, Bengal terrorists continued carrying out assassination attempts and robberies. The need to obtain weapons was always an important objective for Indian terrorists. Various attempts were made to fulfil the need and the second phase of terrorism is notable for one such event. On 26 August 1914, a daring theft was committed at Calcutta's Rodda and Company and fifty Mauser pistols and forty-six thousand rounds of ammunition were taken in this single heist. The government immediately discovered that most of the pistols were distributed amongst the various terrorist groups operating in the province and, consequently, there was a surge in the number of political robberies and murders.[10]

The First World War presented an opportunity to Bengal terrorists to seek outside help in furthering their cause. Accordingly, contact was established with German diplomatic officials based in North America and the Dutch East Indies to ensure shipment of German arms to Bengal.[11] The complex plan, however, came to nothing. In the years after 1915, terrorist acts in Bengal were limited to sporadic acts of political robberies. The exigencies of the First World War provided an opportunity to the colonial government to severely clamp down on the unrest in Bengal.[12] The Defence of India Act was introduced in the province in 1915. This Act, which was originally introduced as a wartime emergency measure, gave the government the right to arrest and hold, without trail, suspected terrorists. The threat of terrorism subsided, albeit for a short while.

The third wave (1919–34)

With the end of the First World War in Europe and the announcement of a series of constitutional reforms in India, the government felt confident enough to lower its vigilance and most of the detainees held in prison under the 1915 Act were released.

The newly freed terrorists did not resume any terrorist activities but were almost immediately caught up in M. K. Gandhi's non-violent Non-Cooperation movement. This movement lasted from December 1920 to February 1922 and witnessed the main terrorist parties, *Anushilan* and *Yugantar* surreptitiously becoming involved with the Congress Party. Members of both groups affiliated themselves with the Bengal Provincial Congress Committee and took part in anti-government agitation led by Congress. District Congress Committees and Calcutta Municipal Corporation offices were used by the terrorists as a pool from which they could find new recruits and finance their activities.[13] This reorganization soon manifested itself with a sudden increase in terrorist activities in 1923 and 1924. Again, a series of arrests were made and, by 1925, the situation in Bengal was brought under control, only for it to relapse again in 1928.

Interestingly, during this time, certain changes were taking place within the terrorist organizations themselves. Long periods of detention had led the terrorists to ask critical questions about their aims and means. A feeling that some sort of regrouping, rethinking and planning was needed began to percolate amongst the members of both *Anushilan* and *Yugantar*. Very soon, the young members began to carve out their own path and formed groups such as *Revolt* or *Advance* group, *Shree Sangha, Deepali Sangha*, and *Benu*. These were small, semi-autonomous groups, with tenuous links to either of the parent bodies. Amongst them, *Benu* changed its name to *Bengal Volunteers* (or 'BV' was it was popularly known) after 1928, and it was this group which, in the following years, became one of the most active and violent terrorist groups in Bengal with most of its attacks directed against Europeans.[14]

Fundamental tactical differences also arose between the old guard and the young activists, with the former strongly against immediate and isolated acts of violence and calling for longer periods of preparation. To the latter, such Fabian tactics reflected the lethargy that seemed to have affected the existing groups.[15] It was also decided that attempts would be made to initiate large-scale revolutionary uprising and pursue guerrilla warfare instead of the individual terrorist acts that had been their modus operandi in the past.[16]

In reality, however, localized actions that sought to make 'examples by deed' continued to take place. A series of suicide attacks continued to be directed against British officials throughout the 1930s.[17] However, it was the Chittagong Armoury Raid of 18 April 1930 that marked the apogee of Bengal terrorism. The attack was planned and led by Surya Sen, a former member of *Yugantar* who had subsequently become a member of the *Revolt* group. The objective of the attack, which targeted government officials and the weapons depot located in Chittagong, a city in the south-east part of the province of Bengal, was to seize control of the district and fight a pitched battle against the British forces, a re-enactment of the Dublin Easter Rising of 1916. Calling themselves the Indian Republican Army, Surya Sen and his group decided to strike during the Easter week of 1930. The raid failed but the sheer audacity of the plan and the involvement of female terrorists in the cause ultimately lent a sense of aura over the Chittagong Uprising of 1930.[18]

Surya Sen's arrest in 1933 and subsequent execution a year later brought an end to the Chittagong Uprising. In fact, it was the swan song of Bengal terrorism. The following years saw changes in the political milieu of India, which left little space for terrorists to operate. Moreover, the years spent in the jungles of Chittagong while evading British police and soldiers had made the terrorists realize the importance of mass contact and a broader concept of the meaning and objective of revolution. Members of Surya Sen's groups who were spared death sentences reflected upon such experiences as they spent years behind bars in the various prisons of Bengal and the penal colony of Andaman Islands.[19] This experience was not only confined to members of the Indian Republican Army. Members of other terrorist groups operating in Bengal also had similar experiences as they spent time in prison and it is interesting to note that a sizeable number of these erstwhile terrorists were imbibed with Marxist teachings and became members of the Communist Party of India or other leftist organizations upon their release from prison. This turn to communism by former terrorists was to have a profound impact upon the subsequent history of Pakistan and Bangladesh.

The composition and motivation of Bengal terrorist groups

The quest for understanding the nature and factors behind the rise and spread of terrorism in early twentieth century Bengal must take into account the nature of indigenous Bengali society and the relationship between its various components. While Muslims made up slightly more than half of Bengal's population, Hindu society itself was divided into various castes and among them there were three upper castes, Brahmans, Vaidyas, and Kayasthas. It was these three castes that were the most important in colonial Bengal as landholders and who also monopolized higher education and the lower and middle-rungs of the colonial civil service.[20] J. Broomfield identified members of these three castes as members of common dominant elite and observes that, in the cities, towns and villages, there was one group of Bengalis who demanded and were accorded recognition as superior in social status to the mass of their fellows. For Broomfield, these were the *bhadralok*, literally the 'respectable people', the 'gentle men'.[21]

In her study of Bengal politics in the last two decades of British colonial rule, Joya Chatterji describes the *bhadralok* as someone whose prosperity was dependent neither on trade nor industry but, rather, land. The Permanent Settlement Act of 1793 had established new property relations in Bengal. It led to the emergence and entrenchment of a *rentier* class, who acquired intermediary tenurial rights to rents from the land.[22] The *bhadralok* was a group that did not work its land but lived off the rental income the land produced. The *bhadralok* gentleman, Chatterji points out, was the antithesis of the calloused peasant working in the field. It was this abhorrence to manual labour that differentiated the 'Babu' from his social inferiors. Thus, 'the title "Babu" – a badge of bhadralok status – carried with it connotations of Hindu, frequently upper caste exclusiveness, of landed wealth, of being master (as opposed to servant) and latterly of possessing the goods of education, culture and Anglicisation'.[23]

The terrorist movement in Bengal was almost exclusively dominated by the *bhadralok* class. Given the fact that it was the *bhadraloks* who benefited the most from British rule in India, it begs the question why members of this group joined the terrorist movement. The following paragraphs attempt to shed light on this conundrum.

The genesis of the terrorist movement in Bengal can be traced to the establishment of *akharas* (gymnasia) in the metropolitan city of Calcutta. The first such gymnasium was set up in 1866 by one Nabagopal Mitra, who also introduced the Hindu mela (fair) in Bengal. 'National' Nabagopal, as he was called, decided that promotion of physical education should be a prominent feature of the Hindu fair, and young men were encouraged to shed their physical weakness through vigorous physical exercise. Indeed, the objective was to transform the human body into a 'sharpened weapon' ready for use. The *bhadralok* had come to see the development of physical faculties as an essential element of 'culture'.[24]

By the beginning of the twentieth century, availing oneself of gymnasium facilities to develop one's physique had become something like a craze among Calcutta's young men. However, to see these gymnasia as venues for developing one's physical prowess would be a mistake. Nirad C. Chaudhuri writes that these institutions were similar to the Prussian gymnastic clubs organized by the poet Friedrich Ludwig Jahn to motivate the German youth to develop themselves as a prelude to their opposition against Napoleon's rule. Similarly, Bengali youths were to be imbibed with the ultimate objective of organizing an armed uprising against British rule. Military power was seen as the key to the political problem.[25] Sarala Debi, a member of one of the famous families of Calcutta, played an important role in setting up gymnasiums and traditional sports meets during the 1890s. In her quest to arouse the militant nationalist physical culture among Bengali youths, she drew her inspiration from the emerging nationalist leader, B. G. Tilak, and Bankimchandra Chattopadhyay's Bengali novels. Swami Vivekananda, an ardent supporter of the need for physical education as a prerequisite for national regeneration, also inspired Sarala Debi and, between them, they influenced some of the leaders of the terrorist movements.[26]

Such an atmosphere was invigorated by events that took place beyond India's borders. The Boer War at the turn of the century triggered mixed feelings amongst the *bhadraloks*. On the one hand, there was a sense of shared triumph as the British defeated the Boers but there was also a part of society which wanted to emulate the Boers.[27] However, it was the Russo-Japanese war of 1905 that triggered a wave of unabashed enthusiasm for Japan.[28] In later years, Bengal terrorists were also encouraged in their use of terrorism by the success of the Irish Republicans in gaining virtual independence for Southern Ireland.

While all of the above-mentioned causes were responsible for the emergence of terrorism, the event that opened the floodgates and led to the long phase of terrorism in Bengal was the partition of the province on 16 October 1905. The partition created resentment among the *bhadralok* class as it was deemed a blatant attempt to divide their motherland and circumscribe their influence in India's political and social fields. A series of political counter-measures were initiated. However, as the limits of the

Swadeshi movement became obvious, terrorism seemed to many as the only way political changes could be brought about in colonial India. As Sumit Sarkar points out in his magisterial study of the *Swadeshi* movement, it was the popular upsurge of 1905 which saved these terrorist groups from a premature demise.[29]

Religion also played a prominent role in the birth and development of terrorism in Bengal. An astute observer of the period had no qualms in admitting that militant nationalism in Bengal rested on twin rocks – the ardent patriotic call of Swami Vivekananda based on the philosophical teachings of Vedanta and Gita, and the religious patriotism propagated by Bankimchandra Chattopadhyay through his book *Anandamath*.[30] In Bengal, Vivekananda called for the betterment of the poor and the downtrodden through education and social service. The chosen instrument for this social change was an order of dedicated monks and nuns who were to be distinguished by their renunciation of the world. Such renunciation was considered by Vivekananda as essential for true service to the motherland. Spirituality and patriotism were not deemed by Vivekananda to be separate from one another.

Bankimchandra's writings from the mid-nineteenth century also provided a powerful stimulus to the terrorist movement. Bankim, a progenitor of modern Bengali literature, wrote *Anandamath* which epitomized the religious patriotism embraced by the terrorist movement. The story revolves around a band of *Sanyasins* (Hindu holy men who have renounced the world) who have come together to rescue their motherland from the anarchy and oppression engulfing it.[31] The *Sanyasins* manifest Bankim's need for a spiritual discipline based on a cultivation of all human faculties, including the physical. Their purpose is to serve one's country in a spirit of total detachment.[32] The *Sanyasins* tried to realize God through their country, a motherland, once glorious, but now reduced to a pitiful entity. She is identified with the mother goddess worshipped as Sakti; that is, power incarnate and, in Bankim, through his famous hymn to the Mother, *Bande Mataram*, the weapon in her ten arms, her infinite strength, and the sharp swords in the hands of her numerous children evoke an image of great power.[33] The powerful imagery of Bankim's *Anandamath* realized its true potential when after 1905, the book became the Bible of the terrorists and *Bande Mataram* was adopted as the unofficial national anthem of the *Swadeshi* movement whose participants were bound to avenge the insult partition had heaped upon Bengal.

Vivekananda and Bankimchandra's ideas provided the impetus for the terrorist movement in Bengal but soon a powerful voice was heard that not only lent a theoretical rationale to the terrorist movement but did so in a way the like of which had seldom been seen before or repeated since in Bengal. Aurobindo Ghosh, the son of a Kayastha doctor, was born in 1872. Educated in England, he returned to India in 1892 and took a bureaucratic position in the native state of Baroda. For the next fourteen years, he worked and wrote from Baroda before shifting to Calcutta and starting a new career in journalism. In Calcutta, Aurobindo became involved with a newspaper called *Yugantar*, and it was from the group of young men who gathered around the newspaper that the terrorist group bearing the same name ultimately evolved.

While at Baroda, Aurobindo wrote a series of articles on Indian politics under the title 'New Lamps for Old'. The articles reflected Aurobindo's mastery of the classics and ancient and modern European history and posed provocative questions about the state of Indian politics.[34] While 'New Lamps for Old' was popular with the people, it was soon overshadowed by a small pamphlet written by Aurobindo in Baroda sometime around the middle of 1905. The piece called *Bhawani Mandir* (Temple of Goddess Bhawani) resembles Bankim's *Anandamath* in that both picture a band of *Sanyasins* who have renounced the world and have dedicated themselves to the service of the country, which is seen as the Mother. However, *Bhawani Mandir's* presiding deity is Durga or Kali and interestingly, Aurobindo used the name Bhawani and thereby established a link between the Maratha general Shivaji who worshipped the mother goddess in the form of Bhawani and said he was acting under her inspiration.[35] Aurobindo was not contented to picture Bhawani as just a deity of the Hindu pantheon. Rather, she was 'the Infinite Energy, which streams forth from the Eternal'. The world envisaged in *Bhawani Mandir* is in constant flux and rejuvenated by a different aspect of the female principle. 'In the present age, the Mother is manifested as the mother of Strength, She is pure Shakti'.[36]

This Shakti was now being put into use by the great empires of the West and Japan, but India was not able to join this group as she has abandoned Shakti. However, all was not lost and India could be reborn:

> For what is a nation? What is our mother country? It is not a piece of earth, nor a figure of speech, nor a fiction of the mind. It is a mighty Shakti, composed of the Shaktis of all the millions of units that make up the nation, just as Bhawani Mahisha Mardini sprang into being from the Shakti of all the millions of gods assembled in one mass of force and welded into unity. The Shakti we call India, Bhawani Bharati, is the living unity of the Shaktis of three hundred million people; but she is inactive, imprisoned in the magic circle of Tamas, the self-indulgent inertia and ignorance of her sons. To get rid of Tamas we have but to wake the Brahma within.[37]

Aurobindo also identified a mission for India. She was 'to purge barbarism (*Mlechchhahood*) out of humanity and to Aryanise the world'.[38] Nowhere in *Bhawani Mandir* does Aurobindo mention the British but what is even more intriguing is that Aurobindo either completely ignores the Muslims or includes them with the barbarians. Leonard Gordon points out that British officials recognized and pointed out in the officials notes they exchanged with each other that by encouraging nationalism in a religious direction men like Aurobindo were exploiting the religious sentiments of the majority Hindus but pushing out and alienating the Muslims. This, Gordon notes, reflects the fact that Aurobindo was following the implicit or explicit anti-Muslim line of the Hindu nationalists and ideologues of the later half of the nineteenth century.[39]

The anti-Muslim stance adopted by Hindu nationalists was constructed and in many instances reinforced by *bhadralok* authors who were at the forefront of Bengali literature. The call for a rejuvenated Bengal went hand in hand with a search for a glorious Hindu past.[40] The literary outpourings of this era aimed at creating a spirit of national pride and self-confidence amongst the *bhadralok* class. The objective was to highlight a tradition of patriotism and glorify Hindu heroes of the past who had bravely fought 'Muslim domination'. Rabindranath Tagore, Bengal's greatest poet, thus eulogized Shivaji and Guru Gobind as nation-builders. Many of Rabindranath's ballads focused upon the patriotism and chivalry of fearless Rajputs, Marathas, and Sikhs as they fought the Muslim Mughal rulers.[41] Others were not far behind. Dwijendralal Roy penned *The Fall of Mewar*, which described the struggle of Mewar against the Mughals. Commenting on these and other literary works, Joya Chatterji observes that such exercises helped construct a direct line of descent from Hindu heroes of the past to modern Bengal and helped the Hindu *bhadralok* to 'appropriate as its ancestors the lesser Rajput and Maratha chieftains who "resisted" the Mughals'.[42]

The terrorist movement in Bengal that took off in the early years of the twentieth century thus owed its origins to a specific cultural and political milieu. Valentine Chirol in his book *Indian Unrest* points out that the *Swadeshi* movement was essentially a movement of Hindu revival.[43] While one may question the neutrality of Chirol in assessing what was a severe challenge to British rule in India, it is interesting to note that Nirad C. Chaudhuri wholly endorses Chirol's observation and writes that it was not the liberal political thought prevailing within the Indian National Congress but the Hindu revivalism of the last decades of the nineteenth century that provided the rationale behind the anti-partition agitation of 1905 and subsequent years.[44] Under such circumstances, it becomes important to ask how the Muslims of Bengal reacted to this movement. The following section shows the reaction of the Muslim community to the events of 1905 and beyond.

Bengali Muslims and Bengal terrorism

In the one hundred and fifty years since the battle of Plassey, which saw the establishment of British rule over Bengal and subsequently over India, Bengali Muslims experienced a traumatic reversal of fortunes. With the end of Muslim rule in Bengal and the introduction of new revenue and education policies by the British rulers, the community lost its hitherto dominant position in Bengal. A series of Muslim uprisings against the British did nothing to endear the community to the new rulers of India.[45]

At the same time, the upper-class Hindus had embraced the opportunities offered by the British and as a result, by the beginning of the twentieth century held an easy and absolute supremacy in the sphere of education and, in consequence, literate professions. This dominance was also manifested in the economic sphere. The Permanent Settlement Act of 1793 had dealt a mortal blow to the Muslim land-owning class and the resulting lacuna had been filled by upper-class Hindus, the group which ultimately came to be identified as the *bhadralok* class. The Act invested the right of proprietorship of the land to the landlord or *zamindar* for perpetuity and consequently, placed the cultivators at the mercy of the *zamindar*. The cultivators were, to all purposes, reduced to a state of semi-bondage.[46] What made the situation complex was the fact that the majority of the cultivators in Eastern Bengal were Muslims while land-holding, professional, and mercantile occupations were dominated by upper-caste Hindus.[47] While there is no reason to believe that Hindu peasants or tenants were treated any better by Hindu *zamindars* and Muslim peasants got an easy ride from the handful of Muslim *zamindars*, the reality is there was always a possibility of communal antagonism lurking beneath the surface. The situation was further aggravated by the fact that the *zamindars* regularly collected illegal 'abwabs' or 'benevolence' from the tenants. Particularly galling were *abwabs* extracted during celebration of Hindu religious festivals, but little could be done against the power of the landlords.[48] The emergence and predominance of a Hindu money-lending class, a direct result of the Permanent Settlement Act, further intensified the misery of the peasants. As a result, the majority of the Muslims cultivators were heavily indebted to the money-lenders' class, almost all of whom were Hindus. Such was the situation in Bengal when the *Swadeshi* movement was launched in 1905.

The partition of Bengal was welcomed by the majority of the Muslims residing in the province. The perceived benefits of a new province in the form of access to education, employment opportunities, and increase in political power made them realize partition would be a boon for them. The *Swadeshi* movement which was started with the objective of rescinding the partition plan certainly did not endear itself to the Muslims. For one thing the movement, originating as it did amongst the *bhadralok* class, could not shake off its religious hue. The movement started with an offering to the Goddess Kali at the Great Kali Temple in Calcutta. While such religious symbolism made it possible for the Hindu masses to identify themselves with the movement, it could not help but arouse uneasiness and hostility in average Muslim minds.[49] Sumit Sarkar points to the various initiatives introduced with a view to bringing the Muslims under the aegis of the *Swadeshi* movement but concedes that such steps were matched and surpassed by the celebration of traditional Hinduism values which acted as a morale-booster for the activists and was the primary political means used by the intelligentsia to mobilize the masses.[50]

There was also an economic rationale behind the apathy of the Muslims towards the *Swadeshi* movement, for it called for a boycott of cheap British manufactured goods and promoted the use of locally manufactured products which were costlier. Refusal to stock and sell such products on the part of Muslim shopkeepers and reluctance on the part of Muslim peasants to buy them often led to instances of 'strong persuasion' by *Swadeshi* activists. Faced with the rhetoric of *Bande Mataram*, which highlighted the Hindu identity of Bengal, pressure on poor Muslims to buy costly *Swadeshi* products and the strong-handed tactics of the Hindu activists, things began to take turn for the worst in Bengal.[51] Riots broke out in various parts of Bengal in 1906–07 and these further imperilled Hindu–Muslim relations.

The terrorist movement in Bengal was spearheaded by *Anushilan* and *Yugantar* and both of these groups found their rationale in *Swadeshi* politics. As the above discussion makes clear, it was difficult for Muslims to identify themselves with the *Swadeshi* cause. Moreover, the upper caste membership of the groups virtually closed any chance of Muslims becoming members of such organization. Also, groups such as *Anushilan* categorically made it clear that under no circumstances were Muslims to be inducted into the organization.[52] That such restrictions continued as late as 1928 was clearly stated by M. Waliullah, a political activist who twice tried to join terrorist organizations operating in Bengal and was rebuffed on both occasions by the groups owing to his religious identity.[53]

The anti-Muslim nature of the terrorist groups did not go unnoticed by the fledgling Muslim press in Bengal. Muslim newspapers were at pains to prove that any terrorist activities would harm the interest of the Bengali Muslims and more importantly, they were concerned at the extreme Hindu nationalist nature of the terrorists. It is therefore not surprising to hear a vernacular newspaper such as *Islam-Pracharak* describe the physical training of Hindu boys as a prelude to an all-out struggle against the British and Muslims and warn that this was to have severe repercussions throughout Bengal. The newspaper warned Muslims against joining such movement which would automatically incur the wrath of the colonial government.[54] The difficulty for Bengali Muslims to identify with the terrorist movement becomes more obvious when one examines the Bengali literature of the period.

In 1926, the novelist Saratchandra Chattopadhyay published one of his most politically significant novels, *Pather Dabi* (The Right of the Way). *Pather Dabi* had begun to appear serially in *Bangabashi* from 1922. It was published in a book form in 1926 and was immediately confiscated by the colonial authorities. The immensely popular novel revolves around the activities of a Bengali terrorist striving for India's freedom. The protagonist, Sabyasachi, is a romantic, larger-than-life figure who lives in the constant shadow of death and leads a life that intrigues and terrifies the audience simultaneously.[55] The same year that *Pather Dabi* was published as a book, Bengal again experienced a series of communal riots. Saratchandra now came out strongly with his own idea of India. In *The Hindu–Muslim Problem of Today*, a paper read at a Hindu *Sabha* meeting in 1926, he categorically said 'Hindustan is the land of Hindus', and Muslims had little or no role to play in India's freedom movement. Muslims were far behind the Hindu community and such a lacuna made it inevitable that differences will continue between the two communities for 'unity can only exist among equals'.[56] While Saratchandra's opinion was certainly influenced by the riots of 1926 and the atrocities committed by both of the communities against each other, it is interesting to note that *Pather Dabi* also contained traces of Saratchandra's views about the exclusive nature of the terrorist movement then prevailing in Bengal. As noted before, *Pather Dabi* came out in 1926 and had a powerful formative influence and provided a deep inspiration to a whole generation of terrorists.[57] What marks out *Pather Dabi* is the belief of the protagonist in terrorism and the futility of other means of political mobilization. No other agents than the *bhadralok* terrorists are deemed qualified enough to lead the movement. As the novel draws to an end, Sabyasachi asks the poet Sashi to forget the peasantry. Instead, Sashi is requested to sing paean to the glorious rebellion of the community of the *bhadralok*; that is, the educated and cultured.[58] Given the fact that the overwhelming section of Bengal's Muslims comprised the peasant class, it is but a small wonder that they could never identify themselves with this movement, which epitomized the yearnings of a tiny hegemonic section of Bengali society.

The contradiction of a terrorist movement led by a tiny elite striving to achieve mass support and its inability to connect with the majority of the population becomes even more obvious when one notices that the terrorist movement in Bengal was unable to tap into the main sources of discontent prevailing within the society. Instead, the terrorist movements themselves tried to maintain the status quo and thereby lost a golden opportunity to mobilize Muslims in particular to their cause. However, given the very nature of the *bhadralok* class, dependent as it was upon rent from the land, it was not possible for the terrorist movement to deal with issues related to the economic life of Bengal, for that would have undermined the very class and way of life for which they were waging this struggle. Perhaps Barbara Southard provided the best summing up of the terrorist movement that prevailed in Bengal for the first three decades of the twentieth century. In her insightful study of Aurobindo Ghosh, she notes that Hindu religious ideology and imagery along with a secular appeal to the political and economic interest of the *zamindar* class were successfully used by Bengali English-educated elite to mobilize the larger rural upper caste group. However, the inability of the ideologues of the terror movement to contemplate the reaction of the Muslims and low-caste Hindu groups to the use of such religious symbols and the apathy of the movement to issues of land and tax reform turned this into a risky strategy which ultimately pushed the Muslims into forming their own organizations, which would take up these issues and struggle for the amelioration of the burdens afflicting the Muslim community of Bengal.[59]

By the early 1930s, some members of Bengal terrorist groups were asking critical questions about the nature and failings of the terrorist movement. Exposure to Marxist literature, contact with members of terrorist organizations of North India who were already strongly influenced by Marxist views, doubts about the utility of a nationalist appeal couched in religious imagery, and the realization that contact with the mass of people was a necessity for any movement to succeed slowly but surely pushed erstwhile terrorists into the fold of Communism.[60] Hatch-Barnwell observes that organizations, even when they have lost their *raison d'être*, try to survive by seeking a new role and the Bengal terror groups were no exception to this rule either. He notes that by the time the Indian subcontinent was partitioned into India and Pakistan both the *Yugantar* and *Anushilan* groups had passed smoothly into the Communist Party of India and into the East Pakistan Communist Party as well.[61]

Conclusion: Pakistan and Bangladesh and Bengal terrorism

As India and Pakistan became two independent states in August 1947, the Communist Party of India tried to reconcile itself with the changed scenario. At the first Party Congress held in February 1948 in Calcutta, the report on the state of the Communist Party in Pakistan was presented by Bhowani Sen. Taking the queer geographical situation of Pakistan into account, Sen called for strengthening the Party as it tried to make inroads into areas where feudalism dominated and trade unions or peasants movements were absent.[62] The Congress also decided that the East Bengal (or East Pakistan) Party would be guided by the West Bengal Communist Party and would retain its link with to the Communist Party of India.[63] Given the fact that the majority of the members of the East Bengal Communist Party were Hindus, and most moved to India in the immediate aftermath of the partition, the party was left with only a couple of hundred members. They, too, were under constant harassment by the East Pakistan government and by 1954 the Communist Party of Pakistan was a banned organization. However, members of the East Pakistan Communist Party, in accordance with decision from party high-ups and Cominform, started joining the Awami League, a party which was soon to become the dominant political party in East Pakistan.[64]

The subsequent history of the development of leftist movement in East Pakistan, its internal squabbling, emergence of different factions, doctrinaire tussles, and its submergence into the Awami League and attempts to break free of it have been admirably covered elsewhere.[65] What is important is that, while the hope of Pakistan as a 'promised land for the chosen people' gradually turned into a faded dream of unfulfilled promise,[66] and disenchantment arose among the people of East Pakistan with Pakistan itself, memories of old, long-forgotten figures were gradually resurrected and began to serve as a tool for the political mobilization of Bengalis or East Pakistanis against the domination of West Pakistan. A process of social diffusion,[67] which was spurred on by affinities such as common Bengali heritage and language, helped in the creation of new Bengali identity that gradually came into conflict with the religious identity responsible for the creation of Pakistan. Cultural activists played a prominent role in this process and given the fact that leftist-inspired activists were at the forefront of this cultural renaissance, it is not surprising to note that events that high-lighted Bengali achievements were increasingly brought to the forefront.[68] The 1952 language movement, the love–hate relationship with the West Pakistani ruling elite, and the gradually felt need for autonomy that trans-formed into a call for independence all saw the emergence and development of an East Bengali culture that acted as a domain – a collec-tive resource that fuelled Bengali solidarity across societal, economic, and religious divisions.[69] Thus, the 1971 war that led to the birth of Bangladesh as an independent state saw the use of Surya Sen and his female associate, Pritilata Waddadar, as inspiring figures urging Bengalis to fight for freedom and led to the reinstatement of Bengal terrorists of the early twentieth century as national heroes in Bangladesh.[70] Perhaps, the renaming of M.A. Jinnah dormitory at the University of Dhaka after Surya Sen immediately after the independence of the country in 1971 symbolizes, more than anything else, the ambiguity which has characterized the Bengali Muslims view about Bengal terrorism.

Bengal terrorism is a somewhat forgotten episode in the annals of terror-ism. This is not surprising given that it took place in a far-off part of the British Indian Empire. However, as this chapter has shown, Bengal terror-ists emerged at a particular juncture of India's colonial history and epitomized the cross-currents that flowed in colonial Bengal. Moreover, Bengal terrorism divided Muslim opinion and this chapter has tried to portray this little-discussed aspect of Bengal terrorism. While the term 'revolutionary' was often used to describe Bengal terrorism, I argue that it was not the case. Rather, terrorism in Bengal was initiated and sustained by a tiny social elite. This elite's religious orientation and economic and polit-ical views prevented the terrorists from reaching out to Bengali Muslims, who constituted more than half of Bengal's population. The creation of Pakistan in 1947 and the emergence of Bangladesh in 1971 did little to resolve the conundrum of Bengal terrorism to Bengali Muslims. How and why Bengal terrorism became a cultural and political landmark for East Pakistanis-turned-Bangladeshis is an interesting field that deserves an academic discussion of its own.

Notes

1   For a brilliant description of the partition plan and its impact, see S. Sarkar, *The Swadeshi Movement in Bengal 1903–1908*, New Delhi: People's Publishing House, 1973.
2   On the Delhi Durbar of 1911, see B.D. Metcalf and T.R. Metcalf, *A Concise History of Modern India*, 2nd ed., Cambridge: Cambridge University Press, 2006, pp. 161–2.
3   I have borrowed the idea of waves of terrorist activities from David C. Rapoport. See D.C. Rapoport, 'The Fourth Wave: September 11 in the History of Terrorism', *Current History*, 2001, vol. 100, pp. 419–24.
4   K. Kumar Banerjee, *Indian Freedom Movement Revolutionaries in America*, Calcutta: Jijnasa, 1969.
5   On Bal Gangadhar Tilak's life, the murder of Walter Rand, and the Chapekar brothers, see V. Chirol, *Indian Unrest*, London: Macmillan and Co. Limited, 1910, pp. 37–63; S. Roy, *Bharater Jatiyatabadi Baiplabik Sangram (1893–1947)*, Kolkata: Radical Impression, 2006, pp. 43–57.
6   A. Kumar Gupta, 'Defying Death: Nationalist Revolutionism in India, 1897–1938', in M. Gupta and A. Kumar Gupta (eds), *Defying Death: Struggles against Imperialism and Feudalism*, New Delhi: Tulika, 2001, p. 40.
7   On the genesis of terrorist groups in Bengal and their modus operandi, see R.C. Majumdar, *History of the Freedom Movement in India, Volume II*, Calcutta: Firma K. L. Mukhopadhyay, 1963, pp. 266–8.
8   R.C. Majumdar, *History of the Freedom Movement in India, Volume II*, Calcutta: Firma K. L. Mukhopadhyay, 1963, p. 268.
9   An excellent description of the Maniktola secret society can be found in P. Heehs, *The Bomb in Bengal: The Rise of Revolutionary Terrorism in India 1900–1910*, Oxford: Oxford University Press, 1993.
10 D.M. Laushey, *Bengal Terrorism and The Marxist Left: Aspects of Regional Nationalism in India, 1905–1942*, Calcutta: Firma K. L. Mukhopadhyay, 1975, p. 11; also see L.A. Gordon, 'Portrait of a Bengal Revolutionary', *Journal of Asian Studies*, 1968, vol. 27, pp. 208–9.
11 K. Kumar Banerjee, *Indian Freedom Movement Revolutionaries in America*, Calcutta: Jijnasa, 1969, pp. 31–6.
12 On the challenges facing the colonial government in using law to suppress terrorists in Bengal, see V. Lal, 'The Rhetorical and Substantive Basis of the "Rule of Law" under Colonialism: The Suppression of Terrorism in Bengal in the early Twentieth Century'. Available online: www.vinaylal.com/9.html (accessed 3 September 2011).
13 D. Ghosh 'Terrorism in Bengal: Political Violence in the Interwar Years', in D. Ghosh and D. Kennedy (eds), *Decentring Empire: Britain, India and the Transcolonial World*, Delhi: Orient Longman, 2006, p. 278.
14 D.M. Laushey, *Bengal Terrorism and The Marxist Left: Aspects of Regional Nationalism in India, 1905–1942*, Calcutta: Firma K. L. Mukhopadhyay, 1975, p. 61; see S. Roy, *Bharater Jatiyatabadi Baiplabik Sangram (1893–1947)*, Kolkata: Radical Impression, 2006, pp. 258–97.
15 T. Sarkar, *Bengal, 1928–1934: The Politics of Protest*, Delhi: Oxford University Press, 1987, pp. 33–4.

16   D.M. Laushey, *Bengal Terrorism and The Marxist Left: Aspects of Regional Nationalism in India, 1905–1942*, Calcutta: Firma K. L. Mukhopadhyay, 1975, p. 43.

17   D.M. Laushey, *Bengal Terrorism and The Marxist Left: Aspects of Regional Nationalism in India, 1905–1942*, Calcutta: Firma K. L. Mukhopadhyay, 1975, p. 76.

18   On the Chittagong Uprising of 1930, see M. Chaterjee, *Do & Die: The Chittagong Uprising 1930–1934*, Basingstoke: Picador, 2010.

19   T. Sarkar, *Bengal, 1928–1934: The Politics of Protest*, Delhi: Oxford University Press, 1987, p. 154.

20   B. Southard, 'The Political Strategy of Aurobindo Ghosh: The Utilization of Hindu Religious Symbolism and the Problem of Political Mobilization in Bengal', *Modern Asian Studies*, 1980, vol. 14, p. 354.

21   J.H. Broomfield, *Elite Conflict in a Plural Society: Twentieth-Century Bengal*, Berkeley/Los Angeles: University of California Press, 1968, p. 5.

22   R. Guha, *A Rule of Property for Bengal: An Essay on the Idea of Permanent Settlement*, 2nd ed., New Delhi: Orient Longman, 1981.

23   J. Chatterji, *Bengal Divided: Hindu Communalism and Partition, 1932–1947*, Cambridge: Cambridge University Press, 2002, pp. 4–5.

24   T. Raychaudhuri, *Europe Reconsidered: Perceptions of the West in Nineteenth-Century Bengal*, New Delhi: Oxford University Press, 2006, p. 153.

25   N.C. Chaudhuri, *The Autobiography of an Unknown Indian*, New Delhi: Jaico Publishing House, 1991, p. 251.

26   J.Rosselli, 'The Self-Image of Effeteness: Physical Education and Nationalism in Nineteenth-Century Bengal', *Past and Present*, 1980, vol. 86, p. 130.

27   N.C. Chaudhuri, *The Autobiography of an Unknown Indian*, New Delhi: Jaico Publishing House, 1991, p. 108.

28   A. Ghosh, 'The Bourgeois and the Samurai', in Sri Aurobindo (ed.) *On Nationalism: Selected Writings and Speeches*, 2nd ed., Pondicherry: Sri Aurobindo Ashram, 1996, pp. 335–54.

29   T. Sarkar, *Bengal, 1928–1934: The Politics of Protest*, Delhi: Oxford University Press, 1987, pp. 472–83.

30   R.C. Majumdar, *History of the Freedom Movement in India, Volume II*, Calcutta: Firma K. L. Mukhopadhyay, 1963, p. 67.

31   B. Chattopadhyay, 'Anandamath', *Bankim Rachanabali Volume I*, Calcutta: Sahitya Sangsad, 1982, pp. 663–736.

32   T. Raychaudhuri, *Europe Reconsidered: Perceptions of the West in Nineteenth-Century Bengal*, New Delhi: Oxford University Press, 2006, p. 135.

33   Ibid.

34   A. Ghosh, 'The Bourgeois and the Samurai', in Sri Aurobindo (ed.) *On Nationalism: Selected Writings and Speeches*, 2nd ed., Pondicherry: Sri Aurobindo Ashram, 1996, pp. 9–62.

35   P. Heehs, *The Bomb in Bengal: The Rise of Revolutionary Terrorism in India 1900–1910*, Oxford: Oxford University Press, 1993, pp. 65–6.

36   A. Ghosh, 'The Bourgeois and the Samurai', in Sri Aurobindo (ed.) *On Nationalism: Selected Writings and Speeches*, 2nd ed., Pondicherry: Sri Aurobindo Ashram, 1996, p. 67.

37   A. Ghosh, 'The Bourgeois and the Samurai', in Sri Aurobindo (ed.) *On Nationalism: Selected Writings and Speeches*, 2nd ed., Pondicherry: Sri Aurobindo Ashram, 1996, p. 69.

38 A. Ghosh, 'The Bourgeois and the Samurai', in Sri Aurobindo (ed.) *On Nationalism: Selected Writings and Speeches*, 2nd ed., Pondicherry: Sri Aurobindo Ashram, 1996, p. 70.
39 L.A. Gordon, *Bengal: The Nationalist Movement 1876–1940*, New Delhi: Manohar, 1974, p. 114.
40 P. Chatterjee, *The Nation And Its Fragments: Colonial And Postcolonial Histories*, Delhi: Oxford University Press, 1995, pp. 76–115; also see S. Sen, *Muslim Politics in Bengal 1937–1947*, New Delhi: Impex India, 1976, pp. 23–4.
41 R.C. Majumdar, *History of the Freedom Movement in India, Volume II*, Calcutta: Firma K. L. Mukhopadhyay, 1963, pp. 142–4.
42 J. Chatterji, *Bengal Divided: Hindu Communalism and Partition, 1932–1947*, Cambridge: Cambridge University Press, 2002, p. 160.
43 V. Chirol, *Indian Unrest*, London: Macmillan and Co. Limited, 1910, pp. 24–36.
44 N.C. Chaudhuri, *The Autobiography of an Unknown Indian*, New Delhi: Jaico Publishing House, 1991, pp. 231–2.
45 S. Islam, 'Resistance Movements and Rebellion in Eighteenth and Nineteenth Century', in Sirajul Islam (ed.) *History of Bangladesh: 1704–1971, Volume I*, Dhaka: Asiatic Society of Bangladesh, December 1993, pp. 126–55.
46 S. Sen, *Muslim Politics in Bengal 1937–1947*, New Delhi: Impex India, 1976, p. 18.
47 R. Ahmed, *The Bengal Muslims 1871–1906: A Quest for Identity*, New Delhi: Oxford University Press, 1998.
48 For an interesting description of '*abwab*' and the rancor it generated, see A. Mansur Ahmed, *Fifty Years of Politics As I Saw It*, 2nd ed., Dhaka: Nawroz Kitabistan, 1970, p. 22.
49 S. Ahmed, *Muslim Community in Bengal 1884–1912*, Dhaka: Oxford University Press, 1974, pp. 258–9.
50 S. Sarkar, 'Hindu–Muslim Relations in Swadeshi Bengal, 1903–1908', *Indian Economic and Social History Review*, 1972, vol. 2, pp. 176–7.
51 B.D. Metcalf and T.R. Metcalf, *A Concise History of Modern India*, 2nd ed., Cambridge: Cambridge University Press, 2006, p. 159.
52 S. Roy, *Bharater Jatiyatabadi Baiplabik Sangram (1893–1947)*, Kolkata: Radical Impression, 2006, p. 78.
53 M. Waliullah, *Juga-Bichitra (A Reminiscence)*, Dhaka: Mowla Brothers, 1997, p. 201.
54 E. Ma'az, 'Bharater rajnaitik sbastha o Musalman jatir kartabya', *Islam-Pracharak*, 8th year, no. 4, *Jyaistha*, 1314 B.S. (1907) quoted in M. Nurul Islam, *Bengali Muslim Opinion as Reflected In The Bengali Press 1901–1930*, Dhaka: Bangla Academy, 2003, p. 45.
55 H. Kabir, *The Bengali Novel*, Calcutta: Firma K. L. Mukhopadhyay, 1968, p. 79.
56 S. Chattopadhyay, 'Bartaman Hindu-Mussalman Samasya', in *Sarat Sahitya Shomuho, Volume II*, Calcutta: Ananda Publishers Private Limited, 1986, pp. 2134–6.
57 T. Sarkar, 'Bengali Middle-Class Nationalism and Literature: A Study of Saratchandra's "Pather Dabi" and Rabindranath's "Char Adhyay"', in D.N. Panigrahi (ed.) *Economy, Society and Politics in India*, New Delhi: Vikas, 1985, p. 454.
58 S. Chattopadhyay, 'Bartaman Hindu-Mussalman Samasya', in *Sarat Sahitya Shomuho, Volume II*, Calcutta: Ananda Publishers Private Limited, 1986, p. 1245.

59   B. Southard, 'The Political Strategy of Aurobindo Ghosh: The Utilization of
     Hindu Religious Symbolism and the Problem of Political Mobilization in
     Bengal', *Modern Asian Studies*, 1980, vol. 14: 375–6.
60   T. Sarkar, 'Bengali Middle-Class Nationalism and Literature: A Study of
     Saratchandra's "Pather Dabi" and Rabindranath's "Char Adhyay"', in D.N.
     Panigrahi (ed.) *Economy, Society and Politics in India*, New Delhi: Vikas, 1985,
     p. 123; D.M. Laushey, *Bengal Terrorism and The Marxist Left: Aspects of Regional
     Nationalism in India, 1905–1942*, Calcutta: Firma K. L. Mukhopadhyay, 1975,
     pp. 99–120.
61   S. Hatch-Barnwell, *The Last Guardian: Memoirs of Hatch-Barnwell, ICS of Bengal*,
     Dhaka: The University Press Limited, 2011, p. 25.
62   H. Malik, 'The Marxist Literary Movement in India and Pakistan', *Journal of
     Asian Studies*, 1967, vol. 26, p. 659.
63   K. Asdar Ali, 'Communists in a Muslim Land: Cultural Debates in Pakistan's
     Early Years', *Modern Asian Studies*, 2011, vol. 45, pp. 513–14.
64   T. Maniruzzaman, *The Bangladesh Revolution and Its Aftermath*, Dhaka: The
     University Press Limited, 2003, pp. 35–6.
65   S. Mahmud Ali, *Understanding Bangladesh*, New York: Columbia University Press,
     2010, pp. 296–308.
66   On the sense of disappointment of Bengali Muslims with the state of Pakistan,
     see A. Kamal, *State Against The Nation: The Decline of the Muslim League in Pre-
     Independence Bangladesh, 1947-54*, Dhaka: The University Press Limited, 2009.
67   On social diffusion, see, P. Kowert and J. Legro, 'Norms, Identity, and Their
     Limits: A Theoretical Reprise', in P.J. Katzenstein (ed.) *The Culture of National
     Security: Norms and Identity in World Politics*, New York: Columbia University
     Press, 1996, pp. 474–5.
68   J. Sarker, *Pakistaner Janmomrittu Darshon*, 2nd ed.,Dhaka: Jatiya Sahitya Prakash,
     2007, p. 452.
69   W. Van Schendel, *A History of Bangladesh*, Cambridge: Cambridge University
     Press, 2009, p. 158; on the role of East Pakistani communists in the 1952
     Language Movement, see B. Umar, *Language Movement in East Bengal*, Dhaka:
     Jatiya Grontha Prakashan, 2000.
70   W. Van Schendel, *A History of Bangladesh*, Cambridge: Cambridge University
     Press, 2009, p. 208.

10 SWAPO, the United Nations, and the struggle for national liberation

Shaloma Gauthier

Introduction

During the wave of decolonization in Africa, armed struggle was used by a number of liberation movements as a means to carry out their 'inalienable' right to self-determination. Such was the case regarding Namibia's turbulent road to independence. Between 1960 and the attainment of its independence in 1990, the South West Africa People's Organization (SWAPO) fought tenaciously for the liberation of Namibia from South African occupation. At the outset of its emergence, this movement maintained, 'we have no alternative but to rise up in arms and bring about our liberation'.[1] SWAPO had widespread international support, as evidenced through many United Nations (UN) General Assembly and Security Council Resolutions. Leading scholar on terrorism, David C. Rapoport classifies the events regarding movements of national liberation within the third 'wave' of modern terrorism, as this violence was a manifestation of the struggle to assert self-determination.[2] In essence, it was a dimension of terrorism that was characterized by the resistance 'against larger political power…specifically designated to win political independence or autonomy'.[3] In this chapter, terrorism will be viewed as the deliberate use of violence or the threat of violence against civilians with the intent of achieving a specific ideological or political objective. Terrorism is also linked to generating an atmosphere of violence within a specific population.[4]

During this wave described by Rapoport, the lines became increasingly blurred between terrorism and the activities that were centred upon revolutionary goals. This was particularly the case for a number of nationalist groups that arose in Asia, Africa, and the Middle East in the 1940s through to the 1960s. Violence invoked against colonial domination was seen in a different light. In a statement to the UN General Assembly in November 1974, former Palestine Liberation Organization chairperson Yasser Arafat maintained:

> The difference between the revolutionary and the terrorist lies in the reason for which each fights. For whoever stands by a just cause and

fights for the freedom and liberation of his land from the invaders, the settlers and the colonialists, cannot possibly be called terrorist.[5]

Hence, in this line of argumentation, if the propelling motivations for the fight were 'just', the violent acts were deemed to be within reason. However, is this really the case? Could some of the activities carried out by SWAPO be referred to as incidents of terror?[6] Today, a number of liberation movements, such as the African National Congress, the Zimbabwe African National Union, and Frente de Libertação de Moçambique (Frelimo), to name a few, are referred to as 'terrorist organizations'.[7] It is interesting to note that SWAPO is similarly listed among these organizations.

A re-examination of some of the activities carried out by SWAPO raises the issue of the use of force by national liberation[8] movements and instances where they veered towards 'terror' methods. Contemporary Western jurists point to the dangers of a sweeping and broad application of the principle of self-determination that could result in the use of terror-violence.[9]

This chapter begins with a brief historical overview of the events that transpired regarding the status of South West Africa, followed by a review of the establishment of SWAPO. The proactive stance taken by the UN General Assembly and other UN committees and its close relationship with SWAPO are examined. South Africa was firm in maintaining that SWAPO perpetrated acts of 'terrorism'. In this vein, South Africa pursued a vigorous campaign to quell the activities of the organization, including the prosecution of alleged SWAPO terrorists. The 1970s marked a phase of increased violence within SWAPO, not only against South Africa, but against individuals from its organization. During this period, the UN had significant difficulty in determining a clear definition of 'terrorism'.[10] However, it could be deduced from some of the discussions in the UN that violence was not to be carried against innocent civilians. For instance, General Assembly Resolution 2444 proscribed violence against civilians and requested that a 'distinction be made at all times between persons taking part in the hostilities and members of the civilian populations'.[11] Did SWAPO remain committed to these principles? Did the significant international support that SWAPO was granted by the UN signify that it was able to use any force at its disposal? There is a vast historiography on Namibia's struggle and tumultuous road to independence.[12] Various authors have explored the excessive use of violence employed by SWAPO against its own members.[13] However, this chapter seeks to go a step further by re-evaluating these aspects and examining the UN's rapport with SWAPO. This study draws significantly from documents at the UN Archives in New York and the British National Archives in Kew, as well as a wide array of monographs, legal journals, and newspaper articles.

South Africa's hold over South West Africa

South Africa's possessive hold over South West Africa began during the First World War.[14] According to the terms of the 1919 peace settlement, it was decided that the territory would be placed under a League of Nations mandate to be administered by the Union of South Africa.[15] After the dissolution of the League of Nations in 1946, the mandate system was supplanted by the trusteeship system under the UN. In lieu of transferring South West Africa under this form of international administration, South Africa had alternate plans. In November 1946, South Africa issued a request before the UN General Assembly for the incorporation of South West Africa into its territory.[16] However, the General Assembly passed a unanimous resolution repudiating the request. Instead, it suggested that South West Africa be put under the trusteeship system.[17] South Africa pursued a policy of gradual encroachment, as was evident in the contentious South West Africa Affairs Amendment Act 23 in 1949. This legislation sought to establish a 'closer association' between the territory and South Africa.[18] South Africa began to treat South West Africa as though it were its fifth province. The racially discriminatory laws and regulations of the apartheid[19] policy were also applied in the territory, resulting in considerable outrage at the UN.[20]

The UN raised the issue of South Africa's legal obligations towards South West Africa before the International Court of Justice (ICJ) in 1946. An intense legal debate ensued and several advisory opinions were issued throughout the 1950s.[21] The UN officially terminated the League of Nations mandate in accordance with General Assembly Resolution 2145 on 27 October 1966 and 'assumed direct responsibility of the Territory of South West Africa',[22] thus marking the beginning of the special relationship between the UN and South West Africa. The ICJ judgment with the most weight was issued in 1971 after the Security Council requested that the issue be re-examined by the Court.[23] The ICJ deemed South Africa's continued presence in Namibia[24] to be illegal and urged South Africa to remove itself from the territory.[25] Some of the opinions had implications for movements of national liberation. For instance, Judge Ammoun of the ICJ stated that the Namibia case demonstrated that the international community considered the use of arms to be legitimate in the pursuit of self-defence.[26] The other Member States of the UN were likewise encouraged to affirm that South Africa's occupation of Namibia was illegal.[27] Accordingly, they were to refrain from partaking in any activity that might serve to uphold or support South Africa.[28] Furthermore, Member States of the UN were encouraged to provide assistance and to support its position towards Namibia.

In 1974, the Security Council reiterated and affirmed the ICJ advisory opinion.[29] The UN's commitment to resolve the situation was further evident in Security Council Resolution 435, which called for a ceasefire and

UN supervised elections in Namibia.[30] It was under the auspices of this mission that the United Nations Transition Assistance Group (UNTAG) was created, with the objective of assisting Namibia with free and fair elections. SWAPO would be a pivotal player in this process, as it was acknowledged that many of these talks would have to take place between SWAPO and South Africa.[31] This historical background serves to illustrate the degree to which the UN upheld South West Africa's struggle against South Africa.

SWAPO: the face of Namibian liberation

Within South West Africa, a number of organizations were established in protest of South African occupation and its racially discriminatory policies. Pockets of resistance began to emerge among some of the inhabitants of South West Africa.[32] The Ovamboland People's Congress was one of the first groups to emerge in Cape Town in the late 1950s, under the leadership of Andimba Toivo JA Toivo. It later became part of the Ovamboland People's Organization,[33] which was led by Sam Nujoma.[34] There was a flurry of activism during this period, as a number of other groups, such as the South West African National Union (SWANU) came into being. In 1959, the Ovamboland People's Congress was renamed South West Africa People's Organization. The strained relations between South Africa and South West Africa reached a climax in 1959, when the former tried to enforce the compulsory removal of inhabitants of the 'Old Location' in Windhoek, in order to conform to the newly introduced apartheid-structured townships of Katutura. In response, Nujoma led a protest, which resulted in the death of twelve protestors. The organizers of the 'dissidence' were pursued and detained by the South African security forces, with the exception of Nujoma, who was able to seek refuge across the border.[35]

It was at this juncture that Nujoma, the charismatic leader and public face of SWAPO, became proactive in fostering networks abroad. In an effort to garner support, Nujoma went to the UN General Assembly in New York. He presented himself in front of the 4th UN Decolonization Committee, where he discussed his 'Hands off South West Africa' platform.[36] In 1961, SWAPO established an office in Dar es Salaam in Tanzania. The first SWAPO national congress was convened in Windhoek in that same year, during which the launching of an 'armed revolution'[37] was proclaimed. Various measures were immediately taken in this regard. The People's Liberation Army of Namibia (PLAN) was established in 1962 to carry out the armed struggle. In 1964, the newly established 'Liberation Committee' of the Organization of African Unity (OAU)[38] asked both SWANU and SWAPO if they were prepared to use armed force against South Africa's occupation of Namibia. SWANU hesitated, whereas SWAPO indicated that it was eager to do so.[39] As a result, the OAU acknowledged

SWAPO as the 'official' liberation organization.[40] The willingness to resort to force in the pursuit of their objective was captured by Nujoma, who declared on 18 July 1966, 'we must at once begin crossing the many rivers of blood on our march towards freedom'.[41] Hence, the discourse on liberation was closely related to the use of violence. The elevation of one organization over the other is highly relevant. Deputy Secretary General of the OAU, Mr. Mohamed Sahnoun, stated in April 1969:

> Because SWANU is not serious, it does not want freedom; its leaders and members are all in Europe and not in Africa; the leaders of other parties are in Africa, I see them; some are even in my own country (Algeria) in military training camps. Other parties such as the African National Congress (ANC), Zimbabwe African Peoples Union (ZAPU), SWAPO are fighting in a guerrilla warfare, and you are not.[42]

In essence, SWANU was not deemed to be a committed organization, as it expressed a hesitancy to resort to the use of force. However, the organization maintained that it firmly believed in the importance of having a clearly defined mandate and in the necessity of being backed by a number of people instead of just being a 'handful of roving disorganized refugees having their bases in far-away places like Cairo, Algeria, Dar es Salaam'.[43]

The leaders of SWAPO clearly conveyed the fact that military efforts needed to be pursued in tandem with political aims. They deemed these two facets to be largely 'complementary, and not contradictory'.[44] SWAPO was proactive in bolstering its military experience. Trainees were sent to Algeria, China, Cuba, Egypt, and North Korea.[45] There was also a significant degree of support from the Eastern bloc, as a number of individuals led by SWAPO went to the USSR in October 1969.[46] Upon its founding, SWAPO's ideology was that 'Our struggle is not an ideological struggle...the only influence is the oppression we are getting from the Boers...We didn't need any ideology to convince these people'.[47] Hence, their mandate was centred upon the termination of colonial domination over the territory and the attainment of self-government for the people of South West Africa.[48] From the outset, Nujoma affirmed, 'As long as South Africa does not meet our demands, we of SWAPO will continue, extend and intensify the armed liberation struggle'.[49] However, as the years progressed, SWAPO started to demonstrate a proclivity towards the tenets of 'scientific socialism'.[50] However, this was not an aspect that SWAPO was keen on broadcasting. As Nujoma stated, 'We believe in socialism, we want to create a socialist state, but we don't want to announce it'.[51]

An important aspect to retain is that the leaders of SWAPO were largely in exile and were therefore cut off from the people that they were representing.[52] However, the organization used this aspect to its advantage and sought to draw as much support as possible from the international community through a series of comprehensive diplomatic manoeuvres.[53] A significant degree of support emanated from the UN. This was evidenced through the establishment of the UN Council for Namibia on 19 May 1967. The Council was the '*de jure* government of the territory'[54] and was supposed to oversee the administration of the territory. Upon the attainment of independence, the responsibilities acquired by the Council were to be handed over to the 'people of Namibia'.[55] The UN's consistent support was further evidenced in March 1969, when the Security Council stated:

> the continued presence of South Africa in Namibia is illegal and contrary to the principles of the Charter and the previous decisions of the United Nations and is detrimental to the interests of the population of the territory and of those of the international community.[56]

The fruits of the diplomatic endeavours undertaken by SWAPO were confirmed by the 1973 General Assembly Resolution 3111, which maintained that SWAPO was the 'authentic representative of the Namibian people'.[57] This was rather symbolic and significant, as it endowed SWAPO with a 'quasi-international personality'.[58] The UN deemed it to be the voice and 'true representative of the Namibian people'.[59] This served to grant SWAPO international legitimacy and further endorsed their armed struggle against South Africa.

These decisions coincided with a vocal stance endorsing movements of national liberation.[60] General Assembly Resolution 3103 denounced colonialism as a 'crime'[61] and recognized the 'inherent right to struggle by all necessary means at their disposal against colonial Powers and alien domination in exercise of their right of self-determination'.[62] SWAPO reiterated this link between self-determination and the right to wage a war of national liberation. For instance, in a statement issued by the movement of national liberation:

> The Declaration [on the Granting of Independent to Colonial Countries and Peoples] treats it as a part of the legal duties stemming from the Charter and it may be argued that it forms a part of the *jus cogens* of international law. It is a right which accrues in favour of a people. If it is forcibly denied then, under article 51 of the Charter of the United Nations, they have a right to defend themselves and their territory; the more so, against an illegal occupier. A people's liberation war can be clearly identified as defensive action within the meaning of the Charter.[63]

When discussing the legitimacy of SWAPO's activities and, more generally, movements of national liberation, contemporary Ghanaian jurist, Edward Kwakwa, argued that the current situation in the world was supportive of the activities of various liberation groups such as SWAPO, who were fighting for self-determination and that 'the present state of international relations suggest the legitimacy of the use of force in pursuit of basic human dignity'.[64]

However, this opinion was not unanimously upheld. According to contemporary American jurist, Robert Friedlander, Resolution 3103 'provides to these insurrections and rebellions the colour of legitimacy under international law'.[65] He further maintained that this resulted in creating an 'unholy alliance of nationalism and terrorism'.[66] To what extent could the principles of self-determination justify the widespread use of violence in the pursuit of national liberation? Furthermore, there were a number of studies published at this time that were critical of the UN's endorsement of groups such as SWAPO.[67] For example, one study commissioned by the Heritage Foundation in Washington maintained that the UN General Assembly was approving and endorsing the activities of a 'terrorist group'.[68] These two viewpoints represent some of the diametrical opinions that were expressed on the issue of SWAPO's use of force. Such ambiguity was, however, not to be found in the UN, as the latter's involvement with SWAPO steadily increased.

South Africa and SWAPO 'terrorists'

The first armed outbreak between South African security forces and SWAPO occurred on 26 August 1966. SWAPO's strategy consisted of hit-and-run raids against South African military camps and other targets.[69] SWAPO also carried out guerrilla attacks in Ovamboland against white farmers and chiefs who supported South Africa.[70] The South African Defense Forces (SADF) launched a vigorous counter-insurgency and a programme to denounce the SWAPO 'terrorists'. In 1966, it pursued the widespread arrests of political leaders of SWAPO, individuals implicated with the organization, or those who had received military training.[71] These individuals were imprisoned for a year until South Africa passed the Terrorism Act, No. 83 of 1967. Thirty-seven South West Africans were tried for their involvement in 'terroristic activities'. For instance, Section 2 of the Act stipulated that any individual who wilfully sought to imperil the maintenance of law and order in South Africa and South West Africa was 'liable on conviction to the penalties for treason, which include the death penalty'.[72] Thirty of the detained were convicted by the Court of having committed offences under the Terrorism Act and three were guilty on 'alternative charges of contravening' the Suppression of Communism Act. Nineteen of the above-mentioned were condemned to life imprisonment.[73] In his defence statement, SWAPO member Toivo Herman JA Toivo, stated:

> Is it surprising that in such times my countrymen have taken up arms? Violence is truly fearsome, but who would not defend his property and himself against a robber? And we believe that South Africa has robbed us of our country.[74]

These actions by South Africa immediately generated a great deal of criticism, as General Assembly Resolution 2324 denounced the 'illegal arrests, deportation and trial' of the individuals.[75] This resolution further maintained that South Africa no longer had jurisdiction over the territory and could, therefore, not proceed with the trying of these individuals.

SWAPO's military strategy and incursions into the disputed territory were bolstered by the events in neighbouring Angola. After five centuries of domination, the Portuguese presence in Angola came to an end.[76] Angola was declared independent on 25 June 1975. This was a momentous event for SWAPO, as it opened a new door for entry into Namibia from the Angolan border and clearly demonstrated that independence could be obtained through armed struggle.[77] This also added a further dimension to the conflict as it now encompassed neighbouring countries.[78]

South Africa was vocal about its tumultuous relationship with the South West African guerrilla forces. South Africa documented lists of violations and sent them to the UN and other governments. This 'creature of violence'[79] was accused of carrying out shootings of innocent civilians, attacks on various villages, rapes,[80] knifings, using grenades, and terrorizing local populations.[81] A letter from the South African Minister of Foreign Affairs declared:

> Neither the United Nations nor the South African Government can afford to allow them to be held ransom by an organization of violence which, as recently as last week, has plainly demonstrated by its truculent attack that it intends to install itself in power by *force and terror*. It has as recently as this year on more than one occasion indicated in statements that this indeed is its chosen path.[82]

There is a similar record of this information from South Africa which outlines the military attacks carried out by these 'terrorists'.[83] It was reported, in April 1977, that one hundred and twenty children and six teachers were taken from a school in northeast Owambo. Other kidnappings were also carried out on 24 February 1978 when two hundred and forty children were abducted from a school on the border and taken to guerrilla training camps.[84] As the conflict between SWAPO and South Africa persisted, a South African Permanent Representative maintained 'SWAPO terrorists were moving southward to attack the civilian population of South West Africa/Namibia'.[85]

However, within the UN, there was more of a focus on the 'repression of Namibians' and 'internal repression', which was consistently being enforced by South Africa.[86] South Africa expressed dismay at the lack of action taken by the UN in light of these reports and maintained that it was ignoring the 'acts of terror perpetrated by SWAPO'.[87] The UN's stance was demonstrated in the following statement issued by the Council for Namibia, 'the Pretoria regime, flaunting the decisions of the Security

Council, is manoeuvring to install in Namibia a puppet regime of hand-picked tribal elements and racist supporters of apartheid'.[88] Therefore, little regard was given concerning these claims of 'terrorism' perpetrated by SWAPO.

The reports issued by South Africa were drastically de-legitimized by the fact that the SADF pursued a repressive campaign of terror as a means to curb SWAPO's activities. For instance, in the Cassinga incident on 4 May 1978, South African forces killed over six hundred Namibian refugees, including a number of women and children.[89] Moreover, South African battalions frequently went into Angola and attacked not only SWAPO guerrillas, but Angolan civilians as well.[90] One author maintains that, when comparing and contrasting the force used by South African Defence Forces and SWAPO, 'SWAPO's... guerrilla operations were small-scale (and) caused only limited casualties and avoided indiscriminate attacks on civilians'.[91]

One critical voice that was levelled against SWAPO emanated from the United States (US). In fact, claims that SWAPO was perpetrating terrorist acts were not so easily dismissed by the US. Throughout this struggle, the US had a rather particular relationship with the organization. This was heavily linked to the superpower rivalry and competition in the region.[92] In the first weeks of President Ronald Reagan's Presidency, the National Security Council convened to discuss the issue of 'terrorism'. It was at this juncture that the Central Intelligence Agency definition of terrorism was expanded to encompass the actions of movements of national liberation in the Third World. There was a general wariness with a number of liberation groups such as SWAPO. This was also due to the fact that they received considerable training and funding from the Soviet Union.[93]

The 1970s: a decade of violence

Regarding its use of violence, SWAPO endeavoured to project a certain image. For instance, concerning civilians, at the International Conference of Namibia and Human Rights convened in Dakar, Senegal in 1976, SWAPO declared 'the Namibian Army must and does comply with the laws and customs of war as set out, in particular in the Geneva Conventions of 1949, and South Africa's armed forces are bound by these provisions'.[94] Further to this, SWAPO informed the International Committee of the Red Cross on 15 July 1981 that it would adhere to the Geneva Conventions and its Additional Protocols.[95] Nevertheless, this did not coincide with the activities of the organization. In fact, the 1970s marked a phase of increasing violence. Looking back at some of the activities of the organization, legal scholar Simon Chesterman maintains that SWAPO was in violation of the laws of war regarding how it treated civilians.[96] In this case, the 'civilians' also encompassed members of SWAPO. The decade began with a six-day conference convened at the organization's principle headquarters in

Tanga.⁹⁷ Nujoma reaffirmed the principle objectives of the organization
and stated that it was the start of a new period, during which the 'Namibian
people would fight bitterly, leaving no stone unturned and sparing no life
or blood when called for in order to see Namibia free and independent'.⁹⁸
SWAPO intensified its use of violence, not only against the 'enemy' but also
against individuals from within its own ranks. This was evident when assessing how SWAPO dealt with a leadership crisis in the organization, which
has been described as a 'war within a war'.⁹⁹

The internal conflict began in 1974, when the Youth League of SWAPO
voiced criticism about the lack of transparency and accountability in the
organization's leadership. In 1975, the Youth League presented a memorandum to the SWAPO leadership. They asked for an overturning of the
'no questions' asked policy, whereby reservations and concerns about the
organization were deemed to be treasonous.¹⁰⁰ This critical regard was not
viewed lightly. There was widespread concern within the SWAPO leadership that the 'moderate group' had become 'a serious threat' to Sam
Nujoma.¹⁰¹ This discontentment was not solely within the Youth League.
The tension escalated when PLAN fighters revolted at SWAPO bases in
Zambia.¹⁰² The SWAPO leadership responded to the internal disunity,
through harsh methods of suppression. SWAPO asked both the Tanzanian
and Zambian military to take action against those within SWAPO who were
challenging the leadership. The Zambian government lent its support to
SWAPO to defeat the rebels out of concern that the unrest could trickle
over and cause instability in their country.¹⁰³ The sources vary, but the
consensus is that approximately one thousand people were imprisoned.¹⁰⁴
Ripangura Kanguatijivi, a member of SWAPO reported, 'I lived in a pit
underground...We were beaten, we had no medicine and we feared for
our lives every day'.¹⁰⁵ Many died from torture or illness and a number of
those imprisoned were unaccounted for. These arrests resulted in generating an atmosphere of fear.¹⁰⁶

According to one news source, after having been forced to confess that
they were spies for South Africa, the prisoners were 'beaten, burned, given
electric shocks, hung upside down and buried alive'.¹⁰⁷ SWAPO used
'organized violence' as a means to consolidate their hold on power.¹⁰⁸
Coercion, in this case, was directed towards the people who were supposed
to be united together in the colonial struggle. SWAPO was evidently not a
state, but as the 'legitimate' and 'sole' representative of the Namibian
people, they formed the embryo of the forthcoming independent state. In
essence, in the pursuit of its objectives for liberation, SWAPO underwent
its own variation of a 'reign of terror'.¹⁰⁹ This was a manifestation of revolutionary terror.¹¹⁰ Hence, the revolutionary rhetoric that was replete with
ideals based upon freedom, liberty, equality, and justice could also be used
against any 'dissidents' within the movement.¹¹¹ The purges that transpired
within SWAPO have been described as a 'witch hunt'¹¹² and have been
likened to the activities carried out by Stalin.¹¹³

It is interesting to note that while these events were ongoing, SWAPO was lobbying Amnesty International and the International Committee of the Red Cross for the release of prisoners being held by South Africa.[114] These events demonstrate that SWAPO was using human rights discourse to petition various groups. However, a double standard was applied when it came to the treatment of its own prisoners. The internal situation within SWAPO steadily deteriorated as it became increasingly difficult for the organization to decipher between friend and foe.

The UN and the final stages of the struggle

These events coincided with UN Security Council Resolution 385 that was passed on 30 January 1976, which has been referred to as the 'fulcrum of international strategy'.[115] The documents located at the UN Archives in New York demonstrate that there was an awareness of what was going on as far as the prison camps were concerned. In 1989, it was decided that as a result of the increasing 'allegations'[116] a mission would be sent to the camps located in Angola and Zambia.[117] This mission was comprised of the UNTAG and representatives of the United Nations High Commissioner for Refugees. Their objective was to locate the prisoners and to ensure their 'prompt voluntary repatriation and participation in the electoral process',[118] as well as to guarantee that they would not be subjected to further coercion and intimidation. Andreas Shipanga, a former SWAPO member who had been imprisoned, grasped the UN's 'reluctance' to investigate these charges.[119] The timing was rather precarious, as the visits to the camps took place a few months before the upcoming November elections. Censuring and harshly reprimanding SWAPO would have been a dangerous endeavour, as it could have resulted in significantly damaging their legitimacy on the eve of independence. According to Chesterman, 'the international community turned a blind eye to human rights abuses, viewing the goal of Namibian independence as of greater importance'.[120] Although one of SWAPO's principle platforms was to combat a system that contravened basic human rights, they were in the process of perpetuating a system that denied these rights.[121]

The final stages of decolonization in Namibia, which was facilitated by the UN, were made possible by an amalgamation of local, regional, and global factors. It exceeds the scope of this chapter to enter into these components. In November 1989, under the auspices of UNTAG, the Namibian people moved closer to complete autonomy. On 21 March 1990, after over two decades of an uphill struggle, Namibia gained independence. Sam Nujoma was officially sworn in and recognized by the UN Secretary General as the nation's first President.

However, the issue of the treatment of various individuals during SWAPO's liberation struggle has been an ongoing issue of sensitivity. In 2006, a Namibian non-governmental organization, Namibian National

Society for Human Rights presented a submission to the International Criminal Court for reconciliation.[122] One of the components of this complaint dealt with the human rights violations carried out by SWAPO in the pursuit of liberation. There was a hostile reception to these claims as President Hifikepunye Pohamba stated, 'Those who are attacking and vilifying Comrade Nujoma are engaging in a dangerous game that can take our country down a very slippery slope and plunge Namibia into the dark depths of instability and mistrust'.[123] This issue continues to be exceedingly controversial today.

Conclusion

Franz Fanon predicted that the road towards the pursuit of national liberation and nationhood would be violent and tumultuous.[124] SWAPO was no exception, as the organization stated that 'Imperialists, colonialists and racists change only when revolution changes them and not through dialogue'.[125] Set amidst the backdrop of apartheid and illegal occupation by South Africa, SWAPO was the recipient of significant international support. The conflict in South West Africa was unique. Not only was it backed by a number of General Assembly and Security Resolutions, but SWAPO was also well-integrated in networks abroad. A re-examination of some of the activities carried out by SWAPO re-opens the portholes of a delicate debate. The UN criticized South Africa's attempts to bring several SWAPO 'terrorists' to justice and rapidly dismissed claims of terrorism committed by SWAPO. However, another form of violence manifested itself within the organization. When faced with internal disunity, SWAPO ordered the use of repressive methods against individuals from their own ranks with the intent of fostering an atmosphere of fear. The leadership of SWAPO under Nujoma wanted to send a message to all potential dissidents. Although a mission was sent by the UN to investigate these allegations, SWAPO was not overly criticized for these activities. In essence, it was eclipsed by the much broader goal of the pursuit of self-determination. Although the label of 'terrorist' organization for SWAPO might not be entirely fitting, its path to independence was certainly marked by a 'reign of terror'.

Notes

1   Department of Information and Publicity/SWAPO of Namibia, *To Be Born a Nation*, quoted in P. Katjavivi, *A History of Resistance in Namibia*, Paris: UNESCO Press, 1988, p. 59.
2   D.C. Rapoport, 'The International World as Some Terrorists Have Seen it: A Look at a Century of Memoirs', in D.C. Rapoport (ed.) *Inside Terrorist Organizations*, London: Frank Cass Publishers, 2001, p. 34.
3   D.C. Rapoport, 'The Fourth Wave: September 11 in the History of Terrorism,' *Current History*, 2001, vol. 100, p. 420.

4   A.E. Gerringer, *Terrorism from One Millenium to the Next*, Lincoln: Writers Club Press, 2002, p. 2.

5   L. Richardson, *What Terrorists Want: Understanding the Terrorist Threat*, London: John Murray, 2006, p. 19. The Palestine Liberation Organisation was created by the Arab League in 1964 and had the mandate of reclaiming land in Israel. They adopted increasingly violent tactics, as could be seen in attacks on the Israeli Olympic team at the Munich Olympics in September1972.

6   A. Hübschle, 'The T-word: Conceptualising Terrorism', *African Security Review*, 2006, vol. 15, p. 9.

7   See, for example, The Global Terrorism Database, Available online: www.start.umd.edu/gtd/search/Results.aspx?perpetrator=2432 (accessed 20 May 2012).

8   National liberation has been defined as 'political independence in a sovereign state under a government representing the majority of the people who had hitherto been excluded from full participation in a society through the imposed apartheid system'. H. Melber, *Re-examining liberation in Namibia: Political culture since independence*, Uppsala: Nordic Africa Institute, 2003, p. 14.

9   R.A. Friedlander, 'Terrorism and National Liberation Movements: Can Rights Derive from Wrongs?' *Case Western Reserve Journal of International Law*, 1981, vol. 13, p. 288.

10 For a further discussion on the task of defining terrorism within the UN, see B. Blumenau, 'The United Nations and West Germany's Efforts against International Terrorism in the 1970s', Chapter 4 in this volume.

11 General Assembly Resolution 2444, 'Respect for human rights in armed conflicts', 19 December 1968.

12 O. Levinson, *South West Africa*, Cape Town: Tafelberg, 1976; J.P. Bruwer, *South West Africa: The Disputed Land*, Cape Town: Tafelberg, 1966; R.B. Ballinger, *South-West Africa: The Case against the Union*, Johannesburg: South African Institute of Race Relations, 1961; R. First, *Namibia: The Struggle for Liberation*, Geneva: World Council of Churches, 1971; Département de l'information et de la publicité de la SWAPO de Namibie, *Devenir une nation: la lutte de libération de la Namibia*, Luanda: SWAPO, 1985; R. First, *South West Africa*, Harmondsworth: Penguin Books, 1963; J. Lissner, *Namibia 1975: Hope, Fear and Ambiguity*, Geneva: Lutheran World Federation, Department of Studies, 1976.

13 C. Leys and J.S. Saul have written a few articles in this regard. C. Leys and J.S. Saul, 'Liberation Without Democracy? The SWAPO Crisis of 1976', *Journal of Southern African Studies*, 1994, vol. 20: 123–47; C. Leys and J.S. Saul, *Namibia's Liberation Struggle: The Two Edged Sword*, London: James Currey, 1995. See also, L. Dobell, *SWAPO's Struggle for Namibia, 1960–1991, War by Other Means*, Basel: Basler Afrika Bibliographien, 1998; L. Dobell, 'Review: Silence in context-truth and/or reconciliation in Namibia', *Journal of Southern African Studies*, 1997, vol. 23: 371–82; S. Groth wrote a firsthand account of these events in *The Walls of Silence: the Dark Days of the Liberation Struggle*, Wuppertal: Peter Hammer Verlag, 1995.

14 The Union forces under the leadership of General Botha and General Smuts occupied South African ports in July 1915, which had formerly been a German colony.

15 The mandate system, which was entrenched in Article 22 of the Covenant of the League of Nations, was a new international institution created to pursue

the principle of 'no annexation'. For a discussion on this, see S. Slonim, *South West Africa and the United Nations: An International Mandate in Dispute*, Baltimore: John Hopkins University Press, 1973, pp. 11–59.

16 S. Slonim, *South West Africa and the United Nations: An International Mandate in Dispute*, Baltimore: John Hopkins University Press, 1973, p. 79.

17 See General Assembly Resolution 141, 'Consideration of Proposed New Trusteeship Agreements, If any: Questions of South West Africa', 1 November 1947.

18 J. Dugard, 'South West Africa and the 'Terrorist Trial', *American Journal of International Law*, 1970, vol. 64, p. 120.

19 Apartheid can be defined as 'a comprehensive and systematic pattern of racial discrimination...comprising a complex set of practices of domination and subjection, intensely hierarchized and sustained by the whole apparatus of the state, which affects the distribution of all values'. See M. McDougal, H. Lasswell and L. Chen, *Human Rights and World Public Order*. New Jersey: Yale University Press, 1980.

20 This was first conveyed in General Assembly Resolution 103, 'Persecution and Discrimination', 19 November 1946.

21 The first advisory opinion which was issued in 1950 stipulated that the territory 'remained subject to the mandate; and that the UN was substituted for the League as to the supervision of the mandate; and but that South Africa was not legally obligated to place the territory under the trusteeship system'. There was also the 1955 International Court of Justice case pertaining to Voting Procedures on Questions Relating to Reports and Petitions Concerning the Territory of South West Africa. This was followed by the Admissibility of Hearings of Petitioners by the Committee on South West Africa in 1956 which affirmed that Special Committees on South West Africa could be convened in order to hear oral petitioners. Ethiopia and Liberia tried to start proceedings against South Africa in 1960, but their request was rejected by the court.

22 General Assembly Resolution 2145, 'Question of South West Africa', 27 October 1966.

23 The Security Council issued Resolution 284 (1970) 'Considering that an advisory opinion from the International Court of Justice would be useful for the Security Council in its further consideration of Namibia and in furtherance of the objectives the Council is seeking'.

24 South West Africa was renamed 'Namibia' according to UN General Assembly Resolution 2372 of 12 June 1968.

25 Legal Consequences of States of the Continued Presence of South Africa in Namibia (South West Africa) 1971 ICJ.

26 He stated in *Legal Consequences for States of the Continued Presence of South Africa in Namibia* (South West Africa) Notwithstanding Security Council Resolution 276 (1970) (Advisory Opinion) 'in law the legitimacy of the peoples' struggle cannot be in any doubt, for it follows from the right of self-defence, inherent in human nature, which is confirmed by Article 51 of the United Nations Charter'.

27 Legal Consequences of States of the Continued Presence of South Africa in Namibia (South West Africa) 1971 ICJ.

28 Legal Consequences of States of the Continued Presence of South Africa in Namibia (South West Africa) 1971 ICJ.

29   Security Council Resolution 366, 'The Situation in Namibia', 17 December 1974.

30   Security Council Resolution 435, 29 September 1978.

31   Rumki Basu, *The United Nations: Structure and Functions of an International Organization*, New Delhi: Sterling Publishers, 2004, p. 98.

32   According to a 1960 census, the population of South West Africa was composed of 525,000 people, of whom 75,000 were white, Afrikaaners from South Africa. The rest of the population consisted of tribes such as the Berg-Damara, the Bantu-speaking Ovambo. See also Herero. E. Landis, *South West Africa and the International Court of Justice*, New York: Consultative Council on South Africa, 1965, p. 1.

33   L. Dobell, 'Review: Silence in context-truth and/or reconciliation in Namibia', *Journal of Southern African Studies*, 1997, vol. 23, p. 27. Although mostly composed of 'Ovambo membership of partly urbanized migrant labourers, the organization welcomed all members who supported its aims'.

34   Nujoma was born 12 May 1929 in Owambo, South West Africa.

35   R. Vigne, 'SWAPO of Namibia: a movement in exile', *Third World Quarterly*, 1987, vol. 9, p. 88.

36   See 'South West Team at UNO Increased,' *Southwest News*, 25 June 1960, quoted in D. Henrichsen (ed.), *A Glance at our Africa: Facsimile reprint of Southwest News-Suidwes Nuus*, Basel: Demasius Publications, 1960, p. 5.

37   H.-R. Heitman and P.Hannon, *Modern African Wars 3 – South West Africa*, London: Osprey Publishing, 1991, p. 4.

38   The OAU was established in 1963 in Addis Ababa. It called for the 'absolute dedication to the total emancipation of the African territories which are still dependence' Article 3(6).

39   I. Taylor, 'China and SWAPO: The role of the people's republic in Namibia's liberation and post-independence relations', *South African Journal of International Affairs*, 1997, vol. 5, p. 110.

40   This was key for Sam Nujoma, according to Colin Leys and John S. Saul, it granted Nujoma 'membership in the League of African presidents, and this in turn encouraged him to expect, even demand, the deference and largely unquestioned loyalty that his presidents, such as Nyerere and Kaunda, received', C. Leys and J.S. Saul, *Namibia's Liberation Struggle: The Two Edged Sword*, London: James Currey, 1995, p. 125.

41   R. Vigne, 'SWAPO of Namibia: a movement in exile', *Third World Quarterly*, 1987, vol. 9, p. 90.

42   Excerpt of an article in SWANU's South West Africa Review, quoted in A. de Braganca and I. Wallerstein (eds), *The African Liberation Reader, Volume 2 The National Liberation Movements*, London: Zes Press, 1982, p.134.

43   A. de Braganca and I. Wallerstein (eds), *The African Liberation Reader, Volume 2 The National Liberation Movements*, London: Zes Press, 1982, pp. 134–5.

44   Quoted in E. Kwakwa, 'The Namibian Conflict: A Discussion of the Jus Ad Bellum and the Jus in Bello', *New York Law School Journal of International and Comparative Law*, 1988, vol. 9, p. 200.

45   H.-R. Heitman and P.Hannon, *Modern African Wars 3 – South West Africa*, London: Osprey Publishing, 1991, p. 4.

46   V. Shubin, *The Hot Cold War: the USSR in Southern Africa*, London: Pluto Press, 2008, p. 201.

47 SWAPO commander R. Kahimise, quoted in L. Dobell, 'Review: Silence in context-truth and/or reconciliation in Namibia', *Journal of Southern African Studies*, 1997, vol. 23, p. 44.

48 L. Dobell, 'Review: Silence in context-truth and/or reconciliation in Namibia', *Journal of Southern African Studies*, 1997, vol. 23, p. 28.

49 Sam Nujoma, South West Africa People's Organisation, 'Press Briefing Given by Mr. Sam Nujoma, President of SWAPO, June 13 1975' World Council of Churches Library and Archives. Available online: www.aluka.org (accessed 14 September 2011).

50 C. Saunders and S. Onslow, 'The Cold War and Southern Africa', in M.P. Leffler and O. Arne Westad (eds) *The Cambridge History of the Cold War*, Cambridge: Cambridge University Press, 2010. Concretely, this entailed the creation of a 'classless society…abolishment of all forms of exploitation of man by man and the destructive spirit of individualism and aggrandizement of wealth and power by individuals, groups or classes'. SWAPO party program quoted in L. Dobell, 'Review: Silence in context-truth and/or reconciliation in Namibia', *Journal of Southern African Studies*, 1997, vol. 23, p. 58.

51 V. Shubin, *The Hot Cold War: the USSR in Southern Africa*, London: Pluto Press, 2008, p. 213.

52 L. Dobell, 'Review: Silence in context-truth and/or reconciliation in Namibia', *Journal of Southern African Studies*, 1997, vol. 23, p. 11.

53 The UN Archives in New York are replete with Sam Nujoma's visits to the General Assembly. He also travelled extensively throughout the US and the United Kingdom. SWAPO also had an office in New York.

54 General Assembly Resolution 2248, 'Question of South West Africa', 19 May 1967.

55 'The implementation of the Programme of Work of the United Nations Council for Namibia in Light of Recent Developments Related to the Independence of Namibia, 28 March 1989', S-0308-0013-014 in Namibia (Mareck Goulding File) 2/2/1989-27/4 1989, United Nations Archives, New York. It also proceeded forward with the renaming of the territory to 'Namibia' in 1968.

56 Security Council Resolution 264, 'The Situation in Namibia', 20 March 1969.

57 General Assembly Resolution 3111, 'Question of Namibia', 13 December 1973.

58 I.I. Dore, 'Self-Determination of Namibia and the United Nations: Paradigm of a Paradox', *Harvard International Law Journal*, 1986, vol. 27, p. 165.

59 United Nations Council for Namibia- Summary Record of the 307th Meeting, 20 October 1979, S-0308-0020-010 in South West Africa People's Organization (SWAPO) 2/2/1979-10/12/1980, United Nations Archives, New York.

60 For a further discussion on the UN's support for a host of other movements of national liberation, see P.J. Travers, 'The Legal Effect of United Nations Action in Support of the Palestine Liberation Organization and the National Liberation Movements in Africa', *Harvard International Law Journal*, 1976, vol. 17, p. 561.

61 General Assembly Resolution 3103, 'Basic Principles of the Legal Status of Combatants Struggling Against Colonial and Alien Domination and Racist Regimes', 12 December 1973.

62 Ibid.

63 Conference Dakar. Published by the International Institute of Human Rights, published in, J. Dugard, 'SWAPO: The Jus ad Bellum and the Jus ad Bello', *South African Law Journal*, 1976, vol. 93, p. 145.

64   E. Kwakwa, 'Namibian Conflict: A Discussion of the Jus ad Bellum and the Jus in Bello,' *New York Law School Journal of Contemporary International Law*, 1988, vol. 9, p. 196.

65   R.A. Friedlander, 'Terrorism and National Liberation Movements: Can Rights Derive from Wrongs?' *Case Western Reserve Journal of International Law*, 1981, vol. 13, p. 284.

66   Ibid., p. 268.

67   See M. Norval, *Death in the Desert: The Namibian Tragedy*, Washington: Selous Foundation Press, 1989.

68   'How the U.N. Aids Marxist Guerrilla Groups' – The United Nations Assessment Project Study, Washington: The Heritage Foundation, 1982, p. 1.

69   R. Warren Howe, 'War in Southern Africa', *Foreign Affairs*, 1968, vol. 46, p. 152.

70   G. Lamb, 'Militarization's Long Shadow: Namibia's legacy of armed violence', *Economics of Peace and Security Journal*, 2006, vol. 1, p. 35.

71   J. Dugard, 'South West Africa and the 'Terrorist Trial'', *American Journal of International Law*, 1970, vol. 64, pp. 19–41.

72   Ibid., p. 22.

73   Ibid.

74   Statement by SWAPO member Toivo Herman JA Toivo, during trial of South West Africans in Pretoria, 1 February 1968 in A. de Braganca and I. Wallerstein (eds), *The African Liberation Reader, Volume 2 The National Liberation Movements*, London: Zes Press, 1982, p. 56.

75   General Assembly Resolution 2234, 'Question of South West Africa', 16 December 1967.

76   For an overview of these events, see W.M. James, *A Political History of the Civil War in Angola, 1974–1990*, New Jersey: Transaction Publishers, 1992.

77   Statement by SWAPO to Representatives of People's Movement for the Liberation of Angola (MPLA) Workers Party and Members of SWAPO Central Committee Foreign and Commonwealth Office, hereafter FCO 105/137, The National Archives, London.

78   The South African Defence Forces launched the 'hot pursuit' and were involved in armed conflict with the Angolan army. Moreover, the situation was further complicated by the eruption of civil war in Angola between the Cuban and Soviet Union backed MPLA on one side and UNITA (the National Union for the Total Independence of Angola) and FNLA (National Liberation Front of Angola).

79   'Letter dated 14 February 1979 from the Minister of Foreign Affairs of South Africa addressed to the Secretary General' S-0308-0019-08 in South Africa-Exchange of Letters between the Secretary General and South Africa Foreign Minister re SWAPO terrorist attack on South African base on 13 February 1978 14/2/1979-20/2/1979, United Nations Archives, New York.

80   'Letter dated 22 February 1980 from Minister of Foreign Affairs of South Africa addressed to the Secretary General from R.F. Botha Minister of Foreign Affairs' S-0308-0020-010 in South West Africa People's Organization (SWAPO) 2/2/1979-10/12/1980, United Nations Archives, New York.

81   Ibid. SWAPO was also accused of collaborating with the ANC of carrying out terrorist tactics.

82   Emphasis added. 'Letter dated February 1979 From the Minister of Foreign Affairs of South Africa addressed to the Secretary-General', S-0308-0019-08 in

South Africa- Exchange of Letters between the Secretary-General and South Africa Foreign Minister re SWAPO terrorist attack on South African base on 13 February 1978 14/2/1979-20/2/1979, United Nations Archives, New York.

83   Armed Incidents Between SWAPO and South African Forces, Letter from South African Embassy, 10 December 1979, FCO 105/137, The National Archives, London.

84   'Enclosure of the atrocities which SWAPO terrorists committed since January 1978' S-0308-0020-010 in South West Africa People's Organization (SWAPO) 2/2/1979-10/12/1980, United Nations Archives, New York. See also H.-R. Heitman and P.Hannon, *Modern African Wars 3 – South West Africa*, London: Osprey Publishing, 1991, p. 8.

85   Quoted in H.-R. Heitman and P.Hannon, *Modern African Wars 3 – South West Africa*, London: Osprey Publishing, 1991, p. 72. In February 1988, an explosion in a Namibian bank resulted in the death of 18 civilians.

86   United Nations Council for Namibia- Summary Record of the 307th Meeting, 20 October 1979, S-0308-0020-010 in South West Africa People's Organization (SWAPO) 2/2/1979-10/12/1980, United Nations Archives, New York.

87   'Enclosure II: Press statement by the South African Minister of Foreign Affairs, the Hon. R. F. Botha, 1 November 1979', S-0308-0020-010 in South West Africa People's Organization (SWAPO) 2/2/1979-10/12/1980, United Nations Archives, New York.

88   'Statement made on 30 April 1979 by the Acting President of the United Nations Council for Namibia on the Arrest of SWAPO leaders by the Illegal South African Administration in Namibia', S-0308-0020-010 in South West Africa People's Organization (SWAPO) 2/2/1979-10/12/1980, United Nations Archives, New York.

89   W. Minter, *Apartheid's Contras: An Inquiry into the Roots of War in Angola and Mozambique*, London: Zed Books, 1974, p. 30.

90   Ibid.

91   Ibid., p. 42.

92   For a further discussion on this, see C. Saunders and S. Onslow, 'The Cold War and Southern Africa', in M.P. Leffler and O. Arne Westad (eds) *The Cambridge History of the Cold War*, Cambridge: Cambridge University Press, 2010.

93   V. Shubin, *The Hot Cold War: the USSR in Southern Africa*, London: Pluto Press, 2008, p. 205.

94   Quoted in E.K. Kwakwa, *The International Law of Armed Conflict: Personal and Material Fields of Application*, Dordrecht: Kluwer Academic Publishers, 1992, p. 71.

95   C. Ewumbu-Monomo, 'Respect for International Humanitarian Law by Armed Non-State Actors', *International Review of the Red Cross*, 2006, vol. 88, p. 908.

96   S. Chesterman, *Civilians in War*, Colorado: Lynne Rienner Publisher, 2001, p. 28.

97   South West Africa People's Organisation Extract from 'Standard' Tanzania 'SWAPO Congress opens in Tanga' Jan 1970, FCO 45/ 740, The National Archives, London.

98   Ibid.

99   Ed. A. Rao, M. Bollig and M. Böck, *The Practice of War: Production and Communication of Armed*, New York: Berghan Books, United States, 2007, p. 75.

100 C. Leys and J.S. Saul, *Namibia's Liberation Struggle: The Two Edged Sword*, London: James Currey, 1995, p. 145.

101 SWAPO, 'Moderate Kicked out', 27.7.79 FCO 105/87, The National Archives, London.
102 T. Sellstrom, *Sweden and National Liberation in Southern Africa: Solidarity Volume II: Solidarity and Assistance 1970–1994*, Uppsala: Elanders Gotab, 2002, p. 308.
103 G. Lamb, 'Militarization's Long Shadow: Namibia's legacy of armed violence', *Economics of Peace and Security Journal*, 2006, vol. 1, p. 31.
104 This uncertainty is largely due to the fact that a number of prisoners were missing and unaccounted for. Leys and Saul state that there were 1,600–1,800 prisoners taken; see C. Leys and J.S. Saul, *Namibia's Liberation Struggle: The Two Edged Sword*, London: James Currey, 1995, p. 49. Whereas Dobell says that there were approximately 1,600 to 2,000; see L. Dobell, 'Review: Silence in context-truth and/or reconciliation in Namibia', *Journal of Southern African Studies*, 1997, vol. 23, p. 49.
105 'Namibia Prisoners Report Brutality', *The New York Times*, 5 July 1989.
106 C. Leys and J.S. Saul, *Namibia's Liberation Struggle: The Two Edged Sword*, London: James Currey, 1995.
107 C.S. Wren, 'Namibian Election Rivals Say SWAPO Tortured Its Prisoners', *The New York Times*, 20 September 1989.
108 H. Melber, *Re-examining liberation in Namibia: Political culture since independence*, Uppsala: Nordic Africa Institute, 2003, p. 9.
109 See H. Melber, *Re-examining liberation in Namibia: Political culture since independence*, Uppsala: Nordic Africa Institute, 2003, p. 47, for a further discussion. Reign of terror has been commonly used to refer to the reign of terror during the French Revolution which started in September 1793. See O. Connelly, *The Wars of the French Revolution and Napoleon, 1792–1815*, New York: Routledge Publishing, 2006.
110 B.M. Leiser, 'Terrorism, Guerilla Warfare and International Morality', *Stanford Journal of International Law*, 1977, vol. 39, p. 48.
111 Ibid.
112 G. Lamb, 'Militarization's Long Shadow: Namibia's legacy of armed violence', *Economics of Peace and Security Journal*, 2006, vol. 1, p. 32.
113 Stalin's regime of terror, which began in the 1930s and lasted until his death in 1953, has been referred to as a manifestation of state terrorism. During this period, he removed all of his political opponents and relied upon a significant degree of coercion and repression. His political purges caused the death, exile, and imprisonment of millions. For more on this see, B. Hoffman, 'Defining Terrorism', in R.D. Howard and R.L. Sawyer (eds) *Terrorism and Counterterrorism*, Guilford: McGraw-Hill/Dushkin, 2002, p. 11; and P. Trewhela, 'SWAPO and the Churches: An International Scandal', *Searchlight South Africa*, 1991, vol. 2, p. 66.
114 South West Africa People's Organisation, Letter from W.J. Vose of the West Africa Department, London. FCO 45/ 740.
115 Resolution 385, 30 January 1976.
116 Guidelines for A Mission to Angola (and Zambia) To investigate Detention Allegations 1989 S 308-12-0018 in 'Military Matters-Mission to Angola (and Zambia) to investigate detention allegations by SWAPO' 23/8/1989, United Nations Archives, New York.
117 Code Cable To Goulding in New York from Ahtisaari, in Windhoek, 23 August 1989S 308-12-0018 in 'Military Matters-Mission to Angola (and Zambia) to

investigate detention allegations by SWAPO' 23/8/1989, United Nations Archives, New York.

118 Ibid. Many of these prisoners were brought to the UNHCR refugee camp at Meheba in north-western Zambia, where they stayed until 1989. See T. Sellstrom, *Sweden and National Liberation in Southern Africa: Solidarity Volume II: Solidarity and Assistance 1970–1994*, Uppsala: Elanders Gotab, 2002, p. 313.

119 'Namibia Prisoners Report Brutality', *New York Times*, 5 July 1989.

120 S. Chesterman, *Civilians in War*, Colorado: Lynne Rienner Publisher, 2001, p. 28.

121 T. Sellstrom, *Sweden and National Liberation in Southern Africa: Solidarity Volume II: Solidarity and Assistance 1970–1994*, Uppsala: Elanders Gotab, 2002, p. 309.

122 S. Höhn, 'International justice and reconciliation in Namibia: The ICC submission and public memory', *African Affairs* 2010, vol. 109 (436), p. 472.

123 O. Shivute, 'Namibia: President warns of 'havoc' as heroes laid to rest at Eanhana', *The Namibian*, 30 August 2007. Available online: www.afrika.no/noop/page.php?p=Detailed/14848.html&print=1 (accessed 15 September 2011).

124 F. Fanon, *The Wretched of the Earth*, New York: Grove Press, 1963, p. 35.

125 'SWAPO A Big Western Diplomatic Spectacle on Namibia Eclipsed. Press Release from Solidarity, Freedom, Justice. 15 May 1979' FCO 105/87, National Archives, London.

11 The 'Claustre Affair'

A hostage crisis, France, and civil war in Chad, 1974–77

Nathaniel K. Powell

Introduction

The 'Claustre Affair' represented, in some respects, one of the most consequential hostage crises in recent history. The events following the April
1974 kidnapping of one German and two French citizens in the northern
Chadian desert had fateful repercussions for the subsequent political
history of Central Africa. It also constituted an important turning point in
the roles of France and Libya in the region. The small group of rebels
responsible for the hostage-taking managed to skilfully drive a wedge
between the Chadian government and its French protector. The nature of
this changing relationship openly exposed the Chadian regime's dependence upon French military might, as well as the incapacity of the French to
impose a favourable political order upon the country. The January 1977
resolution of the affair also opened a crucial outlet for Muammar Gaddafi's
expansionist designs in Chad. The resulting series of conflicts and shifting
political configurations fed and expanded a civil war which, to some extent,
continues to this day.

This chapter examines the nature of French negotiations with the rebel
leadership and its consequences. However, this story has broader implications for a number of issues of importance to the question of international
terrorism. Indeed, the tortuous evolution of the entire affair may also have
contributed to French intransigence over the terrorism negotiations at the
United Nations later in the decade.[1]

Like many acts of terrorism, the political outcome of this kidnapping far
outstripped the military weight of the kidnappers. The crucial questions of
regime legitimacy and foreign dependency have strong parallels today. This
poisonous combination in Chad constituted a weak link that committed
rebels could exploit to their advantage. The Chadian case provides a good
example of how the legitimacy–dependency relationship can create conditions of insecurity and conflict that permit the use of terrorism as an
effective political tactic. Furthermore, the Saharan/Sahelian region of
Africa has more recently become an area of international concern over
Islamist armed groups, kidnappings of westerners, and, notably in Mali,

regional rebellions. As this chapter should at least partially demonstrate, these concerns are not new. However, it should also serve as a warning to policymakers that state repression has, and does, create insecurity in the region. Providing purely military assistance to these states in their fight against terrorism may do little more than strengthen the repressive apparatuses of their respective regimes.

Given the relative importance of the so-called 'Claustre affair', both for the history of the region and of French involvement in Central Africa and the Sahel, no recent literature addresses the issue in any depth. The most reliable sources come from the archives of the French Foreign and Cooperation Ministries. Both, particularly the latter, played important roles in the elaboration and implementation of French policy towards Chad during this period. Although the best material in these collections post-dates the events described here, the available documentation combined with memoirs and existing secondary material, provide a rich source of information.[2] This chapter provides the first account of this crisis using this material.

France and Chad

At its independence from France in 1960, most of the small number of Chadians educated in the colonial system came from the country's south. This meant that southerners dominated the new government of a country two and a half times the geographical size of France. Although the French maintained their colonial administration in the northern Bourkou-Ennedi-Tibesti (BET) region until 1965, the unbalanced nature of political power quickly resulted in growing tensions.

The *Front de libération nationale du Tchad* (Frolinat), founded in 1966, became the focal point of armed resistance against the Chadian government of François Tombalbaye. By 1969, the rebellion had spread throughout large swathes of the country, particularly in the north and east. Like many former French African colonies, Chad and France had signed a secret convention providing for French assistance in the domestic 'maintenance of order'.[3] According to this agreement, Chad could request direct French military participation in the repression of local rebellions. Under these circumstances, command of the Chadian military would pass directly under French control.[4]

By early 1969, heavy fighting between elements of Frolinat and the Chadian army in the north and east of the country ended disastrously for governmental forces. Under pressure from his military commanders, Tombalbaye requested French intervention to crush the rebellion.[5] After some hesitation, much of it due to Tombalbaye's perceived incompetence and testy personal relations with the French, President Charles de Gaulle acceded to the Chadian request. However, he conditioned French intervention on Tombalbaye's acceptance of a *Mission de réforme administrative*

(MRA), which aimed to help reform and improve the Chadian administration in order to prevent rebellion in the future.[6]

In total, France deployed some two thousand eight hundred soldiers, in addition to some six hundred personnel on detached duty as 'advisors' and training cadres in the Chadian army.[7] For more than three years, until September 1972, the French-led military campaign managed to destroy or dismantle Frolinat groups in central and eastern Chad. However, the French never managed to fully 'pacify' the BET.[8]

Robert Buijtenhuijs, one of the most informed observers of the period, estimated that French military operations cost the lives of some ten thousand people in the targeted areas.[9] Although French ground troops officially ceased active military operations against the rebels in September 1972, their mission changed to one of logistical assistance and air support.[10] Furthermore, although the rebellion had seemingly suffered a severe military defeat, pockets survived in many parts of the country, especially in the BET. The MRA, initially deployed to rectify government malpractice, morphed into something of a public works administration.[11] This left the political roots of the rebellion unaddressed.

Despite close collaboration, Tombalbaye did not always maintain a friendly relationship with his French ally. On a number of occasions, he tried to distance himself via quasi-official propaganda campaigns aimed against France and French interests.[12] Although Tombalabaye relied too much upon France to make a clean break, he and fellow Chadian elites suffered from a chafing resentment at the need for such a relationship.

A kidnapping in the desert

On the night of 21 April 1974, an armed group under the command of Hissène Habré stormed the remote garrison town of Bardaï in northern Chad. Defecting *gardes nomades* of the local army presence, auxiliaries of the Chadian regime, assisted the rebel units in the capture of Marc Combe, who worked for the MRA, and Françoise Claustre, a French archaeologist. The rebels also kidnapped Christoph Staewen, a West German doctor who provided medical treatment to residents in the vicinity. Stray bullets hit Staewen's wife, who died on the spot. Within minutes, the rebels, with the three hostages in tow, quickly loaded up three Land Rovers found on the site with fuel and supplies, as well as Combe's radio. The local garrison responded to the sound of gunfire and tried to pursue, but in the darkness of the desert, it was already too late.[13]

In the Chadian capital of N'Djamena, Pierre Claustre learned of what had happened just hours after the event. Claustre headed the MRA and was also the husband of Françoise Claustre. As MRA chief, he had access to an agency airplane, which he flew to the northern town of Faya-Largeau. There, he hoped to move onto Bardaï to learn more about the situation.

Over the next days and weeks, Pierre was the only French official in relatively constant contact with the kidnappers. Partly, this resulted from the timing of the kidnapping, which occurred just days after the French Ambassador, Fernand Wibaux, had left the country. Raphaël Touze, Wibaux's replacement, would not arrive until the 27th. Furthermore, these events also occurred during an interregnum in French politics. President Georges Pompidou had died on 2 April, and the final round of the presidential election would not occur until 19 May. Thus, for several crucial weeks, French authorities acted without a central policymaking anchor. This did not stop the Chadian government from acting, however. Chad's military assistance and defence agreements with France meant that the regime enjoyed a strong French troop presence that provided air and logistical support to far-flung government garrisons.[14] Tombalbaye ordered a Chadian army company flown to reinforce the garrison at Bardaï. However, both Claustre and the Chadian prefect in Faya-Largea felt strongly that the rebels might execute the hostages in response to military actions. Luc Baldit, the French *chargé d'affaires*, immediately received instructions from Paris, however, that under no circumstances would the French provide support for military operations that could put the hostages' lives in danger.[15]

By early May, two West German envoys had already arrived, ready to begin negotiations. French authorities also designated a high-level official in the Cooperation Ministry, Robert Puissant, to negotiate on the French behalf. However, it would take him some days to arrive. Meanwhile, Franz Wallner, one of the German envoys, joined Pierre Claustre who had since moved up to Bardaï. On the morning of 10 May, Habré informed them of the conditions for the release of the hostages. The leadership of the Forces *armées du nord* (FAN), the *Conseil de commandement des forces armées du nord* (CCFAN) demanded the liberation of thirty-two political prisoners in Ndjamena, publication of a CCFAN political manifesto, and an 'indemnity' for the property of local populations, particularly for the villages, palm groves, crops, and goods which Habré claimed French and Chadian government forces had destroyed.[16]

These demands placed the French in an uncomfortable position. France's new ambassador to Chad, Raphäel Touze, feared that the nature of the demands would lead the Germans to negotiate separately with Habré for the release of Dr Staewen alone. Also, by conditioning the release of European hostages upon the release of prisoners held by the Chadian government, the CCFAN helped to drive a wedge between the French and Chadian authorities. The latter, understandably, did not feel that they had a stake in this particular crisis. Releasing potentially dangerous political prisoners to placate French opinion did not sit well with Tombalbaye or his entourage. Given the somewhat strained nature of relations with the Chadian president, French policymakers wanted to carefully avoid giving the impression of threatening the authority of the Chadian government. Indeed, several Chadian officials, including the prefect of the BET, began to urge Tombalbaye to ban direct contacts between the rebels and Franco-German envoys.[17] This forced the French to 'negotiate on two fronts' in order to maintain their position.[18]

On 14 May, Touze and Puissant met with West German diplomats in N'Djamena to discuss the negotiations. The Germans explained that, while they were willing to coordinate their negotiating strategy with the French, they would negotiate separately as long as the rebels maintained their demands for a prisoner release, since these could not concern the German government.[19] The Germans had already offered to broadcast a CCFAN manifesto over *Deutsche Welle* for three days in French and Arabic. Wallner also told Habré that Germany would agree to provide financial indemnities of fifty million CFA for the burned villages.[20] Habré appeared to accept this offer in principle.[21] In the course of the meeting with Touze and Puissant, the Germans expressed their desire to keep any liberation of the hostages, particularly that of Staewen, secret from Chadian authorities. To that end, they planned to fly out from Bardaï directly to Tunis, before the Tombalbaye regime could react.[22] Indeed, the broadcast of anti-government manifestos over German radio, as well as the delivery of a large ransom to the CCFAN, would infuriate Chadian officials.

The French began to pressure Tombalbaye to consent to some kind of prisoner release. Puissant, in a meeting with the Chadian foreign minister, insisted that the demand for the prisoners represented a purely Chadian affair, and expressed fears that governmental inaction would lead to the failure of the negotiations.[23] The regime refused to budge, although it seemed willing to accept the fulfilment of the other two conditions posed by the rebels.[24]

On 18 May, Puissant, along with Claustre and Wallner, met Habré for the first time in the village of Zoui, twelve kilometers to the east of Bardaï.[25] Habré presented the French with a demand for one billion CFA, equal to twenty million French francs, along with the other conditions described above.[26] The next day, the delegation again drove to Zoui, where Wallner officially accepted Habré's conditions for Staewen's release.[27]

Two days later, the negotiators returned to Zoui, where the Germans hoped to finalize the negotiations. According to Claustre, during the meeting Puissant threatened Habré that, if he killed any of the hostages, 'terrible reprisals would fall upon the populations of Tibesti'.[28] Indeed, on 26 May, Chadian troops in Bardaï, perhaps at the instigation of the new garrison commander, decided to take revenge on the families of the *gardes nomades* who had deserted to the rebellion the night of the kidnapping. The gendarmes burnt their homes, without letting them save their belongings. In the evening, the garrison commander ordered the palm grove burnt to the ground. The fire lasted for several days.[29] The Chadian sub-prefect, with tears in his eyes, lamented to Claustre, 'They're crazy, how could the population not hate them?'.[30]

Meanwhile, the situation became worrisome for the French. The rebels would soon release Staewen under circumstances that could incite the

Chadian government to hinder further negotiations. French policymakers decided to pressure Tombalbaye to release the political prisoners demanded by Habré. Former Ambassador to Chad, Hubert Argod, who had close relations with Tombalbaye, arrived in Chad at month's end. Tombalbaye gave Argod assurances that he would release prisoners with a view towards ending the hostage crisis.[31]

However, instead of a prisoner release, Tombalbaye gave an inflammatory speech on 2 June. After vaguely indicating that he had already agreed to amnesty 'all of those led astray by the lies of Frolinat', he flipped Habré's demand on its head. Only if Habré released his hostages, would the government now consider releasing their prisoners. Tombalbaye went one step further and threatened Habré's family. He declared that Habré should now know that 'his relatives, his brothers of the Anakaza tribe, are now guarantees for his hostages ... the safety of the relatives and brothers of Hissène Habré now depend upon him alone'. Tombalbabye further threatened that if Habré hurt the hostages, 'the Chadian people ... would yield to anger. The authorities would then doubtless have difficulty in preventing the worst [from happening]'.[32] Indeed, Chadian forces imprisoned some sixty of Habré's relatives, including his mother and son.[33] Claustre received word from one of his MRA subordinates that the prisoners were even carried aboard French Nord-Atlas transport aircraft.[34]

Ten days later, Habré finally released Staewen in exchange for four million French francs and the broadcast of a Frolinat '2nd Army' manifesto over *Deutsche Welle*.[35] West German officials evacuated Staewen to Libya via Land Rover in order to avoid problems with the Chadian authorities.[36] That same day, the German Ambassador, Werner Seldis, met with an unhappy Tombalbaye.[37] He did not manage to assuage the Chadian president. On the 12th, Tombalabaye declared a break in diplomatic relations between Chad and West Germany.[38] The official government communiqué also made vague accusations against Pierre Claustre, implying that he had tried to make a separate and secret deal with Habré.[39] The Chadian government declared Claustre, who had already returned to France, *persona non grata*.[40]

On the 13th, Touze met with Tombalbaye and argued that the recent actions taken by the Chadian government played into the hands of the rebellion. Touze suggested that he open a dialogue with different elements of the opposition in order to improve the situation.[41] Touze warned, prophetically, that the rebels and their sympathizers probably hoped that the Bardaï affair would result in a serious break in Franco–Chadian relations. They then began to discuss a new plan for the hostage negotiations. At Tombalbaye's request, the French named Commandant Pierre Galopin to accompany their Consul General, Georges Estrade, in the renewed negotiations with the CCFAN.[42]

Galopin' to glory

The choice of Galopin as a negotiator provoked controversy. Upon Staewen's arrival in Libya, he warned the French that Habré considered Galopin a 'piece of scum', guilty of subverting the unity of the northern Toubou communities.[43] Claustre also repeatedly warned French authorities that the choice of Galopin as an emissary could cause serious problems for the negotiations.[44] He suspected that Tombalbaye had asked for Galopin upon the instigation of Camille Gourvennec, the head of his intelligence services. Galopin had played an important role in Chadian intelligence as Gourvennec's deputy in the late 1960s and early 1970s. Numerous Frolinat and French sources attest to the many abuses, including the use of torture by Chadian intelligence officers, many of whom were French.[45] Some, like Galopin, continued to serve as active duty officers on detached service.[46]

Goukouni Weddeye, who led the CCFAN along with Habré, nurtured a special grudge against Galopin. Indeed, Galopin led negotiations which, in 1969, resulted in the defection to the government side of a substantial part of the Toubou rebellion in the BET.[47] Goukouni's elder brother died during a fire fight against a unit led by one of his erstwhile allies.[48] Strangely, Galopin seemed to think that Goukouni held him in some esteem from their contacts several years earlier.[49]

Galopin also enjoyed warm personal relations with Gourvennec.[50] Galopin's history of services to the Chadian regime, and Gourvennec in particular, explain Tombalbaye's desire to see him as a negotiator. Tombalbaye, rightly, feared a deal outside of Chadian government auspices. Galopin would fill this gap since Gourvennec trusted him completely. This way, the Chadian government could remain informed of the negotiations.

Indeed, this state of affairs did not escape French officials in the Foreign Ministry. Its instructions to the Embassy in N'Djamena commanded that Galopin could only remain accountable to French authorities, not to the Chadian government.[51] Furthermore, the instructions noted that the release of Staewen, and Tombalbaye's decision to take Habré's family hostage, had changed the situation. Now the cooperation of the Chadian regime had become absolutely essential. Touze now had orders to make it clear to Tombalbaye that he must make concessions or face French wrath.[52] These pressures may have had an effect. Tombalbaye began to make vague promises of a future release of Habré's family and other prisoners.[53] He also seemed willing to agree to a French ransom, as well as the broadcast of a communiqué.[54]

Meanwhile, Galopin and Estrade reported that the entire Toubou population of Bardaï had fled and joined the rebellion. Only small marginalized ethnic communities had remained in the village. This resulted from the recent fire and destruction of the palm grove by the Chadian army.[55] Finally, in early July, Habré agreed to reopen negotiations and they had their first meeting. Touze saw this as confirmation that, despite fears to the contrary, Habré accepted Galopin as a negotiator.[56] For the release of the hostages, Estrade and Galopin had authorization to agree to a broadcast of a FAN communiqué, as well as the payment of a ransom.[57]

Matters came to a head on 4 August. In the course of the meeting between the rebels and the French negotiators, Habré decided to arrest Galopin.[58] A few weeks later, Habré told a horrified French negotiator, Martial Laurens, that the CCFAN had, 'decided for a long time to appre-hend Commandant Galopin due to his activities against the Toubous. With France "having presented him [to us] in wrapping paper," it would have been stupid not to seize the opportunity'.[59] Goukouni, though absent at the time, later reported that Habré and other rebels present accused Galopin of exploiting his position as negotiator to encourage some of the former *gardes nomades* to defect back to the government side.[60] Goukouni added that, though he could not confirm the accuracy of Habré's accusations, he would have had Galopin arrested anyway, due to his past misdeeds.[61]

Evidence from the French archives lends weight to this version of events. A note from Gourvennec to Galopin suggests that Galopin's mission as emissary went beyond that of a simple negotiator. First, Gourvennec wrote that Galopin should gather information on the state of the rebellion, particularly its relationship with Frolinat's formal leadership in Tripoli, and on Goukouni's position *vis-à-vis* Habré. Then, Gourvennec referred to a possible return of Bardaï's inhabitants who had fled to the rebellion follow-ing the Chadian army's reprisals, as well as the *gardes nomades* who had defected to the rebels. He wrote, 'for the return of the inhabitants and guards to Bardaï = for the former, no problem – for the latter, they should be disarmed while waiting to be brought to N'Djamena where their case will be studied by my agency'.[62]

Indeed, the Chadian government and the French had some evidence suggesting dissension within rebel ranks, particularly among the former *gardes nomades* who had defected during the hostage operation in April.[63] Thus, as Gourvennec's note suggests, Galopin's mission aimed both at intelligence gathering and facilitating the redefection of the *gardes nomades* (who would probably not have enjoyed getting disarmed and shipped off to N'Djamena for interrogation by Gourvennec's men).

With Galopin's capture, the stakes increased. Now, the rebels demanded weapons. Goukouni felt that Galopin's arrest represented an enormous boon for the rebellion. A lack of substantial weaponry and munitions constituted the FAN's most serious handicap. However, since Galopin had extremely close relations with both Gourvennec and Tombalbaye, the rebels now felt that they could ask for anything in exchange for his release.[64] On 31 August, the CCFAN presented their formal demands for arms. Of the one billion CFA (twenty million French francs) they had asked for, they now wanted six hundred million of this amount to take the form of weapons deliveries.[65]

Stalled negotiations, a rogue lover, and a dead soldier

Galopin's arrest added a sense of urgency to the negotiations, both for the French and for Tombalbaye. However, the negotiations with the CCFAN made little progress. Martial Laurens, the French Embassy's First Secretary, replaced Estrade as the official envoy. Laurens described the series of meetings between 30 September and 3 October as consisting of little more than, 'on the one hand "we want weapons and ammunition," and on the other "France rejects this condition"'.[66] Laurens asked him why he could not simply buy weapons on the black market with the four million francs the Germans had already paid. Habré admitted that it was not so simple.[67]

Meanwhile, Pierre Claustre, on a leave of absence, made his way alone and illicitly to Chad via Libya in an attempt to see his wife and possibly make an independent deal for her release. Touze feared that his presence with the rebels would complicate negotiations.[68] Claustre risked joining the growing ranks of Habré's hostage pool, and his presence could provoke renewed mistrust from Tombalbaye. On 4 October, French Foreign Ministry officials began to pressure the Libyan authorities to prevent Claustre's passage through to Tibesti in Northern Chad.[69] By this time, however, Claustre had already crossed the border.[70]

Claustre's presence, however, actually had a positive effect on the negotiations. He managed to convince Habré and Goukouni to slightly modify the form of their demands.[71] They agreed and he passed the message on to Paris, which he reached on 24 November.[72] The proposals involved the liberation of Combe, followed by Françoise Claustre, in exchange for each of whom the rebels would receive one-third of the ransom money, and the release of ten political prisoners from Tombalbaye's jails.[73]

In order to force the matter, on 10 December, the rebels announced that they would execute Galopin if the French refused to name a high-level envoy. Two days later, Robert Puissant, again named special envoy to the rebels, arrived in Bardaï.[74] By early January 1975, Puissant and Habré had agreed on the conditions originally proposed by Claustre. In lieu of the ransom, however, the rebels would receive two Land Rovers, two and a half tons of food, two radios, one hundred uniforms, and two thousand liters of gasoline for each hostage.[75]

This time, the French met with Tombalbaye's refusal. He would only agree to these conditions if the rebels released Galopin first. French President Valéry Giscard d'Estaing sent a personal message demanding that Tombalbaye conform to the conditions, regardless of which hostage the rebels released first. The Chadian president, however, refused to budge, claiming that, according to his sources, Galopin suffered mistreatment.[76]

Thus, the negotiations had stalled once again, with the French unable to satisfy both of their interlocutors at the same time. Eventually, as negotiations remained frozen, Habré announced that the rebels would execute Galopin on 4 April if the French did not agree to deliver weapons.[77]

According to Goukouni, the rebels did not actually intend to execute Galopin on the day their ultimatum expired. However, on the 4th, Goukouni claims that the rebels received a mysterious message from Bardaï. He did not know whether it came from the French or the Chadian garrison, but it threatened, 'Free Galopin, you'll have nothing. If you don't free him, you ragheads [loqueteux] will be decimated'.[78] Goukouni, Habré, and the rest of the CCFAN saw this as an imminent threat, and thus resolved to kill Galopin. Goukouni goes on to mention that, despite Galopin's request for a firing squad, the rebels decided to hang him. To this day, Goukouni does not regret the execution.[79] While no archival evidence supports this version, Touze provides a hint in his diary. On the night of 3 April, he sent a message to Estrade and Laurens in Bardaï, ordering them to remind Habré of the serious consequences of his threat.[80] Habré's treatment of Galopin had apparently traumatized Estrade, his co-negotiator the previous year.[81] Had he sent the threatening message?

A coup d'état and a deal gone sour

Habré's threats on Galopin's life provoked panic among the French. On 1 April 1975, Claustre met Puissant in his office in Paris. To a stunned Claustre, Puissant asked him if he could procure arms for the rebels by finding an arms dealer.[82] However, on 12 April, after learning of Galopin's death, the French reduced their offer. Puissant now proposed ten million francs, four million of which would take the form of non-military material. Nevertheless, Puissant indicated that Claustre could help Habré contact an arms dealer.[83] This turn of events indeed seemed to satisfy both Habré and Goukouni.

The next day, high-ranking Chadian military officers overthrew and killed Tombalbaye in a coup d'état. Over the next few days, the officers leading the coup, including several recently freed from prison, formed the *Conseil supérieur militaire* (CSM) as the new governing entity.[84] The new President, General Félix Malloum, had been on Habré's list of prisoners he wanted the Tombalbaye regime to free in exchange for the hostages. The reasons behind the coup d'état do not particularly concern this chapter. However, one should note that one of its triggers lay in Tombalbabye's attempt to purge elements of his security apparatus following an escape attempt by members of Habré's family, whom the regime had detained the previous year.[85]

Soon after taking power, the CSM made a number of statements which reassured the French. Particularly, it arrested few members of the former regime, and openly declared its desire for national reconciliation. Malloum called on the different Frolinat factions to return to the fold.[86] Nonetheless, Habré remained deaf to these overtures. Since the regime had released a number of prisoners, Habré did agree, however, to remove that condition from his list of demands.[87]

In May 1975, Stéphane Hessel, a famous former resistance figure and Buchenwald survivor, and now high-level official in the Cooperation Ministry, became the lead negotiator for the release of the hostages.[88] However, the situation had changed from the previous month. Marc Combe, whom the rebels had used as a chauffeur and mechanic for their Land Rovers, managed to take advantage of his privileged position and escaped. As Françoise Claustre remained the only hostage, Hessel would offer less to the rebels than promised before. In a meeting with Malloum, Hessel explained his instructions: a four million franc ransom, as well as a number of non-military goods.[89] By June, Malloum had agreed to these conditions.[90]

After several attempts to meet Habré, Hessel finally arranged to a meeting on 14 July. Hessel told Habré and Goukouni, in front of a number of FAN fighters, that Claustre had acquired weapons and, at that very moment, he was delivering them in a chartered DC-4 aircraft to the rebel stronghold of Yebi-Bou.[91] At this news, the rebels agreed to begin discussing the modalities of the prisoner release. Hessel even gave the rebels his Land Rover, so that they could reach Yebi-Bou more quickly in order to verify the weapons delivery. On 1 August, Hessel would deliver the ransom and bring Françoise Claustre to freedom. In N'Djamena, Hessel held a press conference announcing the imminent liberation of Françoise Claustre.[92]

Indeed, after a return visit to the BET, Pierre Claustre had returned to France in order to arrange matters with potential arms dealers. Habré and Goukouni threatened Combe's life if he failed.[93] Taking this threat seriously, Claustre returned to Chad in less than three weeks, this time with famous French documentary film-maker, Raymond Depardon, and photographer Marie-Laure de Decker. Not only would Depardon defray some of the costs of the voyage, but Claustre also felt that some publicity could help his case.[94] In any event, Goukouni gave Claustre one million francs in order to procure weapons.

Claustre managed to charter a DC-4 which would fly to Ghana to buy rifles. From there, it would deliver the weapons to Yebi-Bou. Unfortunately, this plan ended disastrously. The arms that his providers purchased lacked ammunition and consisted of light submachine guns good for combat at close quarters, but not for the kind of fighting engaged in by the FAN.[95] The value of the arms delivered to the rebels was far less than the one million francs given to Claustre. This infuriated the rebels. Furthermore, on the return journey, the DC-4, which now carried the French journalists, made a forced landing in Niger. The Nigerien authorities, discovering the true mission of the aircraft, impounded the plane, and deported its passengers. They also seized the film and recording equipment belonging to Depardon and de Decker. Given the public nature of such an action, the Chadian government quickly learned of the failed mission, thus confirming their worst fears about French duplicity.[96]

On 24 July, the CSM strictly forbade the French from making further direct contacts with the CCFAN. Instead, they announced to the French that any solution to the hostage situation would occur under the auspices of a general negotiated political settlement. French policymakers, seeing little choice in the matter, agreed. However, at the end of August, the rebels announced that they would execute Françoise Claustre if the French failed to pay the ransom agreed upon with Hessel by 23 September.[97]

Meanwhile, Pierre Claustre had again returned to Tibesti with Depardon. The latter managed to conduct an interview with Françoise Claustre, whose broadcast would eventually push the French government into action. On 22 August, however, as Depardon returned to France, the rebels decided to keep Pierre Claustre as a hostage due to the failure of his mission.[98]

Bad break-ups and new friends

On 10 September 1975, the French television station, TF1, broadcast Depardon's moving tearful interview with Françoise Claustre. She notably declared that her austere and isolated conditions were such that 'within three years, I'll go insane!'.[99] The interview provoked a substantial public outcry which forced the French authorities to act. On the 25th, a French Transall aircraft landed and delivered four million francs to the CCFAN.[100] Several days later, according to Pierre Claustre, up to sixteen different French aircraft dropped clothing, blankets, shoes, and food.[101] Such an enormous demonstration did not pass by the CSM unnoticed.

Furious, the CSM accused French authorities of violating Chadian sovereignty by authorizing or tolerating arms deliveries, as well as 'subversive' activities by its citizens in the rebel zone.[102] On 27 September, Malloum gave French forces one month to evacuate the country. The CSM also demanded a renegotiation of cooperation and defence agreements linking the two countries.[103] On 28 October, as the last French forces left Chad, government army units launched a major attack against Zoui, the oasis and village east of Bardaï where many of the negotiations had taken place. Touze noted that French mercenaries piloting Chadian air force planes had observed fires burning around the oasis.[104] Claustre later claimed that the Chadian army killed some sixty of its inhabitants in cold blood.[105] If the CSM wanted to encourage national reconciliation, these tactics did not help.

Franco-Chadian talks stalled until December. Through the mediation of Gabonese president, Omar Bongo, French and Chadian emissaries agreed to begin negotiations on a new set of cooperation accords.[106] In early March 1976, French Prime Minister Jacques Chirac, visited N'Djamena to sign a new set of cooperation agreements. However, this did not help the French in their efforts to free the Claustres.

Fed up with the CSM's consistent refusal to authorize French negotiations with the CCFAN, French diplomats opened a Libyan backchannel to pressure the rebel leadership. With the arrival of Muammar Gaddafi in power in 1969, Libyan authorities began to see Chad as a Libyan zone of influence. Beginning in 1973, Libya unofficially annexed a large band of territory extending as far as one hundred and fifty kilometers south of Libya's internationally recognized frontier. This area, known as the 'Aozou strip', later became a major bone of contention in Chadian–Libyan relations.[107] In fact, the only serious opposition to Libyan designs on Northern Chad came from Hissène Habré and his allies within the CCFAN. Libya, however, served as an important rear base for the FAN. Furthermore, Frolinat, the organization to which the FAN officially belonged as its 'Second Army', had its headquarters in Tripoli. However, the CCFAN had had serious disagreements with the Frolinat Secretary General, Abba Sidick.[108] Thus, until 1975, the Second Army received extremely limited support from Libya. This began to change in late 1975 when Libyan relations with Sidick began to deteriorate. According to Goukouni, Libyan intelligence began sending feelers to the CCFAN. In February 1976, the CCFAN received Libyan envoys and sent emissaries of their own to Tripoli. In addition to providing a few weapons and other goods, the Libyans offered training for medics, drivers, and radio operators.[109]

However, Habré maintained his anti-Libyan enmity. He even refused a personal request from Gaddafi for a meeting in late May. The CCFAN sent Goukouni instead. According to him, Gaddafi expressed a willingness to aid the rebellion, but also wanted the FAN to free the Claustres via Libya.[110] Libyan overtures soon led to divisions within the CCFAN. For example, at the end of June, a FAN detachment ambushed Libyan soldiers south of Aozou and took a large number of prisoners. After difficult negotiations, during which Habré initially refused to return the prisoners, the FAN agreed to release the soldiers.[111]

The CCFAN faced a difficult position, stuck between the government in N'Djamena and growing Libyan ambitions in the North. Pulled between competing threats and options, tensions within the CCFAN reached the breaking point. Habré, viscerally anti-Libyan, resented Libyan interference and wanted to fight against its occupation of the Aouzou strip.[112] Goukouni, on the other hand, felt that Frolinat could not handle a two-front war and should thus focus its efforts against the Chadian government.[113]

In September 1976, the CCFAN and various Frolinat factions held a meeting in Gouro in order to coordinate a common position. However, the meeting soon turned into a clash of personalities, particularly that of Goukouni and Habré. The gathering ended with Habré's decision to leave Gouro and the CCFAN with his supporters, while keeping the acronym FAN for his troops. Habré moved his forces out of Tibesti towards Central Chad. Eventually, under heavy government assaults, he crossed over into Sudan.[114]

With Habré out of the way, Goukouni could begin to build a profitable relationship with Libya. However, Gaddafi continued to press for the release of the Claustres, and provided little or no assistance until their release.[115] Indeed, by linking military assistance to the release of the hostages, Libya signalled that from now on it would have a seat at the Chadian table. Libya henceforth became an indispensible interlocutor for anyone looking to make peace in Northern Chad.

In late 1976, the CSM had begun receiving disturbing reports that the French had begun negotiations with the Libyans for the release of the hostages. Until the very moment of the Claustres' liberation via Libya, the French government continued to assure its Chadian protégés that it had not negotiated with the rebels. On 14 December 1976, in response to Chadian suspicions of this nature, the French ambassador, Louis Dallier, assured the Chadian Foreign Minister, Wadal Abdelkader Kamougue, that the French did not, and would not negotiate with the rebellion for the two hostages. Dallier maintained the official line that France now expected their liberation to result from a general negotiated settlement of the rebellion.[116]

Though not technically a lie as no evidence suggests that France had indeed negotiated with the rebels, it simply covered up the fact that it had begun negotiations with Libya to secure the release of the hostages. At the end of January 1977, Goukouni, now exclusively in charge of the Claustre situation, released the Claustres to the French embassy in Tripoli. Needless to say this infuriated Malloum and his government.[117]

Giscard's letter to Malloum following the release of the Claustres tried to calm Malloum's understandable anger. Giscard wrote 'I am convinced that your tireless policy of national reconciliation, of contact and dialogue, as well as the climate of appeasement and hope...have powerfully contributed to this act of wisdom and humanity [the liberation of the Claustres]'.[118] Although meant to calm the anger sure to arise after the news of the Claustres' release, this missive sounded insulting. Shortly afterwards, the CSM publically denounced France's role in the Claustres' liberation and highlighted France's violations of Chadian sovereignty.[119] Nonetheless, unlike 1975, the CSM took no steps to break relations.

On 3 February, the French newspaper *Le Monde* claimed that Libya provided Goukouni with five million francs, one hundred Kalashnikov assault rifles, and one hundred thousand rounds of ammunition in exchange for the Claustres.[120] Goukouni has since denied these claims.[121] Nonetheless, French documents attest to the veracity of the report, and even suggest that Gaddafi's assistance far surpassed that suggested in *Le Monde*.[122] Thus, this backdoor deal made France indirectly responsible for Goukouni's massive rearmament. French documents also attest to the key role played by French negotiations in Libyan pressure on the Second Army to release the Claustres.[123] France helped to open a door and legitimize a role for Gaddafi in Chad that would have fateful consequences for the country in the years to come.

Goukouni's rearmament and training allowed the Second Army to launch a major offensive in mid-June 1977.[124] Within a month, Goukouni's forces managed to capture the entirety of Tibesti, including Bardaï and substantial portions of Borkou prefecture.[125] This signalled the resumption of a war which has, in various forms, continued until today.

Conclusions

The Claustre affair demonstrated the capacity of a small band of desert guerrillas to substantially alter the nature of French relations with a client regime. By forcing the French into a situation of perpetual two-level negotiations, they managed to go a long way towards realizing their political aspirations. The evolution of the hostage crisis also unmasked the counterproductive nature of French policy in Chad and, by extension, much of Africa. By reinforcing and enabling a tyrannical regime in the repression of its own citizens, the French almost ensured a situation of continuous warfare.

Between 1974 and late 1975, rebel demands seemed almost specifically designed to sow discord between the French and the Chadian regime. This bet paid off brilliantly with the evacuation of French forces. However, their lack of weaponry still meant that they could not make significant headway against government forces. Thus, the question of opting for Libyan support became crucial. It also divided the CCFAN, an event which ultimately had dreadful consequences.

Politically, the Claustre affair had important consequences for the future of Chad. First, it demonstrated the inherent and continual weakness of the Chadian regime, both under Tombalbaye and the CSM. Outside of the few towns in the BET, the rebellion could operate freely, and the hostage crisis gave this fact a good deal of publicity. Also, French negotiations with the rebels eventually revealed the limitations of Chadian sovereignty, and its ultimate dependence upon its former colonial master.

The Claustre affair also allowed Libya to assert itself as an important player in Chadian politics. Although Muammar Gaddafi had ordered the occupation of Aouzou several years previously, the liberation of the Claustres provided him with a triumphal port of entry into the country. French negotiations with Gaddafi over the Claustres represented implicit French recognition of a Libyan sphere of interest in Northern Chad. Libyan meddling would have a disastrous effect on Chadian politics over the next decade and a half.

The evolution of Chadian political configurations resulting from the Claustre affair would ensure that both Goukouni and Habré would have ample future opportunities to demonstrate their commitment to peace and democracy. Neither of them fulfilled their revolutionary promises. Habré later gained a bloody reputation as one of the continent's more ruthlessly efficient dictators, and Goukouni long played Gaddafi's game of civil war.

Notes

1   See B. Blumenau, 'The United Nations and West Germany's Efforts against International Terrorism in the 1970s', Chapter 4 in this volume.

2   For further reading, see Mohamed Tétémadi Bangoura, *Violence politique et conflits en Afrique: le cas du Tchad*, Paris: L'Harmattan, 2005; Robert Buijtenhuijs, *Le Frolinat et les guerres civiles du Tchad: 1977–1984*. Paris: Karthala, 1987; and Millard Burr and Robert O. Collins, *Darfur: The Long Road to Disaster*, Princeton, New Jersey: Markus Wiener Publishers, 2008. This is an updated and cleverly renamed version of their book, *Africa's Thirty Years War: Libya, Chad, and the Sudan, 1963–1993*, Boulder, Colorado: Westview Press, 1999.

3   MAE La Courneuve, Direction des Affaires Africaines et Malgaches, Tchad 1975–1979, Carton 98, Dossier 98/2 Notes de la direction, Note A/S. Intervention militaire française au Tchad (Avril 1969–Septembre 1972), 06 June 1978, p. 1.

4   Accords et conventions de maintien de l'ordre dans les etats africains et malgaches, Cours supérieur interarmées, 1966–1967. Available online: www.rue89.com/files/20070726Defense.pdf (accessed 30 November 2009), p. 2.

5   Direction des Affaires Africaines et Malgaches, Carton 98, Dossier 98/2 Notes de la direction, Note A/S. Intervention militaire française au Tchad (Avril 1969–Septembre 1972), 06 June 1978, p. 2.

6   Ibid., p. 2.

7   Ibid., p. 3.

8   Ibid., p. 4.

9   R. Buijtenhuijs, *Le Frolinat et les guerres civiles du Tchad: 1977–1984*, Paris: Karthala, 1987, p. 425.

10 Direction des Affaires Africaines et Malgaches, Carton 98, Dossier 98/2 Notes de la direction, Note A/S. Intervention militaire française au Tchad (Avril 1969–Septembre 1972), 06 June 1978, p. 4.

11 MC Archives Fontainebleau, Fonds des chargés de mission géographique au Tchad, Carton 2, A4/2, Note, A/S: Evolution de la Mission de réforme administrative au Tchad, 31 October 1974, p. 2.

12 Direction des Affaires Africaines et Malgaches, Carton 90, Dossier Relations franco-tchadiennes–Visite du Premier ministre Jacques Chirac, Voyage du Premier ministre au Tchad 5–6 Mars 1976, Note A/S: les relations franco-tchadiennes, 01 March 1976, p. 2.

13 P. Claustre, *L'affaire Claustre: autopsie d'une prise d'otages*, Paris: Editions Karthala, 1990, pp. 16–17.

14 Direction des Affaires Africaines et Malgaches, Carton 98, Dossier 98/2 Notes de la direction, Note A/S. Intervention militaire française au Tchad. (Avril 1969-Septembre 1972), 06.06.1978, p. 4.

15 Fonds des chargés de mission géographique au Tchad, Carton 2, A4/1 Dossier Affaire Bardaï 21 Avril 1974, Telegram no. 129/30 from Direction des Affaires Africaines et Malgaches to Baldit, 23 April 1974, p. 2.

16 P. Claustre, *L'affaire Claustre: autopsie d'une prise d'otages*, Paris: Editions Karthala, 1990, p. 62.

17 Fonds des chargés de mission géographique au Tchad, Carton 2, A4/1 Dossier Affaire Bardaï 21 Avril 1974, Telegram no. 376/380 from Touze to Paris, 13 May 1974, p. 2.

18 Direction des Affaires Africaines et Malgaches, Carton 90, Dossier Relations franco-tchadiennes – Visite du Premier ministre Jacques Chirac, Voyage du Premier ministre au Tchad 5–6 Mars 1976, Note A/S: les relations franco-tchadiennes, 01 March 1976, p. 3.

19 Fonds des chargés de mission géographique au Tchad, Carton 2, A4/1 Dossier Affaire Bardaï 21 Avril 1974, Telegram no. 389/392 from Touze to Paris, 15 May 1974, p. 2.

20 Fonds des chargés de mission géographique au Tchad, Carton 2, A4/1 Dossier Affaire Bardaï 21 Avril 1974, Telegram no. 371/373 from Touze to Paris, 13 May 1974, p. 1.

21 Ibid., p. 1.

22 Ibid., p. 2.

23 Fonds des chargés de mission géographique au Tchad, Carton 2, A4/1 Dossier Affaire Bardaï 21 Avril 1974, Telegram no. 393/396 from Touze to Paris, 15 May 1974, p. 2.

24 Ibid.

25 P. Claustre, *L'affaire Claustre: autopsie d'une prise d'otages*, Paris: Editions Karthala, 1990, pp. 76–7.

26 Ibid., pp. 77–8.

27 Ibid., pp. 80–1.

28 Ibid., p. 83.

29 Ibid., pp. 84–5.

30 Ibid., p. 85.

31 Fonds des chargés de mission géographique au Tchad, Carton 2, A4/1 Dossier Affaire Bardaï 21 Avril 1974, Telegram no. 604/609 from Touze to Paris, 15 June 1974, p. 2.

32 Fonds des chargés de mission géographique au Tchad, Carton 2, A4/1 Dossier Affaire Bardaï 21 Avril 1974, Note from Touze to Paris, A/S: Affaire de Bardaï, 05 June 1974, La Position du Conseil exécutif du M.N.R.C.S. sur les événements de Bardaï, p. 5.

33 P. Claustre, *L'affaire Claustre: autopsie d'une prise d'otages*, Paris: Editions Karthala, 1990, p. 83.

34 Ibid., p. 93.

35 Al Hadj Garondé Djarma, *Tchad, témoignage d'un militant du Frolinat*, Paris: L'Harmattan, 2003, p. 124.

36 Fonds des chargés de mission géographique au Tchad, Carton 2, A4/1 Dossier Affaire Bardaï 21 Avril 1974, Telegram no. 572/575 from Touze to Paris, 12 June 1974, p. 1.

37 Ibid., p. 2.

38 Fonds des chargés de mission géographique au Tchad, Carton 2, A4/1 Dossier Affaire Bardaï 21 Avril 1974, Note from Touze to Paris, A/S: Affaire de Bardaï. Rupture par le Tchad de ses relations avec la R.F.A. 17 June 1974, Communiqué du Conseil exécutif du M.N.R.C.S. diffusé dans la soirée du 12 juin 1974, p.5.

39 Ibid., p. 3.

40 P. Claustre, *L'affaire Claustre: autopsie d'une prise d'otages*, Paris: Editions Karthala, 1990, p. 114.

41 Fonds des chargés de mission géographique au Tchad, Carton 2, A4/1 Dossier Affaire Bardaï 21 Avril 1974, Telegram no. 600/603 from Touze to Paris, 15 June 1974, p. 1.

42   MAE Nantes, N'Djamena Ambassade, Carton 7, Dossier Documents et notes trouvés dans la valise du Cdt Pierre Galopin le 18 February 1976 (qu'il parait inopportun de restituer à sa famille), Telegram from Direction des Affaires Africaines et Malgaches to N'Djamena Embassy, Otages de Bardaï, 12 June 1974, p. 1.

43   Fonds des chargés de mission géographique au Tchad, Carton 2, A4/1 Dossier Affaire Bardaï 21 Avril 1974, Telegram no. 663/666 from Tripoli Embassy to Paris, 19 June 1974, p. 2.

44   P. Claustre, *L'affaire Claustre: autopsie d'une prise d'otages*, Paris: Editions Karthala, 1990, pp. 112–13.

45   R. Buijtenhuijs, *Le Frolinat et les révoltes populaires du Tchad 1965–1976*, The Hague: Mouton, 1978, p. 237.

46   Ibid., p. 156.

47   Ibid., p. 273.

48   L. Correau, *Goukouni Weddeye: Témoignage pour l'histoire du Tchad*, Entretiens publiés par Radio France Internationale, 2008. Available online: www.rfi.fr/actufr/images/104%5CGoukouni_Weddeye_Entretiens.pdf (accessed 27 May 2012), p. 19.

49   Fonds des chargés de mission géographique au Tchad, Carton 2, A4/1 Dossier Affaire Bardaï 21 Avril 1974, Mémorandum sur l'affaire des otages du Bardaï (Tchad), 12 May 1975, p. 4.

50   MAE Nantes, N'Djamena Ambassade, Carton 7, Dossier Documents et notes trouvés dans la valise du Cdt Pierre Galopin le 18 February 1976 (qu'il parait inopportun de restituer à sa famille), Handwritten note from Camille Gourvennec to Pierre Galopin, 04 July 1974, p. 2.

51   MAE Nantes, N'Djamena Ambassade, Carton 7, Dossier Documents et notes trouvés dans la valise du Cdt Pierre Galopin le 18 February 1976 (qu'il parait inopportun de restituer à sa famille), Telegram from Direction des Affaires Africaines et Malgaches to N'Djamena Embassy, Otages de Bardaï, 12 June 1974, p. 1.

52   Ibid.

53   Fonds des chargés de mission géographique au Tchad, Carton 2, A4/1 Dossier Affaire Bardaï 21 Avril 1974, Telegram no. 604/609 from Touze to Paris, 15 June 1974, p. 2.

54   Ibid., p. 2.

55   Fonds des chargés de mission géographique au Tchad, Carton 2, A4/1 Dossier Affaire Bardaï 21 Avril 1974, Telegram no. 643/45 from Touze to Paris, 22 June 1974, p. 1.

56   Fonds des chargés de mission géographique au Tchad, Carton 2, A4/1 Dossier Affaire Bardaï 21 Avril 1974, Telegram no. 691/92 from Touze to Paris, 06 July 1974, p. 1.

57   MAE Nantes, N'Djamena Ambassade, Carton 7, Dossier Documents et notes trouvés dans la valise du Cdt Pierre Galopin le 18 February 1976 (qu'il parait inopportun de restituer à sa famille), Telegram from Direction des Affaires Africaines et Malgaches to N'Djamena Embassy, Otages de Bardaï, 12 June 1974, p. 2.

58   Fonds des chargés de mission géographique au Tchad, Carton 2, A4/1 Dossier Affaire Bardaï 21 Avril 1974, Mémorandum sur l'affaire des otages du Bardaï (Tchad), 12 May 1975, p. 4.

59 Fonds des chargés de mission géographique au Tchad, Carton 2, A4/1 Dossier Affaire Bardaï 21 Avril 1974, Compte Rendu de la mission effectuée à Bardaï du 30 Septembre au 3 Octobre 1974, by Martial Laurens, p. 7.
60 Interview with Goukouni, in L. Correau, *Goukouni Weddeye: Témoignage pour l'histoire du Tchad*, Entretiens publiés par Radio France Internationale, 2008. Available online: www.rfi.fr/actufr/images/104%5CGoukouni_Weddeye_ Entretiens.pdf (accessed 27 May 2012), p. 60.
61 Ibid.
62 MAE Nantes, N'Djamena Ambassade, Carton 7, Dossier Documents et notes trouvés dans la valise du Cdt Pierre Galopin le 18 February 1976 (qu'il paraît inopportun de restituer à sa famille), Handwritten note from Camille Gourvennec to Pierre Galopin, 04 July 1974, pp. 1–2.
63 Fonds des chargés de mission géographique au Tchad, Carton 2, A4/1 Dossier Affaire Bardaï 21 Avril 1974, Telegram no. 752/753 from Baldit to Paris, 17 July 1974, p. 1.
64 Interview with Goukouni, in L. Correau, *Goukouni Weddeye: Témoignage pour l'histoire du Tchad*, Entretiens publiés par Radio France Internationale, 2008. Available online: www.rfi.fr/actufr/images/104%5CGoukouni_Weddeye_ Entretiens.pdf (accessed 27 May 2012), p. 60.
65 Fonds des chargés de mission géographique au Tchad, Carton 2, A4/1 Dossier Affaire Bardaï 21 Avril 1974, Mémorandum sur l'affaire des otages du Bardaï (Tchad), 12 May 1975, p. 4.
66 Fonds des chargés de mission géographique au Tchad, Carton 2, A4/1 Dossier Affaire Bardaï 21 Avril 1974, Compte Rendu de la mission effectuée à Bardaï du 30 Septembre au 3 Octobre 1974, by Martial Laurens, p. 3.
67 Ibid., p. 8.
68 Fonds des chargés de mission géographique au Tchad, Carton 2, A4/1 Dossier Affaire Bardaï 21 Avril 1974, Note from Touze to Paris, A/S: Déroulement de l'affaire de Bardaï, 14 November 1974, p. 4.
69 Ibid., p. 4.
70 Al Hadj Garondé Djarma, *Tchad, témoignage d'un militant du Frolinat*, Paris: L'Harmattan, 2003, p. 125.
71 L. Correau, *Goukouni Weddeye: Témoignage pour l'histoire du Tchad*, Entretiens publiés par Radio France Internationale, 2008. Available online: www.rfi.fr/ actufr/images/104%5CGoukouni_Weddeye_Entretiens.pdf (accessed 27 May 2012), p. 173.
72 Ibid.
73 Ibid.
74 Fonds des chargés de mission géographique au Tchad, Carton 2, A4/1 Dossier Affaire Bardaï 21 Avril 1974, Mémorandum sur l'affaire des otages du Bardaï (Tchad), 12 May 1975, p. 5.
75 Ibid., p. 6.
76 Ibid., p. 6.
77 Ibid., p. 7.
78 Interview with Goukouni, in L. Correau, *Goukouni Weddeye: Témoignage pour l'histoire du Tchad*, Entretiens publiés par Radio France Internationale, 2008. Available online: www.rfi.fr/actufr/images/104%5CGoukouni_Weddeye_ Entretiens.pdf (accessed 27 May 2012), pp. 60–1.
79 Ibid., p. 62.

80 R.L. Touze, *370 jours d'un ambassadeur au Tchad*, Paris: Editions France-Empire, 1989, p. 364.

81 Ibid., p. 157.

82 P. Claustre, *L'affaire Claustre: autopsie d'une prise d'otages*, Paris: Editions Karthala, 1990, pp. 223–4.

83 Ibid., p. 243.

84 Fonds des chargés de mission géographique au Tchad, Carton 2, A4/4 Note from Touze to Paris, A/S: Après le coup d'Etat du 13 avril, p. 4.

85 Fonds des chargés de mission géographique au Tchad, Carton 2, A4/1 Dossier Affaire Bardaï 21 Avril 1974, Telegram no. 395/97 from Touze to Paris, 03 April 1975, p. 1.

86 Fonds des chargés de mission géographique au Tchad, Carton 2, A4/4 Note from Touze to Paris, A/S: Après le coup d'Etat du 13 avril, p. 5.

87 Fonds des chargés de mission géographique au Tchad, Carton 2, A4/1 Dossier Affaire Bardaï 21 Avril 1974, Mémorandum sur l'affaire des otages du Bardaï (Tchad), 12 May 1975, p. 8.

88 Al Hadj Garondé Djarma, *Tchad, témoignage d'un militant du Frolinat*, Paris: L'Harmattan, 2003, p. 128.

89 S. Hessel, *Danse avec le siécle*, Paris: Seuil, 1997, p. 208.

90 Direction des Affaires Africaines et Malgaches, Carton 90, Dossier Relations franco-tchadiennes – Visite du Premier ministre Jacques Chirac, Voyage du Premier ministre au Tchad 5–6 Mars 1976, Note A/S: les relations franco-tcha-diennes, 1 March 1976, p. 4.

91 S. Hessel, *Danse avec le siécle*, Paris: Seuil, 1997, p. 210.

92 Ibid.

93 P. Claustre, *L'affaire Claustre: autopsie d'une prise d'otages*, Paris: Editions Karthala, 1990, p. 260.

94 Ibid., p. 274.

95 Ibid., p. 310.

96 Ibid., pp. 314–15.

97 Direction des Affaires Africaines et Malgaches, Carton 90, Dossier Relations franco-tchadiennes – Visite du Premier ministre Jacques Chirac, Voyage du Premier ministre au Tchad 5–6 Mars 1976, Note A/S: les relations franco-tcha-diennes, 1 March 1976, p. 6.

98 P. Claustre, *L'affaire Claustre: autopsie d'une prise d'otages*, Paris: Editions Karthala, 1990, pp. 330–4.

99 Al Hadj Garondé Djarma, *Tchad, témoignage d'un militant du Frolinat*, Paris: L'Harmattan, 2003, p. 132.

100 P. Claustre, *L'affaire Claustre: autopsie d'une prise d'otages*, Paris: Editions Karthala, 1990, p. 348.

101 Ibid., pp. 351–2.

102 Direction des Affaires Africaines et Malgaches, Carton 90, Dossier Relations franco-tchadiennes – Visite du Premier ministre Jacques Chirac, Voyage du Premier ministre au Tchad 5–6 Mars 1976, Note A/S: les relations franco-tchadiennes, 01 March 1976, p. 6.

103 Ibid., p. 6.

104 Fonds des chargés de mission géographique au Tchad, Carton 2, A4/1 Dossier Affaire Bardaï 21 Avril 1974, Telegram no. 1941/1942 from Touze to Paris, 29 October 1975, p. 1.

105 P. Claustre, *L'affaire Claustre: autopsie d'une prise d'otages*, Paris: Editions Karthala,

1990, p. 362.

106 Direction des Affaires Africaines et Malgaches, Carton 90, Dossier Relations franco-tchadiennes – Visite du Premier ministre Jacques Chirac, Voyage du Premier ministre au Tchad 5–6 Mars 1976, Note A/S: les relations franco-tchadiennes, 01 March 1976, p. 6–7.

107 For an in-depth discussion of Libyan influence in Chad during this time, see R. Otayek, 'La Libye face à la France au Tchad: qui perd gagne?', *Politique Africaine*, 1984, vol. 16, pp. 66–85.

108 For an extensive analysis of this split, see Buijtenhuijs, op cit., pp. 241–54.

109 Interview with Goukouni, in L. Correau, *Goukouni Weddeye: Témoignage pour l'histoire du Tchad*, Entretiens publiés par Radio France Internationale, 2008. Available online: www.rfi.fr/actufr/images/104%5CGoukouni_Weddeye_Entretiens.pdf (accessed 27 May 2012), p. 64–5.

110 Ibid., p. 65.

111 Ibid., p. 66.

112 R. Buijtenhuijs, *Le Frolinat et les révoltes populaires du Tchad 1965–1976*, The Hague: Mouton, 1978, p. 32.

113 Interview with Goukouni, in L. Correau, *Goukouni Weddeye: Témoignage pour l'histoire du Tchad*, Entretiens publiés par Radio France Internationale, 2008. Available online: www.rfi.fr/actufr/images/104%5CGoukouni_Weddeye_Entretiens.pdf (accessed 27 May 2012), p. 67.

114 R. Buijtenhuijs, *Le Frolinat et les révoltes populaires du Tchad 1965–1976*, The Hague: Mouton, 1978, p. 42.

115 Interview with Goukouni, in L. Correau, *Goukouni Weddeye: Témoignage pour l'histoire du Tchad*, Entretiens publiés par Radio France Internationale, 2008. Available online: www.rfi.fr/actufr/images/104%5CGoukouni_Weddeye_Entretiens.pdf (accessed 27 May 2012), p. 70.

116 MAE Nantes, N'Djamena Ambassade, Carton 7, Dossier Général Malloum, Note from Dallier to the Chadian Foreign Minister, 14 December 1976.

117 MAE Nantes Carton 3, Dossier Rapport de fin de mission de l'Ambassadeur Dallier, Rapport de fin de mission, p. 5.

118 MAE Nantes, N'Djamena Ambassade Carton 7, Dossier Relations Tchado-Libyennes, Telegram no. 73/75 from Georgy to Dallier, 31 January 1977.

119 Mouric, Nelly, 'La politique tchadienne de la France sous Valery Giscard d'Estaing: vers la prise en compte de la rébellion', *Politique Africaine*, 1984, no. 16: 92.

120 R. Buijtenhuijs, *Le Frolinat et les révoltes populaires du Tchad 1965–1976*, The Hague: Mouton, 1978, p. 39.

121 Interview with Goukouni, in L. Correau, *Goukouni Weddeye: Témoignage pour l'histoire du Tchad*, Entretiens publiés par Radio France Internationale, 2008. Available online: www.rfi.fr/actufr/images/104%5CGoukouni_Weddeye_Entretiens.pdf (accessed 27 May 2012), p. 71.

122 Fonds des chargés de mission géographique au Tchad, Carton 2, A4/4, Note, La rébellion tchadienne, 08 July 1977, p. 2.

123 MAE Nantes, N'Djamena Ambassade, Carton 3, Dossier Rapport de fin de mission de l'Ambassadeur Dallier, Rapport de fin de mission, p. 5.

124 Fonds des chargés de mission géographique au Tchad, Carton 2, A4/4, Note, La rébellion tchadienne, 08 July 1977, p. 2.

125 R. Buijtenhuijs, *Le Frolinat et les révoltes populaires du Tchad 1965–1976*, The Hague: Mouton, 1978, p. 39.

12 Reagan and Libya

A history of pre-emptive strikes and (failed) regime change

Mattia Toaldo

Introduction

From 1981 to 1986, Libya and the United States (US) confronted each other over the issue of terrorism. The policy adopted by the Reagan administration showed some elements of what would later become George W. Bush's War on Terror: the use of military force to strike against a regime that was considered to be a major sponsor of international terrorism.[1] Nevertheless, comparisons between the events of the 1980s and the post-9/11 world should be handled with care. Reagan was acting during the Cold War and he was deeply influenced by this context and its constraints. Qadhafi, although being a client of Soviet weapons, was not a Soviet puppet and was hit exactly because of that: his regime was targeted because it would send a signal to other countries, like Syria, that supported terrorism without incurring a major Soviet reaction.[2]

Mu'ammar Qadhafi came to power on 1 September 1969 in a bloodless coup d'état that he subsequently labelled as a revolution. His group of seventy military officers overthrew the pro-Western Sanusi dynasty and established the Revolutionary Command Council (RCC) as the top authority of the country. The first acts of the RCC exposed the mix of political Islam and pan-Arab feelings that lay at the heart of Qadhafi's political project and it was not by chance that Article 2 of the new constitution approved in 1970 said clearly that Islam was the official religion of Libya.[3] Towards the West, Qadhafi mixed realpolitik with ideology: he expelled Italian settlers, closed American and British military bases, nationalized oil companies, while at the same time striking arms deals with France, and gradually establishing a good economic partnership with Italy that allowed him to have enough oil revenues to distribute benefits to his population and stabilize his regime. Ideological background was provided by his plan for a 'Muslim Cultural Revolution' outlined in the *Green Book*. His 'Third Universal Theory' claimed that by returning to the fundamentals of Islam, Libyans could build a 'Third Way' toward development that rejected both Western capitalism and communism. As François Burgat has argued, Qadhafi's policy at home and abroad in the 1970s, with all its ambiguities, significantly contributed to the shift from pan-Arab Nasserism towards Political Islam as the dominant discourse in the Arab world and beyond.[4]

Initially, this reference to Islam led some US policy-makers to believe that he would be harmless, if not become an ally. To their chagrin, relations between the US and Libya were strained by the end of the 1970s because of his support for terrorism and subversion worldwide: the first US sanctions against Libya were started by president Jimmy Carter in 1978 when Qadhafi was denied aircraft for military use and tractors capable of hauling tanks. In December 1979, Libya was designated as a country supporting terrorism and the following month exports making direct contribution to Libya's military potential were blocked.[5] As in other fields of foreign policy, the Reagan administration would be partially in continuity with Carter's and built its confrontation with Qadhafi on an already strained US–Libyan relationship.

Ronald Reagan won the 1980 presidential elections thanks to a campaign in which he promised to restore America's standing in the world after the humiliations of the war in Vietnam and after what he perceived as the failure of the Carter administration to stop a Soviet offensive in the extra-European world. In 1979, Nicaragua had fallen into the hands of the Marxist Sandinista guerrillas, while the Soviets had invaded Afghanistan, and the pro-Western Pahlavi dynasty in Iran had been overthrown by an Islamist revolution.

In November 1979, American diplomats were taken hostage in Tehran. They would only be freed after four hundred and forty-four days in captivity, on Reagan's inauguration. A failed rescue mission under Carter had probably increased the American perception of a decline in the military capabilities of the superpower, further enhancing what was labelled as 'Vietnam syndrome'.

Middle Eastern terrorism was therefore high on the agenda of the administration right from its first days in office. Receiving the hostages who had returned from Tehran, Reagan promised to deliver 'swift and effective' retribution to terrorists.[6] It was not just a matter of restoring the American people's confidence in the military power of their country; US policy-makers thought there was a credibility crisis with their regional allies. America had to show that it could stand by its friends and that it was ready to confront its foes. And Qadhafi was among the major regional foes, for several reasons. The Director of the Central Intelligence Agency (CIA) William Casey emphasized the multiple dimensions of Qadhafi's threat to US power in the region and in the world: his use of terrorism; his unclear relationship with the Soviet Union; his efforts to destabilize the US-friendly regimes in the Middle East, Africa, and Latin America; and his development of weapons of mass destruction.[7]

Even though he was ideologically hostile and politically independent from the Soviet Union, some members of the Reagan administration and of the conservative foreign policy community saw striking at Qadhafi as part of the global Cold War.[8] Before the administration was inaugurated, the Heritage Foundation (a well-organized conservative think tank) had identified eight extra-European countries where Soviet influence could be rolled back. Libya was among them.[9] As Howard Teicher, Director of the Near East and South Asia bureau in the National Security Council (NSC), wrote in his memoirs, 'a perception of Qadhafi as a leading agent of Soviet subversion took hold in Washington' as soon as Reagan established himself in the White House.[10] When asked whether Libya was acting as a Soviet surrogate in Chad, Chester Crocker, then Assistant Secretary of State for African Affairs, emphasized the 'overlap in the interests and motivations of the Soviets and the Libyans'.[11]

Nevertheless, as Robert Gates (Deputy Director of the CIA under the Reagan administration) wrote in his memoirs, Libya was preferred to Syria and Iran as a target for 'retribution' against states that supported terrorism also because of his lack of strong ties with the Soviet Union.[12] For several reasons, Qadhafi looked to be an attainable goal. Libya's military and demographic situation was not comparable to that of Iran while it did not have the formal Friendship Treaty with the Soviet Union that Syria had. Finally, Qadhafi was a regional outsider for whom few regimes would shed tears. Borrowing the words of later National Security Advisor John Poindexter, Libya looked like 'low hanging fruit'.[13]

1981–82: sanctions instead of war

The Reagan administration started the harvest early on. The first meetings about Libya of which we have some form of record were held in March 1981.[14] On 4 May, Reagan approved the closing of the Libyan embassy (official name: People's Bureau) in Washington. In his diary Reagan referred to events, such as the damage inflicted to the US embassy, which had occurred during the Carter years and which had made his decision easier to justify and more consequential.[15] Other reasons were the attempts by the Libyans to kill members of the opposition exiled to the US and all the Libyan 'subversive' activities in Chad, Sudan, and Egypt.[16]

On 1 June, the NSC approved naval manoeuvres in the Gulf of Sidra, which Libya claimed entirely as territorial waters. 'I'm not being foolhardy but he's a madman', Reagan wrote in his diary, 'it's time to show the other nations there Egypt, Morocco, *et al.* that there is different management here'.[17] The 'Freedom of Navigation' (FON) exercises in the Gulf of Sidra took place between 18 and 20 August 1981. A Libyan aircraft fired upon two American F-14s and was eventually shot down. Tension with Qadhafi continued to escalate throughout the following autumn because of a presumed death threat to the president coming from Libyan death squads at work in the US. Indeed, three days after the confrontation in the Gulf of Sidra, Qadhafi met Ethiopian dictator Menghistu and, in the presence of a high-level CIA source, had promised that 'he was going to have president

Reagan killed'. The threat became even more serious when the National Security Agency intercepted a phone conversation in which Qadhafi vowed again to kill the US president.[18]

A constant flow of intelligence kept the threat alive, turning Qadhafi's Libya into an emergency issue that lasted until December 1981. On the 6th, the Libyan dictator appeared on American TV to deny any assassination attempt against US officials: 'We refuse to assassinate any person . . . This is silly, this administration and this president'.[19]

Although anthropologically and politically unconventional, Qadhafi was not the 'mad man' or the 'clown' that Reagan described in his diary: he was a rational actor who understood that a trap was ready for him. Any kind of provocation, be it a terrorist attack or an assassination attempt against Americans, would trigger an American reaction.

As a matter of fact, in those weeks several options were under scrutiny by the Interagency meetings in Washington. They remained valid despite the end of the assassination threat because all of the other, more strategic, reasons for concern about Libya remained in place. The list of options included the withdrawal of US business personnel from the country, a unilateral oil embargo, and 'enhanced security assistance to friendly regional states'. Secretary of State Alexander Haig did not rule out 'further contingency planning concerning US Military response to Libyan aggression'.[20] Less prominent members of the administration were even more explicit on the use of the military. Raymond Tanter, a member of the Political Affairs Directorate of the NSC, wrote that 'Military options include open assistance to anti-Libyan elements in Chad and elsewhere; urging of Egyptian military action against Libya; and blockade of Libyan ports'.[21]

The prerequisite for military action was the withdrawal of US citizens in Libya. This was crucial to avoid having a new hostage crisis. On 10 December, Americans living in Libya were encouraged by their government to leave the country. By the end of January 1982 there would only be two hundred Americans left in the country.[22] While America was getting ready to retaliate against a Libyan-sponsored terrorist attack, Qadhafi seemed careful to avoid it. He had been previously warned to show restraint towards the US, a private demarche which had been envisaged in National Security Decision Directive (NSDD) 16 approved in December and which had apparently worked. Some members of the Reagan administration seemed to have learned the lesson, as it is evident from the document prepared by Dennis Ross and Francis Fukuyama, at the time both part of the Policy Planning Staff headed by Paul Wolfowitz, and drafted in view of top level discussions in January and February 1982.[23]

This paper predicted that, while a public confrontation would lead to an escalation of Qadhafi's actions instead of restraint, a privately conveyed message would alter his behaviour as already happened with the demarche in December. Indeed, the Libyan dictator had sent an emissary to convey the message that he was restraining terrorist attacks and that he would dismantle training camps. The Policy Planning staff, however, did not take these claims too seriously and thought this was 'a tactical manoeuvre'. Nonetheless, Qadhafi was described as a 'survivor' and as acting much more rationally than previously predicted.[24]

Thanks also to Qadhafi's momentary restraint, American preparations for military confrontation were not implemented in 1982. Eventually, the Reagan administration would approve a limited oil ban against Libya through NSDD 27, signed by the president on 9 March 1982. Under the heading 'Economic Decisions for Libya', the Directive explicitly called for the prohibition of the importation of Libyan crude oil into the US.[25] The following day, the General Accounting Office released a study on the effects of the oil ban on Libya. In the short-term there might have been a revenue loss but in the long-term the effect on either the Libyan or US economy would be small.[26]

The Ross–Fukuyama paper helps to explain why, despite the limited effects of the oil ban, this option was preferred. Arab allies would not have understood a US strike in the absence of a clear cut provocation and therefore military options that had been reviewed during the fall had to be ruled out.[27]

The paper therefore argued for the implementation of a unilateral oil ban which, despite not decisively affecting Libya's economy, would signal American willingness not to support or fund terrorist activities. Being unilateral, it would not further strain relations with the Europeans: the allies in the old continent, especially after the imposition of sanctions against Poland and the USSR, thought that the US was using this measure around the world too much. Sanctions, they thought, would further isolate Qadhafi and push him into the arms of the Soviets. On this point, the export ban also had to be carefully designed not to disrupt the business activities of Western Europeans already under stress because of the Polish sanctions. The export ban, therefore, would not be enforced extraterritorially.[28]

Confrontation between Libya and the US would wind down in the following two years as the Reagan administration became involved in the Lebanese civil war after the Israeli invasion of 6 June 1982. Qadhafi, on his part, was already experiencing economic problems before the oil ban went into effect and had to take care of the domestic situation and the war in Chad. Libyan oil production fell by seventy per cent from the last quarter of 1981 to the first quarter of 1982, while actual revenues dropped by only fifty per cent. This decline was due to the combination of several factors of which the end of deliveries to the US was just one: worldwide recession, the oil glut, and the 'phase-outs in production and the annulment of existing contracts by multinational companies'. This decline in oil revenues (which accounted for almost one hundred per cent of the country's total revenues) deprived the regime of its main weapon in addressing popular concerns and stabilizing its rule over the country. Moreover, Libya was not just overly dependent from only one source – namely oil – it was also rely-ing heavily on the contribution that expatriates gave in that sector as well as in the management and agriculture. To make things even worse, the purchase of sophisticated weapons did not stop.[29]

The problem for Qadhafi was, therefore, the loss of oil revenues, due mainly to the world economy and to his domestic choices, not the confrontation with the US, which, instead, was politically welcome for him. In his speeches and publications, the Libyan dictator emphasized the confrontation with the Italian colonialists and with Westerners in general as crucial elements of a common national history. Later on, Qadhafi would bluntly state that 'the Americans today are like the Italians yesterday'.[30] The rhetoric used by the Reagan administration only reinforced the 'David-versus-Goliath image Qadhafi was able to use for his own internal purposes'.[31]

1984–85: a new offensive against terrorism and Qadhafi

The tension would rise again after the 1984 US presidential elections that Reagan won in a landslide over his Democratic opponent. A few days before Americans went to the polls, the Secretary of State George Shultz delivered an illuminating speech on the issue of the fight against terrorism. At the Park Avenue Synagogue in New York City, he called for a policy that went beyond 'passive defence to consider means of active prevention, pre-emption and retaliation' while giving the executive branch more autonomy in deciding who, what, and when was going to be hit by US military might: 'We will need the flexibility to respond to terrorist attacks in a variety of ways, at times and places of our own choosing' he added.[32]

Shultz's ideas, however, were not shared throughout the administration. Secretary Weinberger, for instance, in a veiled attack against him criticized those who sought 'instant gratification from some kind of bombing attack without being too worried about the details'.[33] Vice President George H.W. Bush sought to limit the use of force against terrorists.

Those in favour of a tougher stance against terrorism could count on several points that made an impression both on the president and on public opinion and allowed the pro-intervention agenda on Libya to move forward throughout 1985. The US withdrawal from Lebanon in the face of deadly terrorist attacks only reinforced the impression that the scars of Vietnam, with the fear of American body bags and long-term military entanglement, still haunted policy-makers and hampered US credibility in the Middle East. Furthermore, 1985 would be an '*annus horribilis*' for the US fight against terrorism: first the hijacking of flight TWA-847, which lasted almost three weeks and resulted in the death of Navy Petty Officer Robert Stethem; second, the hijacking of the Italian cruise ship Achille Lauro with twelve Americans on board, among them Leon Klinghoffer, a man in a wheelchair who was killed by the Palestinian terrorists; and third, the shootings in the airports of Vienna and Rome on 27 December which left nineteen people dead and had, according to the US government, clear Libyan fingerprints on them.[34]

These incidents, however, would only add further momentum for a new confrontation against Libya that had started to build up early in 1985. In January, Shultz prompted Casey and the CIA to find out what could be done to 'develop more aggressive action against terrorists'. According to Gates' memoirs, the Secretary of State 'wanted to see some action to let the terrorist groups know that there is a risk in this'. On Valentine's Day, Robert Gates sent Casey 'a first assessment of Iranian, Syrian, and Libyan support to terrorism and their respective vulnerability to retaliation...We did targeting studies of Libyan and Iranian ports and military facilities, and examined similar targets in Syria'. Syria and Iran were ruled out: the former because of its links with the Soviet Union; the latter because economic pressure might bring it closer to the Soviets while military retaliation was 'too hard'. So, as Gates wrote, 'The process of elimination brought CIA to Libya' which was 'in the poorest position to sustain itself against US actions – military or economic' and thus 'became the target for US retaliation against all state-supported terrorism'.[35]

In fact, Qadhafi provided the opportunity to achieve simultaneously several goals. On 15 February, Vincent Cannistraro[36] and Donald Fortier[37] wrote a memo on 'the Qadhafi problem' to National Security Advisor Robert McFarlane, in which they argued for a more 'active' US policy against Libya, saying that it could have 'sobering effects not only on the Soviets, but on Tehran and Damascus as well. This could in turn promote other positive political-military trends'.

The link between striking at Libya and winning a battle in the global Cold War was once more stressed. After the US setback in Lebanon, Fortier and Cannistraro argued, there was a pressing need to show 'that we can protect our friends' on the one hand, and that 'being a friend of the Soviets is not cost free' on the other hand. Therefore, they proposed a multifaceted strategy based on four elements: first, 'spending Qadhafi into bankruptcy'; second, support for domestic opposition given that 'we now have a relationship with Iraq that might allow for some options along these lines'; third, working immediately with Egypt towards a 'reorientation of its military posture toward the Libyan border' to 'create hedges against further improvements in the Soviet posture in Libya'; and fourth, 'conduct a sustained campaign of diplomatic, military and economic pressure' in order to force Qadhafi to turn inward. 'Without foreign policy victories', they predicted, 'and with a steadily deteriorating economic position, Qadhafi's internal position could slowly erode until he was deposed'.[38]

Regime change and Qadhafi's overthrow had been one of the topics for discussion inside Reagan's White House since early 1982.[39] On 8 May 1984, a coup was staged by the National Front for the Salvation of Libya (NSFL), the united front of the Libyan opposition, but it failed and provoked wide purges in the military by Qadhafi.[40] The National Front for the Salvation of Libya was established in October 1981, had a radio station broadcasting anti-Qadhafi propaganda from Sudan, and recruited exiles to abolish the Qadhafi regime through violence, if it was needed. According to Joseph Stanik, the CIA was allowed to support it by an intelligence finding signed by Reagan which called for the provision of 'non-lethal aid'.[41]

Fortier's and Cannistraro's suggestion that the US get involved in the overthrow of Qadhafi was therefore part of a relatively old line of thinking within the administration. This would be the main goal of the 'Flower' plan that developed during the summer of 1985. The plan actually included two different options: 'Tulip' was a covert operation to overthrow Qadhafi with the help of Egypt and through the dissident NSFL; 'Rose' on the other hand was a pre-emptive military strike on Libya in concert with Egypt.[42]

Flower was presented on 22 July to the National Security Planning Group (NSPG) by Robert McFarlane, the same man who was carrying out the Iran–Contra plan, in which the US would deliver weapons to the Iranian regime in exchange for the liberation of Americans held hostage by the pro-Iranian terrorists in Lebanon. While proposing negotiations with the main sponsor of terrorism, McFarlane was advocating action against the easiest one. The goals were similar to the ones described in Fortier's and Cannistraro's February memo: send a signal to other countries supporting terrorism and hitting a Soviet friend. The will to test the new Soviet leadership under Gorbachev was also mentioned in Fortier's notes for McFarlane's presentation to the NSPG. Moreover, action against Libya would signal a policy-shift: 'finally', wrote Fortier to McFarlane, 'what we are after is not so much punishment as pre-emption – and we can already identify important new threats to pre-empt'.[43]

The Rose option, however, was the one that included a pre-emptive strike and it got the coolest reception. According to Gates, at the 22 July meeting 'not a single principal' in the NSPG supported it. With that meeting the invasion plan 'was dead' as he wrote.[44] The president, instead, signed a finding that gave support and assistance to Egypt and Algeria which, in turn, were going to support the NSFL.[45] This made pursuing the 'Tulip' option possible. Backed by Secretary Shultz, the covert operation to overthrow Qadhafi was presented to the Senate and House intelligence committees, which approved it with the thinnest possible majorities: eight to seven in the Senate, nine to seven in the House. Congressmen feared that supporting dissidents in Libya meant supporting assassination. Also, they wanted to avoid the start of another secret war like the one that was currently raging in Nicaragua.[46]

Despite this approval, even the 'Tulip' version of the Flower plan was never implemented. It faced several problems especially after it was leaked by the journalist Bob Woodward on 3 November.[47] The leaks, according to a 1986 memo by John Poindexter, had provoked the withdrawal of Algerian support while Egypt's had been wavering because of Qadhafi's own pressure on Mubarak.[48]

By the time Woodward's article appeared in the *Washington Post*, however, events were heading in a different direction. The hijacking of the Italian ship, Achille Lauro, in October proved to many hardliners in the Reagan administration how unreliable a law enforcement approach could be in the fight against terrorism. Then, at Christmas time in 1985, the shootings in the European airports by Libyan-supported terrorists would lay the ground for a direct US intervention against the Libyan dictator.

Towards the strike against Libya

Among those who were supported by Qadhafi was Abu Nidal, whose real name was Sabri al-Banna. Al-Banna had broken away from the PLO in 1974 when Arafat claimed to have banned terrorist attacks beyond Israel and the Occupied territories. He received support first from Saddam's Iraq and then from Syria. His organization, the Fatah-Revolutionary Council (also known as ANO), was behind the assassination attempt against the Israeli ambassador in London that eventually led to the invasion of Lebanon on 6 June 1982. In 1985, he was still changing patrons and was temporarily working mainly on his own. His common cause with Qadhafi was therefore an alliance between outsiders.[49]

On Friday, 27 December, this alliance produced two bloody attacks against civilians. In all, nineteen people were killed by terrorists in the Fiumicino Airport in Rome and in the Schwechat Airport in Vienna. More than one hundred were wounded in both attacks.[50]

Shortly after the attacks, a man called a Spanish news service to claim that the actions had been carried out by Fatah, the Revolutionary Council. The same was claimed by Muhammad Sarham, the lone surviving terrorist of the Rome assault. The official Libyan news agency Jana defined the attacks 'daring' and 'heroic operations'.[51]

In a memo to the President on 30 December, Donald Fortier explained that 'Tripoli's foreknowledge of the attacks in Rome and Vienna' seemed 'likely' since in the previous months Abu Nidal had become more 'closely aligned with Qadhafi' as a consequence of a general agreement reached between the two in the spring of 1985 on the need 'to cooperate in targeting moderate Arab states, Israel and the US'. Qadhafi was particularly interested in the relationship given ANO's track record of 'successful operations' although, Fortier warned, 'increased funding by Libya is unlikely to win Qadhafi real leverage over the group, which was not wholly responsive to Syrian direction'.[52]

Why, then, was the US targeting only Libya instead of focusing on Abu Nidal's organization? One reason can be found in a memo written by Donald Fortier several months later. Trying to win the support of other G-7 partners in the American fight against terrorism, Fortier emphasized that:

It should be easier to discipline the behaviour of a government than to catch elusive 'private' terrorist groups. We have means of leverage (underlined in the text) against a regime with a locatable leadership and infrastructure that we don't have against small groups.[53]

Nevertheless, the day after the attacks the US started the contingency planning for retaliation against Libya. With a cable to several military posts around the world, the US Joint Chiefs of Staff had communicated the willingness of the US administration to conduct a strike for which targeting had to start immediately. The codename for the operation would be 'Prairie Fire'.[54] It was never implemented and not just because of the, by then usual, leaks to the press.[55]

President Reagan, in the first place, was cautious. As he wrote in his diary, 'We all feel we must do something yet there are problems including thousands of Americans living & working in the mad clown's country' (the 'mad clown' being Qadhafi).[56] Within the administration, two distinct positions coexisted: one, represented in the NSC staff by Donald Fortier and at cabinet level by George Shultz, asked for a military response to the attacks; the other, represented by Weinberger, was strongly against any retaliation, on the grounds that it could bring about American casualties and would upset relations with the pro-US Arab countries. Finally, Weinberger agreed with what Reagan had written on his diary: the threat to the life of those Americans still living in Libya could be too high in case of an attack.[57]

Having ruled out, for the moment, military retaliation, the administration agreed on a more incremental strategy towards confrontation based, on the one hand, on more extensive economic sanctions (which would be included in NSDD 205) and, on the other hand, on new Freedom of Navigation exercises. Both measures were approved during the NSPG meeting held on 6 January 1986.[58] The following day, the executive order about economic sanctions was signed by the President. Writing to House Speaker, Tip O'Neill, he summed up the main features of this new package, which included a prohibition of purchases, imports, and exports from and to Libya; a ban on maritime and aviation relations; a ban on credits and loans; and a ban on travel to Libya.[59]

On 14 March, the NSPG gave the final go-ahead to the FON exercises going beyond the line of death, namely the limit of what Qadhafi had proclaimed being Libyan territorial waters in the Gulf of Sidra. These exercises were meant to give something more than just the impression of an on-going military build-up against Libya. The hope of many inside the administration was that, in case of confrontation, unspecified 'opposition forces' would act against Qadhafi.[60] Indeed, the big decision taken by the NSPG was that, not only would US aircraft trespass the line of death, they would also respond 'proportionally' to enemy fire.[61] These rules of engagement made a confrontation more likely since US planes were allowed to fire not just against aircraft already firing at them but also against 'possible sources of fire'.

The exercise started on 23 March. The question, as Reagan noted in his diary, was: 'Will he (Qadhafi) open fire or not?'[62] The following day, the mission 'Attain Document' turned into what many hawks had hoped: a provocation to which Qadhafi would respond and which, in turn, would imply a US reprisal. During the FON exercise, some US F-14 aircraft were spotted and missed by Soviet-made SA-5 Libyan missiles. This was, according to Shultz, one of the cases that had been predicted when elaborating the contingency planning in Washington. US missiles soon hit a base from which SA-5 missiles could be shot and in which some Soviet advisers were working. Also, the two Libyan patrol boats *Wahid* and *Ean Mara* were hit and sunk by US aircraft. seventy-two Libyans were killed and six Soviet technicians were wounded in the operation.[63]

Bombing Libya

A chain reaction was set in motion. On the night of 5 April, a bomb blew up in the La Belle discotheque in West Berlin where many US servicemen spent their free time. Two people, one of them a Turkish woman, were killed and one hundred and fifty-five were wounded, one-third of them Americans. According to Bernd Schäfer's research in the Stasi archives, the terrorists had acted on instructions from the Libyan embassy in East Berlin with the knowledge of the East German intelligence agency. They later sent a cable to the Libyan intelligence headquarters in Tripoli to confirm the 'execution of one of the actions' that were eventually intercepted by US intelligence.[64]

The following days at the White House focused on the planning for the attack. Two issues took most of the time for the President and his cabinet: targeting and garnering the support of the West Europeans. On the first issue, the president was clear: 'I'm holding out for mil[itary] targets', he wrote in his diary, 'to avoid civilian casualties because we believe a large part of Libya would like to get rid of the Col[onel]'.[65] On the second issue, two countries were specifically needed in support of what became operation El Dorado Canyon, namely the bombing of Tripoli and Benghazi: Great Britain, where the F-111 planes were located and whose participation in the attack was the precondition to have enough firepower and France, who had to guarantee over-flight rights to these planes. Margaret Thatcher, on the one hand, managed to win approval from her cabinet on the ground that this was an action in self-defence and that 'this is what allies are for'.[66] The French government, on the other hand, denied over-flight rights because it had not received the request far enough in advance. This, the US press would remark after the strike, forced US planes to take a long detour around continental Europe with a deviation of twelve hundred nautical miles.[67]

On 14 April 1986, while the NATO exercise 'Salty Nation' provided the necessary cover to the movement of US aircraft and air-carriers in the

Mediterranean, operation El Dorado Canyon started. At 7 p.m., Washington time, NBC and CNN broadcast the attack live from Tripoli. As Roland Bruce St. John commented, 'conducted on a Monday evening during national news, the Reagan attack was the first prime-time bombing in the nation's history'.[68] As soon as the US bombers approached their targets, the Libyans started shooting SA and Crotale missiles. In the end, an F-111 was shot down and the two US pilots were killed. Eventually, the French embassy in Tripoli was hit by mistake.[69]

The strike, however, was not completely successful. A situation room note at 5 a.m. on 15 April described the aftermath of the strike on Libya. The 'NPIC's initial battle damage assessment' did not give the impression of severe damage: Tripoli and Benina airfields along with the Sidi Bilal port were not severely damaged while 'Qadhafi has reportedly survived the attack, although he has made no public appearance'.[70] Reagan's goal of avoiding as many any civilian casualties as possible was not completely fulfilled: thirty-seven Libyan civilians were killed and ninety-three were wounded. In all, five tons of bombs were dropped on civilians.[71]

The night before this report, at 9 p.m. (Washington time), the president went on air to speak about the strike. He outlined the evidence of Libyan responsibility for the La Belle disco bombing as 'conclusive' and promised: 'Today we have done what we had to do. If necessary, we shall do it again.' The mission was defined both as 'fully consistent' with Article 51 of the United Nations (UN) charter and as a 'pre-emptive action against terrorist installations'. Reagan concluded saying: 'I said that we would act with others, if possible, and alone, if necessary, to ensure that terrorists have no sanctuary anywhere. Tonight we have'.[72]

Despite receiving high domestic support for the strike,[73] Reagan's decision had a cool reception with America's Western European allies. The United Kingdom let it be known that it was not going to support another strike[74] and the administration's expert on the Soviet Union warned against further challenges to the credibility of the USSR in the Mediterranean.[75] In response to the attack, Gorbachev cancelled the Shultz-Shevarnadze meeting.

Rather than changing US policy on terrorism, the strike set a model for the future: a surgical strike, exclusively using air force on a precise target related to terrorism. The model strike allowed the US to use force to achieve a foreign policy goal without committing ground troops and having to devise an exit strategy. Moreover, the losses reported in El Dorado Canyon were quite close to the goal set by the president of striking at terrorism without having to deal with too many American body bags. Several constraints, not least the doubts of Weinberger and Bush Senior, guaranteed that this model was not going to be re-enacted during the Reagan administration. It is fair to say, however, that it served as a source of inspiration for successive US actions.[76]

The spring and the summer of 1986 saw a last attempt at regime change in Libya by the Reagan administration spurred by CIA reports that

Qadhafi's regime had been weakened by the attack.[77] The strategy was now to exploit his paranoia, leading him to think that a US attack was imminent and that some of the men in his inner circle were ready to betray him. This would lead to Qadhafi removing the top level of his security apparatus thus becoming more exposed to attempts at overthrow by domestic dissidents.[78] The imminence of the attack would be further confirmed by naval manoeuvres in the Mediterranean and by fabricated leaks to the press. Implementation of the plan stopped after 2 October 1986, when an article by Bob Woodward at the *Washington Post* disclosed its details.[79]

Conclusions

In November 1986, the outbreak of the Iran–Contra scandal definitely ended the escalation between Libya and the US. Some of its main support-ers inside the administration were removed from office and substituted with officials such as Powell and Carlucci who supported a more nuanced, regionalist, and diplomatic policy towards the Middle East. This shift is evident when reading the memorandum of conversation of the 24 February 1987 NSPG meeting on 'terrorism'. President Reagan started the conversation, recognizing that:

> Experience has taught us there is no clear, easy solution to this prob-lem. Dealing with it requires patience, restraint and flexibility. While there may be instances in which a military response will work, the terrorists are becoming more sophisticated and the targets for such a response are disappearing.[80]

The approach of the new National Security Advisor was rather different from that of some of his predecessors:

> Terrorism is primarily a police and intelligence problem rather than a foreign policy problem. It is very hard to bring the power of the US government to bear on most terrorism situations. In the case of state supported terrorism our policy and procedures are clear. But, in most instances, we will be facing terrorism conducted by small groups whose ties to supporting nations will be unclear and tenuous.[81]

The Reagan administration had tried, albeit unconsciously and without a clear decision, to pursue two alternative strategies against terrorism: one, against Libya, focused on the unilateral use of pre-emptive strikes against states deemed to be supporters of terrorism as advocated by Secretary of State George Shultz; the other, implemented with Iran, focused on back-channel negotiations. The failure of the latter led to the collapse of the former. Nevertheless, the strike against Libya could not be repeated because of several constraints: Soviet credibility and patience could not endlessly be tested; Western Europeans were not, to say the least, enthusiastic about this model; and the danger of entering a 'cycle of action and reaction' was clear to many administration officials, not least because the administration would 'loose the support of the American people'.[82]

The strike against Libya set a model not in the fight against terrorism but in the use of US military power. It was one of those 'wars without tears' that have been discussed by Lawrence Freedman: a brief military operation that caused no American casualties.[83]

Against terrorism, the Reagan administration and its successor George H.W. Bush would implement that patient, restrained approach that was advocated by the president in the 1987 NSC. Libyan terrorism, indeed, would strike again on 21 December 1988 in the skies of Lockerbie, Scotland. A Pan Am flight exploded, killing two hundred and seventy people among passengers and the population of the Lockerbie village. Two members of the Libyan intelligence, 'Abd al-Basit al-Maqrahi and Amin Khalifa Fahima, would be accused of being responsible for the attack but Qadhafi refused to hand them over for trial in foreign courts. No military retaliation took place, instead the US decided to act through the UN Security Council which approved resolution 748 on 31 March 1992, imposing severe international sanctions on Libya. They were withdrawn only in 1999, when Qadhafi finally handed over the two culprits to an aptly created international court in The Hague. American sanctions against Libya, though, remained in place until December 2003, when Qadhafi formally announced that Libya had dropped its weapons of mass destruction program.

Shultz's ideas about pre-emptive strikes against states sponsoring terrorism would again become popular in a different international context, that of the post-9/11 world. Eventually, he would be defined as the 'father' of the Bush doctrine.[84]

Notes

1   For a comprehensive discussion of the Bush doctrine, see R. Singh, 'The Bush Doctrine' in M. Buckley and R. Singh (ed.) *The Bush Doctrine and the War on Terrorism. Global Responses, Global Consequences*, Oxford: Routledge, 2006.
2   For a general outlook on Soviet policy in the region, see G. Golan, *Soviet Policies in the Middle East from World War II to Gorbachev*, Cambridge: Cambridge University Press, 1990.
3   A. Del Boca, *Gheddafi. Una sfida dal deserto*, Bari: Laterza, 2010, p. 65.
4   F. Burgat, *Il fondamentalismo islamico*, Turin: SEI, 1995, p. 31.
5   Memorandum for Larry Speakes from William Martin. 'Materials for distribution to the press', 7 January 1986, James Stark files, Ronald Reagan Library.
6   'Remarks at the Welcoming Ceremony for the Freed American Hostages January 27, 1981'. The Public Papers of President Ronald W. Reagan. Ronald Reagan Library. Available online: www.reagan.utexas.edu/archives/speeches/1981/12581a.htm (accessed 7 July 2006).

7   For a summary of the reasons for concern about Qadhafi, see 'Topic For
     Discussion at DCI Breakfast Meeting with Secretary Haig on 25 August 1981.
     Worldwide Libyan Activities of Concern to the US Government'. Crest database.
8   The best account of the bipolar confrontation in the extra-European world can
     be found in O.A. Westad, *The Global Cold War*, New York: Cambridge University
     Press, 2005.
9   S. Wilentz, *The Age of Reagan*, New York: Harper Collins Publishers, 2008,
     pp. 153–7.
10   H. Teicher, and G. Radley, *Twin Pillars to Desert Storm: America's Flawed Vision in
     the Middle East from Nixon to Bush*, New York: William Morrow and company,
     1993, p. 134.
11   R.B. St John, *Libya and the United States: Two Centuries of Strife*, Philadelphia:
     University of Pennsylvania Press, 2002, p. 123.
12   R.M. Gates, *From the Shadows: the Ultimate Insider's Story of Five Presidents and How
     They Won the Cold War*, New York: Touchstone, 1996, pp. 351–2.
13   T. Naftali, *Blind Spot: The Secret History of American Counterterrorism*, New York:
     Basic Books, 2005, p.168.
14   Memo for Richard Allen from Geoffrey Kemp. 'Update on Pakistan, Sinai and
     Libya SIGs', 24 March 1981, folder: SIG on Libya March 18 81, box 91144, Near
     East and South Asia Bureau Files, Ronald Reagan Library.
15   D. Brinkley (ed.), *The Reagan Diaries*, New York: Harper Collins, 2007, p. 17.
16   B. Gwertzman, 'US Expels Libyans and Closes Mission, Charging Terrorism',
     New York Times, 7 May 1981.
17   D. Brinkley (ed.), *The Reagan Diaries*, New York: Harper Collins, 2007, p. 22.
18   B. Woodward, *Veil: The Secret Wars of the CIA, 1981–1987*, New York: Pocket
     Books, 1987, p. 190.
19   Ibid., p. 211.
20   Memorandum to the President from Alexander M. Haig, Jr, 'Status of Review
     of Libya Policy', 17 November 1981. Reproduced in Declassified Documents
     Reference System.
21   Memorandum from Raymond Tanter to Richard Allen, 'IG on Libya, 1 October
     81', 29 September 1981. Folder: 'IF on Libya Oct 1, 1981', Near East and South
     Asia files, Ronald Reagan Library.
22   Department of State, 'Libya NSC paper', 29 January 1982, folder: Libya
     1981–1984 (3 of 6), box 90754, Donald Fortier files, Ronald Reagan Library.
23   Ibid.
24   Ibid.
25   NSDD 27, 'Economic Decisions for Libya'. 9 March 1982. Presidential
     Directives collection, National Security Archive.
26   J. Stanik, *El Dorado Canyon: Reagan's Undeclared War With Qaddafi*, Annapolis:
     Naval Institute Press, 2004, p. 72.
27   Department of State, 'Libya NSC paper', 29 January 1982, folder: Libya
     1981–1984 (3 of 6), box 90754, Donald Fortier files, Ronald Reagan Library.
28   Ibid.
29   D. Vanderwalle, *A History of Modern Libya*, New York: Cambridge University
     Press, 2006, p. 132, and R.B. St John, *Libya and the United States: Two Centuries of
     Strife*, Philadelphia: University of Pennsylvania Press, 2002, p. 128.
30   D. Vanderwalle, *A History of Modern Libya*, New York: Cambridge University
     Press, 2006, p. 125.

31 Ibid., p. 133.
32 'Excerpts From Shultz's Address on International Terrorism', *New York Times*, 26 October 1984.
33 D. Wills, *The First War on Terrorism*, Lanham, Maryland: Rowman & Littlefield, 2003, p. 190.
34 On terrorism against Americans in this decade, see D. Martin and J. Walcott, *Best Laid Plans: The Inside Story of America's War Against Terrorism*, New York: Harper & Row, 1988; T. Naftali, *Blind Spot: The Secret History of American Counterterrorism*, New York: Basic Books, 2005; D.E. Long, *The Anatomy of Terrorism*, New York: Free Press, 1990; D. Wills, *The First War on Terrorism*, Lanham, Maryland: Rowman & Littlefield, 2003.
35 R.M. Gates, *From the Shadows: the Ultimate Insider's Story of Five Presidents and How They Won the Cold War*, New York: Touchstone, 1996, pp. 351–2.
36 Vincent Cannistraro was Director for Intelligence Programs at the NSC from 1984 to 1987.
37 Donald Fortier, Deputy Director of the Policy Planning Staff and then Deputy National Security Advisor from December 1985.
38 Memorandum for Robert McFarlane from Donald Fortier and Vincent Cannistraro, 'The Qadhafi problem', 15 February 1985. Folder: Libya, January–June 1985 (2 of 4), box 90754, Donald Fortier files, Ronald Reagan Library.
39 Memorandum of conversation, 'National Security Council Meeting on Libya', 21 January 1982. Folder: NSC 00038, 21 Jan 1982 [Libya]. Executive Secretariat, NSC: NSC meeting files, Ronald Reagan Library.
40 R.M. Gates, *From the Shadows: the Ultimate Insider's Story of Five Presidents and How They Won the Cold War*, New York: Touchstone, 1996, pp. 321–2; J. Stanik, *El Dorado Canyon: Reagan's Undeclared War With Qaddafi*, Annapolis: Naval Institute Press, 2004, pp. 81–7.
41 J. Stanik, *El Dorado Canyon: Reagan's Undeclared War With Qaddafi*, Annapolis: Naval Institute Press, 2004, p. 41; also in D. Martin and J. Walcott, *Best Laid Plans: The Inside Story of America's War Against Terrorism*, New York: Harper & Row, 1988, p. 73.
42 B. Woodward, *Veil: The Secret Wars of the CIA, 1981–1987*, New York: Pocket Books, 1987, pp. 509–10.
43 Note for Robert McFarlane from Donald Fortier. 'McFarlane Scene-Setter', 19 July 1985. Donald Fortier files, Ronald Reagan Library.
44 R.M. Gates, *From the Shadows: the Ultimate Insider's Story of Five Presidents and How They Won the Cold War*, New York: Touchstone, 1996, p. 353.
45 Memorandum for the President from John M. Poindexter, 'Supplemental Finding on Libya Covert Action', 10 April 1986. Reproduced in Declassified Documents Reference System.
46 B. Woodward, *Veil: The Secret Wars of the CIA, 1981–1987*, New York: Pocket Books, 1987, pp. 516–17.
47 B. Woodward, 'CIA Anti-Qaddafi Plan Backed', *Washington Post*, 3 November 1985.
48 Memorandum for the President from John M. Poindexter, 'Supplemental Finding on Libya Covert Action', 10 April 1986. Reproduced in Declassified Documents Reference System.
49 D. Martin and J. Walcott, *Best Laid Plans: The Inside Story of America's War Against

Terrorism, New York: Harper & Row, 1988, pp. 266–7; for the background on Abu Nidal's organization see D.E. Long, *The Anatomy of Terrorism*, New York: Free Press, 1990, pp. 38–40.

50 D. Martin and J. Walcott, *Best Laid Plans: The Inside Story of America's War Against Terrorism*, New York: Harper & Row, 1988, pp. 267–8; D. Wills, *The First War on Terrorism*, Lanham, Maryland: Rowman & Littlefield, 2003, pp. 176–8.

51 A. Del Boca, *Gheddafi. Una sfida dal deserto*, Bari: Laterza, 2010, p. 155.

52 Memorandum for the President from Donald Fortier, 10 December 1985. Folder: Libya Sensitive 1986 (2 of 7). Box 91668. Howard Teicher files, Ronald Reagan Library.

53 Terrorism at the Tokyo Summit, Objectives and Talking Points, 25 April 1986. Folder: Libyan Airstrike Aftermath II. Box 30. Oliver North files, Ronald Reagan Library.

54 Cable from JCS, 'Warning Order for Operation Prairie Fire', 28 December 1985. folder: 1-6-86 NSPG Libya. Elaine Morton Files, Ronald Reagan Library.

55 Several articles appeared in the *Washington Post* and *New York Times* between 29 December 1985 and 3 January 1986. See 'Chronology of Press Reports, US actions against Libya Sunday 29 December 1985 – Friday 3 January 1985'. Donald Fortier Files, Ronald Reagan Library.

56 D. Brinkley (ed.), *The Reagan Diaries*, New York: Harper Collins, 2007, p. 380.

57 D. Wills, *The First War on Terrorism*, Lanham, Maryland: Rowman & Littlefield, 2003, pp. 178–9.

58 Ibid., p. 181.

59 Letter to the Speaker of the House of Representatives by Ronald Reagan, 7 January 1986. Fortier files, Ronald Reagan Library.

60 Memorandum from John Poindexter, 'Meeting with the National Security Planning Group', 14 March 1986. Folder: Libya Sensitive 1986 (3 of 7), box 91668. Howard Teicher files, Ronald Reagan Library.

61 C. Weinberger, *Fighting for Peace*, New York: Warner Books, 1990, pp. 182–3; J. Stanik, *El Dorado Canyon: Reagan's Undeclared War With Qaddafi*, Annapolis: Naval Institute Press, 2004, pp. 128–9.

62 D. Brinkley (ed.), *The Reagan Diaries*, New York: Harper Collins, 2007, p. 401.

63 G. Shultz, *Turmoil and Triumph. My Years As a Secretary of State*, New York: MacMillan, 1993, p. 680; J. Stanik, *El Dorado Canyon: Reagan's Undeclared War With Qaddafi*, Annapolis: Naval Institute Press, 2004, pp. 127–43.

64 B. Schäfer, 'New Evidence on 1986 US Air Raid on Libya: A Confidential Soviet Account from the Stasi Archives', Cold War International History Project Archive.

65 D. Brinkley (ed.), *The Reagan Diaries*, New York: Harper Collins, 2007, pp. 402–3.

66 Interview with Charles Powell in D. Strober and G. Strober, *The Reagan Presidency. An Oral History of the Era*, Washington, DC: Brassey's, 2003.

67 E.J. Dionne, 'West Europe Generally Critical of US', *New York Times*, 16 April 1986.

68 R.B. St John, *Libya and the United States: Two Centuries of Strife*, Philadelphia: University of Pennsylvania Press, 2002, p. 137.

69 J. Stanik, *El Dorado Canyon: Reagan's Undeclared War With Qaddafi*, Annapolis: Naval Institute Press, 2004, pp. 185–90.

70 Situation room note. Aftermath of Libyan operations, 0500 EST. Folder: Libyan Airstrike Aftermath II. Box 30. Oliver North files, Ronald Reagan Library.

71 D. Martin and J. Walcott, *Best Laid Plans: The Inside Story of America's War Against Terrorism*, New York: Harper & Row, 1988, p. 310.

72 'Address to the Nation on the United States Air Strike Against Libya April 14, 1986'. The Public Papers of President Ronald W. Reagan. Ronald Reagan Library. Available online: www.reagan.utexas.edu/archives/speeches/1986/41486g.htm (accessed 5 October 2005).

73 T. Wicker, 'After the Raids', *New York Times*, 18 April 1986.

74 D. Martin and J. Walcott, *Best Laid Plans: The Inside Story of America's War Against Terrorism*, New York: Harper & Row, 1988, p. 312.

75 Memorandum from Matlock to Poindexter, 'Possible Soviet Responses to US actions in Libya', 25 April 1986. James Stark files, Ronald Reagan Library.

76 This is the main thesis of J. Stanik, *El Dorado Canyon: Reagan's Undeclared War With Qaddafi*, Annapolis: Naval Institute Press, 2004.

77 Directorate of Intelligence, 'Qadhafi's Political Position Since the Airstrike', 17 July 1986. Declassified Documents Reference System.

78 The outline of this plan can be found in Memorandum from the Office of the Deputy Assistant Secretary of Defense, Near Eastern and South Asian Affairs for the Assistant Secretary of Defense for International Security Affairs, 'Means by which to weaken Qadhafi's internal security apparatus at a propitious time', 18 April 1986. James Stark files, Ronald Reagan Library.

79 B. Woodward, 'Qadhafi Target of Secret US Deception Plan', *Washington Post*, 2 October 1986.

80 'NSPG 24 February 1987 [terrorism]', Executive Secretariat, NSC: NSPG meeting files, Ronald Reagan Library.

81 Ibid.

82 Terrorism at the Tokyo Summit, Objectives and Talking Points, 25 April 1986. Folder: Libyan Airstrike Aftermath II. Box 30. Oliver North files, Ronald Reagan Library.

83 L. Freedman, 'The Third World War?', *Survival*, 2001–2, vol. 43, pp. 61–88.

84 D. Henninger, 'George Shultz, Father of the Bush Doctrine', *Hoover Digest*, no. 3, 30 Jul 2006.

Part IV

Contemporary terrorism and anti-terrorism

13 *Al Qaeda* and the reinvention of terrorism

Social sciences and the challenge of post-globalization transnational political violence

Mohammad-Mahmoud Ould Mohamedou

Introduction

Upon its emergence in the mid to late 1980s, *al Qaeda* ushered in a new phase in the history of terrorism. Over the next quarter of a century, the group formed by Osama Bin Laden and Ayman al Dhawahiri would come to represent the most significant threat to international security, having also conducted the most ambitious attack in the history of terrorism, targeting the United States (US) on its own soil in September 2001. The rapid acquisition of power by this Islamist group – initially set up in Afghanistan in the aftermath of the Soviet invasion of that country – and the global projection of its political violence mark a historical shift and represent a consequential illustration of terrorism of the transnational mode. Whether through the succession of waves or the accumulation of ages, the history of international terrorism had essentially come to a standstill by the early 1980s. By then, the world had come to experience the contemporary era successive terroristic campaigns of anarchists and nihilists, nationalists, radical leftists, and religious groups. For all their many qualitative differences, these variegated incarnations of the modern terrorist shared two fundamental characteristics: (i) a field of activity by and large centred on or springing from one main contiguous territory, and (ii) a reactive purview on the use of violence that ultimately depended more on the initiative of the state authority they were battling than their own.[1] In other words, *delineated territoriality* and *dependent potency* had set the boundaries of how terrorism had been manifested internationally over some one hundred and twenty years since the mid-1860s. Per such foundational matrix, Russian students targeted the Czar and his entourage; Algerian nationalists attacked French colonial soldiery and settlers; German and Italian revolutionary youth threatened their respective governments and societies; and Christian, Muslim, and Jewish militants in different settings visited indiscriminate violence on those regarded as infidels or enemies of their respective faiths.

At times, particularly from the late 1960s onwards, some of these groups found themselves going beyond their immediate territory – for example, Palestinians abducting Israelis in Germany, Germans pursuing combat training in Jordan – and displaying proactive patterns transcending their original idea of symbolic punishing violence. Inexorably, however, the groups and their members remained organically linked to and concerned with their original locus. This unshakable relationship was at once a reflection of the immediacy of their goals and the linearity of the means they had adopted to reach those objectives. The liberation of Palestine still motivated the kidnapping of Israeli athletes temporarily located in Munich in 1972, just as a hope for societal revolution in Germany primarily drove the Red Army Faction to take part in the hijacking of a plane of Westerners in Somalia (1977). Such embryonic deterritorialization was limited both in time and in scope. What mattered fundamentally to the respective groups was the impact of their external actions on their original 'theater of operation', the sought-after trauma (and forced reflection) back home. In summary, up to that point and in one way or another, all terrorism had in effect remained local.

The birth of a transnational non-state armed group known as *al Qaeda* in 1989 would profoundly alter this sequence. Building on these earlier historical forms of terrorism, *al Qaeda* would go on to consciously update them and introduce substantial innovations in the conceptualization of its use of political violence, the materialization of its battle plan, the structuring of its organization, and the communication of its goals. Emerging stealthily throughout the 1990s amid relative lack of attention to its revolutionary nature and lethality, the group would go on to become the leading global threat during the 2000s, following its attacks on New York and Washington on 11 September 2001. By the 2010s, and in the aftermath of the killing of its leader in May 2011, the group had gradually become evanescent while still generating a number of mini-*al Qaedas* around the world with independent remits and concerns and operating on the trademark militarized form of terrorism that *al Qaeda* had elaborated during the previous twenty years.

What is the meaning of *al Qaeda* against the background of the history of terrorism? Close to a quarter of a century after the group was established, terrorism studies are still grappling with the production of a proper contextualized and historicized understanding of the major terrorist organization of its time. This is no small paradox and its implications for social sciences are revealing. For at least three reasons, *al Qaeda* should have become a well-understood manifestation of contemporary non-state armed group political violence. First, largely descriptive in their early years, terrorism studies had gained in theoretical sophistication over precisely the period during which the group appeared and gained notoriety. Secondly, *al Qaeda* itself provided a substantial amount of materials for study ranging from its multiple attacks around the world to its regular audio and video messages (releases up to a high of fifty-eight in 2006 and sixty-seven in 2007) to the manifestations of its different franchises (in the Middle East, Africa, Asia, and Europe). Finally, the publicity that the group has received due to the deadliness of its attacks and the identity of its primary target – the world's sole superpower – generated a global debate on the nature of the organization and its objectives.

Nevertheless, social sciences generally failed to offer much compelling scientific insight into the nature of this new organization;[2] the primary data made available by the group were overlooked, dismissed, misrepresented, or simply misunderstood; and a global debate on the novel entity was surprisingly consensual and monochromatic.[3] In so doing, 'an invisible college of terrorism researchers', as Magnus Ranstorp put it, replayed with *al Qaeda* a perennial deficiency in this academic field through which they 'often recycled empirical information, some with questionable credibility and precision, and interchanged context, frequently without sufficient regard for situational, political, social, or security specificity'.[4] Particularly problematic were analyses, on the one hand, betraying excessive emotionality, and, on the other, putting forth a picture of an idiosyncratic religious organization. Essentially, social sciences missed the mark on providing scholarly tools to understand the identity, behaviour, and ultimate historical significance of not just any newcomer in the field of terrorism. The shortcoming deserves emphasis, for, in effect, the leading contemporary texts on *al Qaeda* have been produced by journalists or intelligence officers, not by academics,[5] whereas one would have expected the reverse to be true. Many a scholar was found to be relying indeed on those media accounts for their own constructs, not merely for raw data (which, again, the group itself in any event made available profusely through its three media branches, Mouassassat Al Sihab, Al Malahem, and Al Andalus, more than any other terrorist entity in history).

This chapter argues that the novelty of *al Qaeda* is the result of the coincidence of a conscious revolutionary decision on the part of a group of Islamist militants to project their use of political violence globally and the materialization of empowering patterns of globalization that enabled the successful operational implementation of this design. It puts forth, secondly, the argument that in indulging overwhelmingly culturalist or theological explanations of *al Qaeda*, social sciences have failed so far to come to grips with the manner in which both the initial direct action of *al Qaeda*, notably its staccato series of lethal attacks in the period 1995–2005, and its latter-day indirect influence, both through its franchises and the overall impact of its ideology, have generated a qualitative shift in the type of terrorism that will be manifested around the world in the coming decades. Driven by media accounts, policy determinants, and, at times, orientalist sheet-anchors, the dominant narrative about *al Qaeda* has escaped contextualized, comparative, and critical analysis of the group's methods and goals and often taken the form of a depiction largely confined to the group's Islamist phraseology. Ultimately, the significance of *al Qaeda* in the history of terrorism is consequential in manifold ways but is due primarily to the fact that the organization has managed to turn itself into an ideology, *al Qaedism*, which is likely to outlast it beyond its post-Bin Laden acephalic phase.

Transnationalizing terrorism and militarizing islamism

The late twentieth century is important in the study of terrorism. It is a period that saw a concomitant appearance of what arguably is the most powerful terrorist organization in history and a revolution in human affairs, globalization, unprecedented in scale since the industrial revolution. It is this dynamic and complex historical backdrop which is the mainstay of *al Qaeda's differentia specifica* – not updated neologism articulations of fourth-age religious terrorism such as '*jihad*ism' or 'Islamofascism'. The first key characteristic of *al Qaeda* is its transnational nature; whereas the emergence of transnational patterns of terrorism was recognized before the 11 September 2001 attacks by *al Qaeda*,[6] only recently has the causality of transnational terrorism been interrogated as potentially different from that of domestic terrorism.[7] Yet the terrorism which *al Qaeda* has been displaying was from its very inception born in that mode.

Al Qaeda's precise lineage is not fully documented but concordant sources allow us to identify its first incarnation as a liaison office set up in 1983 in Afghanistan by a Palestinian teacher, Abdullah Azzam, to provide logistical support to Muslim fighters on their way to the Afghan–Soviet front. Known as *Maktab Al Khadamat lil Mujahedeen* (Office of Works for the Combatants), sometimes referred to as *Maktab Al Dhiyafa* (Hospitality House), this office grew in importance becoming in time an international hub bringing together a group of so-called 'Arab Afghans' who garnered important fighting experience in the period 1983–88. In the immediate aftermath of the Soviet withdrawal from Afghanistan, Azzam, joined by Egyptian surgeon Ayman Al Dhawahiri and Saudi millionaire Osama Bin Laden, turned the *Maktab al Khadamat* into a fuller armed militancy organization in late 1989 with the explicit goal of deploying a transnational form of Islamism meant to transcend borders and attack the enemies of Islam on their own territories. Such ethnogenesis was an unprecedented displacement of the focus both of Islamist groups – which in the Middle East and North African regions had been unsuccessfully battling their respective authoritarian regimes, notably in Algeria, Jordan, and Egypt – and of terrorist groups in general that had featured transnationalism but not grounded their action in it. This strategic shift was explicitly articulated in a formula expressed by the group then; namely that of reorientation taking the fight from *al adou al qareeb* (the near enemy) to *al adou al ba'eed* (the far enemy). In introducing such thought-out redirection, the new group was in effect deciding not to 'waste' its terrorism on the governments of the

Islamic world but rather to reserve it to target the mightier powers, the US primarily, which were regarded as both the masters of these regional governments and the ultimate, more consequential foes of Islam.

The second defining feature of *al Qaeda* is its outlook on political Islam and in particular its enactment of what may be termed a militarization of Islamism. Here too, *al Qaeda* comes at the end of a cycle of three successive 'temporalities'[8] (resistance against colonialism, opposition to the postcolonial state, and struggle against Western imperialism) whereby Islamism had manifested itself in the Muslim world under logics of identity affirmation. As *al Qaeda* entered the field of structural political violence in the 1980s, the scene it sprang from in the Islamic world was thus already substantially transformed by a gradual redefinition of the notion of armed opposition to power. With the advent of the age of colonialism and modernity, the discourses on rebellion had been co-opted by Islamist activists and had undergone major reconstructions.[9] The latest slanting of those reconstructions was to expand the territory of attack but also to endow rebellion with a military identity, less to emulate the state than to actually strip it of its essential function (in the Weberian sense, the monopoly of legitimate violence) having bypassed it spatially in jumping frontiers to assault its external supporter. This martial nature is, hence, formulated expressly from the inception of the group which, in its early days, is accordingly identified alternatively as *Al Jaish al Islami* (the Islamic Army), *al Qaeda al 'Askariya* (the military base), and *Sijil al Qaeda* (the base's registry) before settling on simply *al Qaeda* (the base). In that context, the 'base' refers simultaneously to the headquarters where the 'Arab Afghans' were initially housed, the geographically widespread database of those fighters, as well as the ideological basis in which the movement anchored its action: a military base from which to launch its transnational war.[10] In his 1996 Declaration of War, echoing language from military manuals, Bin Laden is strikingly explicit about the group's rationale and its tactical use of asymmetry:

> Due to the imbalance of power between our armed forces and the enemy forces, a suitable means of fighting must be adopted, namely using fast-moving light forces that work under complete secrecy... It is wise in the present circumstances for the armed military forces not to be engaged in conventional fighting with the forces of the... enemy... unless a big advantage is likely to be achieved; and the great losses induced on the enemy side that would shake and destroy its foundations and infrastructure... spread rumors, fear, and discouragement among the members of the enemy forces.

This construct was not so much a subversion of traditional Islamist militancy (nationally based movements such as *Al Jabha Al Islamiya lil Inqadh*, the Islamist Salvation Front, in Algeria or the *Gamaat al Islamiya*, Islamic Groups, in Egypt) as it was a new politico-military expression of it.

Characteristically present from the inception of this process, these two key dimensions – transnationalism and martiality – merged, giving birth to an original terrorist organization with some ten thousand troops springing from distinct horizons: primarily local disbanded 'Arab Afghans' available in the wake of the Soviet retreat; younger newcomers from Islamic countries attracted by the novelty of the enterprise and its ambition; and group or individual operators in Europe and in North America travelling to Afghanistan to join this project. To the innovative nature of this construct and its forward-looking ambition, we must add the important variable of a sense of strength in which *al Qaeda*'s project was grounded. Such self-empowerment was the result of a perception of victory over the Soviet Union among the *mujahedeen*. In effect, the feeling among the early members of *al Qaeda* was to go on to challenge another superpower having defeated one. Whether the victory was empirical or not was a moot point, what mattered was that the group's leaders were convinced that they could strike the US – they ultimately did – and this conviction was passed on consequentially to their soldiery. Finally, *al Qaeda*'s initiative featured, as well, a clear sense of an Islamist vanguard conducting a sort of neocounter-crusade which at once wrestled the monopoly of force from Islamic states and sought to visit violence on the West on an equal footing.[11] True to a tradition of an invisible martial initiative on the part of its oriental foe,[12] Western analyses were by and large unable to recognize the novelty of this: a new age of terrorism driven by a transnational strategic battle plan with political underpinnings and aimed at shifting the nature of the power balance between the West and Islam by exporting indiscriminate violence into the Western metropolis. *Al Qaeda* was born in war and victory, and this constituted a most powerful anchor for its own revolutionary unpacking of terrorism.

Although widely misunderstood in the popular conception, the *al Qaeda* worldview – objectives, strategy, tactics, ideology, vision of history and of the enemy – emerges with surprising clarity and coherence from the group's own statements.[13] Indeed, one can here be equally epistemological. In a series of statements made in the early 1990s, as well as the two declarations of war issued by *al Qaeda* against the US on 23 August 1996 ('Declaration of War against the Americans Occupying the Land of the Two Holy Places'; that is, Saudi Arabia) and 23 February 1998 ('*Jihad* against Jews and Crusaders'), the organization, using religious phraseology and modes of communication (such as the issuing of fatwas), explained its actions as being driven not by religion but by politics, namely action against Western policies and military presence in the Muslim world and support of Arab dictatorial regimes (for example, 'aggression, iniquity and injustice imposed on [the people of Islam] by the Zionist-Crusaders alliance and their collaborators', 1996). Initially, this primordial aspect of *al Qaeda*'s discourse was centred on the presence of the US in Saudi Arabia and Israel's occupation of Palestinian territories. Subsequently, it would come to integrate the conflicts in Afghanistan, Iraq, and Lebanon following the respective conflicts of 2001, 2003, and 2006 in these countries.

Over the years, Osama Bin Laden articulated this rationale as well as the concomitant strategy of his group, namely a transnational military assault meant to disrupt, confuse, and indeed weaken the Western state enemy per a dynamic of reciprocity and lex talionis ('Reciprocal treatment is part of justice', 'If you were distressed by the deaths of your men and the men of your allies...remember our children who are killed', 'Just as you kill, you will be killed, just as you bomb, you will be bombed', 'Our actions are but a reaction to your acts', and 'Just as you lay waste to our nation, so we shall lay waste to yours'). This central disposition was repeated in particular in the messages released on 12 November 2002, 15 April 2004, 29 October 2004, and 19 January 2006. Similarly, Ayman Al Dhawahiri expressed the same ideas in his two books, *Fursan Tahta Rayat Al Nabi* ('Knights Under the Prophet's Banner', December 2001) and *Tabri'at 'an Umat Al Qalam wa Al Sayf min Manqasat Tuhmat Al Khawar wa Al Du'f* ('Treaty Exonerating the Nation of the Pen and the Sword from the Blemish of the Accusation of Weakness and Fatigue', March 2008). Finally, *al Qaeda* lead strategist, Mustafa Bin Abdelqadir Setmariam Nasar, known as Abu Musab Al Suri, outlined the same vision in his 2004 publication *Da'wat Al Muqawama Al Islamiyya Al 'Alamiyya* ('The Global Islamic Resistance Call').

As a new type of post-colonial, post-modern, and post-globalization entity, *al Qaeda* was in effect eschewing the organization and goals of peaceful national liberation movements and equally transcending the limited remit of nationalistically oriented terrorist groups, even when they behaved transnationally such as with Black September in Munich 1972. Instead, it had organized around ideological principles meant first and foremost to recruit and seek influence in territories that far exceed their places of origin and project a global threat. The strategic implication of such broadened goals is that, whereas the earlier groups were content with limited self-autonomy or the usurpation of the role of states in a country or a region, *al Qaeda* sought to create a wider international sphere of influence and control. Groups that pursue the strategic transformation of regional and international affairs along ideological lines challenge the existence and utility of states.[14] In effect, the self-capacitation of *al Qaeda* is essentially what sets it apart as a new type of terrorist organization. John Gray captured the mechanics of such an eminently modern identity:

> *Al Qaeda* has a clear understanding of the vulnerabilities of Western industrial societies...The logic of its strategic goals requires that its reach be worldwide. *Al Qaeda* is essentially a modern organization. It is modern not only in the fact that it uses satellite phones, laptop computers, and encrypted websites...It is not only in its use of communication technologies that *al Qaeda* is modern. So is its organization. *Al Qaeda* resembles less the centralized command structures of

twentieth century revolutionary parties than the cellular structures of drug cartels and the flattened networks of virtual business corporations. Without fixed abode and with active members from practically every part of the world, *al Qaeda* is a global multinational.[15]

Al Qaeda was therefore, from its inception, a globally oriented group endowed with a military-style structure bent on exporting retribution political violence. It was also from the beginning a network, and although this characteristically would become more pronounced and more consequential in the following decade, the 1990s saw *al Qaeda* put in place a *modus operandi*, which here, too, reinvented the ways of modern terrorism. In that respect, and having completed the conceptual and structural architecture of the organization in the period 1989–92, as well as the training of its foot soldiers in 1993–96, and having announced its intentions in a first war declaration, *al Qaeda* would go on to conduct five transnational operations between 1995 and 2000 in preparation of and leading up to its assault on the US the following year. These were the 13 November 1995 bombing of a Saudi–American base in Riyadh, Saudi Arabia; the 25 June 1996 attack on the Al Khobar towers near Dhahran, Saudi Arabia (housing site of the crews enforcing the no-fly zones over Iraq); the simultaneous bombings of the US embassies in Nairobi, Kenya, and Dar-Salaam, Tanzania on 7 August 1998; and the speedboat attack against the *USS Cole* warship in Yemen on 12 October 2000. The culmination of this sequence took place on 11 September 2001, when *al Qaeda* launched an operation, designed in Malaysia, financed from the United Arab Emirates, rehearsed in Spain, led by a five-nationality nineteen-man commando unit assembled in Germany and trained in Afghanistan, which took the form of a simultaneous hijacking of four American domestic airliners crashed into the World Trade Centre in New York and the Pentagon in Washington killing more than three thousand people.

The founding violent radicalism of *al Qaeda* illustrated by the 9/11 operation – the largest terrorist attack in history as well as the most impactful – was thus a strategic reorientation of contemporary political violence owing its fundamental nature to globalization enablers that had been introduced in the 1990s. Rather than the steady pursuit of a locally oriented Islamist conquest of power scenario, the material manifestation of this transnational terrorism was more so an approximation of a military conception of operational delivery underscored by an up-tempo battle plan proactively designed and explicitly communicated:

[E]very one [within *al Qaeda*] agreed that the situation cannot be rectified ... unless the root of the problem is tackled. Hence, it is essential to hit the main enemy who divided the Umma [Muslim nation] into small and little countries and pushed it, for the last few decades, into a state of confusion.[16]

Decentralizing operations and empowering franchises

Whereas *al Qaeda* was acting out such transnationality and manifesting mili-tarized terrorism every step of the way (public declarations of war, commando-style simultaneous operations, strategically targeted use of weaponry, lengthy preparations, articulation of a notion of the 'responsi-bility of the citizenry' of the enemy state, extended video and audio briefing by leaders and middle-operators, and so on), the knowledge imparted about it remained the result of a static perception informed primarily by reporters that had encountered Bin Laden during the 1990s. Overwhelmingly emotional rather than scientific, most scholarship on *al Qaeda* remained divided into three categories, arguing the group's irra-tionality, fundamentalism, and hatred, collapsed into an unshakable threefold narrative: (i) 'We' do not know what *al Qaeda* is, does it even exist? (ii) *al Qaeda* is made up of impoverished ragtags, alienated drifters merely channelling their free-floating anger animated by homicidal animosity, and (iii) *al Qaeda* wants to destroy the Western world and its way of life, and impose a worldwide caliphate. Despite being ahistorical and reductionist, such storytelling perspective came, however, to dominate the social sciences discourse on *al Qaeda* when the group overnight became a household name in the wake of its lethal attacks on New York and Washington on 11 September 2001.

Yet hiding *al Qaeda*'s *casus belli* when it has repeatedly communicated it, ignoring the bourgeois make-up of its leadership, and locating the causes of *al Qaeda*'s resort to force in the fermentation of contemporary religious Islamic culture, rather than the militarization of the politics of sub-state Islamist armed groups with transnational ambitions masks three key notions: the *sui generis* aggrandizement of the principle of 'reactive neces-sity' within which armed political violence is illegally channelled as war (purportedly reacting to the Arab and Muslim states' failure to protect their citizens), the literalization of (Western) civilian responsibility as targets of a new type of post-modern terrorism (in the name of alleged elec-toral support to aggressive policies), and the tactical acknowledgement of technological imbalance with a view to use structural weakness as opportu-nity (instrumentalization of asymmetry through modification of the *locus* and *tempo* of operations) rather than impediment.

The narrative of *al Qaeda* as an apocalyptic organization would have logi-cally yielded inflexibility on its part in the face of stepped-up counter-terrorism. Yet it is precisely the opposite which materialized in the aftermath of the group's attacks on the US. Here too, *al Qaeda* renovated modern terrorism in identifying and implementing a proactive strategy of survival-cum-regeneration. This strategy took the form of the creation and empowerment of what came to be known as regional franchises. In the face of advancing US and United Kingdom troops hunting for its leadership in Afghanistan and Pakistan in 2001–02, and introducing important policy regulations internationally to disrupt its operations (movement and financing were affected in particular), *al Qaeda* was still able to conduct a number of attacks on targets around the world: synagogue in Djerba, Tunisia (11 April 2002); Sheraton hotel in Karachi (8 May 2002); nightclub in Bali (12 October 2002); French oil tanker Limburg near Al Mukkala, Yemen (6 October 2002); Israeli-patronized hotel and chartered airplane in Mombasa, Kenya (28 November 2002); Western housing compounds in Riyadh (12 May and 8 November 2003); Western and Jewish targets in Casablanca (16 May 2003); Marriott hotel in Jakarta (5 August 2003); two synagogues in Istanbul (15 November 2003); central train station in Madrid (11 March 2004); subway and bus system in London (7 July 2005); and three Western housing hotels in Amman, Jordan (9 November 2005).

In the second half of the 2000s, *al Qaeda* formally created five official branches round the world: *al Qaeda* in Mesopotamia (*Tandhim al Qaeda fi Bilad Al Rafidayn*), *al Qaeda* in the Arabian Peninsula (*Tandhim al Qaeda fil Jazira Al Arabiya*), *al Qaeda* in Europe (*Qaedat Al Jihad fi Europa*), *al Qaeda* in Egypt (*Tandhim al Qaeda fi Misr*) and *al Qaeda* in Afghanistan and Pakistan (*Qaedat Al Jihad fil Khorasan*). In addition, in September 2006, Ayman al Dhawahiri announced that the Algerian Islamist organization *Al Jama'a Al Salafiya lil Da'wa wal Qital* (Salafist Group for Predication and Combat) had formally been integrated in *al Qaeda*, emerging officially in January 2007 as *al Qaeda* in the Islamic Maghreb (*Tandhim al Qaeda fil Maghreb Al Islami*). Moreover, a short-lived, non-official *al Qaeda* in Palestine (*al Qaeda fi Filistin*) issued a communiqué in October 2006, the Lebanese group *Fatah Al Islam* claimed, in May 2007, inspiration from *al Qaeda* and expressed readiness to follow Osama Bin Laden's fatwas. The Somali rebel group al Shabaab unilaterally declared that it was joining *al Qaeda*'s global *jihad* campaign in February 2010, as did the Nigerian organization Boko Haram in 2011. Finally, sporadic reports emerged about an *al Qaeda* in Turkey and in Syria.[17] During this late phase, *al Qaeda* was still able to conduct a complex operation targeting the heart of US intelligence with the double-agent mission of *al Qaeda* operator, Humam Khalil Al Balawi, who had posed as an upper-level defector from the group only to penetrate the Khost, Afghanistan-based Central Intelligence Agency top team in charge of anti-*al Qaeda* counter-terrorism, and kill its seven members in December 2009.[18]

At the close of its second decade – after twenty major international attacks, six franchises, and several inspired or associated groups – an *al Qaeda* whose transcendence is very much of this world and not the after one had completed its initial trajectory. In enacting a strategy of decentralization and moving towards emancipated franchises,[19] *al Qaeda* had in effect rebooted both its own narrative and generated discussion of a new terrorism whose global characteristics it had illustrated. Ultimately, however, this overstretched global presence came at a price, namely the evanescence of the mother *al Qaeda* and the hybridization of its legacy.

Beyond Al Qaeda: Al Qaedism

The foundations of terrorism studies in historical research are not very deep.[20] Continuity is privileged and rupture usually escapes identification. Indeed, the central interrogation which should have been raised early on in relation to *al Qaeda* was whether its perceptible manifestation of a type of post-modern and post-colonial type of political violence was consequential in the long term. Instead of exploring such interrogation, as noted, an easy and reductionist narrative of irrationality and apocalyptic terrorism was substituted to proper historical contextualization. It would take a while before inquiry into this dimension of *al Qaeda*'s saga would begin.[21] The intentionality of the new design was not fully registered and social sciences indulged an anthropology of terrorism (in the form of '*jihad*ology') that had not been assigned explanatory power in previous generations. In that sense, the dominant analyses resulted in an inability of policy makers to identify the self-perception of *al Qaeda*, which also generated consequential strategic counter-terrorism errors[22] stubbornly depicting an organization characterized by incompetence, miscalculation, and zeal and inhabiting a largely spent landscape. A sort of terrorism essentialism is what emerged from the analyses predicated upon excessive emphasis on religiosity (*jihad*ism, islamo-fascism) and thanatopolitics (martyrdom, sacrifice). *Al Qaeda*'s success is primarily the result of a redefinition of its ambit of action coupled with a militarized *modus operandi* and an emasculation, indeed a bypassing, of the state. In resorting to analogical frameworks, terrorism studies prioritized an understanding of *al Qaeda* predicated upon a projection of ideas related essentially to Christian fundamentalism or Asian suicide operations (such as the Tamil Tigers) whereas politics (not religion) and survival (not the cult of death) have more often quantitatively driven *al Qaeda*.[23]

Al Qaeda has also invented a communication technique whose impact is an important component of its story and which will remain a central element of its legacy. From the press conferences convened by Bin Laden in February and May 1998 (in which he announced that *al Qaeda* would be 'bringing the war home to America') to the lengthy videotapes of the early 2001 days shipped to Al Jazeera to the late 2000s messages delivered electronically in multiple formats (MP3, AVI, mobile, and PDF), it has indulged digital versatility including multimedia messages with computer simulation featuring computer graphics (re-enacting attacks), statistical data (for example, on the US economy), excerpts from documentaries (such as those on the US–Saudi alliance), commentary on the group (for example, by media analysts), quotations from current affairs books (such as Bob Woodward's *Plan of Attack*), and thematic hour-long online documentaries (with specific titles such as 'Message of One Concerned', 'The Power of Truth', 'The Wills of the Heroes of the Raids on New York and Washington', 'One Row', 'Legitimate Demands', 'From Kabul to

Mogadishu', 'The Path of Doom', 'Security...a Shared Destiny', 'The West and the Dark Tunnel'). The engineering of such communication is inherently linked to a post-modern nature of the group whereby, as David Harvey terms it, time and space are experienced as 'sources of social power'.[24]

Above and beyond these innovations, a proper understanding of *al Qaeda* remains necessary to further a fuller historiography of terrorism. To truly reclaim the importance of ideas for an understanding of modern terrorism requires being able to show the inner dynamic, the immanent necessity, that moves from the ideas to the shape of terrorist violence itself, not the 'opportunist implementation' or justification for terrorist violence.[25] Against that background, for all the common perception, *al Qaeda*'s essential story is in point of fact neither Arab nor religious. It is political and Asian – *al Qaeda* is born in Khost, Afghanistan in August 1989 and Osama Bin Laden dies in Abbottabad, Pakistan in May 2011.[26] During the twenty-two years that separate those two dates, the group went on to write a story whose essential grammar is transnationalism. Paradoxically, while the organization was pursuing a global design, its understanding was ever more ascribed local meaning in the West.[27]

Today, it is no longer possible to speak of *al Qaeda* in the singular. The group's saga spans some consequential two decades, and its exit arguably predates the death of its leader, Osama Bin Laden, in May 2011. By 2007, the franchises had begun demonstrating substantial independence in both operational initiative and strategic decision making. In the next few years, these two tendencies would become steadily confirmed, notably in the case of *al Qaeda* in the Arabian Peninsula and *al Qaeda* in the Islamic Maghreb. As Bin Laden's messages became increasingly less consequential on both international security and the franchises' daily activities, and, indeed, in time with his death, the franchises became perceptibly less concerned with the directives sporadically coming from the mother *al Qaeda*. That situation was in many ways paradoxical for if decentralization worked as Bin Laden and Al Dhawahiri had envisioned, generating a critical mass of multiplied threats around the world for their enemies, the cogency of the vision once articulated in Khost two decades ago had indeed evaporated. In the event, the narrative became 'from the near to the far enemy...and back'. The franchises began demonstrating concern less with the global agenda of their headquarters organization but with eminently local issues: *al Qaeda* in Iraq was immersed in insurgency tactics against the US and internal quarrels between Iraqi groups about the situation in Mesopotamia; *al Qaeda* in the Arabian Peninsula successively battled the Saudi Arabia police and Yemeni military in a replay of a conflictuality that had long beset the territory at the border of the two countries; and, most tellingly, *al Qaeda* in the Islamic Maghreb borrowed the name of Bin Laden's group only to perpetuate the Salafist Group of Predication and Combat political economy of terrorism illustrated by hostage-hustling, drug-trafficking, and arms-dealing. Ultimately, the necessary elasticity *al Qaeda* adopted – partly voluntarily, partly as a way to adapt to the international post-9/11 counter-terrorism campaign – created an ever-growing distance with already independent units, which in time embraced opportunistically that autonomy, being now loosely inspired by *al Qaeda*, now acting on their own (even when, for the sake of publicity, they claimed *al Qaeda* links). 'Spirits that I've called, my commands ignore', would have said Goethe's apprentice sorcerer.

In the final analysis, *al Qaeda* sprang forth as a terrorist project built upon the relocation of authority, the circumvention of the state, and the militaristic empowerment of a non-state actor. Spawning on the failed experience of other Islamist groups, it proliferated transnationally and militarily only to be constrained by its own regionalization and decentralization. Yet *al Qaeda*'s impact on global politics is an affair of long standing and its ubiquitous presence in international security matters defined in a lasting manner the last decade of the twentieth century and the first decade of the twenty-first century. More importantly, *al Qaeda* has in effect reimagined contemporary terrorism with the introduction of patterns that are already giving birth to a new generation of post-*al Qaeda* terrorists: privatization of the resort to political violence, self-radicalization on a 'heroic' military mode, active use of information technology and interconnectedness enablers to beam globally, merging of actual and symbolic violence from battlefield to battlespace, concurrent acceleration and deceleration of simultaneous attack mode, ability to carry inexpensive high-impact operations, and organizational self-capacitation. In overseeing imperfectly the democratization of its own brand of militarized transnational terrorism, what was once *al Qaeda Al 'Askariya* has nonetheless 'bottled' a new terrorism concept. The legacy of such open source *al Qaeda* and in particular the emerging picture of an individualized terrorism has already been featured in several cases such as those of David Headley in Chicago in November 2008, Nidal Malik Hassan in Texas in November 2009, Umar Farouk Abdulmuttalab in the Netherlands in December 2009, Colleen LaRose in Pennsylvania in March 2010, Faisal Shahzad in New York in May 2010, Anders Breivik in Norway in July 2011, and Mohamed Merah in France in March 2012. Paradoxically echoing the early days of anarchist terrorism, these new patterns were also displaying a back to the future logic and aesthetic indicative, too, of a circularity of terrorism.

Notes

1   This does not discount the sporadic presence of transnational patterns of action in previous terrorism ages, notably in the 1970s, or the manifested proactive disposition of the pre-*al Qaeda* terrorist. However, whenever present, these tendencies were additional traits, limited in time and scope, and the essential nature of earlier terrorism did not arguably feature prominently those elements as central characteristics.

2   For a focused critical study of *al Qaeda* using comparative theory, see M. Finn, *Al Qaeda and Sacrifice – Martyrdom, War, and Politics*, London: Pluto Press, 2012.

3   For a review of the dominant themes of the literature on *al Qaeda*, see Chapter four, 'Fallacies and Primacies' in M.-M. Ould Mohamedou, *Understanding al Qaeda – Changing War and Global Politics*, London: Pluto Press, 2011.

4   M. Ranstorp, 'Mapping Terrorism Studies after 9/11: An Academic Field of Old Problems', in R. Jackson, M. Breen Smyth and J. Gunning (eds) *Critical Terrorism Studies – A New Research Agenda*, London: Routledge, 2009, p. 14.

5   See, notably, L. Wright, *The Looming Tower – al Qaeda and the Road to 9/11*, New York: Knoft, 2006; A. Bari Atwan, *The Secret History of al Qaeda*, Berkeley: University of California Press, 2006; P. Bergen, *The Longest War – Inside the Enduring Conflict Between America and al Qaeda*, New York: Free Press, 2011; and M. Scheuer, *Osama Bin Laden*, New York: Oxford University Press, 2012. Wright is a staff writer at *The New Yorker* magazine, Atwan is the editor-in-chief of *Al Quds Al Arabi*, Bergen is CNN's security analyst, and Scheuer served as the head of the anti-Bin Laden unit of the Central Intelligence Agency.

6   See, for example, the work of W. Enders and T. Sandler, notably 'Transnational Terrorism in the Post-Cold War Era', *International Studies Quarterly*, 1999, vol. 43, pp. 145–67.

7   See J.K. Young and M.G. Findley, 'Promise and Pitfalls of Terrorism Research', *International Studies Review*, 2011, vol. 13, pp. 1–21. Young and Findley write: 'Scholars do not typically distinguish between domestic and transnational terrorism... This suggests that most of what we know might apply only to a small portion of overall terrorism... From a theoretical perspective, the causal mechanisms underlying domestic and transnational terrorism might be quite different.'

8   F. Burgat provides the most complete analysis of that history in his *Islamism Under the Shadow of al Qaeda*, Austin: University of Texas Press, 2008.

9   K. Abou El Fadl, *Rebellion and Violence in Islamic Law*, Cambridge: Cambridge University Press, 2001, p. 5.

10 On the multilayered meaning of *al Qaeda*'s name and its different usage as a 'pragmatic precept', see F. Miller, 'Al Qaida as a "Pragmatic Base": Contributions of Area Studies to Sociolinguistics', *Language and Communication*, 2008, vol. 28, pp. 386–408.

11 The feeling of a historical updating of that mission is embodied in Bin Laden's and Al Dhawahiri's upper echelon social status as the vanguard of an old Islamic mission. On echoes of that trajectory, see M. Bonner, *Aristocratic Violence and Holy War – Studies in the Jihad and the Arab-Byzantine Frontier*, New Haven: Yale University Press, 1997.

12 See, for instance, P. Porter, *Military Orientalism – Eastern War Through Western Eyes*, New York: Columbia University Press, 2009. Porter notes: '*Al Qaeda* may seem like a medieval throwback from another world. But it is highly modern, spawned out of globalization and its circulation of ideas and methods... And its murderous methods do not just enact its identity but have a dark strategic logic' (p. 2).

13 J. Alexander Geltzer, *US Counter-Terrorism Strategy and al Qaeda – Signalling and the Terrorist Worldview*, New York: Routledge, 2010, p. 95.

14 For a full examination of this point, see the report by A.J. Dew and M.-M. Ould Mohamedou, *Empowered Groups, Tested Laws, and Policy Options – The Challenge of*

Transnational and Non-State Armed Groups, Harvard University, 2007.

15 J. Gray, *Al Qaeda and What It Means to Be Modern*, London: The New Press, 2003, p. 78.

16 Osama Bin Laden, 'Declaration of War against the Americans Occupying the Land of the Two Holy Places', 23 August 1996.

17 See G. Steinberg, 'A Turkish *Al Qaeda*: The Islamic *Jihad* Union and the Internationalization of Uzbek *Jihad*ism', *Strategic Insights*, Center for Contemporary Conflict, Naval Postgraduate School, Monterey, California, July 2008; and '*Al Qaeda* in Syria?', *The National* (Abu Dhabi), 20 February 2012.

18 See J. Warrick, *The Triple Agent – The Al Qaeda Mole Who Infiltrated the CIA*, New York: Doubleday, 2011.

19 See C. Hellmich, *Al Qaeda – From Global Network to Local Franchise*, London: Zed Books, 2011; and the report by the Center for Strategic and International Studies, *A Threat Transformed – al Qaeda and Associated Movements in 2011*, Washington: CSIS.

20 I. Duyvesteyn, 'The Role of History and Continuity in Terrorism Research', in M. Ranstorp (ed.) *Mapping Terrorism Research – State of the Art, Gaps, and Future Direction*, New York: Routledge, 2007, p. 67.

21 See E. Boehmer and S. Morton (eds), *Terror and the Postcolonial*, London: Wiley-Blackwell, 2010.

22 See W. El-Ansary, 'The Economics of Terrorism: How Bin Laden has Changed the Rules of the Game', in J.E.B. Lumbard (ed.) *Islam, Fundamentalism, and the Betrayal of Tradition*, Bloomington, Indiana: World Wisdom, 2009, pp. 197–242.

23 Robert Pape's research on this issue is important. See R. Pape, *Dying to Win – The Strategic Logic of Suicide Terrorism*, New York: Random House, 2005; and R. Pape, *Cutting the Fuse – The Explosion of Global Suicide Terrorism and How to Stop it*, Chicago: University of Chicago Press, 2010. Pape reports that: 'The strategic logic of suicide terrorism is aimed at political coercion. The vast majority of terrorist suicide attacks are not isolated or random acts by individual fanatics but rather occur in clusters as part of a campaign by an organized group to achieve a specific political goal. Suicide terrorist campaigns are primarily nationalistic, not religious, nor are they particularly Islamic...Even *Al Qaeda* fits this pattern' (Pape 2005, p. 23).

24 D. Harvey, *The Condition of Postmodernity*, Oxford: Blackwell, 1989, p. 226.

25 G. Cameron and J.D. Goldstein, 'The Ontology of Modern Terrorism: Hegel, Terrorism Studies, and Dynamics of Violence', *Cosmos and History – Journal of Natural and Social Philosophy*, 2010, vol. 6, p. 86.

26 See S. Saleem Shahzad, *Inside al Qaeda and the Taliban – Beyond Bin Laden and 9/11*, London: Pluto Press, 2011.

27 See R. Hülsse, 'The Metaphor of Terror: Terrorism Studies and the Constructivist Turn', *Security Dialogue*, 2008, vol. 39, pp. 571–92.

14 The US response to contemporary terrorism

Abraham R. Wagner

Introduction

Even though insulated by two oceans, the US has not been entirely immune to the various waves of contemporary terrorism that have troubled much of the world for over a century. When President William McKinley was assassinated by a terrorist in September 1901, his successor, President Theodore Roosevelt, vowed to eradicate worldwide terrorism, but clearly failed to achieve this noble objective. During the 1970s, terrorists hijacked US aircraft, largely outside the US, with the American response being enhanced security at airports. In the 1980s and 1990s, *al Qaeda* operatives and other Islamic extremists undertook attacks on US facilities in Lebanon, Saudi Arabia, Africa, as well as the *USS Cole* – all of which were far from the US homeland.

The impact of the 9/11 attacks

The 11 September 2001 *al Qaeda* attacks on the US homeland represented an entirely new national security challenge, and as a result the Bush administration embarked on military campaigns in Afghanistan and Iraq in a 'Global War on Terror', seeking to deal with both foreign and domestic threats. The new administration recognized not only the intelligence failure that preceded 9/11, but also the need for new government institutions, laws, and capabilities to deal with this evolving threat. Within days of the 9/11 attack, Bush received Congressional approval for the Authorization for the Use of Military Force (AUMF), a statute which was then used fearlessly to run roughshod over the Constitution, federal law, and anything else that stood in the path to 'making the nation safe'.

Three days after 9/11, Bush visited the World Trade Center site and addressed a gathering via megaphone while standing on a heap of rubble: 'I can hear you. The rest of the world hears you, and the people who knocked these buildings down will hear all of us soon'. Later, he addressed a joint session of the Congress condemning Osama bin Laden and *al Qaeda*, issuing an ultimatum to the Taliban regime in Afghanistan, where bin

Laden was operating, 'hand over the terrorists, or...share in their fate'. Bush announced a 'Global War on Terrorism', and, after the Taliban regime was not forthcoming with Osama bin Laden, ordered the invasion of Afghanistan to overthrow the Taliban. In his January 2002 State of the Union address, Bush further asserted that an 'axis of evil' consisting of North Korea, Iran, and Iraq was 'arming to threaten the peace of the world' and 'pose[d] a grave and growing danger' declaring that the US had a right and intention to engage in pre-emptive war, also called preventive war, in response to perceived threats, forming the basis for what became known as the Bush Doctrine.

Following 9/11, Bush saw an understandable and compelling need to save the nation. Even with Osama Bin Laden and *al Qaeda* identified as the source of the attacks, it was unclear what further strikes were planned or under way.[1] Intelligence reports of further attacks were now investigated and taken seriously, even where the substance was bogus or mythical.[2] Even if the intelligence reports were not correct as to their specifics, the US clearly faced a real and increasing threat from Islamic fundamentalists abroad.

The 9/11 attacks came early in the Bush presidency. He had been in office for only eight months, and came to the White House with no serious experience in the area of national security. Of necessity, Bush relied on key personnel including Cheney, national security adviser Condoleezza Rice, Deputy Secretary of Defence Paul Wolfowitz, and others. While Cheney was clearly the most senior, the most experienced, and the one 'in charge' none of the team had ever faced a national security challenge of this type.

In terms of the actual threat, this was the first time that the US homeland had been attacked since the War of 1812.[3] The US was simply not expecting an attack, and did not have an effective infrastructure in place to process the types of intelligence data that were available prior to the attack, and to respond accordingly.[4] The failure to anticipate and detect the attack was seen as a major intelligence failure – clearly the most significant failure since the 1962 Cuban Missile Crisis. Unlike most other nations, the US has no domestic intelligence service, and reorganization to deal with new domestic threats from terrorists posed a major challenge.[5]

Enormous uncertainty existed over the threat of future *al Qaeda* attacks. While US intelligence agencies had failed to 'connect the dots' and foresee the 9/11 attacks, clearly the intelligence systems were not in a position to anticipate what else might be coming from these new enemies. If Bush and his administration overreacted or reacted badly, it was not because they misused a well-functioning intelligence system that they inherited from their predecessors, particularly with respect to domestic intelligence and the integration of national foreign intelligence data. In many respects, they were 'flying blind' in the early post-9/11 days.

The 9/11 attacks also took place in a radically changed media environment, namely the new world of 24/7 network news, internet sites, and a level of attention orders-of-magnitude greater than in any prior crisis. To a great extent the magnitude of the attack was magnified by the media, while Bush and Cheney helped to fuel the media fires, beating the 9/11 drums endlessly for the next seven years of their administration. Certainly, the three thousand casualties on 9/11 were a horrible outcome, but it was not the end of the republic. Nor did it justify a long and costly war against Iraq and other outcomes not directly related to the 9/11 attacks at all.

The experience of the Bush administration following the *al Qaeda* attacks was one in which many questions were raised that have yet to be fully resolved. Following 9/11, which the US regarded as a national security crisis, the nation embarked on military campaigns, in Afghanistan, Iraq, and elsewhere, as well as in what came to be called a 'Global War on Terror'. Here, the nation sought to deal with threats both at home and abroad, including some that were real and others that were largely imagined.[6]

Doubtless many of these concerns are well-placed. Bush came to the White House with what most historians will agree was, at best, a limited understanding of the Constitution or, as his critics hold, much of anything else.[7] In the wake of the 9/11 attacks, Bush, Cheney, and others engaged in measures to deal with the crisis that sorely strained the concept of the chief executive under the Constitution, a large body of federal statute, and Supreme Court Decisions going back over two centuries. In some cases the law was subverted by what was perceived to be a compelling need to save the nation from future terrorist attacks at home and abroad from Islamic fundamentalists.

Authorization for use of military force and the Bush doctrine

Shortly after 9/11, Bush requested, and the Congress enacted into law, the AUMF, which authorized the President to:

> use all necessary and appropriate force against those nations, organizations, or persons he determines planned, authorized, committed, or aided the terrorist attacks that occurred on September 11, 2001, or harbored such organizations or persons, in order to prevent any future acts of international terrorism against the United States by such nations, organizations or persons.[8]

Here, Bush recognized a need for not only effective intelligence against apparent domestic threats but also military actions against these threats, including some non-state actors such as terrorist organizations. While most legislators saw this as an interim measure that would enable the president to use military resources against *al Qaeda*, few saw the extent to which the Bush administration would use it as legal cover for military and intelligence operations against terrorist threats.

Subsequently, Bush and others in his administration used this statute to avoid the Constitution, federal law, and anything else that stood in their path to 'making the nation safe' and prosecuting perceived foes wherever they might be. While the ultimate objectives were noble, the path taken leaves questions about their legality, as well as whether or not they were operationally useful at all. The most serious of these concerns involve various intelligence and domestic surveillance programs intended to aid counter-terrorism efforts, the detainment of foreign nationals, as well as the torture of prisoners and detainees.

While not enacted into law as the AUMF, the 'Bush Doctrine' delineated in the 2002 National Security Strategy of the United States, further supported actions taken by Bush to combat terrorism worldwide.[9] This strategy saw the terrorist threat as different from what the US had previously faced and went on to say:

> the first duty of the United States Government remains what it always has been: to protect the American people and American interests. It is an enduring American principle that this duty obligates the government to anticipate and counter threats, using all elements of national power, before the threats can do grave damage. The greater the threat, the greater is the risk of inaction – and the more compelling the case for taking anticipatory action to defend ourselves, even if uncertainty remains as to the time and place of the enemy's attack. There are few greater threats than a terrorist attack with WMD.

To forestall or prevent such hostile acts by our adversaries, the United States will, if necessary, act preemptively in exercising our inherent right of self-defense. The United States will not resort to force in all cases to preempt emerging threats. Our preference is that nonmilitary actions succeed. And no country should ever use preemption as a pretext for aggression.[10]

The Bush Doctrine was used as the basis for pre-emptive US military action in Afghanistan and Iraq, and represented a major US policy change from strategic globalism. Combined with the AUMF, it also provided far greater latitude for dealing with those foreign nations that harboured terrorists or supported terrorism.

Organizational responses

Organizationally, the US quickly created a new cabinet level Department of Homeland Security (DHS) as a focal point for its counter-terrorism operations. The new DHS incorporated some thirty-one existing federal agencies or activities, and created several new ones such as the Transportation Security Administration for airport security.

The US also attempted to deal with failings in the intelligence apparatus with the 2004 Intelligence Reform and Terrorism Protection Act (IRTPA), which created a Director of National Intelligence (DNI) to oversee the intelligence community, and an important operating activity, the National Counter-Terrorism Centre. Bush received broad bi-partisan support in recognition of the fact that the nation was long overdue for a major intelligence reorganization and authorizing statute. Here, the IRTPA was one significant attempt to address the problem, by far falling short of meeting the requirements at a complete or even acceptable solution to the entire set of problems identified.[11]

The intelligence available immediately after 9/11 was both limited and often conflicting. Even after the Cold War, intelligence collection and analysis of terrorist organizations and Middle East states were not given either high priority or major resources within the intelligence community.[12] The Central Intelligence Agency's (CIA) Counter-Terrorism Centre was badly managed, understaffed, and underfunded. The White House Counter-Terrorism Coordinator lacked resources and was largely engaged in inter-agency squabbles. Bush had inherited a counter-terrorism system from his predecessors that was in many respects dysfunctional, and even if he personally did not realize the extent of this problem at the outset, many at the White House, the NSC, and elsewhere in his administration did understand it. Much of what they did subsequently, in the name of national security was aimed at overcoming these now obvious shortfalls as quickly as possible, and obtaining reliable information as well as 'actionable intelligence'. If this meant pushing the limits on executive power, it was done as part of an effort to gain information the administration regarded as vital to protecting the nation.

A legacy inherited by the Bush administration was an intelligence community and federal law enforcement establishment not organized, authorized, or equipped to deal with terrorists. The post-Second World War organization of the intelligence community and the establishment of the CIA provided for national foreign intelligence but essentially no mechanism for the effective detection of domestic threats.[13] Animosity between the CIA and the Federal Bureau of Investigation (FBI) had become institutionalized over the years, and cooperation between these two agencies that might have aided in dealing with foreign threats to the US homeland was exceedingly limited in the pre-9/11 days.[14]

As the 9/11 Commission found, in considerable detail, the FBI did not effectively operate as a domestic intelligence service prior to 9/11 and 'failed to connect the dots' with the information they did have at hand. Apart from the existing statutes and Executive Orders, which many argued would have enabled the FBI to do a better job, the existing organization and culture of the FBI as a law enforcement organization – and not an intelligence service was a major stumbling block both before and after 9/11, with limited ability to detect threats from *al Qaeda* and others. Neither effort has been a complete success, while debate in the US continues over ongoing counter-terrorism operations as well as the nature of the future terrorist threat, both to the homeland as well as US assets abroad.

Intelligence and surveillance programs

Throughout the Cold War, the vast majority of all useful intelligence came from technical intelligence collection programs, largely signals intelligence where the intercept of foreign communications provided for attack warning and analysis of potential threats. The National Security Agency (NSA), CIA, and other federal agencies were strictly prohibited by law from intercepting 'domestic' communications as well as those of any 'US persons' wherever located.[15] Enabling statutes for the NSA, CIA, and other federal agencies strictly prohibited and constrained the intercept of both 'domestic' communications as well as any 'US persons' wherever they were located.

Following 9/11, it was clear that the existing legal environment was inadequate for current threats and also that the technology environment had radically changed, including vast increases in international communications as well as cell phone and Internet use. These constraints were clearly inadequate for the new threats to the US, in light of the vast increases in international communications using cell phones, the Internet, and other modern advances. Here the US moved from a 1930s model of telecommunications, with landlines linked with identified parties to cellular systems and hybrid devices, not tied to any identified user.

Legal authority for domestic collection was tied to Title III of a 1968 federal statute – a law now four decades old and a multitude of technology generations out of date.[16] Similarly, the 1978 Foreign Intelligence Surveillance Act (FISA), covering intelligence collection was also out of date and largely unworkable in the modern environment.[17] Bush approached this problem by fiat, largely ignoring the law as well as the Congressional oversight committees for intelligence and justice.

Shortly after 9/11, the NSA implemented an electronic surveillance program named the Terrorist Surveillance Program (TSP) as part of a broader surveillance program conducted under the overall umbrella of the Global War on Terrorism in an effort to intercept *al Qaeda* communications overseas where at least one party was not a US person.[18] The controversy that arose following disclosure of the highly secret program in the *New York Times* in late 2005 concerns surveillance of persons within the US incident to the collection of foreign intelligence by the NSA, which was authorized by executive order to monitor phone calls, emails, internet activity, text messaging, and other communication involving any party believed by the NSA to be outside the US, even if the other end of the communication lies within the US, without warrants.

While the exact scope of the program has not been fully revealed, the NSA was provided total, unsupervised access to all fibre-optic communications going between some of the nation's major telecommunication companies' major interconnect locations, including phone conversations, email, web browsing, and corporate private network traffic. Critics and legal scholars have held that such 'domestic' intercepts require authorization under FISA, while Bush maintained that the authorized intercepts are not domestic but rather foreign intelligence integral to the conduct of war and that the warrant requirements of FISA were implicitly superseded by the subsequent passage of the AUMF.[19] It was further claimed that this program operated without the judicial oversight mandated by FISA and legal challenges to the program are still undergoing judicial review.

Following disclosure in the *New York Times*, Attorney General Alberto Gonzales stated that the program authorized warrantless intercepts where the government 'has a reasonable basis to conclude that one party to the communication is a member of *al Qaeda*, affiliated with *al Qaeda*, or a member of an organization affiliated with *al Qaeda*, or working in support of *al Qaeda*' and that one party to the conversation is 'outside of the United States'.[20] This raised immediate concern among elected officials, civil right activists, and scholars about the constitutionality of the program and the potential for abuse. Subsequently, the controversy expanded to include the role of the press in exposing a highly classified program; the responsibility of Congress in its oversight function; and the extent of Presidential powers under Article II of the Constitution.

Bush stated that he reviewed and reauthorized the program approximately every forty-five days and that the leadership of the Intelligence Committees of both the House and Senate were briefed on it since the initiation of the program. They were not, however, allowed to make notes or confer with others, or even to mention the existence of the program to the full membership of the Intelligence Committees.

When the program leaked to the press, its legality was immediately called into question, looking to whether this program was subject to FISA; and, if so, did the President have any authority to bypass FISA? Since FISA explicitly covers 'electronic surveillance for foreign intelligence information' performed within the US, and there is no court decision supporting the theory that the President's constitutional authority allows him to override statutory law. This was emphasized in a statement by fourteen prominent constitutional law scholars, noting:

> The argument that conduct undertaken by the Commander in Chief that has some relevance to 'engaging the enemy' is immune from congressional regulation finds no support in, and is directly contradicted by, both case law and historical precedent. Every time the Supreme Court has confronted a statute limiting the Commander-in-Chief's authority, it has upheld the statute. No precedent holds that the President, when acting as Commander in Chief, is free to disregard an Act of Congress, much less a criminal statute enacted by Congress that was designed specifically to restrain the President as such.[21]

The disclosure also brought forth a number of challenges in federal court. In August 2006, US District Judge Anna Diggs Taylor in Michigan initially ruled the TSP unconstitutional and illegal.[22] On appeal, the decision was overturned on the procedural grounds that the American Civil Liberties Union (ACLU) lacked the standing to bring the suit, and the lawsuit was dismissed without addressing the merits of the claims, although further challenges are still pending in the federal appellate court.[23]

In January 2007, Attorney General Gonzales informed Senate leaders by letter that the program would not be reauthorized by the president, but would be subjected to judicial oversight. 'Any electronic surveillance that was occurring as part of the Terrorist Surveillance Program will now be conducted subject to the approval of the Foreign Intelligence Surveillance Court.'

In January 2009, President Obama, adopting the same position as Bush, claimed that the state secret privilege entitled them to engage in warrant-less intercept and monitoring, when it urged the court to set aside a ruling in *Al-Haramain Islamic Foundation, et al. v. Obama, et al.*[24] In March 2010, the federal district court ruled against Obama and held that the State Secrets Privilege did not 'trump FISA' or permit the government to engage in warrantless electronic surveillance of suspected terrorists.[25] Obama also sided with Bush in his legal defence of 2008 legislation that immunized the nation's telecommunications companies from lawsuits accusing them of complicity in the eavesdropping program.

The constitutional debate surrounding the authorization of warrantless surveillance is principally about separation of powers, and if no 'fair reading' of FISA can be found in satisfaction of the canon of avoidance, these issues will have to be decided by the federal appellate courts, where the burden of proof is placed upon the Congress to establish its supremacy in the matter: the Executive branch enjoying the presumption of authority until the court rules against it.

The extent of the President's power has never been fully defined, and continues to be a matter of both scholarly debate and legal challenge.[26] Whether 'proper exercise' of war powers includes authority to regulate the gathering of foreign intelligence, which in other rulings has been recognized as 'fundamentally incident to the waging of war', is a historical point of contention between the Executive and Legislative branches.[27]

Passage of the 1978 FISA and the inclusion of such exclusive language reflects Congress's view of its authority to limit the President's use of any inherent constitutional authority with respect to warrantless electronic surveillance to gather foreign intelligence, at least where there is a 'US person' involved in at least one end of the conversation.[28] Application of the Fourth Amendment to the Constitution to electronic surveillance has had a varied history. The Constitution makes no mention of intelligence at all, and at the time of its adoption in 1787 electronic communications did not even exist.[29] While the Fourth Amendment guards against 'unreasonable' searches and seizures, such 'reasonable' searches or seizures require a court order (warrant). Neither the Executive nor Legislative branch can lawfully abrogate this right, nor can any law make an unreasonable search reasonable, or a reasonable search unreasonable.[30]

Whether or not communications intercept was a violation of privacy rights did not even reach the Supreme Court until 1928 when the Court held in *Olmstead v. United States* that warrantless wiretapping and electronic intercept did not violate the Fourth Amendment protections against unreasonable search. The Olmstead decision was finally reversed in 1967 in *Katz v. United States*, when the Court held that the monitoring and recording of private conversations within the US constitutes a 'search' for Fourth Amendment purposes, and therefore the government must generally obtain a warrant before undertaking such domestic wiretapping.[31]

Privacy is clearly not a reasonable expectation in communications to persons in the many countries whose governments openly intercept electronic communications, and is of dubious reasonability in countries against which the US is waging war. The law also recognizes a distinction between domestic surveillance taking place within US borders and foreign surveillance of non-US persons either in the US or abroad.[32] The US Supreme Court has never ruled on the constitutionality of warrantless searches targeting foreign powers or their agents within the US, although there have been several circuit court rulings upholding the constitutionality of such warrantless searches.[33]

Capture, detainment, and interrogation terrorist suspects

No nation has ever expressed greater concern than the US with respect to those suspected or accused of crimes, no matter how offensive or heinous. Responding quickly to the 9/11 attacks, the US and its allies engaged in both military activities and covert operations in Afghanistan and elsewhere to deny *al Qaeda* use of bases and training camps. The inevitable result of these operations was the capture of a significant number of foreign nationals, some of whom were known terrorists and others who were either 'suspected' terrorists and many that were simply in the wrong place at the wrong time. These were difficult military operations in Third World areas, and there was no way to entirely avoid such outcomes. Even if some of those captured were not terrorists, it was reasonable to assume they might have knowledge of intelligence value. The critical questions then become ones of what is their status under international and domestic law; where should they be detained; how should they be interrogated; and what procedures should be followed for their trial or release?

Those captured and detained who were not clearly foreign military, were initially held overseas in various prisons, such as the one established at Bagram Air Force Base in Afghanistan, as well as some CIA 'secret prisons' in Poland, Romania, Tunisia, and elsewhere. Such facilities were in part a logistics convenience, but they also served to keep these detainees away from the gambit of US Constitutional law.[34] It did not keep those captured away from international law and the Geneva Conventions, which the Bush administration frequently argued did not apply since the detainees were not 'enemy combatants'.[35]

The greatest concerns here have been the writ of *habeas corpus*, as well as the right to trial guaranteed under the Constitution, as these individuals were clearly in US custody. Cases filed on behalf of Guantanamo detainees during the Bush administration have already been heard by the Supreme Court which held that Bush had clearly exceeded his authority. In 2006, the Court held that the military commissions set up to try the detainees at Guantanamo lack 'the power to proceed because its structures and procedures violate both the Uniform Code of Military Justice and the four Geneva Conventions signed in 1949'.[36] Subsequently, in 2008, the Court held in *Boumediene v. Bush*, that the detainees held in Guantanamo have the right to challenge their detention in US courts and are entitled to the protections of the US Constitution.[37] The five to four decision by Justice Kennedy overruled prior cases and recognized that fundamental rights afforded by the Constitution extend to Guantanamo.

Closely related to the detention of persons captured in counter-terrorist operations outside the US were efforts to obtain actionable intelligence from the detainees. Interrogations have been conducted in a number of prisons, including the various 'secret prisons', Abu Ghraib in Afghanistan and Guantanamo Bay, Cuba.[38] Interrogations conducted by the CIA and the military often employed 'enhanced interrogation techniques', which critics categorized as 'torture' that violated the law as well as ethical and moral standards.[39]

However unconstitutional, distasteful, or immoral, these interrogations were not undertaken in a legal vacuum. Early on the CIA requested legal advice on detainee interrogation from the White House, which in turn asked the Justice Department for an analysis and opinion on the subject. The CIA's request was routed to the Justice Department's Office of Legal Counsel (OLC) by then White House General Counsel, Alberto Gonzalez, who desired the 'ability to quickly obtain information from captured terrorists and their sponsors'. The CIA wanted to know whether, after the terrorist attacks of 11 September 2001, it could aggressively interrogate suspected high-ranking *al Qaeda* captured outside the US.[40] The result of this analysis was the now famed 'Bybee Memo' prepared by the US Department of Justice's OLC in response to the CIA request to the White House, which describes the limitations on the behaviour of US government interrogators outside the US as governed by the United Nations Convention Against Torture.[41]

The analysis concludes that torture is defined as 'acts inflicting... severe pain or suffering, whether mental or physical'. Physical pain 'must be equivalent in intensity to the pain accompanying serious physical injury, such as organ failure, impairment of bodily function, or even death'. Mental pain 'must result in significant psychological harm of significant duration, e.g., lasting for months or even years' as well as threats of imminent death; threats of infliction of the kind of pain that would amount to physical torture; infliction of such physical pain as a means of psychological torture; use of drugs or other procedures designed to deeply disrupt the senses, or fundamentally alter an individual's personality; or threatening to do any of these things to a third party.

In a second memo, Bybee goes into great detail on ten techniques, a number of which have been referred to as torture, and why they are legal to apply to CIA prisoner Abu Zubaydah, who at the time was held in a covert CIA 'black site'. This memo's detailed legal analysis has subsequently been repudiated by the new OLC personnel who simultaneously promised to defend and indemnify any government employee who ever relied on that advice to commit violations of domestic and/or international law.

The torture memos have been widely criticized. Harold Koh, Yale Law School Dean, and currently State Department Legal Adviser called it 'perhaps the most clearly erroneous legal opinion I have ever read' which 'grossly overreaches the president's constitutional power'.[42] John Yoo's legal opinions were controversial, even within the Bush administration. Secretary of State Colin Powell strongly opposed the invalidation of the Geneva Conventions, while Navy general counsel Alberto Mora campaigned internally against what he saw as the 'catastrophically poor legal reasoning' and dangerous extremism of Yoo's legal opinions. Philip D. Zelikow, former State Department adviser to Condoleezza Rice, testified to the Senate Judiciary Committee, 'It seemed to me that the OLC interpretation of US Constitutional Law in this area was strained and indefensible. I could not imagine any federal court in America agreeing that the entire CIA program could be conducted and it would not violate the American Constitution.' Zelikow also alleged that Bush administration officials not only ignored his memos, but attempted to destroy them.

The torture memo was rescinded by Jack Goldsmith, a Harvard Law School professor who had taken over the OLC, calling it 'deeply flawed' and 'sloppily reasoned' but nevertheless asserted that he 'hadn't determined the underlying techniques were illegal'.[43] Goldsmith has defended the memo's authors. 'I don't impugn the integrity of anyone. I really do believe that everyone, both me and the people I disagreed with, were acting in good faith. And it's quite possible that I made mistakes as well – we were all acting under intense pressure' in the post 9/11 climate.

Notwithstanding the ultimate legality of the enhanced interrogation or 'torture' employed by the CIA and others during the Bush administration are some very real questions as to whether such methods are in fact torture; whether they have actually yielded any operational intelligence; and at what cost to the nation and its international standing. While clearly objectionable by most standards, the methods discussed have been viewed by many as 'torture light' as compared to the satanic torture employed by other nations.[44]

The question as to whether such techniques yielded actionable intelligence is still a matter of ongoing debate. Cheney continues to maintain that these practices did in fact yield highly useful intelligence and were of great benefit to the nation. Others familiar with the specific interrogation cases disagree. Indeed, most experts agree that torture seldom yields accurate, actionable intelligence, and those subjected to various levels of 'enhanced interrogation' simply provide information that is inaccurate or useless to alleviate their situation.[45] Most recently, the capture of Osama Bin Laden was tied to at least some information obtained by 'enhanced interrogation' which has rekindled the debate anew.

An additional question is whether the US has abandoned its own Constitutional concepts, including a fundamental respect for human dignity by engaging in such practices. Does the US have some special provenance to make its own rules, not tainted by Old World conventions and treaties? Indeed, has the US given up the moral high ground for nothing? Some argue that in the post-9/11 era the debate is one between a New Reality vs. Old Morality. In the Global War on Terror, the nation is waging a real war against concealed fanatics who travel the globe at will and are capable of mass killing without warning. This is a newly vulnerable, porous world. This vision holds that 'due process is for sissies' and that human rights fetishists are fighting the last war. Old rules are now quaint.

A human rights counter-vision sees Abu Ghraib and Guantanamo as outposts in a global American gulag where the innocent and guilty alike are illegally detained and tortured, and where little or no useful intelligence is gained from such treatment. The US is seen as squandering moral capital for trash, and torture is viewed as the refuge of the stupid and lazy. Real intelligence services don't use torture. Rather they learn their captives' language and culture and interrogate people with patience, respect, and often tea and cookies.[46] Under Bush, the US turned against civilized opinion since Aristotle; abandoned the Geneva Conventions and the 1994 anti-torture law; and a century of progress toward basic human rights, compromising the ideals of freedom and democracy and became a pariah state where any Muslim was fair game for torture.[47]

The legal strategy for all of these actions were the result of a White House 'War Council' or triumvirate led by David Addington, and included Timothy Flannigan, deputy White House Council, and Alberto Gonzales, White House Council. Bush himself was above the fray.

> With a staff manufacturing propaganda for him, Bush felt liberated from the obligations of reasoned discourse the rule of law largely a matter of self-restraint. "I'm the commander...I don't need to explain...why I say things. That is the interesting thing about being

president. Maybe somebody needs to explain to me why they say something, but I don't feel like I owe anybody an explanation".[48]

In the case of Bush, it is important to note how quickly these programs became known and the speed with which the courts have dealt with the problem. Most of these involved highly classified programs; secret prisons; and covert activities known only to a very few within the government. The speed with which they were revealed in the media almost defies imagination, forcing the Bush administration, the Congress, and the courts to deal with these transgressions more quickly than anyone might have imagined only a few years earlier. If nothing else, future presidents will know that breaking the law and abusing the Constitution cannot be done in secret for long, if at all. Forced transparency and enhanced oversight will certainly act to constrain secret government action and its abuses in the future, even if they cannot be eliminated forever.

Notes

1 Report of the *National Commission on Terrorist Attacks Upon the United States,* US Congress. August 21, 2004. Available online: www.911commission.gov/report/911Report_Ch9.htm (accessed 20 May 2012).

2 Possibly the most interesting was a report from an agent code-named 'DRAGONFLY', which told of a terrorist nuclear weapon in New York City which was obviously not true.

3 At the time of the Pearl Harbour attack, Hawaii was not a state, and thus the Japanese attack was not against the US mainland.

4 See G. Posner, *Why America Slept: The Failure to Prevent 9/11,* New York: Random House, 2004.

5 As a result of the National Security Act of 1947 and successive legislation, the US simply had no domestic intelligence service similar to Great Britain's MI-5, Israel's *Shin Bet,* or the equivalent in any number of nations. Under this Act and Executive Order 12333 (1981) the CIA was prohibited from operating as a domestic intelligence agency, and the FBI was not empowered to do so. The IRTPA of 2004, Public Law 108-458 enacted 17 December 2004, did not entirely solve this problem.

6 Unfortunately, this term has remained in use. It is not logically possible to engage in a war against terror, since terror is not an enemy. It is, rather a set of tactics employed by a range of adversaries, ranging from actual nation states to various non-state actors, which are commonly lumped into an overall category of 'terrorist organizations'. See D.C. Rapoport 'The Four Waves of Terrorism' in A. Cronin and J. Ludes (eds) *Attacking Terrorism Elements of a Grand Strategy,* Washington: Georgetown University Press, 2004.

7 There is already an excellent and evolving historical literature on the George W. Bush presidency, including some good accounts from several who served in the administration. Where national security is involved, some of the best works thus far include: B. Woodward, *Bush at War,* New York: Simon & Schuster, 2002; B. Woodward, *Plan of Attack,* New York: Simon & Schuster, 2004; B. Woodward,

State of Denial: Bush at War Part III, New York: Simon & Schuster, 2006; J. Risen, *State of War: The Secret History of the CIA and the Bush Administration,* New York: Simon & Schuster, 2006; and S. Hersh, *Chain of Command: The Road from 9/11 to Abu Ghraib,* New York: Harper-Collins, 2004. Some of the better 'inside accounts' include F. Fukuyama, *After the Neocons: America at the Crossroads,* London: Profile, 2007; and J. Yoo, *War by Other Means: An Insider's Account of the War on Terror,* New York: Atlantic Monthly Press, 2006.

8   Authorization for Use of Military Force. Enacted 18 September 2001. Public Law 107-40 [S. J. RES 23]. 107th Congress.

9   *National Security Strategy of the United States,* 17 September 2002. Available online: www.globalsecurity.org/military/library/policy/national/nss-020920.pdf (accessed 20 May 2012).

10   Ibid., p. 1.

11   The 2004 IRTPA took a few critical steps, the most important of which were the creation of a DNI to oversee all US intelligence activities, rather than 'dual hating' the CIA Director as Director of Central Intelligence.

12   See ; J. Risen, *State of War: The Secret History of the CIA and the Bush Administration,* New York: Simon & Schuster, 2006.

13   See National Security Act of 1947 (Pub. L. No. 235, 80 Cong., 61 Stat. 496, 50 U.S.C. Ch.15); Central Intelligence Agency Act of 1949 (CIA Act) (Pub. L. No. 81-110, 63 Stat. 208); Executive Order 12333: *United States Intelligence Activities.* (December 4, 1981), amended by Executive Order 13355: *Strengthened Management of the Intelligence Community* (August 27, 2004) and Executive Order 13470: *Further Amendments to Executive Order 12333, United States Intelligence Activities* (July 30, 2008) to strengthen the role of the DNI.

14   See Report of the *National Commission on Terrorist Attacks upon the United States,* US Congress. August 21, 2004. Available online: www.911commission.gov/report/911Report_Ch9.htm (accessed 20 May 2012).

15   See here A.R. Wagner (ed.), *Domestic Intelligence: Needs and Strategies,* Santa Monica: Center for Advanced Studies on Terrorism and The RAND Corporation, 2009. NSA's electronic surveillance operations are governed primarily by four legal sources, namely the Fourth Amendment to the US Constitution; the FISA of 1978; Executive Order 12333; and US Signals Intelligence Directive 18 (1976), reissued and superseded in 1993. A pre-9/11 analysis of this issue was provided by NSA to the Congress, as *Legal Standards for the Intelligence Community in Conducting Electronic Surveillance,* February 2000. Available online: www.fas.org/irp/nsa/standards.html (accessed 20 May 2012).

16   Omnibus Crime Control and Safe Streets Act of 1968, PL 90-351, 82 Stat., 18 U.S.C. §§ 2510 *et. seq.* The role of the 'telecoms' expanded greatly to commercial Internet Service Providers; cable system operators; and others that maintain massive file systems and offer various forms of communications services.

17   FISA, PL 95-511, Title I, 92 Stat. 1976 (1978), 50 U.S.C. §§ 1801 *et. seq.*

18   It was later disclosed that some of the intercepts included communications that were 'purely domestic' in nature, igniting the NSA warrantless surveillance controversy. See J. Risen and E. Lichtblau, 'Spying Program Snared US Calls', *New York Times,* 21 December 2005, p. 1. The next day Bush gave an eight-minute television address during which he addressed the wiretap story directly, stating 'I authorized the National Security Agency, consistent with US law and the Constitution, to intercept the international communications of people with

known links to *al Qaeda* and related terrorist organizations. Before we intercept these communications, the government must have information that establishes a clear link to these terrorist networks.' He forcefully defended his actions as 'crucial to our national security' and claimed that the American people expected him to 'do everything in my power, under our laws and Constitution, to protect them and their civil liberties' as long as there was a 'continuing threat' from *al Qaeda*.

19   FISA makes it illegal to intentionally engage in electronic surveillance under the appearance of an official act or to disclose or use information obtained by electronic surveillance under the appearance of an official act knowing that it was not authorized by statute. Further, the federal Wiretap Act (18 USC §119) prohibits any person from illegally intercepting, disclosing, using, or divulging phone calls or electronic communications.

20   The White House, 'Press Briefing by Attorney General Alberto Gonzales and General Michael Hayden, Principal Deputy Director for National Intelligence', 19 December 2005.

21   Letter to Congress regarding FISA and NSA, 14 constitutional law scholars, February 2, 2006, p. 5.

22   *American Civil Liberties Union v. NSA*, 06-CV-10204 (2006). On 19 February 2008, the Supreme Court, without comment, turned down an appeal from the American Civil Liberties Union, letting stand the earlier decision dismissing the case.

23   In August 2007, the US Court of Appeals for the Ninth Circuit heard arguments in two lawsuits challenging the surveillance program. One of the cases is a class action against AT&T, focusing on allegations that the company provided the NSA with its customers' phone and Internet communications for a vast data-mining operation. In the second, the al-Haramain Foundation Islamic charity and two of its lawyers sued the US government for abuse of constitutional rights. Also in September 2008, the Electronic Frontier Foundation, an Internet-privacy advocacy group, filed a new lawsuit against the NSA, President Bush, and other government agencies and individuals who ordered or participated in the warrantless surveillance seeking redress for what they alleged to be an illegal, unconstitutional, and ongoing dragnet surveillance of their communications and communications records.

24   *Al-Haramain Islamic Foundation, Inc. v. Bush*, 451 F. Supp. 2d 1215 (D Or 2006). Pursuant to Fed. R. Civ. P. 25(d), President Obama is substituted in his official capacity as a defendant in this case.

25   *In Re: National Security Agency Telecommunications Records Litigation*, MDL Docket No. 06-1791. The decision and order by federal Chief Judge Vaughn Walker specifically pertains to the *Al-Haramain Islamic Foundation v. Obama* case, Case No. 07-0109. All federal cases with regard to the TSP were consolidated in the Ninth Circuit under the MDL Docket Number M 06-1791.

26   Two US Supreme Court cases are considered seminal in this area, including *Youngstown Sheet and Tube Co. v. Sawyer, Supra*, and *United States v. Curtis-Wright Export Corp, Supra*. See also Johnson, op cit., and J. Yoo, *War by Other Means: An Insider's Account of the War on Terror*, New York: Atlantic Monthly Press, 2006.

27   See Congressional Research Service, 'Presidential Authority to Conduct Warrantless Electronic Surveillance to Gather Foreign Intelligence Information'. Presidents have long contended that the ability to conduct

surveillance for intelligence purposes is a purely executive function, and have tended to make broad assertions of authority while resisting efforts on the part of Congress or the courts to impose restrictions.

28   The Senate Judiciary Committee articulated its view with respect to congressional power to tailor the President's use of an inherent constitutional power, noting that 'The basis for this legislation [FISA] is the understanding – concurred in by the Attorney General – that even if the President has an "inherent" constitutional power to authorize warrantless surveillance for foreign intelligence purposes, Congress has the power to regulate the exercise of this authority by legislating a reasonable warrant procedure governing foreign intelligence surveillance.'

29   At the time of the adoption of the Constitution and Bill of Rights (1787) these communications technologies were not even on the horizon. See A.R. Wagner, *Technology and National Security*, New York: Columbia University, December 2009.

30   The term 'unreasonable' is deliberately imprecise but connotes the sense that there is a rational basis for the search and that it is not an excessive imposition upon the individual given the motivation for and circumstances of the search, and is in accordance with customary societal norms. It is conceived that a judge will be sufficiently distanced from the authorities seeking a warrant that he can render an impartial decision unaffected by any prejudices or improper motivations they may harbour.

31   *Olmstead v. United States*, 277 U.S. 438 (1928), and *Katz v. United States*, 389 U.S. 347 (1967).

32   In *United States v. Verdugo-Urquidez*, 494 U.S. 259 (1990), the Supreme Court reaffirmed the principle that the Constitution does not extend protection to non-US persons located outside of the US, so no warrant would be required.

33   In *USA v. Osama bin Laden*, 93 F.Supp.2d 484 (2000), the Second Circuit noted that 'no court, prior to FISA, that was faced with the choice, imposed a warrant requirement for foreign intelligence searches undertaken within the United States'. In the Bush administration's view, this unanimity of pre-FISA Circuit Court decisions vindicates their argument that warrantless foreign-intelligence surveillance authorities existed prior to FISA and since, as these ruling indicate, that authority derives from the Executive's inherent Article II powers, they may not be encroached by statute. In 2002, the US Foreign Intelligence Surveillance Court of Review (Court of Review) met for the first time and issued an opinion (*In Re Sealed Case No. 02-001*) that echoed that view. Based on these rulings it 'took for granted such power exits' and ruled that under this presumption, 'FISA could not encroach on the president's constitutional power'. Bush's former Assistant Deputy Attorney General for national security issues, David Kris, and five former FISA Court judges, one of whom resigned in protest, have voiced their doubts as to the legality of a program bypassing FISA.

34   See J. Mayer, 'Use of Torture in Secret Prisons', *The New Yorker*, 14 August 2007. Several reports indicate that 'secret prisons' were also set up on US Naval ships.

35   See H.H. Bruff, *Bad Advice: Bush's Lawyers and the War on Terror*, Lawrence: University of Kansas Press, 2009.

36   *Hamdan v. Rumsfeld*, 548 U.S. 557 (2006). Specifically the Court held that that Common Article 3 of the Geneva Conventions was violated and the detainees were entitled to be treated as 'enemy combatants'.

37 *Boumediene v. Bush*, op cit. See also J. Margulies, *Guantanamo and the Abuse of Presidential Power*, New York: Simon & Schuster, 2006; J.L. Goldsmith, *The Terror Presidency: Law and Judgment inside the Bush Administration*, New York: Norton, 2007; K.J. Greenberg and J.L. Dratel (eds), *The Enemy Combatant Papers: American Justice, the Courts and the War on Terror*, New York: Cambridge University Press, 2008; and P.B. Heymann and J.N. Kayyem, *Protecting Liberty in an Age of Terror*, Cambridge: Massachusetts Institute of Technology Press, 2005.

38 See M. Danner (ed.), *Torture and Truth: America, Abu Ghraib and the War on Terror*, New York: New York Review of Books, 2004 and K. Greenberg and J.L. Dratel (eds), *The Torture Papers: The Road to Abu Ghraib*, New York: Cambridge University Press, 2005.

39 Ibid. See also A. Lewis, 'Torture: The Road to Abu Ghraib and Beyond', in K.J. Greenberg (ed.) *The Torture Debate in America*, New York: Cambridge University Press, 2006; C.H. Pyle, *Getting Away with Torture: Secret Government, War Crimes and the Rule of Law*, Washington: Potomac Books, 2009; J. Margulies, *Guantanamo and the Abuse of Presidential Power*, New York: Simon & Schuster, 2006; and J.R. Schlesinger, H. Brown, T.K. Fowler and C.A. Horner, *Final Report of the Independent Panel to Review DoD Detention Operations*, in Mark Danner (ed.) *Torture and Truth: America, Abu Ghraib, and the War on Terror*, New York: New York Review of Books, 2004.

40 In effect, the CIA was asking for an interpretation of the statutory term of 'torture' as defined in 18 U.S.C. § 2340. That section implements, in part, the obligations of the US under the Convention Against Torture and Other Cruel, Inhuman and Degrading Treatment or Punishment.

41 The 'Bybee Memo' is also known as the 'Torture Memo' and the '8/1/02 Interrogation Opinion', and officially titled *Memorandum for Alberto R. Gonzales, Counsel to the President*, from Jay S. Bybee, Assistant Attorney General, Office of Legal Counsel, *Re: Standards of Conduct for Interrogation under 18* U.S.C. §§ 2340–2340A.

42 See H.H. Koh, 'Setting the World Right', *Yale Law Journal*, 2006, vol. 115: 2350–79.

43 J.L. Goldsmith, *The Terror Presidency: Law and Judgment Inside the Bush Administration*, New York: Norton, 2007.

44 In reviewing these methods, Defence Secretary Donald Rumsfeld commented on the method of 'prolonged standing' as less time than he spent standing each day, and that he was well over 70 years old.

45 Israel, for example, where torture of prisoners was allowable under Israeli law for some time, found that these techniques were largely useless and more often than not yielded false or useless information.

46 See A. Berko, *The Path to Paradise The Inner World of Suicide Bombers and Their Dispatchers*, New York: Praeger Publishers, 2007.

47 Not discussed here are various Special Access programs set up within the Department of Defence and authorized by Presidential finding in late 2001. Under these highly classified programs clandestine teams of Special Forces and others were able to defy diplomacy and international law and were authorized to capture or assassinate 'high value' *al Qaeda* targets, operating anywhere in the world. Secret interrogation centres set up in allied countries, with harsh treatment of prisoners, were largely unconstrained by legal limits or public

disclosure. The rules were 'grab whom you must, do what you want'. See S. Hersh, *Chain of Command: The Road from 9/11 to Abu Ghraib*, New York: HarperCollins, 2004.

48   Ibid., p. 7.

15 Terrorism in the twenty-first century

A new era of warfare

Sean N. Kalic

Introduction

Since the 1960s, the United States (US) and its allies have struggled with transnational terrorism. However, during the Global War on Terrorism the terms and conditions of the warfare have changed and the threat is even more complicated. In the aftermath of the Westphalian peace that emerged after decades of war in Europe, an international system emerged as states became the official entity to negotiate and establish the 'fundamental rights and duties of states'.[1] This Westphalian system established the parameters of the international community and developed international laws, treaties, diplomatic missions, and international organizations as it has evolved over 400 years into the traditional international system we have today.[2]

However, on 11 September 2001 *al Qaeda* fundamentally challenged the tenets of the traditional Westphalian system and many people claimed a new era of warfare had begun. This new era emerged as US President George W. Bush on 30 September 2001 announced before a joint session of Congress that the US had initiated a 'war on terrorism that focused on *Al Qaeda*', as well as the 'defeat of every other terrorist group of global reach'.[3] Interestingly, this new era of warfare focused on a transnational terrorist group, not a state as the 'enemy'. Lacking a Westphalian context, *al Qaeda* operates outside the traditional international community. As a result of being outside the traditional parameters of the legitimate community of nations, the US and the international community have had to adapt and evolve a variety of actions to contain, isolate, and eradicate the threat posed by *al Qaeda*. In its quest to secure its objective, the US and its allies have had to blur the lines between war and peace and in the process defined this new era of warfare.

Nineteen days after *al Qaeda* inflicted one of the most catastrophic attacks on the continental US in the history of the nation, President George W. Bush stated, 'our war on terrorism begins with *Al Qaeda*, but does not end... until every terrorist group of global reach has been found, stopped, and defeated'.[4] In this quotation, Bush confirmed the opening of the US-led global war on terrorism. However, this war and this enemy are unique in some very specific ways, yet similar to enemies of the past in others. Therefore, before providing an analysis of the issues and problems as they relate to the new era of warfare, it is necessary to look at how *al Qaeda* and new terrorism evolved to become the primary international security issue, because transnational terrorist organizations have remained resilient and adaptive despite significant attrition.[5]

A new era of terrorism

A new era of terrorism emerged in the late 1960s and the early 1970s, as various terrorist groups sought to achieve their political objectives through the use of violent means to catch the attention of the international community in an effort to advance their cause. In 1972, the Palestinian-based Black September shocked the world by brashly taking Israeli athletes hostage in the midst of the 1972 Olympics. This single event remains one of the most significant terrorist acts that ushered in the new era of terrorism. Under the watchful eye of international news cameras, the events in Munich, Germany unfolded before the world. The bloody climax came when the terrorists and their hostages attempted to leave, and West German police attempted to neutralize the terrorists and free the hostages. Unfortunately, the Israeli hostages as well as the terrorists died in the ensuing gun battle. The tragedy of this single event prompted the US and the international community to recognize two important points. First, terrorism and terrorists posed a threat to national, regional, and international stability. Second, as a direct result of the botched rescue attempt carried out by West German police in 1972, the nations of the international community recognized the need for effective counter-terrorism forces. Because of the terrorists' actions at the 1972 Olympics, terrorism became a permanent and recognized part of the international security environment. Despite the steadfast recognition by European nations that terrorist organizations posed a significant threat to the international community of nations, the US still remained primarily focused on the context and threats within the context of the Cold War.[6] Although US President Richard M. Nixon did enact anti-terrorism legislation after Munich, the threat withered in the shadow of thermonuclear war.

Throughout the 1970s, the international community witnessed sharp spikes in the number of international terrorist events.[7] Specifically in Northern Ireland, Europe, and the Middle East terrorist attacks flourished.[8] Additionally in this period, the hijacking of commercial aircraft became a political tactic of terrorist groups to advance their agenda, as well as provide a quick means of transportation to a terrorist-friendly nation. Interestingly enough, the hijackers seldom harmed crews and passengers, as long as victims cooperated with the terrorists' demands. By the 1990s, flight crews were informed to concede to the demands of hijackers as a quick way to diffuse the situation. Analysis of *al Qaeda*'s attacks on the US on 11 September 2001 speculated that the flight crews of the four hijacked aircraft initially followed this 'proven' method. Seemingly, by the end of the twentieth century, the hijacking of aircraft had become little more than a nuisance, as well as a major inconvenience to the crews and passengers involved. Although the hijacking of aircraft often ended with minimal casualties, the international community took lessons from the 1972 Olympics and began using specialized paramilitary and police forces to neutralize the hijackers.[9] Internationally, counter-terrorism measures increased as the scale and scope of terrorism expanded in the 1970s and 1980s.

In addition to hijacking, terrorists in this new era used bombs, firebombing, vandalism, arson, and kidnapping as methods to advance and gain notoriety for their specific causes.[10] By the 1980s, the hijacking of aircraft had given way to bombing as the preferred method of terrorist groups to advance their agendas. Three specific examples demonstrate the evolution of terrorists toward more violent and destructive acts. In 1983, suspected Hezbollah 'suicide bombers' killed US Marines and French Paratroopers in two attacks at the Beirut airport when a truckload of explosives was driven into the compounds.[11] Second, Sikh terrorists exploded an Air India flight in 1985, killing all three hundred and twenty-eight people aboard.[12] Last, Libyan leader Muammar Qaddafi 'commissioned' the bombing of a Pan Am flight over Lockerbie, Scotland, killing all two hundred and seventy-eight people aboard the aircraft.[13] Combined, terrorists killed a total of eight hundred and forty-seven people in these three individual bombing incidents. In comparison, RAND analysts, Brian Jenkins and Janera Johnson, established that international terrorists killed two hundred and forty-seven people in 1974.[14] Jenkins and Johnson characterized 1974 as a particularly bad year, as the total number of casualties from terrorism surpassed those from the period 1970–1973.[15] By the middle of the 1980s, it appeared that terrorists had begun to target greater numbers of civilians. The number of casualties in the 1970s and the 1980s reaffirms the transition from the traditional terrorist era to the new era as one of increased and indiscriminate violence. Beyond the use of more violent tactics designed to kill greater numbers of people, the 'new' terrorist era witnessed a gravitation of groups away from political and economic ideology toward the theology-driven transnational terrorist organizations that focus on using mass events to gain recognition for their respective causes.

Largely stemming from the takeover in Iran by the radical cleric Ayatollah Khomeini in 1979, militant Islam became an ideological foundation for the perpetuation of terrorism and terrorist organizations within the international security environment. Prior to the rise of Khomeini, the majority of international terrorist organizations tended to focus on nationalist, social, or political issues. Groups such as the Irish Republican Army, *Euskadi Ta Askatasuna*, and the Palestine Liberation Organization (PLO) focused exclusively on the liberation of their people from the control of the British, Spanish, and Israelis, respectively. Each of these terrorist groups easily incorporated the tactics and strategies associated with the new era of terrorism into their organizations and in their fight for national sovereignty. Beyond the advancement of nationalistic goals, terrorist groups such as the Japanese Red Army (JRA), Red Brigades of Italy, and the Baader-Meinhof group of West Germany sought to advance various forms of Marxism within the international community by advocating and practicing the use of terrorism. Like the nationalist-focused terrorist groups, the JRA, Red Brigades, and the Baader-Meinhof Group easily integrated the elements associated with 'new terrorism' into their operational strategies and objectives, but still tended to ally with state-sponsored terrorist organizations for training and funding. Contrary to the argument made by Bruce Hoffman, the above-mentioned terrorist groups blurred the distinction between the traditional and new eras of terrorism.[16] Building on experience gained in the decades prior to the 1970s and 1980s, all six groups remained active participants in the use of terrorism well into the post-September 11 era. Moreover, the rise of the new terrorist era coincided with the political rise of Khomeini and his adherence to radical Islam in Iran. The Iranian support and sponsorship of terrorist organizations in the declared *jihad* against the West additionally characterized the era of new terrorism.

The establishment of a revolutionary 'Islamic theocracy' by Khomeini in Iran in 1979 provided a shining example to militant Shi'ite Muslims around the world as hope for the future. Historian John Murphy observes that Khomeini recognized this attraction and used his position to advance the cause of militant Islam.[17] Specifically, Khomeini, Hussein Ali Montazerti (head of the Council for Islamic Revolution), and Iranian President Ali Khameni stressed that 'Islamic Iran would be the source of funds and training camps for any Muslim anxious to carry out the permanent holy war'.[18] Coincidentally, at the same time Khomeini established Iran as the epicentre of militant Islam, the Soviet Union invaded Afghanistan, and Iran became a major source of funds and training for the Islamic mujahidin freedom fighters in their vicious opposition to the Soviet Union's invasion.

Within the context of the Cold War, the US overlooked the theological underpinnings of the mujahidin fighters and covertly assisted in their arming and training. Beyond the fundamental ideological differences, the US (specifically the Reagan administration) saw the *mujahidin* and their success in the war in Afghanistan as an opportunity to stem communist expansion and weaken the Soviet Union. Only after the demise of the Cold War and the rise of transnational militant Islamists did links between the US and Osama bin Laden surface in the context of the Afghan War in the 1980s. The Afghan War provided an excellent training ground for militant Islamists to become battle hardened and demonstrate their faith in the concept of a perpetual *jihad*. Iran remained at the epicentre of this fundamental change in the international security environment by advocating and supporting like-minded terrorist organizations.

The Iranian revolution and the war in Afghanistan led to the emergence of sympathetic terrorist/political militia groups, such as Hezbollah, designed to advance a militant Islamist cause.[19] Amid the political turmoil and chaos of Lebanon's civil war in the late 1970s and early 1980s, Hezbollah formed to fill a political vacuum in support of Shias in Lebanon, while also striving to halt the 'usurpation of Muslim lands' and to 'serve their community' against the Israelis.[20] Specifically, Hezbollah sought to emulate the Iranian example and establish an Islamic Republic in Lebanon, and believed Lebanon needed to purge 'all non-Islamic influence'.[21] Based upon these beliefs, Hezbollah became vehemently anti-West and anti-Israel.[22] Acting on their beliefs, Hezbollah attacked US and Israeli forces in Lebanon during their peacekeeping operations, which ultimately led President Reagan to remove US Marines from Lebanon.[23] Hezbollah advanced its agenda through the use of bombings as well as guerrilla operations throughout Lebanon and Israel. By the mid-1990s, Hezbollah attempted to distance itself from its terrorist past by recasting itself as a quasi-legitimate political actor within the regional politics of the Middle East as well as within Lebanon, following a model started by the PLO.[24]

Hezbollah was not the only militant Islamic organization that emerged after the Ayatollah Khomeini came to power. The rise of Hezbollah characterizes the essence of new era of terrorism. The rise of militant Islamic terrorist organizations such as Hezbollah evolved in the late 1970s and early 1980s and ascended to their zenith as the Cold War screeched to a halt. In a break with traditional terrorist organizations, these new groups used strong international and transnational ties to support their agendas. Recruitment was not limited to a specific country or region, but strove to attract likeminded Muslims from around the world, who believed in the goals and theology advocated by militant Islamists.[25] Once the groups had recruited from around the globe, they sent their 'soldiers' off to training camps funded and sponsored by states, charity organizations, and wealthy individuals. These camps thrived in the Middle East, Northern Africa, and Central Asia to instruct *jihad*ists in bomb-making, infiltration, communication techniques, and militant theology of the Islamic terrorist organizations. In addition to the training camps, these transnational terrorist groups relied on a complicated web of legal and extra-legal financial resources to support their sustained operations. Ultimately, these terrorist groups believed they were engaged in long-term ideological struggle with the West.[26] By the end of the Cold War, a whole range of highly advanced, well-funded, and substantially armed transnational terrorist organizations existed within the international security environment. These world-wide security threats posed a substantial risk to national, regional, and international stability. In the midst of this environment, *al Qaeda* eventually emerged as the ultimate model of a militant Islamic transnational terrorist organization.

The rise of *al Qaeda*

In the wake of its attacks on the US, *al Qaeda* became the most publicized transnational terrorist organizations in history. Before 11 September 2001, the group and its leader, Osama bin Laden, remained relatively unknown.[27] Evolving from the trained like-minded 'Islamic extremists' in the fight against the Soviet Union's invasion of Afghanistan, Saudi national bin Laden joined the mujahidin resistance in 1979 and later founded *al Qaeda* with Abdullah Azzam.[28] Bin Laden used his family's amassed material wealth to help 'recruit, finance, and train' *mujahidin* resistance fighters for the Afghan War.[29] Having joined the *mujahidin* in the successful defeat of the Soviet Union, bin Laden used his experience gained in Afghanistan to construct a well-funded, trained, and organized transnational terrorist organization designed to combat the 'ideals and influence of unbelievers'.[30] Bin Laden's objective was to re-establish the caliphate by reaching out to support Muslims (Sunni and Shi'ite) oppressed by non-Muslim regimes.[31] As Iran and the Ayatollah Khomeini became the epicentre of the first wave of new terrorism in the early 1980s, bin Laden and *al Qaeda* emerged in the 1990s as the primary transnational terrorist source willing to support, fund, and train militant Islamists committed to *jihad* against the West.

The origins of *al Qaeda* are of profound significance to the status and structure of the organization. During the Soviet Union's invasion of Afghanistan, mujahidin fighters 'portrayed the event as a holy war', which resonated throughout the Islamic world.[32] Islamic freedom fighters committed to ejecting the foreign invaders from Afghanistan converged from around the globe to fight the Soviet Union. In addition to the indigenous support from various local Islamic sources, the mujahidin received substantial support from the US, European, and Saudi Arabian governments.[33] The experiences gained by mujahidin fighters in Afghanistan served as a common force in the creation of *al Qaeda*'s network.[34] The success in Afghanistan led militant Islamists to assume a 'heady sense of confidence' and belief that they assisted in the demise of the once-powerful Soviet Union.[35] The development of an esprit de corps among the radical mujahidin led to an intensified belief in the concept of the *jihad*. The Afghan War provided bin Laden with a 'rolodex' of willing participants in his vision for the future.

In the aftermath of the mujahidin's success in Afghanistan, the global security environment fundamentally changed, significantly influencing the belief and vision of Osama bin Laden. In the summer of 1990, Saddam Hussein invaded the oil-rich kingdom of Kuwait provoking a military response from the US and the United Nations (UN). Saudi Arabia, fearing an invasion, granted permission to the US and its alliance partners to use its military and port facilities to launch Operation DESERT SHIELD and Operation DESERT STORM. In an effort to appease Muslims and Arabs alike, the Saudi government initially required the foreign troops to leave after the cessation of hostilities. However, in the aftermath of DESERT

STORM, Saudi Arabia allowed US and coalition forces to remain in the country to enforce the peace settlement and specifically to enforce the no fly-zones in Iraq. This action by the Saudi royal family led bin Laden to claim they were 'false Muslims' for reneging on their policy concerning the US presence.[36] Bin Laden used the opportunity to call for the installation of a 'true Islamic state in Saudi Arabia'.[37] In response to his claim about the royal family being 'false Muslims', as well as his call for the establishment of a 'new state', the Saudi government deported bin Laden and revoked his citizenship in 1994.[38] As a result of his diplomatic troubles, bin Laden increasingly relied upon the contacts and networks he had fostered while fighting the Soviet Union in Afghanistan.

Using his international contacts and his vast monetary resources, bin Laden energized *al Qaeda* to fight against 'globalization' in Bosnia, Kashmir, the Philippines, and the Muslim republics of the former Soviet Union.[39] Through the early stages of building his new transnational terrorist network, bin Laden and *al Qaeda* moved between bases in Sudan and Pakistan before settling in Afghanistan.[40] With the control of Afghanistan in the hands of the radical Islamic Taliban regime, bin Laden had sympathetic governmental support for his declaration of war against 'foreign unbelievers'.[41] Beyond the charisma of its leader, the revolutionary nature of *al Qaeda*, as a new terrorist group stemmed directly from bin Laden's reliance on an ideology with mass appeal to militant Islamists. Bin Laden relied upon his business education to develop an organizational structure and diverse financial network to support his militant Islamic network of terrorists.

According to *al Qaeda* experts, Rohan Gunaratna and Christina Hellmich, bin Laden and *al Qaeda* subscribe to an ideology that is general and broad in appeal to 'Middle eastern and non-Middle eastern groups that are Islamic in character'.[42] Anti-Western and anti-Israeli rhetoric forms the foundation of *al Qaeda*'s ideological paradigm. *Al Qaeda*'s reliance on using militant Islamic theology to target the US and Israel allows the message to have a 'global and resilient appeal' to militant radical Muslims.[43] To further capitalize on his mass appeal, bin Laden and *al Qaeda* emphasize the development of 'pan-Islam unity' aimed toward the establishment of a 'community of believers or a umma' to displace the hegemony of the West.[44] Within the post-Soviet security environment, the US embraced an expanded interventionist foreign policy in Somalia, Bosnia, and Haiti. Bin Laden used these endeavours as examples to justify his call to combat the expansionist tendencies of Western culture and ideology led by the US. This attack against the West's cultural, political, and military encroachment struck a chord with militant Islamists around the globe, and *al Qaeda* used this to their advantage. Their objective was to organize and fight 'until US troops are removed from all lands of the Muslims, no Muslim is absolved from sin except the mujahidin'.[45] This belief had mass appeal to the militant Islamic community, which is the exact group *al Qaeda* and bin Laden wanted to mobilize for their cause.

To advance his theological paradigm, *al Qaeda* members believed under the direction of bin Laden, that they are fighting a perpetual *jihad* against the West.[46] This 'call to arms' allows *al Qaeda* to cast their struggle as an epic and just cause. From the perspective of *al Qaeda*, the desire to roll back the encroachment of the west demands steadfast beliefs, devout principles, and violent action. Beyond the ideological/theological foundations of *al Qaeda*, bin Laden revolutionized the structure of terrorist organizations by moving away from the strictly centralized model of traditional terrorist organizations.[47] While the core structure of *al Qaeda* is vertically aligned in a traditional manner, the organization also relies heavily upon semi-autonomous cells found in operational territories throughout the globe that are 'horizontally integrated' into the centralized command structure.[48] This flexible and dynamic organizational structure permits the central command to maintain control over specifically identified strategic operations, such as the attacks on the World Trade Centre and the Pentagon, while also allowing the local and regional cells to maintain autonomy over their own local and regional operations. The organizational structure of *al Qaeda* is an important element to its success.

Osama bin Laden was at the pinnacle of the core-centralized structure. Below are the *Shura majilis*, who operate as a 'consultative council' on the day-to-day operational and management details needed to maintain the vast *al Qaeda* network.[49] The *Shura majilis* receive information from four subordinate committees designed to focus on the specific segments of planning and operations. The military, finance, religious/legal, and media committees independently handle compartmentalized portions of current and future *al Qaeda* operations. The military committee, by far the most robust and active of the four committees, is directly responsible for 'recruiting, training, procuring, and launching support and military operations'.[50] Base teams work with field teams in 'planning and preparing attacks', including the analysis and dissemination of intelligence, training and procurement of armaments, and the arrangement of necessary documents such as passports and visas needed to conduct the operation.[51]

In coordination with the military committee, the three additional committees operate to support and sustain *al Qaeda* operations. The finance committee, as the name implies, oversees, develops, and cultivates the 'financial resources needed to sustain Al Qaeda and its operations'.[52] Borrowing from transnational organized crime factions, *al Qaeda* relies on a complicated global system of 'licit and illicit companies, private investors, government sponsors, and religious charities' to fund its operations.[53] Breaking from the other terrorist organizations, *al Qaeda* relies on the use of 'legitimate businesses to generate revenue' to sustain its operations.[54] In addition to the use of legitimate businesses such as 'construction companies, agriculture products, fishing boats, and furniture companies', *al Qaeda* relies on philanthropic 'Islamic NGOs'.[55] Combining the use of legitimate businesses and charity organizations allows *al Qaeda* to retain a substantial capability to generate revenue and large sums of capital, despite actions taken by the US and the UN to freeze the financial assets of the terrorist organization.[56]

The religious/legal and the media committees, although removed from the operational side of *al Qaeda*'s planning, are vital in the overall synergy of the network. The religious/legal committee 'justifies' the actions and operations of attacks within the theological parameters of '*Al Qaeda*'s model of Islam'.[57] In *al Qaeda*'s objective of re-establishing the caliphate, the justification of attacks and operations within the tenets of Islam are necessary because they reinforce the significance of the movement. All actions taken by *al Qaeda* are interpreted within the context of radicalized Islam. To further spread the word of *al Qaeda*'s actions and to build additional support and sympathy for their cause, the terrorist organization relies on a media committee to produce 'news and information' in support of *al Qaeda*'s operations.[58] The actions of the media committee build upon the justifications of the attacks by the religious/legal committee to produce propaganda designed to influence Muslims across the globe to support *al Qaeda*'s cause.

The coordinated actions advocated by the military, finance, religious/legal, and media committees stream in from *al Qaeda* – 'franchise' cells found throughout the globe. These 'franchises' have their own organizational structures and operate both directly in support of centralized directives and upon their own individual plans. This loosely organized cell structure provides *al Qaeda* with regional and operational flexibility by allowing the cells to generate and raise their own capital, as well as plan their own operations.[59] Using this diffused method of organization *al Qaeda* can influence a much broader front across the international political spectrum. While the cells have autonomy, they receive strict, rigid, and detailed training in conducting their business based upon the exacting requirements of bin Laden's *al Qaeda* model.

The organizational structure of *al Qaeda* enables the network to sustain itself and their operations within the increasingly hostile environment of the global war on terrorism. Even after ten years of war and the capture and killing of over seventy-five per cent if its original leadership, in addition to significant arrests, foiled operations, and tighter financial controls, *al Qaeda* remains adaptive and flexible. More than any other terrorist group, *al Qaeda* embodies the complex and complicated nature of new terrorism.

A new era of warfare

In the post-Cold War security environment, transnational threats such as *al Qaeda* filled the void left by the demise of the Soviet Union. However, unlike the days of the Cold War where military and diplomatic solutions provided the best options to combat the expansive enemy, the US and the international community initially remained unsure of how to target and prosecute transnational terrorist organizations. Essentially, the US and other nations used criminal and financial methods to prosecute and bring transnational terrorist organizations to justice for two reasons.

First, the use of criminal proceedings to combat terrorism allows the US government and other nations to apply legislation that has a proven track record in fighting transnational organized crime. By characterizing *al Qaeda* as terrorist/criminal enterprises, the nations of the international community can use the well-established international law networks, such as INTERPOL, to combat the actions and movement of terrorist members. Through the application of criminal legislation, the US and the international community have decapitated and eroded the membership of *al Qaeda* and its affiliates. Experience in fighting transnational organized crime factions provided the model the US and other nations used to attack transnational terrorist organizations and *al Qaeda*.[60]

By using their experiences to combat the influence of transnational organized crime groups, the US and the international community have expanded the scope and application of traditional criminal legislation to apply to terrorist groups. The objective behind the application of criminal statutes is to weaken the leadership of terrorist organizations by degrading their operational capability. Law enforcement, intelligence, and military organizations have successfully applied this approach to capture *al Qaeda*'s leadership and members. However, this method has not curbed membership at the local and regional levels of *al Qaeda* and its franchise organizations.[61]

With the use of criminal legislation, the US and its allies have eroded the operational capability and operations of terrorist organizations by limiting the terrorists' access to finances. Money is a vital component in the operations carried out by terrorist organizations. Therefore, the US and its allies surmise that if the international community can limit a terrorist organization's access to its operating funds, the nations of the world can slowly attrite the operational capability of terrorist organizations, and *al Qaeda* specifically. The use of the Banking Secrecy Act and the Money Laundering Control Act are two examples of legislation used by the US to deprive terrorist organizations of their operating funds.[62] As with the use of criminal legislation, the experience gained from fighting and prosecuting organized crime as well as experience gained after ten years of war provides vital insight into the adaptation and evolution of financial legislation for the war on terrorism.

The US and its allies in the war on terrorism extensively use criminal, financial, and military methods to erode the growing presence of transnational terrorist organizations. US President William J. Clinton established a precedent when he used executive orders as an additional tool to fight transnational terrorism. Specifically, Clinton issued Executive Order 12947 on 23 January 1995 to deter potential terrorists from disrupting or attempting to stop the Middle East peace process. Clinton stated in Executive

Order 12947 that 'grave acts of violence committed by foreign terrorists that disrupt the Middle-East peace process constitute an unusual and extraordinary threat to the national security, foreign policy, and economy of the United States'.[63] The executive order also outlawed an individual or a group's 'financial, material, and technological support and/or assistance' to terrorist organizations identified as hostile to the Middle East peace process.[64] Although Clinton issued Executive Order 12947 to ensure stability in the peace process, the document provides another example of the legislative attempts by the US to reduce the support and influence of terrorist organizations in the years prior to the attacks by *al Qaeda*.

In addition to the use of criminal legislation, financial legislation, and executive orders to fight terrorism, military force is another tool used by political leaders as they attempt to curb the threat posed by *al Qaeda* and its affiliates.[65] However, until the openly declared 'Global War on Terrorism' by President George W. Bush, the military option remained the most reserved and guarded response used by US presidents.

As the US expanded its fight against terrorism in the 1990s, so did the UN. Scholars Jane Boulden and Thomas G. Weiss argue that 'prior to the 1990s, the General Assembly of the United Nations approached the issue of terrorism as a general international problem'.[66] Within this period, the General Assembly strove to develop 'an international framework for cooperation among states', while still directly avoiding a definition of terrorism.[67] Based on increased terrorist activity in the 1990s, the persistent issue of terrorism slowly gravitated toward the jurisdiction of the Security Council and away from the General Assembly. Boulden and Weiss observe that the 'attempted assassination of Egyptian President Hosni Mubarak, the bombing of American embassies, and first attacks on the World Trade Center' led the Security Council to begin issuing sanctions as a way to deal with state sponsorship of terrorism.[68] The Security Council directed these actions against nations such as Libya and Sudan which supported terrorism, and any other nation refusing to cooperate with the rest of the international community in the condemnation of terrorism. In the aftermath of the *al Qaeda* attacks on the World Trade Centre in New York and the Pentagon in Washington DC, the UN and the Security Council fundamentally embraced the position of President George W. Bush in his efforts to eradicate the threat posed by terrorism by initiating a global war on terrorism.

Although efforts to combat terrorism before 11 September 2001 had been well established, the severity and high casualties in the *al Qaeda* attacks reinforced the sentiments within the US and the international community that transnational terrorism needed to be stopped. International actors such as the UN and NATO, as well as individual nations such as Britain and Russia, pledged to assist in the US war to eradicate transnational terrorist groups. The response to terrorism by the US and the nations of the world fundamentally changed after 11 September 2001.

For the US, actions taken against terrorist groups prior to September 2001 focused on the criminal actions and financial assets of transnational terrorist networks in an effort to reduce their operational capability. In the period after the attacks, President George W. Bush established that the US would use all means necessary to combat the forces of terrorism. Bush warned that nations assisting, supporting, or conducting terrorist operations would be held accountable for their actions. Bush openly declared a 'Global War on Terrorism', and broke with previous administrations by arguing that the transnational terrorist threat, posed specifically by *al Qaeda* and its leader bin Laden, demanded overt military force. Bush and his National Security Council viewed the attacks as 'acts of war'.[69] As the administration officially linked *al Qaeda* and bin Laden to the attacks, Bush's cabinet moved to align the nation for a 'campaign against terrorism'.[70] Congress supported the president's decision by 'approving a joint resolution that authorized the use of armed force against those responsible for the attacks'.[71] Secretary of State Colin Powell diplomatically manoeuvred to align nations with the US position, while Secretary of Defence Donald Rumsfeld and his staff at the Department of Defence worked on putting together a military package to use against *al Qaeda* and the Taliban government in Afghanistan.

On 7 October 2001, Operation ENDURING FREEDOM began. The initial stage of the attack consisted of 'aircraft and cruise missile attacks on Taliban forces, Al Qaeda fighters, training sites, command and control systems, and radar installations' in Afghanistan.[72] The second phase of the operations entailed the landing of US Special Forces and US Army Rangers.[73] Behind the Special Forces and rangers, US Marine Corps Expeditionary Units followed to establish a base in the vicinity of Kandahar from which US forces could fight for control of the nation.[74]

The combat operations carried out in Afghanistan by the US were not unilateral. The British, Russian, and Pakistani governments, as well as other nations, overtly supported and contributed to the combat effort.[75] The sustained combat operations in Afghanistan by the US and its allies against the Taliban and *al Qaeda* therefore represent a fundamental break with how nations attempted to combat terrorism prior to September 2001. The use of overwhelming military force is not what made this action different; rather it was the alliance forged in the wake of 11 September 2001 to reduce the international security threat posed by transnational terrorist groups.

In conjunction with the use of military power, the US and the international community recognized that the fight against terrorism demanded the application of a whole government approach. The work done before 11 September 2001 became fundamentally significant because it provided a foundation upon which the US and the international community began to build and expand common links found throughout the national systems. The link of transnational organized crime, arms traffickers, and narcotics traffickers to terrorist organizations proved to be one such connection made and pursued in the international community's fight to eradicate transnational terrorist groups. The use of criminal, financial, and immigration legislation, combined with the use of force by law enforcement and military organizations, converged to offer the nations allied in the 'Global War On Terrorism' a plethora of tools to combat the transnational terrorist activity. In the aftermath of 11 September 2001, the international community worked diligently with the US to establish a loosely grouped cooperative network of national and international laws designed to curtail and eventually eradicate threats posed by *al Qaeda* and other transnational terrorist organizations. The actions taken by the US and the international community discussed thus far describe how *al Qaeda*'s attacks forced the US and the international community to focus on transnational terrorism as an international security issue.

Detailing the development of *al Qaeda* and the response by the US brings us back to the Peace of Westphalia and the subsequent congresses and international agreements that have defined the lexicon of international relations since 1648. At their core, these agreements have detailed and maintained that nations are the primary agent in the course of international relations. Periods of peace and war have come to be representative of strong nations or unified blocs of state power. Seldom has there been a transnational terrorist threat that operated well outside the parameters of the system. Combating *al Qaeda* is a fundamental break with the past and requires wholesale adjustments to the traditional Westphalian system.

Although the US and its allies are involved in a global war against terrorism that maintains active military fronts and a constant state of awareness, there has not been an official declaration of war by the US Congress and this creates a schism between the 'total war mentally' fostered by the Bush administration and the seemingly disconnectedness of the population of the US. The lines of war and peace blur as the military services of the US and its allies continue to conduct combat operations, while the vast majority of the citizens remain far removed from the conflict. US President George W. Bush even tried to convince the public of the wartime stance by consistently referring to the global war on terrorism as the 'first ideological fight of the twenty-first century'. However, the American public remains largely unconvinced.

In many ways, the juxtaposed perceptions between the military's consistent and steady involvement in combat operations and the public's perception of 'life as normal', mimics the nation's treatment of its primary threat – *al Qaeda*. While lacking a traditional national structure, as enemies of the past have tended to have, the US used criminal, financial, immigration, and military processes in an attempt to dissuade the enemy. This blend of military, criminal, and legislative approaches further obscures the distortion between war and peace and makes this era of warfare seem fundamentally different compared to previous eras, even though the actual act of combating terrorism has traditional links to wars of the past.[76]

This new era of warfare is characterized by the US and its allies as focusing on transnational militant Islamists as the primary threat to the international security environment. After a decade of war, the US and its allies have used all means necessary, short of weapons of mass destruction, to combat the enemy. While it appears the traditional Westphalian system has inadequacies, in the context of the 'Global War on Terrorism', it has not outlived its usefulness. The international system does need to be adjusted to meet the demands of the international security environment that encompasses both traditional state actors, as well as transnational terrorist organizations. Until these adjustments are made, the international community will continue to blur the line between war and peace, which has come to be a defining characteristic of this new era of warfare.

Notes

1   A.S. Hersey, 'History of International Law Since the Peace of Westphalia', *American Journal of International Law*, 1912, vol. 6, p. 33.
2   L. Gross, 'The Peace of Westphalia, 1648–1948', *American Journal of International Law*, 1948, vol. 42, p. 20.
3   US Department of State, *Patterns of Global Terrorism, 2001*, Washington DC: US Department of State, May 2002, p. i.
4   Ibid.
5   B. Hoffman, 'Change and Continuity in Terrorism', *Studies in Conflict and Terrorism*, 2001, vol. 24, p. 419; A. Davis, 'Resilient Abu Sayyaf Resists Military Pressure', *Jane's Intelligence Review*, 2003, vol. 15, p. 14; T. Makarenko, 'Transnational Crime and Its Evolving links to Terrorism and Instability', *Jane's Intelligence Review*, 2001, vol. 13, p. 23; R. Gunaratna, '*Al Qaeda* Adapts to Disruption', *Jane's Intelligence Review*, 2004, vol. 16, p. 20.
6   This sentence is not meant to convey the idea that the US has completely ignored the terrorist threat, but rather that the implications and issues framed within the strategic nuclear balance and the Cold War obscured the severity of the security threat posed by the 'new' terrorists.
7   US Department of State, *Patterns of Global Terrorism 1990*, Washington, DC: Department of State, 1992, p. 39; Y. Alexander and M.B. Kraft, *Evolution of US Counterterrorism Policy, vol. I*, Westport: Praeger, 2008, pp. 1–49.
8   B.M. Jenkins and J.A. Johnson, 'International Terrorism: A Chronology (1974) Supplement', Report for the Defense Advanced Research Projects Agency, Santa Monica: RAND Corporation, 1976, pp. 1–3, R-1909-1-ARPA.
9   The most significant examples would be the Israeli 'Raid on Entebbe', France in Marseilles in 1994, and Germany in Mogadishu in 1997.
10 US Department of State, *Patterns of Global Terrorism 1990*, Washington DC: Department of State, 1992, p. 38.
11 J.P. Harik, *Hezbollah: The Changing Face of Terrorism*, London: I.B. Tauris, 2004, p. ix; T.J. Geraghty, *Peacekeepers at War: Beirut 1983 – The Marine Commander Tells His Story*, Dulles: Potomac Books, 2009, pp. 79–122.
12 W. Laqueur, *The New Terrorism: Fanaticism and the Arms of Mass Destruction*, New York: Oxford University Press, 1999, p. 3.

13 Ibid.

14 B.M. Jenkins and J.A. Johnson, 'International Terrorism: A Chronology (1974) Supplement', Report for the Defense Advanced Research Projects Agency, Santa Monica: RAND Corporation, 1976, pp. 1–3, R-1909-1-ARPA, p. 1.

15 Ibid.

16 I. Duyvesteyn, 'How New is New Terrorism', *Studies in Terrorism*, 2004, vol. 27, pp. 439–51.

17 J.F. Murphy Jr, *Sword of Islam: Muslim Extremism from the Arab Conquest to the Attack on America*, New York: Prometheus Books, 2002, p. 123.

18 Ibid., p. 122.

19 J.P. Harik, *Hezbollah: The Changing Face of Terrorism*, London: I.B. Tauris, 2004, p. 1.

20 Ibid.

21 US Department of State, *Patterns of Global Terrorism 1995*, Washington, DC: Department of State, 1996, p. 48.

22 Ibid.

23 T.J. Geraghty, *Peacekeepers at War: Beirut 1983 – The Marine Commander Tells His Story*, Dulles: Potomac Books, 2009, pp. 123–80.

24 J.P. Harik, *Hezbollah: The Changing Face of Terrorism*, London: I.B. Tauris, 2004, p. 1.

25 A.E. Youssef, *Militant Islamist Ideology: Understanding the Global Threat*, Annapolis: Naval Institute Press, 2010, pp. 1–6.

26 A. McCarthy, 'Global War on Terrorism? No, It's a Global War on Militant Islam', *Journal of Counterterrorism and Homeland Security International*, 2004, vol. 10: 53; C. Hellmich, *Al Qaeda: From Global Network to Local Franchise*, London: Zed Books, 2011, pp. 46–56.

27 According to R. Gunaratna, the US government did not learn the 'real name' of bin Laden's group until after its attacks on US embassies in Africa in 1998, see R. Gunaratna, *Inside Al Qaeda: Global Network of Terror*, New York: Berkley Books, 2002, p. xlii. Gunaratna's claim differs from the information provided by the Department of State in *Patterns of Global Terrorism 1997*, which was published in April of 1998, in which the State Department clearly identified bin Laden's groups as *al Qaeda*. See US State Department, *Patterns of Global Terrorism 1997*, Washington DC: Department of State, 1998, p. 30.

28 US State Department, *Patterns of Global Terrorism 1997*, Washington DC: Department of State, 1998, p. 30.

29 Ibid.

30 R. Gunaratna, *Inside Al Qaeda: Global Network of Terror*, New York: Berkley Books, 2002, p. 74.

31 M.-M. Mohamedou, *Understanding Al Qaeda: Changing War and Global Politics*, London: Pluto Press 2011, pp. 46–7; R. Gunaratna, *Inside Al Qaeda: Global Network of Terror*, New York: Berkley Books, 2002, p. 74.

32 B.M. Jenkins, *Counter al Qaeda: An Appreciation of the Situation and Suggestions for Strategy*, Santa Monica: RAND Corporation, 2002, MR-1620-RC, p. 3.

33 R. Gunaratna, *Inside Al Qaeda: Global Network of Terror*, New York: Berkley Books, 2002, p. 74.

34 B.M. Jenkins, *Counter al Qaeda: An Appreciation of the Situation and Suggestions for Strategy*, Santa Monica: RAND Corporation, 2002, MR-1620-RC, p. 3; C. Hellmich, *Al Qaeda: From Global Network to Local Franchise*, London: Zed Books,

2011, pp. 22–4; M.-M. Mohamedou, *Understanding Al Qaeda: Changing War and Global Politics*, London: Pluto Press 2011, p. 48.

35 B.M. Jenkins, *Counter al Qaeda: An Appreciation of the Situation and Suggestions for Strategy*, Santa Monica: RAND Corporation, 2002, MR-1620-RC, p. 3.

36 R. Gunaratna, 'Blowback', *Jane's Intelligence Review*, 2001, vol. 13, p. 43; R. Gunaratna, *Inside Al Qaeda: Global Network of Terror*, New York: Berkley Books, 2002, p. 74.

37 R. Gunaratna, *Inside Al Qaeda: Global Network of Terror*, New York: Berkley Books, 2002, p. 43.

38 C. Hellmich, *Al Qaeda: From Global Network to Local Franchise*, London: Zed Books, 2011, p. 44.

39 B.M. Jenkins, *Counter al Qaeda: An Appreciation of the Situation and Suggestions for Strategy*, Santa Monica: RAND Corporation, 2002, MR-1620-RC, p. 3.

40 M. Mohamedou, *Understanding Al Qaeda: Changing War and Global Politics*, London: Pluto Press 2011, pp. 51–3; C. Hellmich, *Al Qaeda: From Global Network to Local Franchise*, London: Zed Books, 2011, pp. 39–45.

41 M. Mohamedou, *Understanding Al Qaeda: Changing War and Global Politics*, London: Pluto Press 2011, pp. 50–1; C. Hellmich, *Al Qaeda: From Global Network to Local Franchise*, London: Zed Books, 2011, pp. 49–51; R. Gunaratna, *Inside Al Qaeda: Global Network of Terror*, New York: Berkley Books, 2002, p. 56.

42 R. Gunaratna, *Inside Al Qaeda: Global Network of Terror*, New York: Berkley Books, 2002, p. 43. Gunaratna observes that bin Laden's theological preaching was influenced by the teachings and ideas of Dr. Ayman Muhammad al Zawahiri.

43 R. Gunaratna, *Inside Al Qaeda: Global Network of Terror*, New York: Berkley Books, 2002, p. 116.

44 Ibid.

45 Ibid., p. 17.

46 O. Bin Laden, 'Declaration of Jihad against the Americans Occupying the Land of the Two Holy Sanctuaries', in G. Kepel and J.P. Milelli (eds) *Al Qaeda in Its Own Words*, Cambridge: Belknap Press, 2008, pp. 47–50.

47 Ibid., p. 72. B. McAllister offers a contradictory position in '*Al Qaeda* and the Innovative Firm: Demythologizing the Network', *Studies in Conflict and Terrorism*, 2004, vol. 27, pp. 297–319. McAllister argues that while the original organization of *al Qaeda* by Osama bin Laden was 'innovative', the actual structure does not 'differ much from other Islamist organizations'.

48 M. Mohamedou, *Understanding Al Qaeda: Changing War and Global Politics*, London: Pluto Press 2011, pp. 52–3; R. Gunaratna, *Inside Al Qaeda: Global Network of Terror*, New York: Berkley Books, 2002, p. 43.

49 R. Gunaratna, *Inside Al Qaeda: Global Network of Terror*, New York: Berkley Books, 2002, p. 43

50 M. Mohamedou, *Understanding Al Qaeda: Changing War and Global Politics*, London: Pluto Press 2011, pp. 51–3.

51 R. Gunaratna, *Inside Al Qaeda: Global Network of Terror*, New York: Berkley Books, 2002, p. 43.

52 Ibid.

53 M. Basile, 'Going to the Source: Why *Al Qaeda*'s Financial Network Is Likely to Withstand the Current War on Terrorist Financing', *Studies in Conflict and Terrorism*, 2004, vol. 27, p. 169.

54 M. Basile, 'Going to the Source: Why *Al Qaeda*'s Financial Network Is Likely to

Withstand the Current War on Terrorist Financing', *Studies in Conflict and Terrorism*, 2004, vol. 27, p. 170. Basile observes that the vast majority of terrorist organizations tend to rely on 'fraud, narcotics trafficking, kidnapping, and extortion' to raise operating capital.

55 R. Gunaratna, *Inside Al Qaeda: Global Network of Terror*, New York: Berkley Books, 2002, pp. 90–1.

56 M. Basile, 'Going to the Source: Why *Al Qaeda*'s Financial Network Is Likely to Withstand the Current War on Terrorist Financing', *Studies in Conflict and Terrorism*, 2004, vol. 27, p. 183.

57 R. Gunaratna, *Inside Al Qaeda: Global Network of Terror*, New York: Berkley Books, 2002, p. 43.

58 Ibid.

59 L. Vidino, *Al Qaeda in Europe: The New Battleground of International Jihad*, Amherst: Prometheus Books, 2006, pp. 291–336; C. Hellmich, *Al Qaeda: From Global Network to Local Franchise*, London: Zed Books, 2011, p. 55.

60 A. Baveja, 'America's 'War' on Terrorism: Can the US Learn from its War on Drugs?', *Journal of Counterterrorism and Security International*, 2002, vol. 8, p. 16.

61 L. Vidino, *Al Qaeda in Europe: The New Battleground of International Jihad*, Amherst: Prometheus Books, 2006, pp. 23–70.

62 P.J. Smith, 'USA Adopts Financial Legislation for Counterterrorism', *Jane's Intelligence Review*, 2004, vol. 16, p. 35.

63 W.J. Clinton, 'Executive Order 12947: Prohibiting Transactions With Terrorists Who Threaten to Disrupt the Middle East Peace Process', *The Federal Register*, 25 January 1995, p. 5079.

64 Executive Order 12947, p. 5079. The US government specifically identified Abu Nidal, Democratic Front for the Liberation of Palestine, Hizballah, Islamic Gama'at (IG), Islamic Resistance Movement (HAMAS), Jihad, Kach, Kahane Chai, Palestinian Islamic Jihad-Shiqaqi Faction (PIJ), Palestine Liberation Front-Abu Abbas faction, Popular Front for the Liberation of Palestine, and Popular Front for the Liberation of Palestine-General Command as the primary terrorist organizations that posed a threat to the Middle East peace process in 1995.

65 President Reagan's authorization of operation EL DORADO CANYON in 1983 and President Clinton's use of cruise missiles against targets in Sudan and Afghanistan in the wake of *al Qaeda* bombing on US embassies remain the two primary examples of the use of military force against terrorists in the years prior to the *al Qaeda* attacks on the US on 11 September 2001.

66 J. Boulden and T.G. Weiss, 'Wider Terrorism and the United Nations', in J. Boulden and T. G. Weiss (eds) *Terrorism and the UN: Before and After September 11*, Bloomington: Indiana University Press, 2004, p. 10.

67 Ibid.

68 Ibid., pp. 6, 11.

69 C.H. Briscoe, R.L. Kiper, J.A. Schroder and K.I. Sepp, *Weapon of Choice: US Army Special Operations Forces in Afghanistan*, Fort Leavenworth, KS: Combat Studies Institute Press, 2003, p. 33.

70 Ibid.

71 T. Anderson, *Bush's Wars*, New York: Oxford University Press, 2011, pp. 82–3. The approval by Congress was not a declaration of war, but rather the authorization and support of the president's decision to use military force against *al*

Qaeda and Osama bin Laden. Under the War Powers Act, the president must inform Congress of his decision to use military force, upon which those forces can only be deployed for sixty days. If the president needs an extension, he may appeal to Congress for an additional thirty days before the troops then either need to be removed or approved by Congress.

72 S.M. Duncan, *A War of a Different Kind: Military force and America's Search for Homeland Security,* Annapolis: Naval Institution Press, 2004, p. 53.
73 Ibid.
74 Ibid., p. 34.
75 Approximately twelve nations supported and assisted the US in its operations in Afghanistan. The activity of support ranged from the commitment of combat forces by nations such as Britain to fly-over rights granted by several republics of the former Soviet Union.
76 S. Wilson and A. Kamen, "Global War on Terror' is Given a New Name', *Washington Post,* 25 March 2009, pp. 1–3. Available online: www.washingtonpost.com/wp-dyn/content/article/2009/03/24/AR2009032402818.html (accessed 17 March 2010).

Part V
Concluding essay

16 The four waves of modern terror

International dimensions and consequences[1]

David C. Rapoport

Introduction

11 September, 2001 was the most destructive day in the long bloody history of terrorism. It led President George W. Bush to declare a 'war [that] would not end until every terrorist group of global reach has been found, stopped and defeated.'[2] But his declaration was not altogether unique. Exactly one hundred years before, when an Anarchist assassinated President William McKinley in September 1901, his successor President Theodore Roosevelt called for a crusade to exterminate terrorism everywhere.[3]

Will we succeed now? No one knows, but we can better appreciate the difficulties ahead by examining the history of non-state terror that is deeply embedded in our culture. That history offers parallels worth pondering, and provides a perspective for understanding the uniqueness of 9/11 and its aftermath.[4] To this end, I will examine modern terror from its initial appearance, emphasizing continuities and changes, particularly with respect to international dimensions and consequences.

The wave phenomenon

Modern terror began in Russia in the 1880s. Within a decade it appeared in Western Europe, the Balkans, and Asia, and in a generation the wave was complete. Anarchists initiated the activity, and their primary strategy – assassination campaigns against prominent officials – was adopted by virtually all contemporary groups, even those with nationalist aims in the Balkans and India.[6]

Significant examples of successful, secular rebel terror existed earlier, but each was particular to a specific time and country. The Sons of Liberty made striking contributions to the American independence struggle as did the Ku Klux Klan (KKK) to the South's ability to segregate blacks after the Civil War, but neither group had international emulators.[7]

The 'Anarchist Wave' was history's first *global* terrorism experience;[8] it began in 1880 and was completed in the 1920s. Three similar, consecutive, and overlapping expressions followed. The 'Anti-Colonial Wave' began in the 1920s and lasted about forty years. The 'New Left Wave' of the 1960s followed subsequently and diminished significantly as the century closed, leaving a few groups active in Nepal, Spain, the United Kingdom (UK), Peru, and Columbia. The 'Religious Wave' emerged in 1979. If it follows the history of its predecessors, it will disappear by 2025, and a new one may then appear.[9]

Academics and governments focus on organizations for good reasons. Organizations launch terror campaigns, and governments are always primarily concerned with disabling those organizations.[10] Moreover, we are obsessed with contemporary groups and contemporary events, and thus are less sensitive to a *wave*,[11] which requires considerable time to complete its cycle.

What is a 'wave'? It is a cycle of activity in a given time period with expansion and contraction phases. Those activities occur in many countries, driven by a common predominant energy shaping the relationship of participating groups. As their names suggest, a different energy drives each wave.

A wave's name reflects its dominant special feature. Nationalist organizations, for example, appear in all waves, but each wave shapes its national elements differently. In the First Wave, Anarchist and nationalist groups used the same tactics and sometimes groups trained each other. Third Wave nationalist groups displayed profoundly Left Wing aspirations, and religious pressures shape nationalism in the Fourth Wave. *All* groups in the Second Wave were nationalist but we named the wave 'Anti-Colonial' because colonial powers were the enemy – an enemy that had become ambivalent about retaining their colonial status and helps explain why the Second Wave produced the first successes. In other waves, that ambivalence was absent or very weak, which is why their nationalist groups rarely succeeded.

A wave consists of organizations, but the two have different life rhythms. Organizations normally break up before the wave originally associated with them does. New Left organizations were particularly striking in this respect, generally lasting only two years. Nonetheless, the wave contained sufficient energy to create successor groups. When its energy cannot inspire new organizations, a wave disappears. Resistance, political concessions, and changes in the perception of generations explain the disappearance.

Occasionally, an organization survives its original wave. The Irish Republican Army (IRA) is the oldest modern terrorist organization, emerging first in 1916, although not as a terror organization.[12] It then fought five campaigns (the 1950 struggle used guerrilla tactics)[13] in two successive waves. At least two of its offshoots, the Real IRA and the Continuity IRA are still active. The Palestine Liberation Organization (PLO), founded by the Arab League in 1964 to serve as a military element in various Arab armies, became independent in 1967 as a terrorist organization. In time, it became the pre-eminent body of the New Left Wave because of its international connections, even though it was primarily a nationalist group. More recently, PLO elements became active in the Fourth Wave, even though the organization began as a wholly secular group. When an organization transcends its particular wave or origin, it reflects the new wave's influences, thereby posing new special problems for the group and its constituencies.

The first three waves lasted about a generation each, a timeframe in which specific dreams inspiring ancestors lose their attractiveness for their descendants.[14] Although the resistance of those attacked is crucial in explaining why terror organizations rarely succeed, the wave's duration also suggests that it has its own momentum. Over time, fewer organizations survive because the problematic nature of the struggle becomes increasingly manifest. The pattern is familiar to students of revolutionary states, such as France, the Soviet Union, and Iran. The heirs of the revolution simply do not value it in the same way its creators did. In the 'Anti-Colonial Wave', the process is also relevant to the colonial powers. A subsequent generation found it much easier to discard colonialism. The wave pattern calls our attention to crucial political themes in general world culture – themes that distinguish different generations.

Why did the First Wave occur when it did? There are many reasons. Technological developments were crucial. New communication and transportation patterns materialized. The telegraph, daily mass newspapers, and railroads flourished in the late nineteenth century. Events in one country were known elsewhere in a day or so. Prominent Russian terrorists travelled extensively, helping to inspire sympathy and groups elsewhere. Sometimes as the journeys of Michael Bakunin indicate, terrorists had more influence abroad than at home. Peter Proudhon spent more time in France than in Russia. Mass transportation enabled mass emigrations to create diaspora communities that affected politics in both their 'new' and 'old' countries. Subsequent innovations continued to shrink time and space. The second technological change was the development of dynamite. Introduced for peaceful engineering and industrial purposes, it became easily accessible for other purposes. Producing bombs was a 'comparatively simple process...and bombs were easily portable, much safer to use than earlier explosives, and their effects were controllable.'[15]

The bomb made it possible for small underground groups to engage in terror. Before that, as the cases of the Sons of Liberty and the KKK indicate, non-state terror was a mob activity. Russian writers created a strategy for terror for successors to use, improve, and transmit. Sergei Nechaev, Nicholas Mozorov, Peter Kropotkin, and Serge Stepniak were leading contributors.[16] The Sons of Liberty and KKK had no emulators, partly because they made no effort to explain their tactics. Likewise, the ancient religious terrorists always stayed within their own religious tradition, the source of their justifications and binding precedents. Each religious tradition produced its own kind of terrorist; sometimes the tactics were so uniform that they appear as a form of religious ritual.[17]

A comparison of Nechaev's *Revolutionary Catechism* with Bin Laden's training manual, *Military Studies in the Jihad Against The Tyrants* shows that they share a paramount desire to become more efficient by learning from the experiences of friends and enemies alike.[18] One major difference is the role of women. Nechaev considers them 'priceless assets'; they were crucial leaders and participants in the First Wave. Bin Laden dedicates his book to protecting Muslim woman, but ignores what experience can tell us about female terrorists. Initially, women did not participate in *al Qaeda*, but *al Qaeda* in Iraq gave them a minor role.[19] In the Fourth Wave, they were more important in Sri Lanka, Chechnya, and Palestine.

Each wave produces major technical works that reflect the wave's special properties, and contributes to a common effort to formulate a 'science' of terror. Between Nechaev and Bin Laden, there were *inter alia*, Georges Grivas' *Guerrilla War* and Carlos Marighella's *Mini-Manual of the Urban Guerrilla*, in the Second and Third Waves.

'Revolution', the overriding aim in every wave, is understood in different ways.[20] Revolutionaries create a new source of political legitimacy. Most often that means national self-determination, a principle introduced by the French Revolution that also made the term 'terror' part of our political vocabulary.[21] The definition of the 'rule of the people', a crucial element of the revolutionary vocabulary, has never been (perhaps never can be) clear and fixed; it provokes recurring conflict even when it is accepted everywhere. Revolution can also mean a radical reconstruction of authority to eliminate all forms of inequality – a cardinal theme in the First and Third Waves. It can mean a new source of legitimacy; sacred texts or revelations dominate the Fourth Wave.

This chapter focuses on the global context, emphasizing five dimensions: terrorist organizations, diaspora populations, states, sympathetic foreign publics, and finally supranational organizations.[22]

The 'First Wave': creating a doctrine

The creators of modern terrorism inherited a world where revolutionaries, depending on pamphlets and meetings, suddenly seemed obsolete. The masses, Nechaev said, regarded traditional revolutionaries as 'idle word spillers'![23] A new form of communication, 'Propaganda by the Deed', was needed. It would be heard and command respect because the revolutionary's act involved serious personal risks, signifying its deep commitment.[24]

The Anarchist analysis contained four major points: 1) society has huge reservoirs of latent ambivalence and hostility; 2) social conventions were devised to muffle and diffuse antagonisms by generating guilt and providing channels for settling grievances and securing personal amenities; 3) one can demonstrate that these conventions are simply historical creations; acts now perceived as immoral are those that our children will hail as noble efforts to liberate humanity; 4) terror is the quickest and most effective means to destroy those social conventions. Perpetrators free *themselves* from the paralyzing grip of guilt to become different kinds of people. Terror forces the governments to respond in ways that undermine the principles governments claim to respect and defend.[25] Dramatic action repeated again and again would invariably polarize society, and revolution would inevitably follow.

A striking incident inspired decades of turbulence. In 1878, Vera Zasulich wounded a Russian police commander who abused political prisoners. When the judge asked why she threw her weapon to the floor, she proclaimed she was a 'terrorist *not* a criminal'.[26] The jury unexpectedly freed her, and crowds greeted the verdict with thunderous applause.[27]

A successful campaign entailed learning how to fight and *die*. The most admirable deed occurred in a court trial in which one accepted responsibility and indicted the regime in the process. Stepniak, a major Russian participant, described the terrorist as 'noble, terrible, irresistibly fascinating uniting the two sublimities of human grandeur, the martyr and the hero'.[28] Dynamite was the weapon of choice. Criminals did not use it, partly because it could kill the criminal in the process.[29]

Terror was violence beyond the moral conventions used to regulate violence: the rules of war distinguishing combatants from non-combatants and the rules of punishment distinguishing the guilty from the innocent. Invariably, most onlookers would label acts of terror as atrocities or outrages. The rebels described themselves as terrorists – not guerrillas – tracing their lineage to the French Revolution. They sought targets that could affect public attitudes.[30] Tactics depended upon the group's political objective and on the specific context. Judging a context constantly in flux was both an art and a science.

Major unexpected political events dramatized a government's vulnerabilities and excited hope (the indispensable lubricant of rebel activity) stimulate a wave.[31] In Russia, the events that exposed the vulnerability of the system began with the dazzling efforts of the young Czar Alexander II, whom the *New York Times* called the 'greatest liberator in history'. In 1861, with a stroke of the pen, he freed the serfs (one-third of the population), promising them funds to buy land. Three years later he established limited local self-government, 'Westernized' the judicial system, abolished capital punishment, relaxed censorship powers, and reduced control over education. Hopes were aroused but could not be fulfilled quickly enough. Funds promised to the former serfs, for example, were insufficient. In the wake of inevitable disappointments, systematic assassination strikes against prominent officials began, culminating in the death of Alexander II himself.

Russian terrorists trained other groups, such as the Armenians and the Polish. Then the Balkans exploded, where many groups found the boundaries of states recently torn out of the Ottoman Empire to be unsatisfactory.[32] When the Russians fled to the West, the most democratic European states (Switzerland, England, and France) gave them the best sanctuaries. In 1905, the Terrorist Brigade had its headquarters in Geneva, launched strikes from Finland (an autonomous part of the Russian Empire), got arms from an Armenian terrorist group that Russians helped train, and was offered funds by Japan laundered through American millionaires.[33] In Europe, they taught Asian students tactics to use in Asia.[34]

The high point of international terrorist activity occurred in the 1890s in the 'Golden Age of Assassination', when monarchs, prime ministers, and presidents were struck down one after another, often by foreign assassins who moved easily across international borders.[35] The most immediately affected governments clamoured for international police cooperation and better border control – a situation President Theodore Roosevelt thought ideal for launching the first international effort to eliminate terrorism. 'Anarchy is a crime against the whole human race, and all mankind should band together against the Anarchist. His crimes should be made a crime against the law of nations…declared by treaties among all civilized powers'.[36]

But the effort did not last. The interests of states pulled them in different directions, a process that continued as the century progressed. Bulgaria gave sanctuary and bases to Macedonian nationalists to aid operations in the Ottoman Empire. The suspicion that Serbia helped Archduke Franz Ferdinand's assassin precipitated the First World War – the first great international overreaction in the history of terrorism.

The 'Second Wave': mostly successful and finding a new language

A 'Wave' by definition is an international event, although the first one was sparked by a domestic political situation. The Versailles Peace Treaty, concluding the First World War, precipitated the Second Wave. The victors used the principle of national self-determination to break up the primarily European empires of the defeated states. The non-European portions of those empires, deemed not yet ready for independence, became League of Nations 'Mandates'. They were administered directly by the victorious powers until they were prepared for independence.

Inadvertently, the victors undermined the legitimacy of their own empires. In 1921, the IRA established the Irish state.[37] The victors of the Second World War reinforced and enlarged Versailles' implications. Once more, the defeated had to abandon empires. This time, the colonial territories (Manchuria, Korea, Ethiopia, Libya, and so on) became independent states, not mandates. The victors began liquidating their own empires as well, albeit not in response to terrorist activity in India, Pakistan, Burma, Ceylon, Tunisia, Egypt, Morocco, the Philippines, Ghana, Nigeria, and so on. This process indicated how firmly committed the Western world had become to the principle of self-determination.[38] The United States, the West's hegemonic power, pressed hardest to eliminate empires.

Terror campaigns were fought in territories where special political problems made withdrawal a less attractive option. Jews and Arabs in Palestine,
for example, had dramatically conflicting versions of what terminating
British rule should mean. The considerable European population in
Algeria did not want Paris to abandon them, and, in Northern Ireland, the
majority wanted to remain British. In Cyprus, the Turkish community would
not accept union with Greece – the terrorists' aim, and Britain wanted to
retain Cyprus as a base for operations in the Middle East. Terrorist activity
persuaded imperial powers to withdraw in these special cases, but this did
not resolve the remaining tensions. Begin's *Irgun* fought to gain the entire
Palestine mandate but settled for partition.[39] IRA elements refused to
believe that Britain would never leave Northern Ireland without the
majority's consent. EOKA (National Organization of Cypriot Fighters)
fought to unify Cyprus with Greece but accepted an independent state.
EOKA then tried to subvert it in the hope that the new government would
join Greece. In Algeria, all Europeans fled, even though the National
Liberation Front of Algeria (FLN) proclaimed that it wanted to establish a
democratic state including the Europeans – objectives never achieved.[40]

Successful terrorist groups developed in all of the empires after the
Second World War and helped establish new states such as Israel, Cyprus,
Algeria. As empires dissolved, the wave receded. The Cold War accelerated
the process as the Soviets were always poised to help rebels. The Soviet
Union's internal life was not affected, partly because it did not recognize
itself as an empire and had no overseas territories. In the period between
the two World Wars, there was terrorist activity in various Balkan states. The
new states that the Versailles Treaty created there lacked overseas territories
and they did not consider themselves colonial powers.

Because the term 'terrorist' had accumulated so many negative connotations, Second Wave organizations understood that they needed a new
language to describe themselves. The Israeli group *Lehi* was the last self-
identified terrorist group. Menachem Begin, the leader of the *Irgun* (*Lehi*'s
Zionist rival), concentrating on purpose rather than means, described his
group as 'freedom fighters' struggling against 'government terror'.[41] So
appealing was this self-description that all subsequent terrorist groups
followed suit. Moreover, as the anti-colonial struggle seemed more legitimate than the First Wave's purpose, the 'new' language became attractive
to potential political supporters as well (even Bin Laden later described
himself as a 'freedom fighter').[42] Governments appreciated the political
value of 'appropriate' language too, and began to describe *all* violent rebels
as terrorists. To avoid being seen as blatantly partisan, the media corrupted
the language further. Major American newspapers, for example, often
described the same persons alternatively as terrorists, guerrillas, and
soldiers in the same description of an event![43]

Tactics changed as well. Because diaspora sources contributed more
money, bank robberies were less common. The First Wave demonstrated

that assassinating prominent political figures was often counterproductive; few assassinations occurred in the Second Wave. The Balkans were an exception. Perhaps that was related to the fact that, although assassinations in the Balkans did provoke the First World War, the Versailles Peace Treaty established some new Balkan states.[44] Elsewhere, only *Lehi* (the British called it the 'Stern Gang') remained committed to assassination as the principal tactic. Martyrdom often linked to assassination seemed less significant as well.

The new strategy was more complicated than the old. A larger array of targets was chosen, and it was important to strike them in proper sequence: First eliminate the police – a government's eyes and ears – through systematic assassinations of officers and/or their families. The military units replacing them would prove too clumsy to cope without producing counter-atrocities that increased social support for the terrorists. If the process of atrocities and counter-atrocities was well executed, it favoured those perceived to be weak and without alternatives.[45] (Note that during the 'Golden Age of Assassination', Anarchists were seen as bizarre, incapable of living peacefully anywhere.) Major energies went into guerrilla-like (hit and run) actions against troops: attacks that still went beyond the rules of war because the assailants had no identifying insignia and concealed their weapons. Some groups, however (such as the *Irgun*), initiated a pattern of giving warnings to limit civilian casualties.[46] In some cases (Algeria), terror was only one aspect of a more comprehensive rebellion that included extensive guerrilla forces.

Second Wave terrorists exploited the international scene more productively than had their predecessors. Different national groups touted an international revolutionary tradition that gave them common bonds, but the heroes invoked in the literature of those groups were almost always their own national heroes.[47] The underlying assumption for this conflict seemed to be that if one strengthened ties with foreign terrorists, other international assets would become less useful.

Diaspora groups regularly displayed abilities not seen earlier. Nineteenth century Irish rebels received money, weapons, and volunteers from the Irish-American community. After the First World War, however, Irish-Americans induced the US to pressure Britain to accept an Irish state.[48] Jewish-Americans exerted similar leverage when the Holocaust horrors became public.

Foreign states with kindred populations were also active. Arab states gave the Algerian FLN crucial political support, and those adjacent to Algeria offered sanctuaries for cells to stage attacks. Greece sponsored the Cypriot uprisings against the British, and then against Cyprus when it became a state. Frightened Turkish Cypriots in turn looked to Turkey for aid. Turkish troops invaded the northern part of the island in 1974 and are still there.

Outside influences obviously depend on the purpose of the terrorist activity and the local context; the different Irish experiences illustrate. The

1920s effort was seen simply as an anti-colonial movement, and that was when the Irish-American community had its most productive impact.[49] The diaspora was less interested in the IRA's brief campaigns to bring Northern Ireland into the Republic during the Second World War and the Cold War.

As the Second Wave progressed, the League of Nations got involved – a matter Townsend discusses in this volume (see Chapter 2).[50] After the Second World War, the United Nations (UN) inherited the League's ultimate authority over the remaining colonial Mandates, now scenes of extensive terrorist activity. When Britain decided to withdraw from Palestine, the UN was crucial in legitimizing the partition. Subsequently all anti-colonial terrorism sought to involve the UN. Most new states admitted to the UN were formerly colonial territories lent and gave the anti-colonial sentiment in that body more power. UN debate participants used Begin's language more and more to describe anti-colonial terrorists as 'freedom fighters'.[51]

The 'Third Wave': excessive internationalism?

The agonizing Vietnam War was the major political event stimulating the 'New Left Wave'. The effectiveness of the Viet Cong's 'primitive weapons' against the American Goliath's modern technology rekindled hopes that the world system was vulnerable. Groups popped up in the Third World and in the West also, where the war stimulated enormous antagonism among the youth toward the existing system. Western groups such as the American Weather Underground, the German Red Army Faction, the Italian Red Brigades, the Japanese Red Army, and the French *Action Directe* claimed to be vanguards for the masses in the Third World – a development the Soviet world encouraged with moral support, training, and weapons.

As in the First Wave, radicalism and nationalism were often intertwined as the Basque, Armenian, Corsican, Kurdish, and Irish cases show.[52] Although every First Wave nationalist movement failed, the linkage was renewed. Ethnic constituencies are always more durable than radical ones. Nationalist groups were the Third Wave's most durable entities, but their failure rate was high and those still struggling will probably fail too. The states attacked – Spain, France, the UK, Turkey, and the former colonial territories that became new states – simply did not consider themselves colonial powers. This pattern was also seen in the Balkan experience in the Second Wave, and thus government ambivalence necessary for rebel success was absent.

When the Vietnam War ended in 1975, the PLO replaced the Viet Cong as the wave's heroic model. Originating after the extraordinary collapse of three Arab armies in the Six Day War (1967), its existence and persistence gave credibility to supporters who argued that only terror could destroy Israel. The PLO's centrality was strengthened because its training facilities in Lebanon were available to other groups, and the PLO got strong support from Arab states and the Soviet Union.

First and Third Waves share striking resemblances. Women in the Second Wave had been restricted to the role of messengers and scouts; now they became leaders and fighters again.[53] 'Theatrical targets', comparable to those of the First Wave, replaced the Second Wave's 'military' ones. International hijacking is one example; some seven hundred occurred during the Third Wave's first three decades.[54]

Planes were often hijacked to secure hostages. Hostages were seized in other ways too, and hostage crises became a wave characteristic. The most memorable happened when Red Brigades kidnapped former Italian Prime Minister Aldo Moro in 1979. When the government refused to negotiate, he was brutally murdered and his body dumped in the street. The Sandinistas took Nicaragua's Congress hostage in 1978, an act so audacious it sparked a popular insurrection that brought down the Somoza regime a year later. The Columbian April 19 Movement (M-19) in 1985 tried to duplicate the feat by seizing the Supreme Court, but the government refused to yield and nearly one hundred people, including eleven justices, perished.

Kidnappings occurred in seventy-three countries, especially in Italy, Spain, and Latin America. From 1968 to 1982 there were forty-nine inter-national kidnapping incidents involving nine hundred and fifty-one hostages.[55] Initially, hostages were taken to give their captors political lever-age, but soon another concern became more attractive. Companies insured their executives and kidnapping became lucrative. When money was the principal issue, kidnappers found that hostage negotiations were also easier to consummate on their terms. Informed observers estimate that the practice 'earned' US$350 million.[56] Some organizations became criminal groups reviving a significant Russian First Wave pattern.[57]

The abandoned practice of assassinating prominent figures was revived. The IRA and its various splinter organizations, for example, assassinated two British ambassadors in 1976 and 1979, Lord Mountbatten in 1979, and then attempted to kill Prime Ministers Margaret Thatcher in 1984 and John Major in 1991.[58] The PLO's Black September assassinated Jordan's Prime Minister in 1971, made an attempt on Jordan's King Hussein three years later, and killed the American Ambassador in the Saudi Embassy in Khartoum in 1973 – the year that the ETA killed Spanish Prime Minister Luis Carrero Blanco.

But First and Third Wave assassinations had a different logic. A First Wave victim was assassinated because he or she held a public office. Third Wave assassinations were more often justified as 'punishments'. Jordan's Prime Minister and King had forced the PLO out of Jordan in a savage battle. The attempt against British Prime Minister Thatcher occurred because she was 'responsible' for the deaths of nine IRA hunger strikers who rejected the practice of treating IRA prisoners as ordinary criminals.[59] When Italy's government refused to negotiate for his life, Aldo Moro was murdered.

For good reason, the term 'international terrorism' was revived. Again, the revolutionary ethos created bonds between separate national groups, which intensified when first Cuban and then PLO training facilities were made available. Emblematic of this new internationalism was that some state sponsors (such as Libya) now supported *all* radical groups.[60] International dimensions were reflected in the targets chosen, too. Some groups conducted more assaults abroad than on their home territories. The PLO, for example, was more active in Europe than on the West Bank, and sometimes more active in Europe than many European groups were themselves were! Different national groups worked together in attacks, such as the Munich Olympics massacre (1972), the kidnapping of OPEC ministers (1975), the hijackings of an Air France flight to Uganda in 1976 and a Lufthansa plane to Somalia in 1977.

On their own soil, groups often chose targets with international significance. Strikes on foreign embassies began when the PLO attacked the Saudi Embassy in the Sudan (1973). The Peruvian group *Tupac Amaru*, partly to gain political advantage over its rival *Sendero Luminoso* and held seventy-two hostages in the Japanese Embassy for more than four months (1996–97) until a rescue operation killed every terrorist in the complex.

The US became a favourite target of most groups. One-third of the international attacks involved American targets in Latin America and the Middle East, where the US supported most governments under terrorist siege.[61] European groups focused on American facilities in NATO members states. Despite its pre-eminent status as a victim and its denunciation of terrorism, Cold War concerns sometimes induced the US to support terror activity in Nicaragua, Angola, and elsewhere – indicating how difficult it was to forgo a worthwhile purpose when deplorable tactics had to be used.

Third Wave organizations paid a large price for being unable to negotiate the conflicting demands imposed by various international elements.[62] The commitment to a revolutionary ethos alienated traditional foreign supporters, particularly during the Cold War. The IRA lost significant support from the Irish-American diaspora when its goal was a united socialist Ireland and accepted aid from Libya and the PLO. The Cold War had to end before the Irish diaspora and the US government could move to resolve the Irish issue.

Involvement with foreign groups forced terrorists to neglect their domestic constituencies. A leader of the German Second of June group said obsession with the Palestinian cause induced it to attack a Jewish synagogue on the anniversary of *Kristall Nacht*, a date many use to mark the beginning of the Holocaust. Such 'stupidity', he said, alienated Germans.[63] When the cooperating entities had unequal power, the weaker found that its interests were ignored. The German Revolutionary Cells, hijacking partners of the Palestine Front for the Liberation of Palestine, discovered that when it could not get that group's help to release German prisoners. '[D]ependent on the will of Wadi Haddad and his group', whose agenda was very different than theirs after all, the Revolutionary Cells terminated the relationship and soon collapsed.[64]

The PLO, always a loose confederation, often found international ties to be costly, complicating serious existing divisions within the organization. In the 1970s, PLO intelligence chief Abu Iyad wrote that the Palestinian cause was so important in Syrian and Iraqi domestic politics that those countries felt it necessary to capture some PLO organizations to serve their own ends, thereby making it even more difficult to settle for a limited goal, as Israel and Cyprus had done earlier.

Entanglements with Arab states created problems for both parties. Raids staged from Egyptian-occupied Gaza helped precipitate a disastrous war with Israel in 1956. Egypt prohibited Palestinians from launching raids from that territory ever again. A Palestinian raid from Syria brought Syria into the Six Day War, and subsequently Syria tightly controlled those operating from its territories. When a PLO faction hijacked British and American planes to Jordan (1970) in the first effort to target non-Israelis, the Jordanian army devastated the PLO and pushed it out of Jordan. Finally, an attempted assassination of an Israeli diplomat in Britain sparked Israel to invade Lebanon (1982), forcing the PLO to leave the land that gave it so much significance among foreign terrorist groups. Tunisia, the PLO's new host, prohibited it from training foreign groups. To a large extent, the PLO's career as an effective terrorist organization seemed to be over. (Ironically, Abu Nidal's renegade faction associated with Iraq, which made two previous attempts to kill the PLO's leader Arafat, organized the assassination attempt, *a fact known to the Israeli government.*[65])

Other state sponsors found promoting terrorist activity expensive. In the 1980s, Britain severed diplomatic relations with Libya and Syria to punish them for sponsoring terrorism in the UK. In 1986 the US, with British aid, bombed Libya. The European Community subsequently imposed an arms embargo.[66] Iraq's surprising restraint during the 1990 Gulf War also revealed some difficulties of state-sponsored terror. Iraq threatened to use terror. Western authorities predicted that terrorists would flood Europe.[67] But the terror never materialized. If it had, the Gulf War might have aimed to bring Saddam Hussein to trial for war crimes. A desire to avoid that result may explain his uncharacteristic restraint.

The Third Wave began ebbing in the 1980s. Revolutionary terrorists were defeated in one country after another. Israel's invasion of Lebanon (1982) eliminated PLO facilities for training terrorist groups. International counter-terrorist cooperation became increasingly effective. The international police cooperation sought in 1904 began to materialize as *TREVI* and Europol were established, respectively, in 1975 and 1994.

Differences between states remained; even close allies could not always cooperate. France refused to extradite PLO, Red Brigade, and ETA suspects to West Germany, Italy, and Spain, respectively. Italy spurned American requests to extradite a Palestinian suspect in the seizure of the *Achille Lauro* cruise ship (1984), and refused to extradite a Kurdish person in 1988 because Italian law (unlike Turkish law), forbids capital punishment. The

US also refused to extradite some IRA suspects. Events of this sort will not stop until that improbable day when the laws and interests of separate states are identical.

The UN's role changed dramatically. Now 'new states', former colonial territories, found that terrorism threatened their interests and they particularly shunned nationalist movements fighting to secede.[68] Major international and UN conventions from 1970 through 1999 prohibited hijacking, hostage-taking, attacks on senior government officials and on foreign states' facilities, and the financing of international activities.

'Freedom Fighter' was no longer a popular term in UN debates. The word 'terrorism' was even used in the title of documents, such as the 'International Convention for the Suppression of Terrorist Bombing' (1997).[69] Evidence that Libya's agents were involved in the Pan Am Lockerbie plane crash produced an unanimous Security Council decision in 1988. It obliged Libya to extradite subjects. A decade later when collective sanctions had their full effect, Libya complied. In 2003, Libya paid compensation to the victims' families.

Very serious ambiguities and conflicts still persist, and reflect the ever-present fact that terror serves different ends, some of which are prized. Ironically, the most important ambiguity concerned the PLO, the wave's major organization. It received official UN status and over one hundred states gave it diplomatic recognition after 1974 when the Arab League finally decided that the PLO (and not Jordan or Egypt) was entitled to receive a share of the Palestine Mandate, destined to be a sovereign state.

The wave produced only four successes, and each was related to special circumstances. Two of the successes were very limited. After the Soviet Union (a major supporter) collapsed, and after losing much of its striking power, the PLO recognized Israel. Israel in turn allowed it to come back to the West Bank in 1992. South Tyrol terrorists struggled for independence from Italy but settled for autonomy in 2001 when Italy finally lived up to its treaty with Austria.

The two African successes were more complete. South-West Africa, a German overseas territory, became a League of Nations Mandate under the jurisdiction of South Africa – a contiguous state. South Africa planned to incorporate the territory. Unlike other nationalist struggles in the Third Wave, they got important international support. However, only after a twenty-four-year struggle, and the end of the Cold War (inducing the Soviets to withdraw their aid), did South Africa yield to allow the state of Namibia to be born in 1990.[70]

In South Africa itself, the African National Congress (ANC) in 2001 achieved the wave's most complete success. Although the government's apartheid policies generated enormous international hostility, it was not until the rebels gave up their New Left commitment, and the Soviet Union fell, that the government agreed to let the ANC participate in elections (which it knew the ANC would win). Just as the weakness of the PLO encouraged Israel to let it return, the carefully restrained attacks in South Tyrol and South Africa made governments there more willing to concede.[71]

The 'Fourth Wave': how unique and how long?

As the Third Wave began to ebb, the Fourth gathered force. Religious elements have always been important in modern terror because religious and ethnic identities often overlap (as the Armenian, Macedonian, Irish, Cypriot, French Canadian, Israeli, and Palestinian struggles illustrate).[72] The early aim was to establish *secular* states; now *religious* states are the object. The Fourth Wave occasionally produced a secular group. When Sri Lanka Buddhists tried to transform the country into a religious state, the secular Tamil Tigers tried to secede and became a significant wave element.

The wave has reshaped the international system profoundly. The collapse of the Soviet Union was partly due to its defeat in Afghanistan – making the US the only superpower, at least for a while. Terrorists played a significant role either as provocateurs or participants in four wars.[73] Contemporary American policies authorizing drone attacks on various states have weakened the principle of sovereignty.[74] While the assassination precipitating the First World War had a greater impact on the international system and virtually eliminated the First Wave too,[75] the impact on the international system is now spread out over the wave's entire life span.

Islam is at the heart of the wave. Islamic groups have conducted the most significant, deadly and most profoundly international attacks. The events providing the inspiration for the wave originated there and influenced religious terror groups elsewhere.[76] After Islam erupted, Sikhs sought a religious state in India. Jewish terrorists attempted to blow up Islam's most sacred shrine in Jerusalem, and in 1995 committed a variety of attacks including the assassination of Israeli Prime Minister Rabin. In that year, Aum Shinrikyo, a strange group combining Buddhist, Hindu, and Christian themes, released nerve gas on a Tokyo subway killing twelve and seriously injuring forty. This attack created a persistent, worldwide anxiety that more chem-bio weapon attacks would occur soon.

Christian terrorism emerged based on racist interpretations of the Bible. In true medieval, millenarian fashion, armed rural communes composed of extended families withdrew from the state to wait for the Second Coming and the 'great racial war'. The violence it produced has not been great except for the Oklahoma City Bombing in 1995.

Four events in 1979 involving Muslims highlight both the importance of religion and the weakness of secular forces. The Iranian Revolution occurred, the Camp David Treaty was signed, a new Islamic century began, and the Soviets invaded Afghanistan.

Street demonstrations in Iran destroyed the Shah's secular state, provided clear evidence that religion had more political appeal than neo-Marxism, because Iranian Third Wave groups mustered only meager support against the Shah. 'There are no frontiers in Islam', Ayatollah Khomeini proclaimed. 'His' revolution reshaped relationships among Muslims and between Islam and the rest of the world. Most immediately, Iranians inspired and assisted Shiite terror movements outside of Iran in Iraq, Saudi Arabia, Kuwait, and Lebanon.

In Lebanon, Shiites (influenced by the self-martyrdom tactic of the medieval Assassins) introduced suicide bombing, quickly ousting American and other foreign troops in the country on a peace mission following the 1982 Israeli invasion. 'Suicide bombing' became the wave's trademark. Despite the conventional wisdom (that only a belief in the rewards of Paradise could inspire these acts), the secular Tamil Tigers, impressed by the success in Lebanon, used the tactic in Sri Lanka to give their movement new life. From 1983 to 2000, they employed more 'suicide bombers' than did all Islamic groups put together, often using women, for the first time in this wave.[77]

The Camp David Peace Treaty between Egypt and Israel demonstrated that the most powerful secular Arab state supporting the PLO changed its policy. Iran then closed Israel's embassy and gave the site to the PLO.

The monumental Iranian Revolution was unexpected, but many Muslims believed that 1979 would be very significant. A new Islamic century began then and would produce a *Mahdi* (redeemer). That expectation had often sparked uprisings in the past when a new Islamic century began.[78] In the first minutes of the new century, several hundred Muslims occupied the Grand Mosque in Mecca, Islam's holiest site. It took several weeks and many casualties to dislodge them. During that siege, numerous examples of Sunni terrorism appeared in Egypt, Syria, Tunisia, Morocco, Algeria, the Philippines, and Indonesia.

The Soviet Union invaded Afghanistan. The Saudi government, undermined by the Mecca attack and anxious to restore its religious authority, aided the resistance. They were joined by the US for Cold War reasons.[79] Abdallah Azzam (1941–89), a former PLO member, wrote several works defining the Afghan struggle as a religious obligation to defend Muslim territories. He was instrumental in bringing numerous Arab volunteers, including Bin Laden, to Afghanistan.[80] The Soviets gave up in 1989. Two years later the stunning and unimaginable collapse of the Soviet Union occurred.

Religion had eliminated a secular superpower – an astonishing event with important consequences for terrorist activity. Lands with a large Muslim population formerly part of the Soviet Union (for example, Chechnya, Uzbekistan and Azerbaijan) became important new terrorist fields. Conflicts in Bosnia attracted foreign volunteers, especially the trained, confident Arab-Afghan War veterans. Kashmir again became a critical issue where the death toll since 1990 has been more than fifty thousand.[81]

The Fourth Wave was more deadly and effective than the Third, but produced fewer terrorist groups. About two hundred groups, mostly Third

Wave, were active in the 1980s – but during the next decade the number fell to forty.[82] The trend is related to the size of the primary audiences. A major religious community is simply much larger than any national one. Different cultural traditions also may be relevant. The huge number of secular terrorist groups largely came from Christian countries; and Christianity always generated more religious divisions than did Islam.[83]

Islamic groups have been the most durable; major groups in Lebanon, Egypt, and Algeria have persisted for over two decades.[84] Moreover, the groups tend to be large. When Bin Laden transformed Abdallah Azzam's group into *al Qaeda,* it contained over five thousand members.[85] The larger Third Wave groups had several hundred active members. The PLO in Lebanon was trying to create a regular army and constitutes a special case with around twenty-five thousand members.

Under Bin Laden, *Al Qaeda's* purpose was transformed and aimed to create a single Islamic state under the *Sharia* (Islamic law). Most volunteers were Arabs; more than sixty countries contributed recruits. In the first three waves, by way of contrast, organizations drew recruits from a single national base.[86] The contrast between PLO and *al Qaeda* training facilities reflects this fact; the PLO trained units from other organizations, whereas *al Qaeda* accepted individuals only. Middle Eastern and African states with dominant Muslims populations were designated as 'The Near Enemy' *Al Qaeda* vigorously supported Islamic terror groups aiming to overthrow those states. Those campaigns, however, were indiscriminate and counter-productive.

During the 1990 Gulf War, Saudi Arabia allowed the US to establish military bases in Islam's holiest land to drive Iraq out of Kuwait. An outraged *Al Qaeda* proclaimed that the permission violated Prophet Muhammad's command that the land should harbour only one religion. The organization asserted it was therefore justified in attacking 'The Far Enemy', confident that this act would ultimately unify the Sunni world.[87] *Al Qaeda* bombed military posts in Yemen and Saudi Arabia but the Americans remained. Strikes against American embassies in Kenya and Tanzania (1998) inflicted heavy casualties, and futile cruise missile responses were made against *al Qaeda* targets 'turn[ing] Bin Laden from a marginal figure in the Muslim world to a global celebrity'.[88]

Unsuccessful efforts to strike targets in America began in 1993.[89] Then there was 9/11; an effort to rejuvenate a failing cause by triggering indiscriminate reactions, perhaps?[90] The response was unprecedented, partly because so many foreign nationals had been killed. Under UN auspices, more than one hundred states (including Iran) joined the effort against *al Qaeda* in Afghanistan. Still, no one expected the intervention to be so quick, or apparently so decisive. Invaders had always found Afghanistan difficult to subdue. Moreover, the history of terrorism demonstrates that even when anti-terrorism forces are very familiar with territories harboring targets, the entrenched had considerable staying power (as was true in the cases of Cyprus, Algeria, Northern Ireland, and Sri Lanka). This time anti-terrorism forces also did not know the terrain.

One reason why *al Qaeda* in Afghanistan collapsed so quickly was that it violated a cardinal rule for terrorist organizations, namely, to always remain underground. *Al Qaeda* stayed visible to operate its extensive training oper-ations.[91] As the Israelis demonstrated in ousting the PLO from Lebanon, visible groups are very vulnerable. *Al Qaeda* did not plan for the possibility of an invasion. Perhaps its contempt for previous American reactions convinced it that the 'paper tiger' would avoid difficult targets like Afghanistan.[92]

Before the invaders finished the job, the US made a reckless decision to carry the battle to Iraq, changing the international scene profoundly, and giving *al Qaeda* many new recruits while the US lost many allies. International overreactions by governments have been a common feature in terrorist history ever since the First World War.[93] One unanticipated consequence of Israel's reckless invasion of Lebanon (to destroy the PLO) was the creation of Hezbollah – the most durable entity of the 'Religious Wave'.

But *al Qaeda* played its hand badly too. As explained in a critical, much-publicized letter from *al Qaeda* central command to al-Zarqawi (leader of *al Qaeda* in Iraq): 'Many of your Muslim admirers among the common folk are wondering about your attacks on the Shia. The sharpness of this ques-tioning increases when the attacks are on one of their mosques. Among the things which the feelings of the Muslims who love and support you, will never find palatable also are the scenes of slaughtering the hostages. We are in a battle and more than half of this battle is taking place in the battle-field of the media. We just don't need this.'[94]

The inclination to attack on Islamic holy days never stopped.[95] Finally, the indiscriminate attacks produced the 'Great Awakening', a crucial watershed in which Sunni tribes – vigorous *al Qaeda* supporters – reversed themselves.

The group's gradual deterioration was punctuated by the use of drones to kill Bin Laden in May 2011 and Atiyah Abd al-Rahman, *al Qaeda*'s second in command two months later. General Douglas Lute, a National Security Advisor, concluded that all of the senior leadership of *al Qaeda* 'could be knocked out in six months'.[96]

Perhaps, but the wave is not over. *Al Qaeda* still has franchises in Yemen and elsewhere.[97] When American troops leave Iraq, *al Qaeda* in Iraq might be revived. The new Libyan regime contains members formerly associated with *al Qaeda*, such as Abdel Beihaj, Chairman of the Military Council in Tripoli. What that means ultimately is unclear, but one should remember that an *al Qaeda* related uprising in Libya in 1998 induced Qaddafi's government to be the first to denounce Bin Laden as an 'international criminal,' and issue a warrant for his arrest (1998).[98]

If American drone attacks transform the Pakistani scene, new groups might be created in a country that possesses a nuclear arsenal. If Pakistan does not resolve the Kashmir problem with India, religious terrorism will probably persist there, and resume its nationalist orientation. Religious–nationalist groups elsewhere (such as Hezbollah, Hamas, and Jewish religious terror groups) will not soon disappear. More new groups, such as the Islamic Boko Haram in Nigeria, could materialize.

Leaving Afghanistan without an agreement with the Taliban could be a disaster. Since the Taliban's basic concern has been Afghanistan, and it has never been interested in international operations, there is reason to believe that it would keep an agreement to prevent international activity – *our* basic concern.

Recent events have reminded students of terrorism that they had neglected the tactics of the 'lone wolf' or 'leaderless resistance'. It was first recommended by Louis Beam (1992), who argued that the vulnerability of Christian groups to government infiltration and entrapment meant a new tactic was necessary – one that could only be responded to only *after* it had occurred.[99] Timothy McVeigh used the tactic in the Oklahoma City Bombing in 1995, the deadliest terrorist act in American history until 9/11. But the act repulsed Christian groups, and the level of violence has still been minimal – so far. Anders Breivik's two attacks in Norway on 22 July 2011 killed seventy-seven people, the Fourth Wave's second-most devastating lone wolf action in the West. He cited American Christian arguments for 'lone wolf' strikes, but much like Timothy McVeigh, he alienated potential supporters.

In 2005, Abu Misab al Suri, a jihadist theorist and veteran leader, noted that the centralized hierarchical structure was no longer suitable for *al Qaeda*. Sanctuaries for training abroad were not available. He recommended 'leaderless resistance' to revitalize Islamic terror, and to exhaust the Western economy[100] – a recommendation that *al Qaeda* in the Arabian Peninsula publicly endorsed in October 2009. A week later, Major Nidal Hasan killed fourteen fellow soldiers at Fort Hood. He was followed by the 'Christmas Day Bomber' passenger from Yemen, and then by the Times Square bomb attempt in May 2010. Another attempt by a US soldier targeted Fort Hood personnel in July 2011.[101] Since 2009, sixteen Islamic lone wolf attacks have been attempted in the US.[102] But so far, the new tactic has only highlighted the organization's weakness.

Ever since *Aum Shinrikyo* used nerve gas, many have been worried that if this wave has been so indiscriminant, the use of chemical and biological weapons would be common. Bin Laden said that *al Qaeda* was 'obligated' to employ them, but its efforts were never successful.[103] Our view is that the concern is unfounded because states that used them found they had little value. Moreover, terrorists need weapons with properties not found in those weapons.[104] It is no accident that the bomb has continued to be the major weapon since modern terror began. Alex Schmid's valuable new *Handbook on Terrorism Research* notes that 'the largest topic (18.9 per cent of all the articles written on terrorism) concerns the threat of weapons of mass destruction', but he devotes only two sentences to the issue! Does he feel we talk too much about it, too?[105]

In 2004, we said that the Fourth Wave would be over by 2025, and we have no reason yet to change our mind.[106]

Concluding thoughts and questions

Unlike crime or poverty, international non-state terrorism is only one hundred and thirty-five years old. It was generated by technology, the spread of French Revolutionary spirit, and the system of sovereign states. The political reason for the First Wave was the failure of a democratic reform program; self-determination inspired the Second. Third Wave groups maintained that the egalitarian principle of the French Revolution was never fully accepted. The Fourth Wave's spirit is explicitly anti-democratic. Democracy requires 'the people' to be sovereign; religion supplied an alternative legitimating principle.

This chapter has emphasized variations in the relationships between the waves and the international world. In the First Wave, the intense hostility of so many states stimulated efforts to eliminate terrorism by making it an international crime, but international police cooperation planned never materialized. Ironically, in view of our situation since the 1960s, democratic states were most likely to provide refuge for foreign terrorists and be most resistant to the international police efforts.

The First Wave transformed the international system in a wholly unanticipated way when Serbian–Bosnian nationalists assassinated the Arch Duke of the Austro-Hungarian Empire. The First World War was precipitated by this event. The resulting peace treaty made self-determination a crucial ingredient of international politics. Europe became a continent of national states, and the first successful terrorist organizations appeared in overseas empires. The world as a whole largely accepted the cause proclaimed, especially since participants in the new wave made their strikes and target choices more discriminate and comprehensible. The language of the debates in the UN, the League of Nations' successor, kept referring to anti-colonial terrorists as 'freedom fighters'. States no longer could expand their boundaries through conquest.

The Third Wave rejected its predecessor's concern with domestic targets – often losing potential domestic constituencies in the process. It revived and significantly extended the First Wave's practice of mutual cooperation in executing attacks. Most activity was directed against Western governments (especially the US) and their Third World allies. For the first time, individual states *overtly* sponsored groups. Indeed, Libya said it would support *all* radical groups and tried to do so. Terrorism became an ingredient of the Cold War as the Soviets covertly supplied many with technical help. But the favourable UN attitude toward terrorism dissolved; many new states became victims of secessionist efforts, or were affected by the wave's new tactics, such as hostage-taking and hijacking. Very few organizations achieved any success, and the few that did limited their strikes and made serious compromises. The ANC in South Africa was the most successful group; its restraint was a factor.

The most destructive and indiscriminate wave by far is the Fourth Wave. No regular tactic produced as many casualties as self-martyrdom or suicide bombing did. 9/11 was in a class by itself, a suicide bombing that killed more people including more of different nationalities than ever before in the history of terrorism. The international scene was dramatically altered. The Soviet Union's collapse was partly due to its defeat in Afghanistan, leaving the world with only one 'superpower' – at least for a while. Terrorists played significant roles either as provocateurs or participants in three other major wars as well. Religious ties and antagonisms enabled the emergence of new forms of cooperation between terrorist groups, and produced hopes that religious communities would produce a different kind of global order. American responses authorizing drone attacks on individuals in various independent, even allied, states threaten the principle of sovereignty – the rock of the international order. Bin Laden said he would bankrupt the West[107] – a claim no one takes seriously.

Will the Fourth Wave's demise mean that George W. Bush's pledge to end global terrorism has been fulfilled? Perhaps. But the terrorism we have been discussing is a strategy that attracts small groups in a technological and international context mirroring that of the late nineteenth century; it is unclear what should (or could) be done to eliminate that context. Our sense is that a Fifth Wave will probably begin before the Fourth Wave ends.

What form will it take? If history is a reliable guide, we will not know *beforehand*. Previously, dramatic and unanticipated political events stimulated each wave. Perhaps the world's enormous economic difficulties may have that effect now.

Acknowledgement

The author wishes to express his gratitude to the Andrew W. Mellon Foundation for an Emeritus Grant which he used to finish the article.

Notes

1   An earlier version of this essay was published as D.C. Rapoport, 'The Fourth Wave: September 11 in the History of Terrorism', *Current History*, 2001, vol. 100, pp. 419–24. A second version is D.C. Rapoport, 'Modern Terror: The Four Waves', in A. Cronin and J. Ludes (eds) *Attacking Terrorism: Elements of a Grand Strategy*, Washington, DC: Georgetown University Press, 2004, pp. 46–73.
2   On 20 September, the President told Congress that 'any nation that continues to harbor or support terrorism will be regarded as a hostile regime. [T]he war

would not end *until every terrorist group of global reach* has been found, stopped, and defeated.' [emphasis added]

3   See R.B. Jensen, 'The United States, International Policing, and the War against Anarchist Terrorism', *Terrorism and Political Violence*, 2001, vol. 13, pp. 5–46.

4   No good history of terrorism exists. Schmid and Jongman's initial monumental study of the terrorism literature did not even list a history of the subject! See A. Schmid and A.J. Jongman, *Political Terrorism: A New Guide to Actors, Authors, Concepts, Theories, DataBases, and Literature*, rev. ed., New Brunswick: Transaction Books, 1988.

5   We lack the space to discuss the domestic scene but the unusual character of terrorist activity made an enormous impact on national life in many countries, beginning in the latter part of the nineteenth century. Every state affected in the First Wave radically transformed its police organizations into tools to penetrate underground groups. The Russian *Okhrana*, the British Special Branch, and the FBI are conspicuous examples. The new organizational form remains a permanent, perhaps indispensable, feature of modern life. Terrorist tactics, *inter alia*, aim at producing rage and frustration, often driving governments to respond in unanticipated, extraordinary, illegal, socially destructive, and shameful ways. Because a significant Jewish element was present in the several Russian terrorist movements, the *Okhrana* organized pogroms to intimidate Russian Jews, compelling many to flee to the West and to the Holy Land. *Okhrana* fabricated *The Protocols of Zion*, a book that helped stimulate virulent anti-Semitism that went well beyond Russia. The influence of that fabrication continued for decades, and still influences Christian and Islamic terrorist movements today. Democratic states 'overreacted' too. In 1901, President Theodore Roosevelt proposed sending all Anarchists back to Europe. Congress was more restrained and simply barred foreign Anarchists from entering the county. More than a decade later, President Wilson's Attorney General Palmer implemented a proposal similar to Roosevelt's, and rounded-up *all* Anarchists to ship them back 'home', regardless of whether or not they had committed crimes. That event produced the 1920 Wall Street Bombing, which in turn became the justification for an immigration quota law – making it much more difficult for persons from Southern and Eastern European states (the original home of most Anarchists) to immigrate for decades. This was a law that Adolph Hitler praised highly. For a discussion of the Spanish situation, see Florian Grafl, 'A Blueprint for Successfully Fighting Anarchist Terror? Counter-terrorist Communities of Violence in Barcelona during the *Pistolerismo*', Chapter 3 in this volume. It is still too early to know what the domestic consequences of 9/11 will ultimately be. One first reaction suggested that we had learned from past mistakes. The federal government made special efforts to show that we were not at war with Islam, and it curbed the first expressions of vigilante passions. The significance of subsequent measures seems more problematic. Our first homeland experience with foreign terror led us to create important new policing arrangements. Congress established a Department of Homeland Security with one hundred and seventy thousand employees – clearly the largest change in security policy in America's history. No one knows what that seismic change will mean. One casualty could be the *Posse Comitatus* law, which prohibits the military from administering civil affairs – a law that, ironically, was passed because we were unhappy with military responses to KKK terrorist activity after

the Civil War! A policy of secret detentions – a common reaction to terrorist activities in many countries – has been implemented. Extensive revisions of immigration regulations are being instituted. Prisoners taken in Afghanistan are not being prosecuted under criminal law, reversing a long-standing policy in virtually all states including our own. Previous experiences suggest that it will take time for the changes to have their effect because so much depends upon the scope, frequency, and duration of future terrorist activity.

6   Rashed Uz Zaman provides a detailed account of the complexities of the Indian situation in 'Bengal Terrorism and the Ambiguity of the Bengali Muslims', in Chapter 9 of this volume.

7   D.M. Chalmers, *Hooded Americanism: The History of the Ku Klux Klan*, 3rd ed., Durham, NC: Duke University Press, 1987, p. 19.

8   The activities of the Thugs and Assassins had international dimensions but were confined to specific regions. More important, there were no comparable groups operating at the same time in this region or elsewhere. See D.C. Rapoport, 'Fear and Trembling: Terror in Three Religious Traditions', *American Political Science Review*, 1984, vol. 78, pp. 658–77.

9   The lineage of rebel terror goes back at least to the first century. Hinduism, Judaism, and Islam produced the Thugs, Zealots, and Assassins respectively; names still used to designate terrorists. Religion determined every purpose and each tactic of the ancient form. See D.C. Rapoport, 'Fear and Trembling: Terror in Three Religious Traditions', *American Political Science Review*, 1984, vol. 78, pp. 658–77.

10   By far, most published academic articles on terrorism deal with organizations and counterterrorism policies. My experience as an editor of *Terrorism and Political Violence* suggests that the proportions are increased further in this direction if we consider the articles submitted for publication, too.

11   See note 2.

12   The rebels fought in uniform and against soldiers. George Barnard Shaw said 'My own view is that the men who were shot in cold blood . . . after their capture were prisoners of war'. Prime Minister Asquith said that by Britain's own standards, the rebel's were honourable, that 'they conducted themselves with great humanity . . . fought very bravely and did not resort to outrage'. *The Manchester Guardian* declared that the executions were 'atrocities'. See D.C. Rapoport, 'Introduction to Part III', in D.C. Rapoport and Y. Alexander (eds) *Morality of Terrorism*, 2nd ed., New York: Columbia University Press, 2001, pp. 219–27.

13   Guerrillas carry weapons openly and wear an identifying emblem, circumstances obliging states to treat them as soldiers.

14   Anyone who has tried to explain the intensity of the 1960s to contemporary college students knows how difficult it is to transmit one generation's experience to its successor.

15   D. Ronfeldt and W. Sater, *The Mindsets of High-Technology Terrorists: Future Implication From an Historical Analog*, Santa Monica: RAND Note, 1981, p. 3.

16   Nechaev's 'Revolutionary Catechism' is reprinted in D.C. Rapoport, *Assassination and Terrorism*, Toronto: Canadian Broadcasting Corporation (CBC), 1971. See M. Bakunin and P. Kropotkin, *Revolutionary Pamphlets*, New York: Benjamin Bloom, 1927; N. Mozorov, 'Terroristic Struggle', in F. Gross (ed.) *Violence and Politics*, The Hague: Mouton, 1972, pp. 102–22; S. Stepniak, *Underground Russia: Revolutionary Profiles and Sketches from Life*, Westport: Hyperion Press, 1973.

17   See D.C. Rapoport, 'Fear and Trembling: Terror in Three Religious Traditions', *American Political Science Review*, 1984, vol. 78, pp. 658–77.

18   It took time for this attitude to develop in Islam. If one compares Bin Laden's work with Faraj's *Neglected Duty* (a work written at the beginning of the Fourth Wave to justify the assassination of Egyptian President Sadat (1981)), the two authors seem to occupy two different worlds. Faraj cites no experience outside the Islamic tradition, and his most recent historical reference is to Napoleon's invasion of Europe! See D.C. Rapoport, 'Sacred Terror: A Case from Contemporary Islam', in W. Reich (ed.) *Origins of Terrorism*, Cambridge: Cambridge University Press, 1990, pp.103–30. I am grateful to Jerry Post for sharing his copy of the Bin Laden treatise. An edited version appears on the Department of Justice website, available online: www.U.S.DaJgove/ag/training manuals.htm (accessed 20 April 2012).

19   Bin Laden's dedication reads:
  'Pledge, O Sister
  To the sister believer whose clothes the criminals have stripped off:
  To the sister believer whose hair the oppressors have shaved.
  To the sister believer whose body has been abused by the human dogs.
    . . .
  Covenant, O Sister. . . to make their women widows and their children orphans'
  While women did participate in supplementary and logistic roles in *al Qaeda*, *al Qaeda* in Iraq is the only group in the movement to use women as fighters, but even here, their role was very limited. It employed four female suicide bombers in the 2005–06 period. It was not clear why they were used; it was al Zarqawi's decision, and it may be that he was running out of male volunteers. See J. Stone and K. Patillo, 'Al Qaeda's Use of Women in Iraq: A Case Study', in L. Sjoberg and C.E. Gentry (eds) *Women, Gender, and Terrorism*, Athens, GA: University of Georgia Press, 2011, pp. 159–75.

20   Our concern is with revolutionary groups in the waves. Right Wing and single-issue (such as abortion) groups are not discussed.

21   The term terror originally referred to actions of the Revolutionary government that went beyond the rules regulating punishment in order to 'educate' a people to govern itself.

22   Vera Figner, the architect of *Narodnaya Volya's* foreign policy, identifies the first four ingredients. A fifth was created later. For a more extensive discussion of Figner, see D.C. Rapoport, *Inside Terrorist Organizations*, 2nd ed., London: Frank Cass, 2001, pp. 125 ff.

23   Nechaev's 'Revolutionary Catechism' is reprinted in D.C. Rapoport, *Assassination and Terrorism*, Toronto: Canadian Broadcasting Corporation (CBC), 1971.

24   The term comes from the Italian Anarchist Carlo Cafiero in 1880.

25   An equivalent for this argument in religious millennial thought is that that the world must become impossibly bad before it could become unimaginably good.

26   A.B. Ulam, *In the Name of the People*, New York: Viking Press, 1977, p. 269 (emphasis added).

27   Newspaper reports in Germany the next day interpreted the demonstrations to mean that a revolution was coming. *New York Times*, 4 April 1878.

28   S. Stepniak, *Underground Russia: Revolutionary Profiles and Sketches from Life*, Westport: Hyperion Press, 1973, pp. 39–40.

29 The bomb was most significant in Russia, although terrorist groups elsewhere used it extensively. The Irish 'Skirmishers' of the 1880s were the only ones who confined themselves to the bomb.

30 A guerrilla force has political objectives but aims to weaken or destroy the enemy's military forces first. The terrorist, on the other hand, strikes directly at the political sentiments that sustain the enemy.

31 Thomas Hobbes may have been the first to emphasize hope as a necessary ingredient of revolutionary efforts. The first chapter of Menachem Begin's account of his experience in *the Irgun*, contains the most moving description of the necessity of hope in terrorist literature. M. Begin, *The Revolt: Story of the Irgun*, Jerusalem: Steinmatzky's Agency, 1997.

32 There were many organizations: the Internal Macedonian Revolutionary Organization, Young Bosnia, Serbian Black Hand, and so on.

33 The Japan's offer to finance Russian terrorists during the Russo–Japanese War (1905) encouraged Indian terrorists to believe that the Japanese would help them too. P. Heehs, *Nationalism, Terrorism, and Communalism: Essays in Modern Indian History*, Delhi: Oxford University Press, 1998, p. 4. Russian terrorists refused the Japanese offer, fearing that the transaction during a time of war would destroy their political credibility.

34 Ibid., Chapter 2.

35 Italians were particularly active as international assassins, crossing borders to kill four heads of state and holders of principal political offices in different countries: French President Carnot (1894), Spanish Premier Casnovas (1896), and the Austrian Empress Elizabeth (1898). In 1900, Italian Anarchist Gaetano Bresci, a member of the Anarchist community in Patterson, New Jersey (the capital of Italian Anarchism in North America), returned to Italy to assassinate King Umberto I. Several other attempts failed. The 'war' of the Italian Anarchists against the US is described by N. Pernicone, 'Luigi Galleani and Italian Anarchist Terrorism in the United States', *Studi Emigrazione/Etudes Migrations*, 1993, vol. 30, pp. 469–89. See also L. Blaisdell, 'The Assassination of Humbert I', *Prologue. The Quarterly of the National Archives*, 1995, vol. 27, pp. 241–7. Richard B. Jensen supplied the Blaisdell reference.

36 Jensen, 'The United States, International Policing, and the War against Anarchist Terrorism', *Terrorism and Political Violence*, 2001, vol. 13, p. 19. See also Jensen's contribution to this volume, 'The First Global Wave of Terrorism and International Counter-terrorism, 1905–14' (Chapter 1). The aim was to deal with terrorists under the law governing piracy.

37 The IRA's success in 1921 occurred when the British recognized the Irish State. Northern Ireland, however, remained British, and the civil war between Irish factions over the peace settlement ended in defeat for those who would not support the treaty.

38 For an interesting useful account of the de-colonization process, see R. Hager Jr. and D.A. Lake, 'Balancing Empires: Competitive Decolonization in International Politics', *Security Studies*, 2000, vol. 9, pp. 108–48. They emphasize that the literature on decolonization 'has ignored how events and politics within the core (metropolitan area) shaped the process' (p. 145).

39 Begin said that his decision was determined by the fact that since many Jews favoured partition, a civil war would occur. M. Begin, *The Revolt: Story of the Irgun*, Jerusalem: Steinmatzky's Agency, 1997, pp. 152–3. He reminds his

readers of the Zealot revolt against the Romans, which culminated in a disastrous civil war. In 'Terror and the Messiah', I discuss this issue in greater detail in D.C. Rapoport, *Assassination and Terrorism*, Toronto: Canadian Broadcasting Corporation (CBC), 1971, pp. 31–3.

40   A. Horne, *A Savage War of Peace*, London: Macmillan, 1977, pp. 94–6.

41   M. Begin, *The Revolt: Story of the Irgun*, Jerusalem: Steinmatzky's Agency, 1997, Chapters 9 and 10.

42   See G. Kepel and J.P. Milelli (eds), *Al Qaeda in its Own Words*, Cambridge, MA: Harvard Univeristy Press, 2009, p. 52.

43   For a more detailed discussion of the definition problem, see D.C. Rapoport, 'Politics of Atrocity', in Y. Alexander and S. Finger (eds) *Terrorism Interdisciplinary Perspectives*, New York: John Jay Press, 1987, pp. 46 ff.

44   Begin points out in *The Revolt* that it was too costly to assassinate prominent figures. Alexander I of Yugoslavia (1934) was the most prominent victim during the Second Wave.

45   The strategy is superbly described in the film *Battle of Algiers,* based on the memoirs of Yaacev Saadi who organized the battle. When attacks against the police occur, police responses are limited by rules governing criminal procedure. In desperation, the police set-off a bomb off in the Casbah, inadvertently exploding an ammunition dump, killing Algerian women and children. A mob emerged, screaming for revenge, and giving the FLN a moral warrant to attack civilians. There is another underlying element that often gives rebel terrorism a special weight in a democratic world. The atrocities of the strong always seem worse than those of the weak because people believe the weak have no alternatives.

46   The 1946 bombing at the King David Hotel in Jerusalem (the administrative centre for British forces) killed 91 people including many civilians. Warnings were given to front desk operators but were never transmitted to the administration.

47   See D.C. Rapoport, 'Politics of Atrocity', in Y. Alexander and S. Finger (eds) *Terrorism Interdisciplinary Perspectives*, New York: John Jay Press, 1987, pp. 46 ff.

48   Irish-Americans have always given Irish rebels extensive support. The Fenian movement was born in the American Civil War. Members attempted to invade Canada from the US and then went to Ireland to spark rebellion there.

49   The First World War increased the American influence. Wilson justified the war with the self-determination principle.

50   C. Townsend, 'Methods Which All Civilized Opinion Must Condemn: The League of Nations and International Action Against Terrorism', in this volume. When a Croatian group assassinated Alexander I of Serbia in Marseilles (1934), the League tried to contain international terror by drafting two conventions, including one for an international court (1937). Neither came into effect. Two League members (Hungary and Italy) apparently encouraged the assassination and blocked the anti-terror efforts, see M.D. Dubin, 'Great Britain and the Ant-Terrorist Conventions of 1937', *Terrorism and Political Violence*, 1993, vol. 5, p. 1.

51   See J. Dugard, 'International Terrorism and the Just War', in D.C. Rapoport and Y. Alexander (eds) *The Morality of Terrorism*, 2nd ed., New York: Columbia University Press, 2001 pp. 77–98.

52   For example: Basque Nation and Liberty (ETA), the Armenian Secret Army for the Liberation of Armenia (ASALA), the Corsican National Liberation Front (FNLC), and the IRA.

53 During periods of the First and Third Waves, the rights of women were also asserted more vigorously than in the general society.

54 S. Anderson and S. Sloan, *Historical Dictionary of Terrorism*, Metuchen, NJ: Transaction Press, 1995, p. 136.

55 Although bank robbery was not as significant as in the First Wave, some striking examples materialized. In January 1976, the PLO – together with their bitter enemies of the Christian Phalange – hired safe-crackers to help them loot the vaults of the major banks in Beirut. Theft estimates range between US$50 and US$100 million stolen. 'Whatever the truth the robbery was large enough to earn a place in the *Guinness Book of Records* as the biggest bank robbery of all time'. J. Adams, *The Financing of Terror*, New York: Simon and Schuster, 1986, p.192.

56 Ibid., p. 94.

57 A. Geifman, *Thou Shalt Kill: Revolutionary Terrorism in Russia, 1894–1917*, Princeton: Princeton University Press, 1993, Chapter 5.

58 The attack on Major was actually an attack on the Cabinet. It is not clear whether or not the Prime Minister was the principal target (Lindsay Clutterbuck told me this in a personal note).

59 The status of a 'political prisoner' was revoked in March 1976. William Whitelaw, who granted the status initially, ranked it as one of his 'most regrettable decisions'.

60 See T. Riegler, '*Quid pro Quo*: State Sponsorship of Terrorism in the Cold War', Chapter 7 in this volume.

61 Sometimes the US supported terrorist activity, such as the efforts of the *Contras* in Nicaragua.

62 When a disappointed office-seeker assassinated President Garfield, Figner's sympathy letter to the American people asserted that there was no place for terror in democratic states – a statement that alienated elements of her radical constituencies in other countries.

63 M. Baumann, *Terror or Love*, New York: Grove Press, 1977, p. 61.

64 Interview with Hans J. Klein in J.M. Bougereau, *German Guerrilla: Terror, Rebel Reaction and Resistance*, Sanday, Orkney, Cienfuegos: Cienfuegos Press, 1981, p. 31.

65 Abu Nidal was himself on a PLO list of persons to be assassinated.

66 Mattia Toaldo discusses the American strikes against Libya in 'Reagan and Libya: A History of Pre-emptive Strikes and (failed) Regime Change', Chapter 12 in this volume.

67 W. Andrew Terrill, 'Saddam's Failed Counterstrike: Terrorism and the Gulf War', *Studies in Conflict and Terrorism*, 1993, vol. 16, pp. 219–32.

68 For a very interesting discussion of West Germany's role in helping to transform UN attitudes, see Bernhard Blumenau's essay, 'The United Nations and West Germany's Efforts Against International Terrorism in the 1970s', Chapter 4 in this volume.

69 In addition to four UN conventions, there are eight other major multilateral terrorism conventions starting with the Tokyo Convention of 1963 (dealing with aircraft safety). See [http://usinfo.state.gov/topical/pol/terror/conven.htm] and [http://untreaty.un.org/English/Terrorism.asp].

70 See S. Gauthier, 'SWAPO, the United Nations, and the Struggle for National Liberation', Chapter 10 in this volume.

71 Virtually all studies of uprisings emphasize the crucial importance of non-violent resistance. See S. Zunes, 'The Role of Non-Violent Action in the Downfall of Apartheid', *Journal of Modern African Studies*, 1999, vol. 37: 137–69; I.W. Wink, *Violence and Non-Violence in South Africa; Jesus' Third Way*, Philadelphia: New Society Publishers, 1988; R. Ross, *A Concise History of South Africa*, New York: Cambridge University Press, 1999.

72 K. Tololyan, 'Cultural Narrative and the Motivation of the Terrorist' in D.C. Rapoport (ed.) *Inside Terrorist Organizations*, 2nd ed., London: Frank Cass, 2001, 217–33.

73 There were two Afghan wars and two Iraqi wars – one with Iran and one with the US. The Iraq–Iran War was the longest conventional war of the twentieth century. The First Gulf War (1990) also occurred in that period. Iraq's invasion of Kuwait was the cause of the Gulf War – not terrorism – but there was significant irritation with Iraq for its record of supporting Third Wave groups that contributed to the US response.

74 For a discussion of the sovereignty issue which focused on *al Qaeda* practices, see S.N. Kalic, 'Terrorism in the Twenty-First Century: A New Era of Warfare', Chapter 15 in this volume.

75 There were serious bomb attacks with high casualties in the 1920s, but they were sporadic and the movement clearly was declining.

76 See D.C. Rapoport, 'Comparing Militant Fundamentalist Movements and Groups', in M. Marty and S. Appleby (eds) *Fundamentalisms and the State*, Chicago: University of Chicago Press, 1993, pp. 429–61.

77 In the period specified, Tamil suicide bombers struck one hundred and seventy-one times. The combined total for all thirteen Islamic groups using the tactic was one hundred and seventeen. Ehud Sprinzak cites the figures Yoram Schweitzer compiled in 'Rational Fanatics', *Foreign Policy*, 1 September 2000: 69. The most spectacular Tamil act was the assassination of Indian Prime Minister Rajiv Ghandi. The Tamil example has other unusual characteristics. Efforts to make Sri Lanka a Buddhist state stimulated the revolt. Although Tamils largely come from India, there are several religious traditions represented in the population, but religion does not define the terrorists' purpose. Religion did not motivate the notorious Kamikaze attacks during the Second World War, either.

78 The most familiar is the nineteenth century uprising in the Sudan, which resulted in the murder of legendary British General 'Chinese' Gordon.

79 There were two other times when secular forces helped launch religious terror activity. Israel assisted *Hamas'* establishment, thinking that it would compete to weaken the PLO. To check Left Wing opposition, President Sadat released religious terrorists from prison who later assassinated him.

80 See T. Hegghammer, 'Introduction, Abdallah Azzam, The Imam of Jihad', in G. Kepel and J.P. Milelli (eds), *Al Qaeda in Its Own Words*, Cambridge, MA: Harvard University Press, 2009, pp. 81–101.

81 P. Bergen, *Holy War Inc. Inside the Secret World of Osama Bin Ladin*, New York: Free Press, 2001, p. 208.

82 See A. Pedahzur, W. Eubank and L. Weinberg, 'The War on Terrorism and the Decline of Terrorist Group Formation' *Terrorism and Political Violence*, 2002, vol. 14, pp. 141–7.

83 The relationship between different religious terror groups is unusual. Groups from different mainstream traditions (such as Christianity and Islam) do not

cooperate. Traditional cleavages *within* a religion (such as Shiite and Sunni Islam) sometimes are intensified. But the Shia do aid Sunni terrorist groups hostile to Israel.

84 I have no statistical evidence on this point.

85 R. Gunaratna, *Inside Al Qaeda: Global Network of Terror*, New York: Columbia University Press, 2002, p. 97.

86 In the First Wave individuals often went abroad and associated with other groups.

87 B. Lewis, 'License to Kill', *Foreign Affairs*, November/December 1998.

88 P. Bergen, *Holy War Inc. Inside the Secret World of Osama Bin Ladin*, New York: Free Press, 2001, p. 225.

89 Those attacks, as well as expected ones that did not materialize, are discussed in a special volume of *Terrorism and Political Violence* in Spring 2002, edited by Jeffrey Kaplan, entitled 'Millennial Violence: Past, Present, and Future'. The issue was also published as a separate volume with the same title by Frank Cass, London, 2002.

90 For a very interesting discussion of the circumstances that provoke American military responses to terrorist attacks, see M. Mavesti, 'Explaining the United States' Decision to Strike Back at Terrorists', *Terrorism and Political Violence*, 2001, vol. 13, pp. 85–106.

91 If the organization understood its vulnerability, it might have thought that an attack on the sovereignty of the state protecting it was unlikely. One reason the *Taliban* government refused repeated UN demands to expel *al Qaeda* was that without *al Qaeda* support it could not survive local domestic opposition. Nonetheless, the failure to plan for the possibility of an invasion is astonishing.

92 R. Gunaratna, *Inside Al Qaeda: Global Network of Terror*, New York: Columbia University Press, 2002.

93 Note 5 deals with overreactions on the domestic scene and with respect to prisoners.

94 The practice of beheading prisoners was also a serious concern. Zawahari, second in command, wrote the letter. He knew from personal experience in Egypt the political dangers of excessive tactics. See M. Scheuer, '*Al Qaeda* in Iraq: Has al Zawahari Reined in al-Zarqawi?', *Terrorism Focus*, 2006, vol. 3.

95 Suicide attacks have generated increasing antagonisms among Muslims toward the organization. The only place suicide bombing is considered acceptable in Muslim countries now is the West Bank where Israelis are present too. The Pew Research Center's Forum on Religion & Public Life. *Muslim Americans: No Signs of Growth in Alienation or Support for Extremism Muslim Americans: Released*, August 30, 2011.

96 E. Schmitt and D. Sanger, 'White House Advisor Says US Has Six Months to "Knock Out" Rattled Qaeda Leadership', *New York Times*, 29 July 2011.

97 *Al Qaeda* in the Arab Peninsula is the largest and most active franchise internationally. It has between three hundred and five hundred members. See A. Harris, *Exploiting Grievances Al-Qaeda in the Arabian Peninsula*, Carnegie Endowment for International Peace, Middle East Program, Number 111, May 2010, p. 14.

98 R. Gunaratna, *Inside Al Qaeda: Global Network of Terror*, New York: Columbia University Press, 2002, pp. 142–3.

99 See L. Beam, 'Leaderless Resistance', *The Seditionist*, 1992, vol. 12. Jeffrey

Kaplan's extremely interesting article 'Leaderless Resistance', *Terrorism and Political Violence*, 1997, vol. 9, pp. 80–95, discusses Beam's work. See also E. Sprinzak, 'Right Wing Terrorism in Comparative Perspective; The Case of Delegitimation', *Terrorism and Political Violence*, 1995, vol. 7, pp. 17–43. W. Pierce's *Turner Diaries* influenced Timothy McVeigh, the Oklahoma City Bomber. Pierce also published a novel on the lone wolf, *The Hunter*, under his pseudonym, Andrew MacDonald.

100 Al Suri uses Beam's term 'leaderless resistance' and includes individuals and autonomous cells in the concept. See L. Wright, 'The Master Plan', *New Yorker*, 11 September 2006, pp. 48–59; and S. Zabel, *The Military Strategy of Jihad*, Carlisle, PA: US Army War College, 2007, pp. 5–7. See Brynjar Lia's comprehensive discussion of Abu Misab al Suri's work in his *Architect of Global Jihad: The Life of al-Qaida Strategist Abu Mus'ab al Suri*, New York: Columbia Press, 2007. Lia's article 'Doctrines for Jihadi Training', *Terrorism and Political Violence*, 2008, vol. 20, pp. 518–42 compares al Suri with other *al Qaeda* theorists.

101 J. Kaplan, 'Leaderless Resistance', *Terrorism and Political Violence*, 1997, vol. 9, p. 80. See also E. Sprinzak, 'Right Wing Terrorism in Comparative Perspective; The Case of Delegitimation', *Terrorism and Political Violence*, 1995, vol. 7, pp. 17–43.

102 Southern Poverty Law Center (SPLC) Report Fall 2011, p. 3. This represents the number of attack in the previous eight years.

103 S. Salama and L. Hansell, 'Does Intent Equal Capability? *Al Qaeda* and Weapons of Mass Destruction', *Non Proliferation Review*, 2005, vol. 12, pp. 615–53.

104 See D.C. Rapoport, 'Terrorism and Weapons of the Apocalypse', *National Security Studies Quarterly*, 1999, vol. 5, pp. 49–67. Reprinted in H. Sokolski and J. Ludes (eds), *Twenty-First Century Weapons Proliferation*, London: Frank Cass, 2001, pp. 14–32.

105 B. McAllister and A.P. Schmid, 'Theories of Terrorism', *Routledge Handbook of Terrorism Research*, London: Routledge, 2011, p. 255.

106 See D.C. Rapoport, 'Terrorism and Weapons of the Apocalypse', *National Security Studies Quarterly*, 1999, vol. 5, pp. 49–67.

107 In a video released in March 2004, Osama bin Laden said that he used the same methods against the Americans as those used by the mujahedeen during the Soviet occupation of Afghanistan. 'We will continue this strategy bleeding America to the breaking point'. See [http://www1.folha.uol.com.br/mundo/967557-bin-laden-tornou-se-sinonimo-de-terrorismo-apos-ataques-nos-eua.shtml].

Index

9/11 terrorist attacks 237, 245–8, 263,
274, 302–3n

Abu Nidal Organization (ANO) 124
Addington, David 256
Afghanistan: al-Qaeda founded 233;
militant Islamists training 266, 268;
political instability 299; US invasion
246, 274, 280n
African National Congress (ANC) 170,
173, 294
al-Assad, Hafez: attacks in Jordan 119;
regional influence 126, 143, 145;
TWA-847 hijack, response to 138,
141, 142, 144
al-Balawi, Humam Khalil 239
al-Dhawahiri, Ayman 233, 236, 241, 297
Alexander I, King of Yugoslavia 34
Alexander II, Czar 2, 286
Alfonso XIII, King of Spain 19–20
Algeria: Algerian War 91; National
Liberation Front of Algeria 288, 289,
306n; TWA-847 hijack negotiations
135, 136–7; US anti-Libyan support
217; US seek rapprochement 134
Al-Haramain Islamic Foundation 252,
259n
al-Qaeda: 9/11 attacks 237, 245–6, 263;
academic analysis, lack of 231–3;
multimedia, integrated use of 240–1;
objectives, ignored indicators 238,
240; operational structure 270–1,
297–8, 299; origins of objectives
233–4, 268–9; reduced force 298,
309n; regional franchises 238–9,
241–2, 271; transnational attacks
237, 239; transnational terrorism,
reason for 235–6, 241; women 285,
304n

al-Rahman, Atiyah Abd 298
al-Suri, Abu Musab 236, 299
al-Wardani, Ibrahim Nasif 22
al-Zawahiri, Ayman see al–Dhawahiri,
Ayman
Amal 135, 138, 139, 143
Ammoun, Fouad, Judge 171
anarchist assassinations 2, 282;
Argentina 21; Egypt 22; Finland 6;
France 34; Greece 21; India 152;
Russia 17; Serbia 22; Spain 19–20,
55; Sweden 21
Andropow, Yuri 117–8
Angola 176, 179
Anushilan 152, 154, 161
Arafat, Yasir 122, 124, 126, 169–70
Argentina 20–1
Argod, Hubert 194
Assayas, Oliver 128
Atwa, Ali 136, 141, 146n
Aum Shinrikyo 295
Austria: Abu Nidal's terrorist attacks
124, 126–7; hostage-taking, Vienna
(1975) 76, 124–5; terrorist
compromise 127–8; Vienna Airport
attacks 218
Austria-Hungary 22, 27
Auswärtiges Amt (AA) 72–3, 75, 77
Awami League 163
Azzam, Abdullah 233, 268, 296

Baader, Andreas 67, 68
Baader-Meinhof 266
Baldit, Luc 192
Banerji, Jatindranath 152
Bangladesh 164
Barbone, Marco 108
Barcelona: anarchist bombings 19,
51–2; *Banda Negra* 57–8, 59;

'*pistolerismo*', communities of violence 52–6, 59; '*pistolerismo*', counter-terrorism 56–8; 'Tragic Week' 20, 52
Barthou, Jean Louis 34
Baum, Gerhart 104, 106
Beam, Louis 299
Begin, Menachem 288, 305–6n
Beihaj, Abdel 298
Benavente, Roserio 54
Bengal: Communism, adoption of 163; Hindu nationalism revived 158–9; Muslim exclusion 160–2; partition, impact of 156–7; Permanent Settlement Act (1793), impact of 155, 160; Swadeshi movement 152–3, 156–7, 159, 160–1; terrorism, cultural motivations 155–7, 160–1, 164; terrorist objectives and tactics 152–5
Bengal Volunteers 154
Benjadid, Chadli 135
Berri, Nabbi 138, 139, 140–1, 142, 144
Bewegung 2. Juni (Second of June) 67–8, 292
Bin Laden, Osama: actions, reasoning behind 236, 268–9, 285; al-Qaeda founder 233, 268; death of 241, 256, 298; Declaration of War (1996) 234; global celebrity 297; Libyan arrest warrant 298; women, dedication to 285, 304n
Black September 71, 264, 291
Boato, Marco 103, 108
Bongo, Omar 200
Bonnici, Carmelo 145
Borghi, Armando 24–5
Brandt, Willy 124
Brass, L.S. 40–1, 45
Bravo Portillo, Manuel 57, 59
Breivik, Anders 299
Bresci, Gaetano 34, 305n
Britain: anti-Raj attacks in India 152–3; Indian legislation, impact of 155, 160; IRA activities 303n, 307n; League convention, legal sovereignty issues 42–5; League convention, skeptic approach to 39–42; Loyalists, intelligence support 118; Russian police, relations refused 23–4; St Petersburg Protocol, objection to 23; terrorism, changing attitude to 47; Tsarist

Regime, impact of 19; US air strike on Libya 220
Buijtenhuijs, Robert 191
Burgat, François 210–1
Bush, George 215, 223
Bush, George W.: Global War on Terror 1, 245, 263–4, 274, 301–2n; intelligence gathering, legality of 250–2, 256–7, 258–9n; national security, overriding issue 246–8

Canalejas, José 20, 26
Cannistraro, Vincent 216–7, 225n
Carlos Group *see* Organization of International Revolutionaries
Carlos the Jackel *see* Ramírez Sánchez, Ilich
Carlson, Kurt 135
Carnot, Sadi 2, 34
Carter, Jimmy 211
Carton de Wiart, Henry, Comte 35, 36, 46
Casey, William 211, 216
CCFAN: kidnaps and initial negotiations 191–4; negotiations ongoing 199; negotiator capture and arms demand 195–8; relations with rebel factions 201, 203; relations with Libya 201
Ceausescu, Nicolae 120–1
Central Intelligence Agency (CIA): links with 'freedom fighters' 118, 217; Middle Eastern intelligence 126, 127; organizational failures 249, 257n; Qaddafi threat 211, 213–4, 216; report on Qadhafi 120; terrorist prisons and interrogation 253–4; *Terror Network* 117
Chad: French expulsion 200; kidnaps, initial negotiations 191–4; kidnaps, provocative negotiations 195–200; Libyan intervention 201; political future 203; political instability and rebellion 190–1; regime change 198
Chapekar, Damodar 152
Chattopadhyay, Bankimchandra 156, 157
Chattopadhyay, Saratchandra 161–2
Cheney, Richard 246, 256
China 17, 22, 28n
Chirac, Jacques 200
Claustre, Françoise 191, 199, 200, 202
Claustre, Pierre: Chad kidnaps 191–2;

initial negotiations 193, 194, 195; negotiations, return to 197, 198; procurement of arms 199; release of 202; taken as hostage 200
Clinton, Bill 272–3
Cold War: GDR assisted terrorism 116, 121–3, 124; Middle Eastern strategies 119–20, 125–8; state sponsored terrorism 116–9, 128–9; terrorist aims and strategies 128–9
Combe, Mark 191, 199
Confederación Nacional del Trabajo (CNT) 52, 55, 57, 58
Conseil supérieur militaire (CSM) 198, 199–200, 202
Convention for the Prevention and Punishment of Terrorism: British objections and abstention 39–45; Committee of Experts formed 35; delegates debate principles 35–7; extradition, national differences 37–8, 39; ineffectiveness of 46; terrorism, definition debate 37–8
counter-terrorism: Convention for the Prevention and Punishment of Terrorism 35–8; criminal legislation 271–3; international strategies 5, 273–6; St Petersburg Protocol (1904) 22–4, 25–7; strategy developments 264–5, 302–3n
Cyprus 288, 289
Czechoslovakia 120

Dallier, Louis 202
Debi, Sarala 156
de Decker, Marie Laure 199
Depardon, Raymond 199, 200
Donat-Cattin, Marco 107, 113n
Dufur, Lluís 53, 54
Durruti, Buenaventura 56

Egypt 22, 217, 296, 308n
Ensslin, Gudren 67, 69
Estrade, Georges 194, 195, 198
European Convention on the Suppression of Terrorism 47
European Political Cooperation (EPC) 72, 77

Fadlallah, Mohammed Hussein 142
Falcon, Ramon 21
FAN (armées du Nord) 192, 196, 199, 201

Fatah-Revolutionary Council (ANO) 218
Federal Bureau of Investigation (FBI) 249–50, 257n
Federal Republic of Germany (FRG) *see* Germany, West
Ferrer Guardia, Francisco 17, 19–20, 52
Finland 6
Flannigan, Timothy 256
Fortier, Donald 216–7, 218–9, 225n
Foucault, Michel 94
France: 1968 student protests 87, 89; Algerian war 91; Chad, post-colonial intervention 190–1; Chad kidnaps, cooperation sort 195–8, 202; Chad kidnaps, initial negotiations 191–4; Chad kidnaps, ransom delivery 200; Constitutional Council 93; Court of State Security 91–2, 94; League convention 37, 44; liberalization and civil rights 93–4; Libyan assistance in Chad 200–1; Paris, anarchist hub 17, 18; radical leftists, activities of 87–8, 90, 92, 94, 99n; radical leftists, authorities response to 88–92, 95; rule of law, expansion of 92–3; Russian anarchists, activities of 19; terrorist extradition 293; UN conventions on terrorism 75, 77; US air strike on Libya 220
Franz Ferdinand, Archduke of Austria 22
freedom fighters 6, 118, 169–70, 217, 288
Frente de Libertação de Moçambique (Frelimo) 170
Friedlander, Robert 175
Frolinat 190–1, 193, 196, 198, 201
Front de libération nationale (FLN) 91
Fukuyama, Francis 213–4

Gaddafi, Muammar *see* Qaddafi, Muammar
Galopin, Pierre 194–8
Gandhi, Mohandas Karamchand 154
Gates, Robert 212, 216
Gauche prolétarienne (GP) 87–8, 89, 90, 94, 98n
Gaulle, Charles de 87, 91, 190–1
Geismar, Alain 88, 89, 92
Genscher, Hans-Dietrich 76, 77
German Democratic Republic (GDR):

admittance to UN 70; Libyan
intelligence links 220; Middle
Eastern intelligence 126–7; Ministry
sponsored terrorism 116, 121–3,
124; RAF, links with 120; self-
determination 72
Germany (pre-1949) 23, 25–6
Germany, West: admittance to UN 70;
agent provocateurs, use of 119;
Auswärtiges Amt, policy role 72–3,
75; Berlin discotheque bombing
220; Chad kidnaps and negotiations
191–4; diplomats, kidnapping of
73–4; 'German Autumn' 68–9;
Munich Olympics hostage crisis 71,
264; national terrorism policy 67–70;
terrorism policy within UN 72–3, 79;
terrorist networks 67–9, 292; UN
anti-terrorism proposal 71; UN
hostage-taking initiative 76–8; UN
Protection of Diplomats Convention
74–6
Ghali, Butrus 22
Ghose, Aurobindo 152
Ghose, Barinda Kumar 152
Ghosh, Aurobindo 157–9, 161
Giscard d'Estaing, Valéry 94, 197, 202
Global War on Terror 1–2, 245–6,
257n, 263–4, 273–5, 301–2n
Goldsmith, Jack 255
Gómez Franquet, Alfredo 54
Gonzales, Alberto 251, 252, 254, 256
Gorbachev, Mikhail 142, 144, 145, 221
Gourvennec, Camille 195–6, 198
Grailly, Michel de 88
Gray, John 236–7
Greece 118, 136, 137–8
Grivas, Georges 285
GSG 9 (Grenzschutzgruppe 9) 68, 69
Guatemala 73–4
Gunaratna, Rohan 269, 277n

Habré, Hissène: CCFAN kidnaps and
demands 191, 192; Galopin's
capture and fate 196, 197–8; kidnap
negotiations 193–4, 197–8, 199–200;
political future 203; relations with
rebel factions 201; relations with
Libya 201
Haddad, Wadi 117–8, 122
Haig, Alexander 117, 213
Halliday, Fred 1
Hartenstein, Abraham 21, 30n

Hartstrich, Jacques 89
Hasan, Nidal, Major 299
Heritage Foundation 175, 212
Hessel, Stéphane 199
Hezbollah 134, 142, 143, 265, 267
Hoffman, Bruce 4, 266

India: anarchist activity 21; anarchists
taught in Paris 17, 18, 28n; Bengali
terrorism 40; Bombay Presidency
attacks 152; Chittagong Uprising
154; Communist Party origins 163;
Hindu nationalism revived 158–9;
National Congress Party 151, 153;
terrorism, cultural motivations
155–7; terrorist objectives and tactics
152–5
International Court of Justice 171
International Criminal Court 35, 36,
44, 45
International Criminal Police
Organization (Interpol) 47
International Law Commission 74
Iran: links with Libya 142; militant
Islamism 265, 266–7, 295–6; TWA-
847 hijack, innocent of 143; US seek
rapprochement 133–4
Iraq 126, 268, 293
Irgun 288
Irish Republican Army (IRA):
assassinations 291; creation of 283;
Irish Free State 287, 303n; targets of
265–6; US sponsorship 292, 306n
Islamic *Jihad* 136, 142, 143
Israel 139–40, 141–2, 288, 296, 308n
Italy: anarchist assassinations 305n;
anti-terrorist legislation 101–2;
bombing in Milan 100; Catholic
Church, role of 109; NATO
supported terrorism 118; repentant
legislation, debated 102–6;
repentant legislation, impact of
106–9; Rome Airport attacks 218;
royal assassination 34, 305n; Russian
anarchists, influence of 29n; St
Petersburg Protocol, objection to 25;
terrorist extradition 293; terrorist
kidnapping 101

Japan 17, 21–2, 25–6
Japanese Red Army 71, 266
Jonathan Institute 116
Jordan 291

July, Serge 88

KGB 117–8
Khameni, Ali 266
Khomeini, Ruhollah 265, 266, 296
Koh, Harold 255
Komarnicki, Titus 37
Kotoku, Shusui 26, 30n
Kreisky, Bruno 124, 126, 127
Kroesen, Frederick 120
Kwakwa, Edward 174–5

Laqueur, Walter 4
Laurens, Martial 196, 197
League of Nations 35–46, 171, 181–2n, 287, 290, 306n
Lebanon: Hezbollah, activities of 267; Israeli invasion 218, 293; suicide bombing 296; TWA-847 hijack, response to 135, 136
Legge Pentiti (Italy): debate and formulation of 102–6; impact on terrorism 106–9
Lehi 288, 289
Lévy, Benny 87
Libya: accessible US enemy 216–9; Chad, political involvement 201, 203; Chad kidnaps 197; economy and US sanctions 214–5; Lockerbie bombing 223, 294; post Qaddafi Regime 298; Qaddafi assumes power 210–1; Qaddafi terrorist links 120, 134, 293; Semtex, purchasing of 120; US air strike 220–1; US provocation strategy 219–20; US sanctions 211, 219, 223
Lorenz, Peter 67–8
Luxembourg 23

MacFarlane, Robert 217
Makins, Roger 41–2
Malloum, Félix, General 198, 199, 200, 202
Malta 145
Marcellin, Raymond 87, 88, 90–1, 93, 94–5
Marighella, Carlos 285
Martínez Valles, Francisco 53, 59
Masdeu Batista, Andrés 54
Maxwell, Alexander, Sir 41, 42
McKinley, William 2, 34, 245, 282
McVeigh, Timothy 299
Meinhof, Ulrike 67

Middle East: government sponsored terrorism 119–20; intelligence agencies 126–7
Mielke, Erich 121
militant Islamism: al-Qaeda, rise of 268–71; Iranian origins 265, 266; transnational terrorism 266–7, 295–7
Ministry for State Security, GDR (MfS) 116, 121–3, 124
Mitra, Nabagopal 156
Mitra, Pramatha Nath 152
Mitterrand, François 94
Montazeri, Hussain Ali 266
Moro, Aldo 101, 120, 291
Morral, Mateo 20
Mugniyeh, Imad: Beirut hostages 144, 145; Sheik Fadlallah's influence 143; TWA-847, hijacking contract 134; TWA-847, hijack of 136–7, 139, 142, 146
Munich Olympics hostage crisis 71, 264

Nacht, Siegfried 24
Namibia: administrated by UN Council 174; independence, UN support for 179, 294; legal ownership debate 171–2; SWAPO, objectives of 172–3, 177–9
Namibian National Society for Human Rights 179–80
National Front for the Salvation of Libya (NSFL) 216–7
national liberation movements: self-determination, UN stance 174–5; terrorists or freedom fighters 169–70; terrorist tactics 3; UN exemptions proposed 74, 75–6, 77
National Security Agency (US) 250–1, 252
National Security Decision Directive (US) 213–4
NATO 118–9
Nechaev, Sergei 284, 285
Nicaragua 118
Nidal, Abu: Austrian compromise 127–8; Gaddafi alliance 218; PLO and pro-PLO targeted 126–7, 293; PLO target 307n; state sponsored 115, 120, 124
Nittel, Heinz 126–7
Nivedita, Sister 152
Nixon, Richard 70, 264

Nujoma, Sam 172–3, 178, 180, 183n

Obama, Barack 252
Organisation de l'armée secrète (OAS)
    91, 96–7n
Organization of African Unity (OAU)
    172–3, 183n
Organization of International
    Revolutionaries 120–1, 123, 127–8
Ovamboland People's Congress 172

Pakistan 163–4, 298–9
Palestine Liberation Organization
    (PLO): *Achille Lauro*, hijack of 215,
    293; bank robberies 307n; Camp
    David Treaty 296; conflict within
    Lebanon 143, 293; creation of 181n,
    290; Nidal's war on moderates 126;
    Soviet training 122; targets of 265–6;
    terrorist networks 292, 293, 297; UN
    status recognized 294
Pallás, Paulino 51
Papandreou, Andreas 137, 138
Pardiñas, Manuel 20
Paris 17, 18, 28n, 91
Pather Dabi (Chattopadhyay) 161–2
Peci, Patrizio 102, 106
Peci, Roberto 102
Peiró, Juan Bautista 54–5
Pella, Vespasian 38
Peres, Shimon 140, 144
'pistolerismo': counter-terrorism 56–8;
    economic motives for violence 52,
    56, 58; terrorist networks 52–5, 59
plane hijacking
Pohamba, Hifikepunye 180
Poindexter, John 217
Poland 37, 45
political crimes, extradition refusals
    37–8, 39
Ponto, Corinna 115–6
Popular Front for the Liberation of
    Palestine (PFLP) 68, 117–8, 121–2
Powell, Colin 222, 255, 274
Primo de Rivera, Miguel 52, 56
Puissant, Robert 192, 193, 197, 198

Qaddafi, Muammar: assumes power in
    Libya 210–1; Chad hostage
    intervention 201–2; links to Greek
    government 138; links with Bruno
    Kriesky 127; Lockerbie bombing
    223, 265; political interference 143;

Reagan assassination denial 212–3;
    Rome and Vienna Airport attacks
    218; TWA-847, hijack involvement
    134, 138, 143, 145
Qadhafi, Muammar *see* Qaddafi,
    Muammar

Radowisky, Simon 21
Rafsanjani, Akbar Hashemi 142
Ramírez Sánchez, Ilich 69, 76, 121,
    123, 128
Rand, Walter 152
Reagan, Ronald: Libyan air strike
    speech 221; Libyan death threat
    denied 212–3; Libyan problem 219;
    TWA-847 hijack, response to 135,
    136–7, 138, 140–1, 144
Red Army Fraction *see* Rote Armee
    Fraktion (RAF)
Red Brigades 101, 102, 120, 266, 291
Red Cross 141
Revolutionäre Zellen (Revolutionary
    Cells) 67, 292
Rice, Condoleezza 246
Rizzo, Aldo 106
Robaldo, Vitale 103
Rodenas, Progreso 55
Rognoni, Virginio 102, 104, 106, 111n
Romania 120–1
Roosevelt, Theodore 18, 245, 287,
    302n
Rosa, Guido 102
Ross, Dennis 213–4
Rote Armee Fraktion (RAF) 67, 68–9,
    115–6
Rull, Juan 51
Rumsfeld, Donald 274
Russia *see also* Soviet Union; 1905
    Revolution, impact of 17, 18–9;
    anarchist activity abroad 21, 27, 284,
    286–7; British police refuse relations
    23–4; Okhrana, formation of 302n;
    Socialist Revolutionaries, influence
    of 17–8, 22; St Petersburg Protocol
    (1904) 23, 25; terrorist values 286

Sahnoun, Mohamed 173
Sales Mollner, Vincente 54
Sales Ortiz, Vincente 54
Saletas Pla, José 54
Sartre, Jean-Paul 86, 88, 94
Saudi Arabia 268–9, 296
Schauman, Eugene 6

Schleyer, Hanns-Martin 68, 69
Schmid, Alex 299–300
Schmidt, Helmut 67–9, 76
Segarra, Rosario 54
self-determination 71, 72, 174–5, 287, 300
Sen, Surya 154, 164
Shipanga, Andreas 179
Shultz, George: anti-terrorism speech 215; terrorism, military targeting 216, 219, 223; TWA-847 hijack, response to 137, 138, 140, 141, 142–3
Simon, John, Sir 39
Socialist Revolutionaries 17–8
Soler, Antonio 57, 58
Sossi, Mario 101
South Africa: African National Congress (ANC) succeed 294; apartheid measures 172, 182n; Namibia, illegal occupation of 171–2, 176, 294; SWAPO conflict 176; SWAPO prosecution campaign 170, 175
South West Africa *see* Namibia
South West African National Union (SWANU) 172–3
South West Africa People's Organization *see* SWAPO
Soviet Union: KGB links with Abu Nidal 124; KGB links with PFLP 117–8; terrorist groups, post collapse 296; terrorist sponsorship 116–7, 118–9, 294; TWA-847, hijack involvement 133–4, 142, 144, 146; US actions in Libya, response to 221
Spadolini, Giovanni 102–3
Spain: bombing in Barcelona 19, 51–2; Catalonian attacks in Argentina 21; Confederación Nacional del Trabajo (CNT) 52, 55, 57, 58; *'pistolerismo'* period 52–8; police force, modernizing of 22, 26; royal assassinations attempts 19–20; *Sindicato Libres* 58; support for 1904 Protocol 23, 26
Spreti, Karl, Count von 73–4
Sri Lanka 296
Staewen, Christoph 191, 193, 194, 195
Stanik, Joseph 217
Stepnick, Serge 284, 286
Sterling, Claire 117
Stethem, Robert 135, 136

Stewart, Findlater, Sir 40
St Petersburg Protocol (1904) 22–4, 25–7
suicide bombing 244n, 296
SWAPO: internal conflict and oppression 178–9, 180; liberation through violence 169, 172–3, 177–8; South Africa's retaliation 175–7; UN recognition and support 174, 176–7, 179, 180
Sweden 68
Switzerland: anarchist expulsion agreements 24–5, 26; anti-anarchist legislation 22–3, 24; Russian anarchists, activities of 19
Syria: attacks on Jordan 119; base for terrorism 293; regional power strategy 126–7, 143

Tamil Tigers 296, 308n
Tanter, Raymond 213
Taylor, Anna Diggs 252
terrorism: Christian 295, 299; concept origins 2–3; definition, ideological divisions 37, 47; definition, various 3–6; first wave (anarchist), causes of 16–22, 282, 284, 285–7, 300; first wave (anarchist), government responses 22–7; fourth wave (religious) 295–300, 301; freedom fighters 6; 'lone wolf' attacks 299; militant Islamism 266–71; national groups, single focus 230–1, 265–6; second wave (anti-colonial) 287–90; terrorists for hire 69; third wave (new left) 290–5, 300–1; transnational 233–7; violence, expansion of 265; wave phenomenon 282–5
Testrake, John 135–6, 137, 138–9
Thatcher, Margaret 291
The Terror Network (Stirling) 117
Tilak, Bal Gangadhar 151–2, 156
Toivo, Andimba Toivo ja 172
Toivo, Herman Toivo ja 175
Tombalbaye, François: death of 198; French dependency 190–1; kidnaps, negotiation involvement 192–5; negotiation demands 197
Touze, Raphäel: Chad kidnaps, negotiation difficulties 192, 194; Chad kidnaps, negotiation role 193, 195–6

Tupac Amaru 292
Turkey 118–9, 289
TWA-847, hijacking of: analysis of
    events 135–6; key terrorists 134,
    136–7, 139–41, 142, 146; Libyan
    involvement 134, 138, 143, 145;
    negotiations in Algeria 135, 136–7;
    Soviet involvement 133–4, 142, 144,
    146; US response 135, 136–8, 140–4

Umberto I, King of Italy 34, 305n
United Kingdom *see* Britain
United Nations (UN): anti-terrorism
    strategies, ongoing 79, 273;
    International Convention against
    Taking of Hostages 77–8; new states,
    new attitudes 294–5; Protection of
    Diplomats Convention 74–6;
    Resolution 2444 170; Resolution
    3034 on terrorism 46–7, 72; self-
    determination, legality of 174–5,
    290; South West Africa, ownership
    debate 171–2, 182n; SWAPO,
    political support of 174, 176–7, 179;
    terrorism, members' conflicting
    agendas 70–2; Third World politics,
    dominance of 70
United Nations Transition Assistance
    Group (UNTAG) 172
United States: 9/11 attacks,
    government response 245–8, 274,
    302–3n; *Achille Lauro*, hijack of 215,
    293; anarchist extradition 302n;
    anarchist scare (1908) 18; anti-
    communism support 292;
    Authorization for the Use of Military
    Force (AUMF) 245, 247, 279–80n;
    Beirut hostages 142–3, 144, 145;
    Bush Doctrine 248; CIA links with
    'freedom fighters' 118, 217; counter-
    terrorism measures 272–3, 279n;
    Foreign Intelligence Surveillance
    Act compliance 250–1, 252, 259n;
    Freedom of Navigation exercises
    212, 219–20; Global War on Terror
    1–2, 245–6, 257n, 263–4, 273–5;
    intelligence agencies, failures of 249,
    257n, 258n; intelligence agencies,
    powers enhanced 250–2;

intelligence gathering, legality of
    252–3, 256–7, 258–9n, 259–60n;
    isolation of Libya 134; liberation
    groups, attitude to 177; Libya,
    accessible enemy 211–2, 216–9;
    Libya, air strike 220–1, 279n; Libyan
    sanctions 211, 213–4, 219; Lockerbie
    bombing 223; 'lone wolf' attacks
    299; Middle Eastern policy (Reagan)
    216, 221–2; mujahidin fighters,
    support of 266; Oklahoma City
    bombing 295, 299; rapprochement
    with Iran 133–4; Soviets and terrorist
    sponsorship 117; terrorism policy
    (Reagan Review) 222–3; terrorist
    interrogation, legality of 254–6;
    terrorist suspects, detainment of
    253–4, 261–2n; TWA-847 hijack,
    response to 135, 136–8, 140–1, 144;
    UN anti-terrorism proposal 71
Urban, Josef 24

Versailles Peace Treaty 287, 288
Vivekananda, Swami 156, 157
von König, Baron 58

Waldheim, Kurt 71, 72
Wallner, Franz 192, 193
Wechmar, Rüdiger von 78
Weddeye, Goukouni: CCFAN and
    Libya 201; Galopin, dislike of 195,
    196, 198; kidnaps, negotiation
    involvement 197, 199, 202; political
    future 203
Weinberger, Casper 215, 219
Williams, John Fischer, Sir 42–4, 45
Wolf, Markus 121, 122
Wolfowitz, Paul 246
Woodward, Bob 217–8

Yoo, John 255
Yugantar 152, 154, 161

Zambia 178, 179
Zasulich, Vera 286
Zealots 2, 3–4
Zelikow, Philip D 255
Zimbabwe African National Union 3,
    170, 173